D0966300

FIVE DOWN, NO GLORY

FIVE DOWN, NO GLORY

Frank G. Tinker, Mercenary Ace in the Spanish Civil War

Richard K. Smith and R. Cargill Hall

Naval Institute Press
Annapolis, Maryland

This book has been brought to publication with the generous assistance of Marguerite and Gerry Lenfest.

Naval Institute Press
291 Wood Road
Annapolis, MD 21402

Library of Congress Cataloging-in-Publication Data

Smith, Richard K. (Richard Kenneth), 1929–2003.
  Five down, no glory : Frank G. Tinker, mercenary ace in the Spanish Civil War / Richard K. Smith and R. Cargill Hall.
    p. cm.
  Includes bibliographical references and index.
  ISBN 978-1-61251-054-5 (hbk. : alk. paper)   1. Tinker, F. G. (Frank Glasgow), 1909–
2. Spain—History—Civil War, 1936–1939—Aerial operations.   3. Spain—History—Civil War,
1936–1939—Participation, American.   4. Air pilots, Military—Spain—Biography.   5. Air pilots,
Military—United States—Biography.   6. Americans—Spain—Biography.   7. Spain—History—
Civil War, 1936–1939—Biography.   I. Hall, R. Cargill.   II. Title.   III. Title: Frank G. Tinker,
mercenary ace in the Spanish Civil War.
  DP269.4.S57   2011
  946.081'48092—dc23
  [B]
                                                                                    2011025670

♾ This paper meets the requirements of ANSI/NISO z39.48-1992 (Permanence of Paper).

Printed in the United States of America.

19 18 17 16 15 14 13 12 11   9 8 7 6 5 4 3 2 1
First printing

Fear

Some men enjoy the gentle walks of life,
And live amid cool serenity.
Immersed in bookish joys, they wall out strife,
Their one desire a calm security.
The man who flies is of a different mould.
His fear is not of rain or driving sleet,
But rather of the chance that he grows old,
Before his round of life has been complete.
The joy of paths to blaze makes him strong.
The thrill of fate uncertain sets afire
A pulse that quickens with a burst of song,
Or races at the urge of sweet desire.
He does not long for never-ending years.
It's only lack of living that he fears.

Flying Cadet F. E. Rouse,
The Randolph Field Tee
1 June 1934

CONTENTS

ILLUSTRATIONS

Photographs

Maps

PREFACE

ichard Kenneth Smith was born on 2 November 1929, four days after the "Black Tuesday" stock market crash that would precipitate a collapse of economies around the world. A true child of the depression, he grew up in Joliet, Illinois, and in Mexico, where his father, a mechanical engineer, found work with the Mexican state railway system in the 1930s. Returning to Joliet after World War II, Smith entered the University of Illinois in 1947 and matriculated for two years. Uncertain about an academic major or a career, in 1949 he abruptly left university and enlisted in the United States Merchant Marine, where he spent the next six years on board merchant ships hauling all manner of goods from port to port around the world. In his many off-duty hours at sea, Smith consumed the "great books" in literature and history, learned German to accompany his Spanish, and fell in love with the works of Rudyard Kipling.

Smith reentered the University of Illinois in the fall of 1957; a year later he pocketed a bachelor of arts degree and, in 1959, a master of arts degree, both in history. He began work on a PhD at the University of Chicago while teaching as a graduate instructor, and, when funds ran short, he returned to sea for one year in 1963. On returning to the University of Chicago, he chose as his dissertation topic "The Airships *Akron* and *Macon*: Flying Aircraft Carriers of the United States Navy." The United States Naval Institute Press published it as a book in 1965, one year before the university awarded him his PhD. In the years that followed, Smith worked at the Smithsonian Institution's National Air and Space Museum, the Milton S. Eisenhower Library at Johns Hopkins University (as a defense contractor), and as an adjunct professor teaching the history of aeronautics in the engineering department at the University of Maryland in College Park, before retiring to Wilmington, North Carolina, in 1986. During his career Smith published a number of seminal books and articles—key among them, his contribution that compassed an airplane's performance: "The Weight Envelope: An Airplane's Fourth Dimension, Aviation's Bottom Line," which appeared in *Aerospace Historian* in 1986 and was quickly picked up and reprinted as a feature article by the International Society of Allied Weight Engineers in 1987.

I first met Dick Smith in Boston, at a session of the American Institute of Aeronautics and Astronautics where we both were presenting papers in the late 1960s. We struck up a friendship that lasted for the rest of his life. Sometimes erratic and almost always irascible, I found him to be one of those "unforgettable characters" that you meet once, maybe twice, in a lifetime. He possessed the remarkable faculty of near-total, encyclopedic recall. I don't know whether he developed that ability at sea or, as I suspect, had it all along. Friends and professional acquaintances could question him about an obscure movie, an airplane, or an aeronautical event, and he would have an answer and an explanation of its importance or unimportance in history, most often citing a source where you could find the details. I have known only one other historian who shares this remarkable faculty.

In 1990, after transferring from the USAF Historical Research Agency in Alabama to a position with the USAF History Program in Washington, D.C., I began spending four or five days with Smith each spring at his home in Wilmington. There, we would reminisce, discuss current historiography, and exchange war stories. It was during one of these visits that I first observed the typewritten biography of Frank Tinker on a shelf in his office. He had begun work on it around the time we met in the late 1960s and had completed a draft in 1983. When asked why he had not pursued publication, he replied that he had lost interest in the project. Typical Smith. I subsequently badgered him about the work, and a few months before his death in October 2003 he gave me the manuscript and said, "See what you can do with it." I told him I would try and see it published.[1]

That opportunity did not present itself until 2009, after my own retirement. What I anticipated to be an editing assignment, however, soon became much more. Some manuscript pages and footnotes were missing, which meant acquiring the works that Smith had relied upon to complete them. More recent scholarship, post-1983, also had to be consulted, and that material provided for refinement and amplification of the biography. Finally, after research trips to Arkansas and California in 2010, new information became available that resulted in changes to chapters 2, 16, and 17. In this endeavor, I found Frank G. Tinker Jr. to be a complex, colorful, and uncommon man—traits that I believe are borne out in the narrative. Both Smith and I relied on Tinker's personal papers and records that are now in the keeping of his niece, Marcia Tinker Morrison, who lives in Fresno, California. She and her husband kindly provided me access to this vital collection. Mrs. Maria Peña, manager of the digitization center at the Henry Madden Library, California State University, at Fresno, assisted in copying the Tinker family photographs that appear in this volume. My own contributions to the biography are identified in the endnotes that bear my initials. Endnotes without initials are Smith's.

A number of colleagues, friends, and associates also contributed to this work, which is far the richer for it. You and I are indebted to them. On learning that I held Smith's Tinker biography, Richard Sanders Allen, before he died in June 2008, sent me valuable material from his Spanish Civil War collection that proved especially helpful. A Russian expatriate, Ilya Grinberg, currently a professor at Buffalo State College in New York, assisted by Andrey Simonov, who supervises search and rescue at the Flight Research Institute (LII—the equivalent of Edwards Air Force Base) in Zhukovskiy, Russia, provided vital information on what became of the Soviet pilots that served with Tinker in the Spanish Civil War. Those pilots appear in the epilogue. Historians Kenneth Werrell, Ian White, William Trimble, Von Hardesty, and Richard Hallion referred me to recent scholarship, read each chapter, and made valuable suggestions and corrections; Hallion also graciously contributed the introduction. They served as Clio's backstop. My first English instructor at Shattuck School, Cecil D. Eby, who coincidentally went on to become an authority on the Lincoln Battalion in Spain, provided literary counsel on the beginning and ending chapters. Ms. Frances Lawson, an editor and longtime friend, helped in innumerable ways, most especially guiding me through the intricacies of using Windows XP Professional. Robert Fleitz, employing his genealogical skills, furnished the birth and death dates for a number of Tinker's colleagues who appear in the epilogue. His wife, San Juana Alcaraz Abrego Fleitz, translated numerous pages from Andres Garcia Lacalle's *Mitos y Verdades*, which allowed me to flesh out various aspects of the air war in Spain. Cartographer Christopher Robinson prepared the maps that appear in this biography. Ms. Shirley Mitchell of the Grand Prairie Historical Society in DeWitt, Arkansas, directed me to key Arkansas research sources and introduced me to some of Tinker's still-living contemporaries. Lemuel C. Brown Jr., who in his youth accompanied Tinker and his father on hunting trips, provided valuable details of the aviator's life in DeWitt in 1938–39 and furnished the photograph of Frank Tinker's JN-4 "Jenny." Finally, Shirley M. Hall, my wife and emeritus English instructor, read the entire manuscript, suggested changes for clarification, and ensured that the grammar and punctuation stood in good order.

Royalties from this publication have been consigned to the American Aviation Historical Society, in keeping with Smith's wishes.

INTRODUCTION:
THE SPANISH CIVIL WAR

F ew civil wars have been less civil than the vicious Spanish Civil War that raged across the Iberian Peninsula from the summer of 1936 until early 1939. Over seven decades have passed since General Francisco Franco y Bahamonde emerged from that conflict as caudillo of Spain. In the more than three decades since his passing in 1975, Spain has evolved into a very different country than it was at the time of his death. Then, the possibility of a Soviet thrust across Western Europe was a very real threat, and Franco's steadfastness as a staunch anti-Communist NATO ally largely tempered reservations about his autocratic, uncompromising rule. Today, Spain is a democratic state, fully integrated into the European Union. Like its European neighbors, it is coping with economic woes, widespread unemployment, and both homegrown and foreign-rooted terrorists. The traveler to its historic cities, rich countryside, and spectacular Mediterranean coast finds little evidence of the civil war, save for an occasional graffiti-embellished monument or weathered commemorative plaque. But a history so painful is not easily forgotten in just seventy years. Never far below the surface of pleasant social interchange, civil war memories still foment contention and divisiveness.[1]

To a surprising degree, that contention holds true across Europe and the United States. Since the cannon fell silent on the evening of 31 March 1939, the debate over the Spanish Civil War has constituted a veritable litmus test for both the political Left and Right. The more partisan of these extremes have accorded the civil war the stature of a veritable holy cause. They employ a shorthand of emotionally suggestive and visually evocative words and expressions to obscure and cloak the war's many complexities. During the war itself, the Left conjured images of impoverished and frustrated landless peasants rebelling against privileged and uncaring aristocratic land barons; the Right evoked images of atheistic Stalinists butchering clergy, burning churches, and destroying Spanish culture and traditions dating to the Middle Ages.[2] Although strong elements of truth exist in both portrayals, distortion still prevails.

If Franco won the civil war, the Left clearly won its history. Virtually from the outset of the fighting, a vigorous, persistent agitprop campaign presented the Spanish government in the best possible light, while it dismissed even the slightest reservations expressed by its own sympathizers and attacked more substantive complaints (most famously, in the case of George Orwell's *Homage to Catalonia*). Accordingly, for decades, most historians, journalists, and other literati have portrayed that war as a clear-cut Manichaean struggle between the causes of "Fascism" and "democracy," pitting privileged "Fascists" or "Nationalists" against freedom-loving "loyalists" or "republicans," largely ignoring what all these words meant within the realm of contemporary propaganda and the range of forces and factions at play on both sides.[3]

Thus, one still finds simplistic and even somewhat cartoonish portrayals of Spain in the 1930s as a free and democratic nation malevolently destroyed by the totalitarian triumvirate of Franco, Mussolini, and Hitler. Nurtured by seven decades of constant repetition, this globally accepted narrative flourished despite later and more balanced scholarship that presented more critical and nuanced viewpoints.[4] Beginning with Hugh Thomas (who authored the first dispassionate overview of the war) and Stanley Payne (who examined the war, its origins, and its outcome within the nature of Spanish social, cultural, and political thought and the international environment of the interwar years), historians have begun to venture beyond the veil of the common narrative, portraying a more layered and complex society, one riven in its prewar period (like Weimar Germany) by a remorseless battle between competing factions of the Left and Right, a partisan struggle for the heart of Spain that mortally wounded its fragile democracy well before Franco arrived in Morocco on 19 July 1936.

Ironically, if the Spanish government had succeeded in defeating Franco and his allies at that moment, the result would have been the imposition of a dictatorship of the Left no less authoritarian than that imposed by the caudillo—for the Spanish government in 1936 was essentially hijacked by Moscow and hitched to a Stalinist red star. Rather than a straightforward contest between Fascists and democrats, the Spanish Civil War was actually a bitter, uncompromising struggle between two expedient and equally ruthless coalitions: a right-wing mélange of Spanish Nationalists, monarchists, clericalists, and Fascists, against a left-wing mix of Communists, Trotskyites, Socialists, anarcho-syndicalists, and trade-unionists, with a leavening of genuinely liberal democrats. Spain's peasants largely split between these two coalitions; the sudden disappearances of their neighbors and the all-too-frequent and dolorous rattle of firing squads emphatically punctuated their daily lives and offered a grim reminder of the risks to them should they display any opposition—actual or suspected—to those of the Left or Right who controlled their local districts. In Spain, the casual brutality found in most civil wars amplified even further, whether by the Right's ruthlessly shooting out-of-hand suspected Socialist and Communist party leaders and local officials, or by the Left's *Terror Rojo*, manifest in widespread desecration of churches and the torturing, murdering, and then mutilating of the corpses of priests, nuns, and various other religious figures.

Like the civil war between the two Koreas a generation later, both sides relied upon foreign powers that sent expeditionary forces whose leaders gradually assumed ever-greater control and execution over strategic, operational, and tactical matters.[5] Fascist Italy and Nazi Germany supported Franco, while the Soviet Union aided the Spanish government that drew upon thousands of Comintern-recruited volunteers from western Europe and the United States. Although neither coalition worked together particularly well, the Left's effort proved a disaster. One can enumerate many reasons for the collapse of the Spanish government before the Nationalist onslaught, but, aside from Stalin's eventual withdrawal of Soviet support, none assumed greater prominence than did the feuds among its senior leaders and their lower-level supporters, their disunity exacerbated further by corruption, organizational disarray, and military incompetency. Spanish leftist infighting over legitimacy and goals frustrated Stalin. His operatives expended at least as much energy in Spain purging perceived undesirables from the ranks of the International Brigades and the Spanish government, while simultaneously trying to instill doctrinal cohesion, as they did fighting Franco and his allies.

Ironically, more than any other single individual, Joseph Stalin, not Franco, Mussolini, or Hitler, bears ultimate responsibility for the final collapse of "Republican" Spain. Stalin, as the Franco-American journalist, biographer, and historian Ted Morgan wrote damningly, "took over the Spanish government and the conduct of the war for his own ends. If nothing else, the Spanish Civil War was a lesson in the creation of a satellite state, which he would later apply to Central Europe."[6] He acted as a ruthless realpolitiker, whose support of the Spanish cause continued only so long as it served his political purposes.

In mid-to-late 1937 Stalin determined that he had extracted as much political and economic profit from Spain as could be obtained. He then judged Japan's bellicosity as of greater significance, and shifted the Soviet Union's strategic focus to the Far East. Whatever his change in focus, Stalin's involvement in Spain proved most profitable: the Soviet Union acquired almost all of Spain's nearly $500 million gold reserves—equivalent to approximately $8 billion in 2010 dollars—and because Stalin artificially pegged the ruble at double its value, he ensured the Spanish government paid twice as much for the aid it received as it was actually worth. (In contrast, later committed to the Chinese Communists, he authorized an "extraordinarily generous" aid package.[7] Morgan concluded: "When it came to arms deals, the Soviets made the capitalists look like amateurs.")[8]

Stalin's betrayal mortally wounded the Loyalists, who up to that point had been fighting steadfastly and generally well. He robbed them of men, matérial, and money precisely at the most critical period of the war, which doomed the Republic to eventual defeat.[9] Nor would he prove particularly grateful to those who had served the Soviet state in this venture. Mussolini's and Hitler's Spanish veterans returned to honors, promotion, and positions of responsibility; Stalin's Spanish veterans returned briefly to the Soviet Union, with many transferred to the Far East. There, they proved crucially important to the Soviet Union's subsequent combat success against the Japanese in China and Manchuria in 1938–39.[10] Many other Spanish veterans and their International Brigades comrades who also returned to the USSR met with xenophobic suspicion, consequent detention, and even death.[11] Only the coming of the "Great Patriotic War" likely saved more of them that otherwise would have disappeared into the anonymous human wasteland of the gulags. Surprisingly, after the end of World War II, large numbers of former Spanish government officials and military personnel, and some International Brigades members, also took refuge in Eastern Europe and the Soviet Union. Not surprisingly, some of them would be caught up in Stalin's last spasms of political terror, only reappearing, if at all, after his death in 1953. Of those among this cohort that survived, a number of them returned to Spain, while others settled in France, Eastern Europe, Mexico, other countries in Central and South America, and (for those Americans who had fought in the International Brigades), the United States.[12]

Stalin, of course, was hardly alone in practicing realpolitik in Spain. So too did Hitler and Mussolini, each supporting Franco for a mix of reasons, most having to do with securing positional advantage for their own nations.[13] A leftist Spain was antithetical to the interests of both Fascist Italy and Nazi Germany, while a rightist Spain could counterbalance both France and Britain's straits-guarding Gibraltar, to the possible benefit of both Italy and Germany in the event of a crisis or war. Supporting Franco and his fellow generals thus made perfect sense.

Franco had proven both a courageous and gifted officer, rising to army chief of staff in the years before the war. Even so, neither Mussolini nor Hitler considered him their equal. Neither shared Franco's passionate Catholicism or viewed the war as a holy crusade, echoing the earlier Reconquista. Il Duce was at best ambivalent in his own religious feelings, and der Führer, for his part, so pathologically detested any aspect of the West's Christian tradition (particularly the Catholic church) that he frequently spoke far more favorably of Islam than Christianity.[14] Though Hitler had a high regard for the fighting qualities of the individual Spanish soldier, he found the caudillo so tiresome that he once famously remarked during World War II that he would rather have "three or four teeth pulled" than endure another meeting with Franco.[15] In their dismissiveness, they seriously underestimated the shrewd and tenacious Spaniard, and it would be Franco, not they, who survived the war and a further three decades. Too astute to be drawn into the Axis camp in World War II, despite the seductively brilliant opening of Hitler's blitzkrieg, Franco profited from both his own innate wariness and warnings from Admiral Wilhelm Canaris, the anti-Hitler chief of Nazi military intelligence who was later arrested, tried, and executed for his part in the failed July 20, 1944, bomb plot against der Führer.[16]

Stalin, Hitler, and Mussolini quickly moved away from matters Iberian as the 1930s neared their close. By the late summer of 1939 (at which point surviving supporters of the Loyalist regime were languishing in refugee camps in France, making their way to exile in other foreign destinations, or in prison or work camps within Franco's Spain), Stalin and Hitler were putting the final touches on their Non-Aggression Pact. Coming after the Spanish defeat and Stalin's Purge trials, the pact cleaved an unmendable rift through the ranks of the Left, exacerbating the long-running battle between the Trotsky and Stalinist camps within the Communist movement, and between Socialists and Marxists who shared an even longer-running struggle. Despite the best efforts of party loyalists, the rift would not close completely, even after Hitler turned on Stalin in July 1941. But united by an expedient treachery in 1939, Hitler and Stalin dismembered Poland, plunging Europe into World War II, their respective Polish assaults spearheaded by many of the German and Soviet veterans first blooded in the war in Spain.[17]

At the outset of the Spanish Civil War, both sides sought to swiftly exploit military aviation, seeing airplanes, in the words of Hugh Thomas, as the "key to victory."[18] Indeed, aviation proved central to the onset of the revolt: to launch it, Franco flew from the Canary Islands to the Spanish enclave in Morocco on board a Dragon Rapide, a small, chartered, British biplane airliner. At once he faced a problem, one that mirrored the Bolshevik revolution nearly two decades previously: Spanish sailors had gone "Red," mutinying and taking over the fleet. What to do? Franco again looked skyward, using approximately thirty transports (composed of Italian, German, and Spanish Savoia-Marchetti, Junkers, and Fokker trimotors, and some Dornier Wal seaplanes) to airlift his Spanish Legion across the straits from North Africa. (Six years later, during one of his frequent anti-Catholic tirades, Hitler exclaimed in frustration to a group of dinner guests, "If I had not decided in 1936 to send him the first of our Junkers aircraft, Franco would never have survived. Today, his salvation is attributed to Saint Isabella!")[19] If not miraculous, the airlift certainly was providential. Without it, the revolt literally could not have left the ground.[20]

Despite the success of the government in enforcing its control over much of Spain, and that of Franco in moving his forces across the straits, neither side was able to swiftly overcome the other, and so the demands of war quickly translated into a drive by both sides to secure men, material, and foreign support sufficient to ensure eventual victory. Thus, both sides vigorously sought to acquire foreign aircraft from a variety of European and American nations, beside Germany, Italy, and the Soviet Union, both legally and covertly.[21] French aviation minister Pierre Cot, a Savoie Radical Socialist and self-acknowledged "Sovietophile," directed an extensive supply, support, and training effort to get French combat aircraft and volunteer pilots into the Loyalist air arm. Jean Moulin, then a young lawyer who served as Cot's principal private secretary, oversaw this effort. (Following the collapse of France in 1940, Moulin became "Max," a legendary resistance leader. He was eventually betrayed, captured, tortured, and murdered at the behest of the notorious Klaus Barbie.[22]) It was through Cot and Moulin that quantities of Dewoitine fighters and Potez bombers were transferred to the Loyalists, as well as many technical support personnel and pilots to fly and maintain them. The best known of these was the French leftist intellectual, adventurer, and author André Malraux, whom Cot sought out to help arrange Spanish support. The flamboyant Malraux, though not really a pilot himself, was an enthusiastic proponent of air power. Working from his Paris apartment on the Rue de Bac, he recruited, organized, and then led a volunteer squadron of airmen, the *escuadrilla España*, flying antiquated Potez bombers in the opening months of the war. The *escuadrilla* experienced indifferent success (and not a few losses) and was replaced near year's end by professional Soviet "Workers' and Peasants' Red Air Fleet" cadres flying Andrei Tupolev's more modern SB-2 bombers.[23]

Both sides worked strenuously to acquire weapons, particularly airplanes, from overseas, complementing the large numbers of German, Italian, and Russian airplanes that served in the conflict. But even the Germans, Italians, and Russians, at least at first, sought to mask the scope of their involvement. In early September 1936, for example, Stalin wrote to Lazar Kaganovich, a key deputy, that "It would be good to sell Mexico 50 high-speed bombers [a reference to the SB-2], so that Mexico can immediately resell them to Spain. We could also pick about 20 of our good pilots to perform combat functions in Spain and at the same time give flight training on the high-speed bombers to Spanish pilots. Think this matter over as quickly as possible."[24]

Arms transfers posed a particular headache for America, whose modern high-speed monoplanes were eagerly sought, particularly by the Loyalists, and early in January 1937 Congress passed a joint resolution banning arms, ammunition, and "implements of war" from the United States to Spain, as long as a state of civil strife existed.[25] But this did not prevent the Loyalists from working strenuously to evade such restrictions. In one telling example described in chapter 16 of this biography, the Bellanca Aircraft Corporation in 1938 tried various approaches to export twenty-two airplanes to Spain, but found its attempts thwarted by the State Department.

Spain served as a proving ground for contemporary and future warfare, but, as in any conflict, it was one in which the experimenters learned and refined as they went along. Despite later assertions, none of the external combatants—Germany, Italy, or the Soviet Union—entered the war with coherent doctrines or strategies that they were able or desirous of immediately "putting to the test." The intervention of German and Russian forces was marked by a certain irony: throughout the 1920s, to mid-1933, German and Soviet soldiers and (particularly) airmen had worked and trained together at Russian training and testing sites to the mutual benefit of each, and it is not inconceivable that some veterans of that earlier cooperation met under far less congenial circumstances in the skies above or upon the dusty terrain of Spain.[26]

Though the war attracted widespread military attention, assessing the lessons of Spanish combat was hardly as straightforward and easy as many have subsequently assumed. Old and new technology clashed, but analysts had to be careful in drawing lessons for the future, particularly for military aviation. To the later consternation of military and civil authorities, many aviation analysts drew the wrong conclusions.[27] Aircraft designer Alexander Yakovlev, a rising star in Soviet aeronautics in the late 1930s, noted how Nikolai Polikarpov's I-16 had initially proven a good match for Willy Messerschmitt's early Bf 109 when it appeared in Spanish skies. Soviet aviation authorities, however, failed to appreciate that in the climate of the late 1930s the I-16 was rapidly obsolescing, while the Bf 109 was just beginning its development, they failed to properly modernize their fighter force to address later and far more powerful and capable "Messers." Consequently, by the time of the Nazi invasion of the Soviet Union in 1941, Germany possessed an undisputed qualitative superiority in fighter (and also bomber) technology over the USSR. "The Germans," Yakovlev concluded bitterly after the war, "made better use of the experience gained in the Spanish war than the Soviet Union."[28]

Airpower proved crucially important in air-land warfare, repeatedly illustrating the vulnerability of troops and vehicles on the move to air attack, the psychological impact of air attack on deployed troops, and the power of synchronized combined arms in air, artillery, and armored assault.[29] Loyalist combat commander Tom Wintringham (who had previously served as an engine mechanic with the Royal Flying Corps in World War I) observed that "by 1938 . . . air power had become capable of taking over a large share of the functions of artillery. . . . Planes could do what guns used to do in Napoleon's hands: blast open a breach in the enemy's position for decisive manoeuvre."[30] Ferdinand Miksche, a Czech Loyalist military adviser who fought in Spain, declared even more forcefully:

The air force has become the hammer of modern war on land. Employed in close co-ordination with tanks, motorized infantry, and other ground forces it can bring battle to swift development. The great mobility of aircraft enables the attacker, because he holds the initiative, to seize almost at a flash the mastery of the air over the battlefield. Aviation gives modern land battle a third dimension: height. Forces no longer fight for surfaces, limited to length and breadth; modern battle is the fight for cubic space.[31]

The Wehrmacht's *Heer* campaigns into Poland, the Low Countries, and France in 1940 would show just how correct Wintringham and Miksche were.

But other lessons were far less straightforward. Indeed, like the Battle of Britain less than eighteen months afterward, Spain is, in many ways, more notable for lessons missed or misunderstood than for those actually learned and taken to heart. Consider, for example, the issue of fighters versus bombers. A debate raged in Europe in the early 1930s over whether, in some future war (as the British politician Stanley Baldwin put it), "The bomber will always get through." Spain offered contradictory lessons. Early in the conflict when rudimentary first-generation monoplane bombers, such as the cumbersome Potez and Junkers Ju 52, confronted nimble high-performance biplanes, such as the Polikarpov I-15 and Fiat C.R. 32, the open-cockpit biplanes had little difficulty in shooting them down. This experience encouraged the Soviet Union, Italy, Britain, and other nations to persist in building fighter biplanes, resulting in airplanes that were utterly outclassed when Hitler launched Europe into World War II in 1939. By the middle of the Spanish Civil War, Russian, German, and Italian streamlined monoplane bombers—aircraft such as the Tupolev SB-2, Heinkel He 111, and Savoia-Marchetti S.79, all representing the latest technological state of the art—had little difficulty outrunning older fighter biplanes. Because of this, many concluded that Baldwin was right: the self-defending bomber always would get through. But when, after August 1939, these monoplane bombers confronted modern streamlined monoplane fighters—airplanes such as the Messerschmitt Bf 109 and Britain's Supermarine Spitfire and Hawker Hurricane—they were savaged. Thus, in a technologically fluid aviation arena, the success of offensive bomber and defensive fighter operations was in fact situational, and, overall, when the technology of bomber and fighter was equivalent, the fighter normally had the upper hand, as the Battle of Poland, the Battle of France, the Battle of Britain, and the opening of the Anglo-American Combined Bomber Offensive against Germany would reveal.

Pilots proved as important as airplanes, and from the outset of the civil war both sides had need of as many skilled airmen as they could find. The Loyalists mobilized committed Communist youth and like-minded Socialists, idealists, and other "fellow travelers" into various International Brigades fighting for the Republican cause, recruiting aviators among these cohorts. In the years since the civil war, however, the role and importance of the International Brigades has been greatly exaggerated and their members romanticized and idealized. Largely a distilled by-product of official agitprop, sympathetic contemporary accounts by leftist sympathizers such as Malraux, Muriel Rukeyser, Ernest Hemingway, and the memoirs and accounts of International Brigades veterans, the mythos of the selfless "anti-Fascist" volunteer has constituted an essential pillar of the Loyalist narrative, periodically retold for newer audiences.[32] Over time, however, historians and other researchers have painted a very different picture, one of a group of individuals who were, on the whole, poorly trained, poorly prepared, and poorly disciplined; who were misused and mistreated (even executed) by their own officers and local Spanish and Russian authorities; and who were, as a consequence, prone to violence against their comrades, desertion, and disruptive action. Indeed, "The thousands of idealistic young men who signed up were deceived into helping Stalin hijack the Republican government," Ted Morgan concluded in 2003; "Anyone who dared criticize the brigades was denounced as a Franco agent."[33] For all of this, they fought as well as they could, and took heavy losses. Their casualties were such that, over time, the Comintern could not replenish the International Brigades with their fellow countrymen, and Spanish Loyalist soldiers replaced the losses.[34]

Not surprisingly, Hollywood played a crucial role in promulgating, refreshing, and repackaging both the common Loyalist narrative of the war and the image of the passionate, idealistic, "committed" international Loyalist volunteer.[35] Producers, directors, actors, and backers all enthusiastically championed the Loyalist cause from the start of the war, beginning with promotion of Dutch Communist filmmaker Joris Iven's *The Spanish Earth*. Even years after the Spanish government's collapse in 1939, Hollywood and foreign motion picture communities continued to propagate and embellish the Loyalist narrative in various films. Four stand out: Sam Woods' *For Whom the Bell Tolls* (based upon Ernest Hemingway's novel of the same name, released in 1943 with Gary Cooper's idealistic and doomed Robert Jordan); Fred Zinnemann's *Behold a Pale Horse* (from a novel by Emeric Pressburger,[36] released in 1964 featuring Gregory Peck's Manuel Artiguez, an aging anticlerical leftist guerrilla who, though disillusioned, cannot remain peacefully exiled in France while Spain remains in the thrall of Franco's civil police); Sydney Pollack's *The Way We Were* (a 1973 drama tracing the evolution of Katie Morosky—Barbara Streisand—from a young idealistic Loyalist sympathizer to a wounded-but-unbowed middle-aged activist); and Ken Loach's *Land and Freedom* (released in 1995, with Ian Hart portraying David Carr, a fervent young British Communist who goes to Spain, is disillusioned by Stalinist infighting and mutual atrocity, and returns to Britain, his fling with international activism carefully hidden from even his relatives until after his death).

Each offered a very different depiction of the war and its aftermath. Faithful to the novel, *For Whom the Bell Tolls* presented a simplistic view of the conflict (ironic, given that its director, Sam Woods, became increasingly conservative). Zinnemann's *Behold a Pale Horse*—with brilliant acting from Peck, Anthony Quinn (as a Spanish police captain), and Omar Sharif (as a priest who attempts to prevent Peck from crossing into Spain)—was more nuanced and forthright in portraying the lingering moral ambiguities in the aftermath of the war. Pollack's *The Way We Were* (which won two Oscars) drew a unwaveringly straight line from the Loyalist cause in Spain through the Hollywood Ten and into the McCarthy era, as lived by a passionate leftist proto-feminist (fittingly played by Streisand), whose uncompromising political activism eventually erodes her marriage with a more malleable and traditionalist scriptwriter (played by Robert Redford). Of the four, the most surprising was Loach's *Land and Freedom*, produced after the end of the Cold War when the workings of Stalinist-era Communism were largely laid bare. Though not free of some sentimental mawkishness, overall it offered a refreshingly accurate depiction of the war's realities.[37] It devastatingly conveyed the widespread sense of betrayal and disillusionment triggered by the Stalinist purging of non-Communists, Socialists, anarchists, and other non-doctrinaire undesirables, no matter how strongly anti-Franco and anti-Fascist they might otherwise be.

Although these films at best only partially addressed the complexities of the Spanish ground war, none of them examined the multifaceted complexity of the air war. The air war pitted Spanish airmen against one another, and against foreign aviators.[38] The foreign airmen were German, Italian, and Russian military pilots sent by Hitler, Mussolini, and Stalin, as well as various mercenaries recruited to fly for a particular side. In somewhat of a microcosm of how the International Brigades were mythologized, the mercenary pilots flying for the Loyalists have received a disproportionate amount of attention. Several left accounts of their experiences, one of whom, Frank Tinker, is the subject of this book.[39] Their exploits, some imagined and others, while real, too often embroidered, have been largely accepted uncritically. They have become the fabric of oft-repeated popular history and fable. Despite all the contemporary publicity attending their exploits (much of it appearing in aviation magazines and newspapers), they were neither as competent and reliable, nor as influential, as popularly portrayed.[40] Many, despite whatever talents they may have possessed, had personal weaknesses and faults that (if masked at the time) eventually led to their downfall. Like many mercenaries over the centuries, steadfastness, loyalty, personal discipline, and a willingness to accept authority within an established chain of command were often lacking. Many had spotty flying records and messy personal lives. Bickering, drinking, and "go-it-alone" tendencies work against developing the smoothly functioning teamwork and trust critical to any military flying organization, the latter attributes particularly characteristic of a professional air force.[41] Most pilot-mercenaries left or were reassigned from active service in Spain by the end of 1937. Thereafter, the air war was decided by professionals from established air arms, not by hired warriors, whatever their background and motivation.[42]

Readers acquainted with the air war in Spain will know that Spanish Nationalist forces frequently referred to encountering "Boeing" and "Curtiss" fighters, and "Martin" bombers. In fact (with the exception of one lone Boeing P-26 monoplane in Spain at the outset of the war), no Boeing, Curtiss, or Martin aircraft flew in Spanish skies. The confusion arose because so little was known of Soviet aircraft developments in the interwar years. When Franco landed in Morocco, the Soviet Union was a nascent aeronautical power with various gifted designers working to transform its military power. Chief among them were Nikolai Polikarpov and Andrei Tupolev. Polikarpov designed a trim fighter biplane, the I-15, which was first thought to be simply a Russian version of the Curtiss Hawk fighter, and a very advanced (for its time) monoplane, the I-16, which was likewise mistaken for the Boeing P-26 (despite the fact that the Boeing had externally braced wings and a fixed landing gear, while the I-16 was a fully cantilever monoplane with a retractable landing gear). Tupolev designed a highly streamlined twin-engine monoplane, the SB-2, which was thought to be a Russian version of the Martin B-10 bomber. Here, too, the SB-2 was an indigenous Soviet design. Tinker spent much of his time flying first the I-15, and then, after it arrived in Spain, the I-16. While the I-15 was the most agile, it was too slow and lacked power to operate much in a vertical plane. The I-16, though agile in its own right, was more powerful and could exploit diving and zoom-climbing ("back to the perch") in the vertical. The two together posed a formidable challenge to Nationalist pilots flying first the Heinkel He 51 (a biplane fighter inferior to the I-15), and then the Fiat C.R. 32 (which was a match for the I-15 but inferior to the I-16). The I-16 proved a match for the early Messerschmitt Bf 109 (as mentioned earlier), and Frank Tinker fought and scored against all three Nationalist fighters: the Heinkel, Fiat, and Messerschmitt.

This book is the biography of Frank Glasgow Tinker Jr., aka "Francisco Gomez Trejo." It was written by Richard K. Smith (1929–2003), whom I was privileged to know, and know well. Smith, one of the most influential figures in aviation historiography, was a meticulous scholar who had an eye for a great and interesting story. Though he would have denied it, he was a romantic, befitting a historian trained first as a professional seaman and naval officer. Something about doomed causes and the "what might have beens" of history struck a deep and resonant chord within him. Among Smith's many interests were flying boats and dirigible airships (two better examples of lost causes could hardly be found), but his most persistent interest—one I recall him telling me about nearly forty years ago—was the Spanish Civil War and the men who flew in it. Smith was not one by nature to accept uncritically the popular and prevailing narrative of such men and their exploits. And so, fluent in Spanish himself, he ventured to Spain, Mexico, France, and other locales where the *aviadores de la República* lived, seeking them out. In time, his interest settled on Tinker, who had already written a less-than-satisfactory autobiography, and had died under mysterious circumstances back in the United States in 1939. Perhaps it was the wanderlust that seemingly dominated Tinker's persona, or perhaps it was, at key moments of his life, his ability to snatch defeat from the jaws of victory that caught Smith's attention. For whatever reason, Smith used every opportunity afforded him to gather and sift through material that might shed light on this man, his contemporaries, and their work—real, not imagined—in Spain.

Five Down, No Glory is the result. Ironically, reflective of Smith's own mercurial, restless, and fickle nature, it was destined not to see publication during its author's lifetime. Indeed, in this writer's opinion, were Smith still alive, it is likely it would remain unpublished. Like the late Gordon Prange (another great historian the author was fortunate to know), Smith was rarely satisfied to let a manuscript go and was forever polishing text and looking for one more source to buttress some argument or elucidate some observation. And so, over time, he actually lost interest in Tinker, and when asked why the draft manuscript sat gathering dust on a shelf, he responded to Cargill Hall, coauthor of this biography, "By the time I finished it, I found that I didn't care for the man."[43] All who knew Smith will not be surprised by that answer.

Tinker, like many of the mercenary airmen (and those who affiliated with the International Brigades, whose association claims him as one of their own), was a complex, driven figure. Like his friends Albert "Ajax" Baumler and Harold "Whitey" Dahl, he came ultimately to a sad end, the bright promise of an early career lost for various reasons. Reading this work, one does find Tinker difficult to like at times, and certainly difficult to categorize. What might he have done had he lived into the World War II era? Was his life overall a life well lived? Of the first, we cannot know. Of the second, the answer is mixed, a balance of some notable accomplishments arrayed against opportunities squandered and lost to time.

But one thing is clear: Tinker's life is well worth reading for what it tells us of how the Spanish air war was fought, and how the international aviators who flew for the Loyalist cause conducted themselves, perceived their role, and interacted with both the Spanish military system and the increasingly dominant Soviet leadership of the Loyalist air arm. Building upon Smith's thorough scholarship, Hall mined new information, consulted sources unavailable to Smith, and, along the way, overturned some myth and misunderstandings.

Certainly, it would have been wonderful if Smith himself could have finished this work and published it within his lifetime. But since that did not occur, the next best outcome was having his good friend Cargill Hall, an outstanding historian in his own right, finish it for him. As for me, it has been a pleasure to associate with them both.

Dr. Richard P. Hallion
Shalimar, Florida
September 2010

1

THE ROAD TO PORT BOU

The young man slouched comfortably in the mohair cushions of the French train compartment, his cheek pressed against the window's cool glass. He might have been studying the passing rural scene if it were not for a far-away smile that tugged at the corners of his mouth. It was a wry, knowing smile that could function as the short fuse to an explosive go-to-hell laugh, and it had nothing to do with the lovely countryside of Languedoc flashing past the tall panes of the railway coach. The monotonous *click-click-click* of the coach's wheels across the butt ends of the French rails, which are laid side by side, vibrated through his cheekbone; it was so different from the rhythmic *clickety-clack* of American rails that have staggered joints. It reminded him of how greatly the tempo of his life had changed during the past thirty days.

His mind was oscillating between past and future, but with its sharpest focus upon the morrow so near at hand. It promised to be what he had always wanted, what he had volunteered for ten years earlier, and for which he had carefully prepared himself—only to be frustrated by the slow-motion chaos of the Great Depression, the muddling of a confused government, and the results of his own restlessness and recklessness. Eighteen months earlier his chosen career had been shattered and its pieces flushed away by humiliation. He had only himself to blame, but perhaps it was all for the best. The humdrum routines fenced in by rules, regulations, and no end of punctilio eventually would have inspired his rebellion. Better sooner than later. His humiliation of 1935 had become his opportunity of 1936, and now at the beginning of a new year he felt nothing but confidence as he mulled over his destiny.

So the young man smiled with sightlessness at the blurred landscapes of Languedoc. That smile, his conspicuous American clothes and lack of a hat, his companions in the *Wagon-Lits* compartment, and the very direction in which he was traveling were more than enough to excite the suspicions of any agent of the French *Sûreté* on this second day of January 1937. And with good reason.

The inside pocket of his suit held a Spanish passport that identified him as Señor Francisco Gomez Trejo. He had to think about that last name. It was pronounced "Tray-Ho." In his suitcase was a large manila envelope with other documents. One certified him as U.S. Naval Aviator No. 4091; another described him as an aviation cadet of the U.S. Army Air Corps; and yet a third was a certificate from the U.S. Commerce Department, which said he was licensed as a second mate on board American merchant ships.

Other men might have been worried about the explanations necessary to unravel these contradictions. But as his train shrieked through Perpignan and Port Vendres toward the French control point at Cerbère on the Iberian frontier, Francisco Gomez Trejo could not have cared less. Soon, after petty functionaries had solemnly exercised their rubber stamps at Cerbère, the frontier's barrier would be lifted and he would travel on to Port Bou; the gateway to Republican Spain and to the chance of a lifetime.

The señor had good reason to feel pleased with himself. Most of his adult life had been a curious series of unusual zigzags that could only arouse suspicions in the carefully ordered bureaucratic mind—a type of intellect he regarded with sly contempt. On the other hand, confusion had become his friend, and among the chaos that reigned in Spain he expected to find the key to his destiny.

This train ride along the Mediterranean shore of France had its beginnings almost eleven years before in the small town of DeWitt, Arkansas. From there it wound its way through the electrical shops of the battleship *Texas*, across the drill grounds of Annapolis, through the flight schools at Randolph Field and Pensacola, from where it hurled down the catapult rails of the cruiser *San Francisco*, through the honky-tonks of Long Beach and Waikiki to the navigating bridge of the Standard Oil tanker *Christy Payne*. From the coastwise oil routes his tracks went back to DeWitt for a moment, and then down the high iron of the Missouri Pacific Railroad to the Spanish Embassy in Mexico City, to the luxurious salons of the great transatlantic liner *Normandie*—to LeHavre, Paris, the Garé d'Orsay, and over the *click-click-click* of the *chemin de fer* to the south. To Cerbère and Port Bou. To Spain—and to the greatest of adventures in a disorderly life that had known few dull moments.

When Francisco Gomez Trejo leaned back from the window of the *Wagon-Lits* coach and raised his left hand to massage his cold cheek, his third finger displayed a massive gold signet ring. In the oval margins surrounding a garnet in its center, raised letters said "U.S. Naval Academy," and on one of its sides were the numerals "1933." On the ring's inside band, hidden against the flesh of the señor's finger, was engraved "Frank G. Tinker." The American papers in his suitcase identified him more completely as Frank Glasgow Tinker Jr. But the initials were the same. Even "Francisco" was Spanish for "Frank."

They seemed to have thought of everything.

2

THE RAGGED EDGE OF INFINITY

Frank Glasgow Tinker Jr. was born on 14 July 1909 in Gueydan, Louisiana, where his father served as the engineer-manager of a rice mill that supported the whole local economy. Located in the far south of the state, Gueydan is situated near Grand Lake, southwest of Lafayette. This is "Cajun country," the Cajuns being descendants of the French colonists whom the British deported en masse from Nova Scotia in 1763 after the end of the French and Indian War. Resettled in what was then French Louisiana, they knew Nova Scotia as Acadia, and as the language of the transplanted Acadians degenerated into a patois, "Acadian" became "Cajun." The Cajuns maintained their own way of life that was neither French nor American, but a peculiar amalgam of both. They spent as much energy celebrating Bastille Day as they did the Fourth of July, and in his younger years Frank was sure that the excitement had something to do with his birthday.[1]

As Frank grew older he came to respect his sister, Lucille, two years his senior, and on 8 December 1914 they were joined by a younger sister Mary Elizabeth. She grew up to despise her name, and within the family she acquired the nickname of "Toodles." She was Frank's first big disappointment in life; he had fully expected his mother to bring home a baby brother.

It was a slow, evenly paced, and pleasant rural world in which Frank Tinker grew to adolescence. For the Tinker family, one of a small handful of Anglo-Saxon families in the area, the ways of the Cajuns prevailed; when the Cajuns were not brawling among themselves on Saturday nights they were a delightful people to live among. The Cajuns were not only Catholics but considered themselves more French than American, so the Tinkers enjoyed not only the regular American holidays but also all of the Catholic feast and saints' days, with some French national holidays thrown in for good measure. These were invariably bright and noisy, with lots of music, dancing, roman candles and firecrackers, everything kept afloat on an ocean of wine. It was a world unique to the flat, swampy bayou country along Louisiana's Gulf Coast where Frank Jr. learned to hunt and fish, and the Tinker family enjoyed it as long as it lasted.

Within the Tinker family, young Frank grew up with an institution far removed from the bayous—the U.S. Navy. This singular aspect of the family was owed to Frank's grandfather, Thomas Christopher Tinker (1835–1915), who immigrated to the United States from England in the 1840s and settled in Wisconsin. When the American Civil War broke out in 1861, he joined the Navy and served under the command of Admiral David Glasgow Farragut in the fight up the Mississippi Delta and the battle of New Orleans, after which he was given an officer's commission. Admiral Farragut was Christopher Tinker's hero and it was no accident that his firstborn son was given the admiral's middle name, which was duly passed on to Frank Jr.

Grandfather Christopher Tinker returned to Wisconsin after the war, took a bride, and after the nationwide financial collapse of 1873, moved to the warmer clime of Louisiana where he became an engineer for various hydraulic projects. He eventually fathered eight children, four boys and four girls, the latter including twins. The boys grew up hearing all about Admiral Farragut, New Orleans, Mobile Bay, and other naval operations on the Gulf Coast during the Civil War, along with all of the virtues of the U.S. Navy. Twenty-six years old when the Spanish-American War broke out in April 1898, Frank Tinker Sr. made his way to the Pensacola Navy Yard, where he enlisted for the emergency. Although the war was over in a few months, he decided that life as a machinist's mate was good enough for him to go regular, and he stayed in the Navy for the next six years. When he finally carried his seabag down the gangway of the USS *Kearsarge* in March 1904, he was a chief petty officer.

At that time Grandfather Tinker was working on an irrigation project near Primeaux's Landing, Louisiana, and Frank Sr. went home to work on it as an engineer. As further mechanization of rice milling developed, he moved from the irrigation works into the mills themselves. It was in these years that he met a little butterfly of a girl named Effie Beatrice Henry, whom he married in 1906.

Thus the household in which young Frank grew up was one whose men had known horizons far beyond Louisiana and had established two generations of naval service. The Tinker household was full of sea stories, some real, many well stretched, and doubtlessly some fanciful, as sea stories will be, but they were enough to fire the imagination of a small boy. And they could keep it fired to adolescence, because this was an age without a mass media to degrade it with the decadent urban cynicism of the self-styled elite. At an early age, Frank Jr. learned that the most honorable career to which a young American could aspire was to be an officer in the U.S. Navy, and the best means of attaining this end was to graduate from the U.S. Naval Academy at Annapolis. To ensure that his children, already avid readers, would learn of other horizons and times, Frank Sr. purchased two sets of encyclopedias: *The Book of Knowledge* and *The*

Encyclopedia Britannica, an investment that put the family on rations for a number of months.

The demands of World War I caused a tremendous boom and expansion of the rice business, especially after the United States entered the war in April 1917. The Tinker family moved with the expansion, to nearby Abbeville in 1917 and to Kaplan in 1918. They lived well, but it was an incredibly simple life when compared with American standards only a quarter century later.

The Saturday motion picture show was the only commercial entertainment available in Kaplan. Shown in a room upstairs over the town's drugstore, they were silent films, as were all movies until 1931. But in Kaplan they were far from "silent." Most of the Cajuns could not speak English, most of them could not read any language, and they all looked forward to Mr. Tinker bringing his family to the movies. Frank Tinker Sr. read the film's English subtitles aloud for the benefit of his children. He always spoke loudly in an authoritative tone of voice, even to family members at home, accustomed as he was to directing others over the noise of rice-milling machines. Those Cajuns who understood English grouped themselves around the Tinker family so they could translate his words into their patois and shout it to the rest of the viewers. Saturday's silent movies were invariably noisy productions in Kaplan, Louisiana.

During World War I commercial rice growers discovered the virtues of the rich wetlands in the delta between the Arkansas and Mississippi rivers, and in the 1920s rice culture flourished in eastern Arkansas, as it still does today. Frank Sr. accepted an attractive offer, and the day after Frank's birthday in July 1924 he moved the family to DeWitt, Arkansas, as engineer-manager for the Smith Brothers Rice Mill then under construction. This was not to the liking of the Tinker children; not only did they have to leave their friends in Kaplan, the move also held a measure of cultural shock.

DeWitt is located about sixty miles southeast of Little Rock, near Arkansas' eastern border and the White River. In the 1920s its population numbered fewer than one thousand. Here, Frank was surprised to discover no big celebration on 14 July; but being a boy he soon adjusted to it and to numerous other changes. He made friends who showed him that hunting and fishing in the creeks and woods of Arkansas could be as good as that in the bayous of Louisiana. The girls, however, more socially conscious, soon loathed DeWitt. When it came time for Lucille to go away to college in 1925, she hastened back to Louisiana to the teachers' college at Natchitoches, and for all practical purposes never returned to Arkansas.[2]

In Louisiana the family had grown up as a tiny Protestant minority among the Cajuns and the Tinker children innocently assumed that only two religions coexisted in the United States. In DeWitt they were perplexed to discover only a few Catholics but all kinds of different Protestants. Society in DeWitt pivoted around the Baptist and Methodist churches, and it seemed to the children that their First Commandment was "Thou shalt have no fun." They sorely missed the Cajuns' lively saints' days, not to mention the everyday cheerfulness of the Cajuns themselves. Compared with Kaplan, life in DeWitt proved drab indeed.

Worse, as the children grew older and extended their intelligence network, they discovered that DeWitt's starched Protestant morality was only a façade. Everything forbidden with much clucking of tongues seemed to be done nevertheless, but out of sight, and it was the height of indiscretion to even hint at that reality. Appearances were what counted and the girls hated it. Frank grew up to laugh at it, which may have marked the beginning of his skepticism toward any "established order" that could not command his respect.

While living among the Cajuns the Tinkers had been known as "the Americans"; in DeWitt they came to be known as "those French people." Coming from the quasi-French environment of Louisiana, the Tinkers customarily served wine with the evening meal. In DeWitt, where the Southern Baptist and Southern Methodist churches held sway with a host of "Thou shalt nots" on the subject of alcoholic beverages, this was considered scandalous. Furthermore, with national Prohibition in effect, the Tinkers' wine was not only immoral, it was illegal!

Then there was all that strange, spicy cooking Mrs. Tinker did that had all those foreign names like "gumbo" and "jambalaya" and "gaspargeaux." The family ate strange things like shrimp, crabs, and lobster shipped in from Louisiana, and Mr. Tinker drove all the way to Pine Bluff to meet the express trains that delivered this fare. No one in DeWitt had seen a live lobster until the Tinkers imported them. One day Frank terrorized the family's washwoman by putting a lobster in her washtub. And then there was the rice. Strange as it may seem, in those years few people in the Arkansas rice country ate rice. But Mr. Tinker bought it at the mill in hundred-pound bags, maybe a dozen bags each year, and the family seemed to have rice on the table every day. The neighbors regarded this as extraordinary. This perception was largely owed to rice culture in Arkansas still being new. The local people did not yet understand how to cook the fine, white grain, and when they attempted it they usually transformed the rice into an unappetizing paste.

One of the strangest things about the Tinker family was the boy Frank. He was forever talking about going to some place called Annapolis where the government had the "Navy school." Annapolis was not only a long way from DeWitt, but everyone knew that a person had to have political connections to get into the Navy school. Mr. Tinker might be a big man at the mill, but he didn't know any congressmen or senators in Arkansas. And that was a fact. But Frank and his father had a way around this problem. When the Navy started its "Preparedness Program" of expansion in 1916, Secretary of the Navy Josephus Daniels slipped in a piece of legislation that reserved to the secretary of the Navy one hundred appointments to the Naval Academy for enlisted men already in the Navy between the ages of seventeen and twenty. These appointments were determined by competitive examinations, and it was one of these that Frank Jr. expected to obtain.

Tinker graduated from DeWitt High School on 21 May 1926, and when 14 July rolled around on the calendar, he wasted no time. At seventeen years of age, he and his mother, Effie, traveled to the state capital of Little Rock where they went to the Navy recruiting office in the post office and she signed the papers for his early enlistment. Frank G. Tinker Jr. raised his right hand and Lieutenant Commander John F. Donelson swore him into the U.S. Navy. Invested with a strong southern drawl, at his

Tinker, high school graduation photo
(*Family photograph*)

swearing-in young Tinker pronounced his surname "Tanker," a pronunciation he retained for the rest of his life. Detained at the mill that day, Frank's father missed the ceremony.

This was a moment of satisfaction for the Tinker family but incomprehensible to their friends in DeWitt. The Great War had been over for seven years and the patriotism and glamour that once attended a naval career had long since become tarnished by the "normalcy" of the 1920s. To the people of DeWitt, the peacetime Navy was a notorious catchall for fugitives, misfits, and petty criminals; and it was not as if Mr. Tinker couldn't afford to send Frank to college. As for Frank himself, he had life bore-sighted, his target standing bright and clear before him. This simple ceremony in the recruiting office was his first step toward the tree-shaded passage of Stribling Walk that leads to the steps of Bancroft Hall.

Within a week Frank Tinker was on board a train rushing eastward through the Ohio Valley and over the Alleghenies to the Navy town of Norfolk, Virginia. In 1926 Norfolk, with a population of about 120,000, was almost twice the size of Little Rock and Tinker regarded it as "a great big city." At the Naval Training Center in nearby Hampton Roads, the service introduced him to a new world in which clothes were not hung on hooks or hangers but were rolled up and stowed in a seabag; floors became decks, walls were bulkheads, and ceilings became overheads; where faucets were valves, his bed was a hammock rigged every night and "triced up" in the morning, and the bathroom was called "the head." The day began with reveille at 0530 when all hands turned out and triced up for inspection; breakfast at 0645, then another inspection, and after that, drill, drill, drill until 1630, when one washed clothes until suppertime at 1800. Tinker was grateful for his experience as a Boy Scout, for it resulted in his becoming a squad leader.

The active regimen of boot camp proved more than enough to keep a restless seventeen-year-old boy absorbed. And beyond the day's routine there was the exciting view of Hampton Roads' anchorage with "a lot of big ships" and the sky above where "every day we see airplanes and seaplanes." There were also Army blimps from Langley Field across the bay, and on two occasions Tinker looked up to see the massive form of the rigid airship USS *Los Angeles* drone by overhead. This was heady stuff for a small-town boy living in an era when books, magazines, and newspapers served to heighten curiosity among those remote from experience, with no television or personal computer to pilfer that experience of its novelty. The year 1926 saw the first flights to the North Pole and across the Polar icecap; as yet no one had flown to the South Pole. Only seven flights had been made across the North Atlantic, and no one had flown transpacific. For all practical purposes there was not a scheduled airline operating in the United States. The world of 1926 was still a very big place.

Among the draft of fifty-seven men with whom Tinker entered boot camp, only one besides him was a high school graduate. Most of them hailed from inland areas and were baffled by the action of the tides. His father had explained to him the function of the moon in this phenomenon, but when he tried to explain it to his fellow recruits they thought he was trying to play them for fools. When he told them that he planned to attend the U.S. Naval Academy, they thought he was out of his mind.

In late September Tinker packed his seabag, rolled up his hammock and triced it around the length of the bag, heaved it to his shoulder, and marched off to his first ship, the battleship *Texas*. He found the *Texas* in the Norfolk Navy Yard where she and her sister ship, the *New York*, had just been modernized by being converted from coal burners to the use of oil, and having their gun elevations increased. Even in 1926 the *Texas* was an old ship. Her construction was authorized in 1910, when the bulk of William Howard Taft filled the White House, and she was not commissioned until 12 March 1914. However, her "age" had less to do with time than technology. Many new ship requirements were discovered as the result of experiences during World War I and few of them could be retrofitted into the *Texas*. This old ship nevertheless was to perform many vital services during World War II.[3]

On board the *Texas*, Tinker was assigned to the electrical division and received instruction on rewiring the ignition circuits of the ship's several motorboats. What fascinated him most, however, were the two Loening OL-6 seaplanes perched near the catapult atop No. 3 turret. It was an exciting moment when he had occasion to check the water in the seaplanes' batteries. He fantasized about the possibility of being taken up for a flight, but as a lowly apprentice fireman he hardly dared say more than "Good morning, Sir," to the aviators on board.

In mid-November he enjoyed an unusual diversion when the Schneider Trophy races were held at Hampton Roads. Jack Schneider, a member of the French family of armaments manufacturers, initiated this international event in 1912 as a seaplane competition between private fliers to foster interest in marine aviation. After 1919, however, it became a competition between national teams financed by governments. By 1926 the contest had been reduced to one between the Americans, British, and Italians, although in this year the British failed to enter and it was an Italo-American event. Three sleek Curtiss R3C biplanes represented the United States. The Italians had three even-more sleek Macchi M.39 low-wing monoplanes. To the unease of the Americans, preliminary speed trials showed that the Macchi monoplanes were almost as fast as the Curtiss racers, and the calm smiles that the Italian pilots shared among themselves suggested that perhaps they had been holding back on their throttles.

On Saturday, 13 November, Frank Tinker numbered among the more than 30,000 spectators who watched the tiny silhouettes on floats dash back and forth across the sky over the triangular race course.[4] The Italians won the race with a speed of 246 mph. Little could Tinker imagine that eleven years later he would be debating, with himself and others, the merits of biplane versus monoplane; although the aircraft in question would not be American versus Italian, but Russian versus Italian and German.

The battleship *Texas* took Tinker on a few pleasant cruises to Cuba and other Caribbean ports, but "economy" was the watchword of the parsimonious Republican governments of the 1920s. Fuel oil cost money, so the *Texas* spent most of her time moored to a pier in Norfolk. Meanwhile, he kept busy with a correspondence course in mathematics to prepare himself for the examinations to the Naval Academy. Back in October he took the preliminary fleet-wide examinations and passed, which permitted him to attend the Navy's preparatory school. The Navy did not permit its enlisted men candidates to go up against the Academy exams cold. Recognizing the fact that the men had been out of school for a year or two, it put them through a six-month prep school that "crammed" them for the examination.[5] This was an expensive procedure, but no less dared

Tinker, enlisted seaman (*Family photograph*)

be done in the procurement of the Navy's future officer material.

From October 1926 to March 1927, Tinker wore down many a pencil to its stub in the prep school at Hampton Roads. Attrition took its toll, and as the months went by he watched the others drop out in ones and twos, which soon added up to dozens. He thought he was doing well until one day in early March he was told to pack his seabag. Three hours later he was crossing the quarterdeck of the new aircraft carrier *Lexington* for transport to the West Coast, where he had orders to report to the battleship *New York*.

This was a demoralizing experience. Tinker received no explanation as to why he had been dropped from the school. Two consolations eased his pain: he could try again next year, and there was the cruise to the West Coast on board the *Lexington*. When he reported to the *Lexington*, it was Lieutenant C. A. F. "Ziggy" Sprague who logged him on board and turned him over to the master at arms who took him to his berthing space. Sprague was the ship's arresting gear officer; he would have a bitter rendezvous with destiny sixteen years later under the guns of Japanese battleships at the Battle of Leyte Gulf. The *Lexington*'s ordnance officer was Lieutenant Forrest P. Sherman, a brilliant air officer who would rise to become chief of naval operations. The ship's air department included Lieutenant A. M. "Mel" Pride, a great test pilot of the interwar years, and Lieutenants Braxton Rhodes, who had been a member of the Navy's transatlantic NC flight operation of 1919.[6] Lieutenant Joseph B. Anderson had been the weather forecaster in the Azores for that flight and was in charge of the ship's aerology department. Lieutenant (jg) D. Ward Harrigan and Lieutenant Frederick M. Trapnell embarked with the *Lexington*'s aircraft squadrons. Both of them would share some unusual years as "trapeze artists" on board the Navy's airplane-carrying airships *Akron* and *Macon*,[7] and Trapnell would directly cross Frank Tinker's career seven years later on board the cruiser *San Francisco*. At that moment, however, all of this was unknown to them. Whatever the future, Frank was more interested in the awesome spaces of the *Lexington* and that, not being a member of the ship's company, he would have a "free ride" to San Diego.

On 8 March 1927 the *Lexington* got under way and four days later anchored at Pensacola where she received on board the remainder of her airplanes. A week later she was en route to the Panama Canal. The *Lexington*'s transit of the canal was a minor disaster. At this date she was the largest ship ever to make the transit, and the canal pilot was perplexed by the ship's bridge being on an "island" on the starboard side instead of across her beam as on most ships. Visibility of the ship's port side relative to the wall of the locks was practically zero. Consequently, hundreds of square feet of paint were scraped off her sides while going through the locks, and there was minor damage. Tinker wrote to his father that in the Gatun locks alone she knocked down five lampposts on the locks' edge and tore off a boat boom and most of the scupper guards on her port side. After this first experience, piloting a large aircraft carrier through the Panama Canal developed into a special technique.

While growing up in Louisiana and Arkansas, Tinker's two sisters had taken to calling him "Brother," or "Bro," a custom common in the South in those days. Like "Toodles" for Mary, it became his family nickname. In all of the many letters that he wrote to his sisters and parents during all the years that followed, Tinker always signed them "Bro."

It was a pleasant cruise up the west coast of Mexico, and as the *Lexington* neared San Diego on the morning of 6 April she launched twenty-six of her Curtiss F6C-3 fighters and a dozen Martin T4M-2 torpedo planes. As the mighty *Lexington* steamed into San Diego bay with an umbrella of her airplanes overhead, the sight of the battleships *California, Maryland, New Mexico, Idaho,* and *Arizona* riding at anchor in the roadstead, their pale gray hulls glittering in the noonday sun, filled Tinker with awe. This was the real American Battle Fleet, or at least a substantial part of it.

When the *Lexington*'s anchors plunged into the mud offshore of San Diego's Point Loma, Tinker's "vacation" ended. Within an hour he was hustled into a motor whaleboat and taken to the *New York,* his home for the next year. The *New York* was a sister ship to the *Texas,* so she held nothing new for Tinker except occasional cruises to the ports of the West Coast and Hawaii. He was absorbed by correspondence courses in mathematics and geometry. He was also keeping up with his career as an enlisted man and was rated as a fireman 2nd class—no small achievement for only two years in the peacetime Navy.

That summer of 1928 Tinker took the preliminary exams for the Naval Academy again, passed, and in October attended the prep school in San Diego. He worked harder than ever this time. By December only 64 of the original 112 of his class were left, and in May 1929 he discovered to his relief and delight that he had won one of the coveted 100 appointments. Physically well joined, the blue-eyed Frank Tinker sported a shock of light brown hair, a height of five feet eleven inches, and a weight of 150 pounds. As his future yearbook picture attested, women would find him definitely attractive.

A few weeks later, in June, he carried his seabag down Annapolis' Maryland Avenue, through the Naval Academy's No. 3 gate, and reported on board the USS *Reina Mercedes*, which had been gathering barnacles in Santee Basin for more than a quarter of a century. The *Reina Mercedes* was an ancient Spanish cruiser that had been the Spanish navy's station ship in Santiago, Cuba. The U.S. Navy took her over as a prize of the Spanish-American War and pressed her into the same service for the Naval Academy, where she served as a barracks ship for enlisted personnel. She also had a collateral disciplinary function as regards the midshipmen. When a midshipman committed a serious offense, he was sentenced to live on board the *Reina Mercedes*—"the ship," as she was known—for a week or more. The offender had to attend classes as usual but otherwise dared not put a foot on the Academy grounds. On board "the ship" he had to sleep in a hammock, submit to endless inspections, and perform all kinds of menial work. The enlisted personnel berthed on board the *Reina Mercedes* had orders to make the life of midshipmen confined to "the ship" as uncomfortable as possible, orders they followed with gusto. When Tinker went on board the *Reina Mercedes* that day, he was a fireman 2nd class; when he went down her gangway a few days later he was a midshipman. Although he subsequently developed a "non-reg" reputation at the Academy, his conduct (or his luck) was good enough that he never again had occasion to spend a night on board the *Reina Mercedes*.

Tinker was accustomed to "aye-aye-Sir" discipline, but the Academy held some shocks for him. A recruit in boot camp was treated with more dignity than a plebe (as a midshipman is called in his first year); at the Naval Academy he was denied it completely. Other things were perplexing. Though a religious family, the Tinkers were only occasional churchgoers; at the Academy he had to attend church on Sunday, like it or not. And then there was hazing.

Although the physical hazing of plebes was forbidden by an act of Congress in 1874, the Academy's authorities did practically nothing to enforce it. Despite the hazing, and within broad limits, the midshipmen not only were permitted to run their own little world, they were expected to do so. The four distinct classes provided a hierarchy through which the middies learned military discipline and leadership by practicing on one another. The officers who administered the Academy seldom intervened in midshipmen affairs, except as problems were brought to them, or in the case of an untoward event provoking pressures from the outside world.

Endowing the midshipmen corps with this quasi-autonomy reflected the old Navy's philosophy of "Tell a man what to do, but don't harass him by constantly telling him how to do it." Coincidentally it served to kindle within the whole body of midshipmen a tough elitism that for four years gave them an "us-versus-them" view of the world beyond their small corps. Most important in the long run, this system served to make them "learn from each other." Odd as it may seem, it was in many ways democratic, and one of its virtues was its long-term flexibility. As a result of the annual turnover in midshipmen, values changed across a term of years, reflecting an approximation of the values of the outside world. They changed slowly, but they changed, thereby avoiding stagnation into hidebound ridiculousness.

To be sure, physical hazing took place within this tight little world of some two thousand young men, and some of it was brutal—favorite instruments being broom handles and cricket bats applied to the derrière. With dark humor, one sadistic drill was called "pile drivers." A hapless plebe was ordered to chin himself on the lintel of a doorway, then raise his legs until they were 90 degrees to his torso. Once in this position and with his buttocks aimed at the terrazzo deck almost five feet beneath him, he was commanded to release his grip on the doorway. It is a marvel that a plebe made it to his second year with a straight spine. Inevitably, there were abuses. The authorities, however, expected upperclassmen endowed with a sense of responsibility to police any malevolence among their peers.

More typically, a plebe's life was simply one of seemingly endless petty harassments. He had to address all upperclassmen as "Sir"; he walked only along the centerline of a hallway with a stiff military posture, eyes dead ahead, thumbs on the seams of his trousers. On changing direction, he turned 90-degree "square corners." At meals he was expected to sit stiffly "braced" on the outboard two inches of his chair, arms not touching the table, and occasionally partake of a "square meal," in which he moved food from his plate to his mouth through a 90-degree angle. Failure to observe these rules brought down on the unfortunate plebe more serious hazing.

Suppertime could be a bad hour. A plebe was always expected to know what was being served for dessert. If an upperclassman asked and he did not know, humiliating penalties followed. The plebe might be ordered to finish his supper under the table, and if someone seated at the table just happened to kick the plebe's plate out of his hands, that was too bad. At any meal the plebe could expect all kinds of inane, humiliating questions from the upperclassmen, to which he was expected to have the correct predetermined answers, such as:

Q. "What is the longest ship in the Navy?"

A. "The battleship USS *Maine*, Sir, because her foremast is in Annapolis and her mainmast is in Arlington Cemetery, Sir!"

Q. "Where are you, plebe?"

A. "I'm at 38 degrees, 58 minutes, and 53 seconds north by 76 degrees, 29 minutes, and 08 seconds west, Sir!" [The latitude and longitude of Annapolis.]

Q. "How long have you been in this Navy, plebe?"

A. "All me bloomin' life, Sir! My mother was a mermaid, my father was King Neptune. I was born on the crest of a wave and rocked in the cradle of the deep. Seaweed and barnacles are my clothes; every tooth in my head is a marlinspike; the hair on my head is hemp. Every bone in my body is a spar, and when I spits, I spits tar! I'se hard, I are, I are, Sir!"[8]

This simply was too much for many of the plebes and before the fall term ended two dozen had resigned. Tinker told his parents that, as far as he was concerned, this was just fine because "I figure that the more that resign the more chance there will be for those who stick it out." He was nevertheless shocked when his roommate broke down and told him he was going to resign. Having worked for three years to get into the Academy, Tinker found it difficult to watch another person throw away the same prize. He talked his roommate out of resigning but managed to make it stick for only two months. His next roommate had come to the Academy by the same enlisted man's route as he had, only he was a Marine by the name of Guy M. Morrow; they became fast friends and remained roommates to graduation.[9]

After three years' hard labor, for a moment Tinker's entrance to the Academy seemed like a happy ending. But the Academy proved to be the Navy prep school all over again, with cramming and more cramming of the books, not just for six months but for four years, eleven months of each year, and with nothing like the leisure he had as a fireman 2nd class. There is an old saying that there are two great disappointments in life: one is the failure to achieve one's heart's desire and the other is achieving it in full. To the latter can be added a small but malignant postlude of bitterness that may occur when the achievement comes late; and this original distortion in timing may lead to subsequent distortions.

Frank Tinker was no academic whiz and remained always in the lowest quarter of his class, but he did much better in his plebe year than in any year thereafter. Coming to the Academy from the discipline of the fleet, he got fewer demerits in conduct during his whole year as a plebe than in either semester of his "youngster" year (as midshipmen in their second year are called). By the summer of 1930, between his first and second years, something occurred that caused him to reassess his position and he began to sour. It may have been a realization that the Academy was not a happy ending; that for all practical purposes he had been hard at it for four years and still had three years of "more of the same" to go.

Aware of it or not, he became angry, cynical, and frustrated. And he often took out his frustrations on the plebes. His peers in the class of '33 recall him as a colorful character who exhibited a "quickness of mind and a keen sense of humor," but some of his juniors in the class of '34 remember him as a capricious bully whom they often went around corners to avoid. Also in 1930, he discovered liquor as an anesthetic to the world. Although not a heavy drinker, his problem was a low threshold of tolerance to alcohol over which he easily tripped into drunken behavior and its corollary realm of extraordinarily bad judgment. It was during this second year at the Academy that he first displayed many of the characteristics of a spit-into-the-wind personality that would serve him badly in the years to come.

In the summer of 1930 there was a cruise to France, Norway, Germany, and Scotland with the midshipmen divided among the old battleships *Florida* and *Utah*, and the somewhat newer *Arkansas*. In Cherbourg, Tinker hired a bicycle for a tour of Normandy. He was at first perplexed by the European bicycle having its brakes on the handle grips, a wholly different form of control as compared to the American coaster brake, but he soon became accustomed to its mechanics. This mechanical detail Tinker would forget during the next seven years—to his later peril in Spain.

The visit to France was marred by one midshipman who went to Paris, locked himself in a hotel room, and shot himself. Tinker shrugged this off; there were simply some who couldn't take it. But he thought a letter of resignation would have made much more sense than a bullet in the head.

The months passed and rolled themselves up into another year. There was no summer cruise for Tinker's class in 1931; they were held at Annapolis for a special aviation course. In the autumn of 1931 he was a second classman. Life was a regimen of one examination after another, anxiously studying the bulletin boards for grades, or looking on "the tree" to see if there was an "unsat" in any courses. Once upon a time at Annapolis a midshipmen's unsatisfactory scores were posted on a tree on the Academy grounds. By the twentieth century "the tree" was long gone, replaced by a special bulletin board in Bancroft Hall, but the name remained in the vernacular. Tinker had few "unsats," and he crammed hard to make them up, always hanging on by what he called "the ragged edge of infinity."

In the Navy system of scoring, 4.0 is perfect, 2.5 barely passing, and Tinker was a 2.9 student. The most irksome of his studies was "Dago," the pejorative used by midshipmen to describe any foreign language course. Before World War II the Academy taught only Spanish and French. Midshipmen of the 1st and 3rd

Battalions took Spanish; those of the 2nd and 4th Battalions took French. It was as simple as that. Being in the 4th Battalion, Frank struggled with French. Of course in those years he could not imagine how useful Spanish would be to him within a few years—not to mention Russian.

The compulsory Sunday church attendance most irritated Tinker, and after his plebe year he decided that he had had enough. He protested to the chaplain that it was against his religion because he was a Muslim. This was an old dodge used by midshipmen in an attempt to avoid the Sunday duty, but a questioning by the chaplain on the major points of the Muslim faith invariably demolished the claim. Tinker, however, took pains to do his homework. He bought a Qur'an, studied it, and in the excellent library facilities of Mahan Hall he did extensive collateral reading. The chaplain was surprised to discover that Tinker knew more about the subject than he did.

The chaplain admitted Tinker's claim but at this point the upperclassmen took over. None of them enjoyed the prospect of this "youngster" lying in bed on Sundays while they had to go to church. They visited his room every day to "supervise" his prayers to Allah. Tinker had a rug that he solemnly oriented toward Mecca and duly went through the Muslim rakats for his audience, day after day, week after week, until the upperclassmen finally wearied of it. Tinker already had the nickname "Salty"; after this he was also called "the Moham-medan." During the next two and one-half years he enjoyed his Sunday mornings lying in the sack reading *Yachting* magazine or such pulps as *Amazing Stories* and *Flying Aces,* while the "Christian dogs" marched off to church.

By his third year he and his roommate Guy Morrow were berthed in room 4346, which claimed a marvelous view of Annapolis and Eastport. They transformed their room into a comfortable den with two Victrolas, an excellent radio, and an illegal electric coffeepot. The coffeepot was a relatively innocuous offense as compared with the liquor most midshipmen had stashed somewhere on the Academy grounds. In spite of Prohibition, and of Navy regulations in general and Academy regulations in particular, clandestine booze was a normal constituent of midshipman life in Bancroft Hall.

Tinker was prepared to entertain anyone who dropped around to their room with some "country music" played on his harmonica or an asthmatic old accordion that he had acquired in high school. He had taught himself to play these instruments by listening to radio station WLW in Nashville, Tennessee. A fondness for music notwithstanding, he was a "Red Mike," an ancient label applied to a midshipman who refused to attend dances and other social functions in which the fairer sex played a part. As early as 1926 he remarked that he "did not approve of modern dancing," and while in Seattle on board the *New York* he looked in on a widely publicized "dance marathon," one of those spectacles of the 1920s that went on for days, and he claimed to be shocked by it.[10] Although the girls found him attractive and personable, he tended to be uncomfortably self-conscious in their presence. He refused to learn how to dance, rationalizing it in terms of something frivolous and unworthy of his attention. If his classmates judged him to prefer the company of his books, sailboats, booze, magazines, and accordion to that of *les girls*, during his four years at the Academy Tinker did correspond with girls that he knew while growing up in Louisiana and Arkansas. Certainly, his interest in the fairer sex would increase noticeably after graduation.

In the autumn of 1931 the midshipmen received news that they might not be commissioned on graduation. This was owed to an old law of 1916 that restricted the number of Navy line officers to 4 percent of the enlisted personnel, and to the economics of the Great Depression that was now two years old. The authorized strength of the Navy's enlisted personnel stood at 137,485 men, but as a result of cutting back on enlistments in the name of "economy," by 1931 there were only 29,700 enlisted men on strength. On the other hand, there were 5,578 officers. This created an apparent excess, and the Academy graduated about 400 new officers each year. Congress seriously considered not granting commissions to the entire graduating class in 1932 and simply dumping them all into civilian life. A compromise resulted in all of the class of '32 being commissioned, but only one-half of those classes graduating thereafter. Tinker's class would graduate in 1933.[11] The one-half to be commissioned were those who ranked scholastically in the upper half of their class, and that was not Frank Tinker's territory.

Meanwhile, back in September 1931 the Japanese seized Manchuria and began squeezing China. While President Herbert Hoover was doing his best to emasculate the Navy in his desperate search for the will o' the wisp of a balanced budget, his secretary of state Henry Stimson chirped moralistic lectures at the Japanese, telling them how naughtily they were behaving. From his eyrie in Bancroft Hall, Midshipman Tinker kept an interested eye on the smoldering "Eastern Question," remarking that "the situation in China is beginning to look very interesting, especially to members of my class. A first class war with Japan is about the only chance we have of getting commissions." Naively, he expected Stimson "to send the Japs an ultimatum just any day now," and added, "If the action does start, they'll probably graduate my class at once, so here's hoping for the best!"

By the spring of 1932, however, Tinker had given up any hopes he may have had of a war salvaging his predicament: "I doubt if we can do anything about the Japanese situation with the present Republican regime in power." Now he was disgusted with Stimson's "note writing." On the other hand, he was aware of the Navy's deplorable condition: "Only five of our battleships are anyways near modern, and they were built during and right after the war, and I doubt if we have any destroyers that could hold up under any kind of extended cruise; right now the

Jap navy could probably beat the tar out of any fleet the U.S. could muster up."[12] The Japanese had arrived at a similar estimate; across the Pacific, they stoically ignored the scoldings of Mr. Hoover and his pedantic secretary of state.

June came around again, the Naval Academy class of '32 was graduated and commissioned, and Tinker and his classmates had the exciting experience of being fitted for their class rings. The rings were made by Tiffany of Fifth Avenue, New York, which inspired him to exclaim, "Some class, eh wot!" He thought that "Tiffany & Co." should be inscribed somewhere on the outside of the ring! And then his class was off for its summer cruise, a short circuit of the North Atlantic to the Azores and Nova Scotia on board the old battleship *Wyoming*. The brevity of the cruise owed to financial restrictions; the Navy had orders not to burn too much oil.

Twenty-one years old by 1932 and scheduled to be scrapped, the *Wyoming* was only a souvenir battleship. Two of her main turrets and all of her armor had been removed a few years before, and her only function was as a training ship. It was a dull cruise, but enlivened by the awesome experience of sailing through the eye of a hurricane. During this event the removal of the old battleship's former topside weights probably saved her and the class of '33 from being transformed into another great mystery of the sea, similar to that of the USS *Cyclops*, which disappeared in the Caribbean in 1918. While in the coils of the hurricane, 90-knot winds and mountainous seas lashed the *Wyoming* and tossed her around like a wood chip. And her rolling became severe when the ship broached. Finally, at one point, she rolled over to 38 degrees to port and seemed to hang there for an eternity. Everyone feared that she was going to capsize. But she snapped back to roll 33 degrees to starboard, after which her oscillations became fewer. But for a few seconds all hands feared that the ship was finished. Belowdecks in the engine room, the engineers marveled that the boilers had not hopped off their footings—a turn of events that most certainly would have initiated the beginning of the end. During this tonic experience it may be assumed that Tinker had a few kind words for Allah.

When classes resumed in the autumn of 1932, a singular mixture of gloom and to-hell-with-it-all existed among Tinker's classmates. These feelings, of course, were restricted to those in the lower half of the class who knew that there would be no commissions for them on graduation day. Faced with this certainty, many chose to rush fate by flagrantly violating the Academy's regulations. Academy officials asked most of them for their resignations, or they were expelled. But not Frank Tinker; he hung on like a bulldog.

In anticipation of being returned to civil life, Tinker busied himself writing letters to steamship companies in quest of future employment. In similar straits, Midshipman Elliot L. "Jesse" James proved more imaginative. He went to Washington and visited his congressman, Lister Hill of Alabama, to ask about the possibility of getting an appointment as an air cadet in the Army Air Corps. Hill was on the Military Affairs Committee that handled the U.S. Army and he had no familiarity with the Navy's problems. James' information about half of the Academy class of '33 being returned to civil life prompted Hill to salvage a part of the government's investment. It cost $14,000 to train a midshipman to graduation; it made no sense to Hill to let this investment in trained manpower go to waste in the name of "economy." The congressman made arrangements for the Army Air Corps to accept seven ex-midshipmen of the class of '33 for flight training.[13] This gesture served to create a small group of officers who would be unique in the annals of U.S. naval aviation.

There had been a great deal of excitement in February 1933 when Congress moved to terminate the nation's disastrous "noble experiment" with Prohibition; bells, whistles, and sirens sounded throughout Annapolis. Still greater excitement ensued in April when beer became legal and a parade of 2,200 truckloads of beer rolled into Annapolis from breweries in Baltimore. All Annapolis was in an uproar and the carillon in the city's clock tower played "How Dry I Am." Some midshipmen went "over the wall" to join the festivities, but not Tinker; he remained determined to protect his graduation. But a few days later, audible groans could be heard from Bancroft Hall to the cemetery on Strawberry Hill when the midshipmen drew their April pay and discovered that the government's Economy Act had slashed all government salaries by 15 percent.

In April it also became manifest that Congress would not give the class of '33 a last-minute reprieve; now it was certain that only one-half of the class would receive commissions. To sweeten the bitter dose for the noncommissioned half, all of the graduating midshipmen would be awarded bachelor of science degrees. This was something new. Until 1933 the Naval Academy had never awarded an academic degree. Those discharged into civil life would be given commissions in the Naval Reserve and a year's pay of $780 (less 15 percent for "economy") by way of severance pay. With this windfall in prospect Tinker bought a 1929 Chevrolet convertible and made arrangements to buy a .45 Colt automatic pistol. He thought the combination might be useful if he had to take up bank robbing for a living—a practice much in vogue in the Depression year of 1933.

When the Navy announced that the Air Corps had vacancies for flight training, Tinker and about a hundred others applied. Only about forty passed the physical exam, and for a while there were doubts about Frank's eyesight. Unbeknownst to Tinker, he had a problem with depth perception, but the medics told him to rest his eyes and come back in thirty days. To put an anchor to windward he took the Commerce Department's examinations for a merchant marine officer's license and emerged with a second mate's ticket. It would be useful two years

GUY MARION MORROW
DECATUR, ILLINOIS
"Guy" "G"

WAY back yonder in the past, Guy decided that military life was just the thing for him, so what do you think he did? No, you're wrong. He went and joined the Marines. However, he rectified his error later on by passing the entrance exams to this our beloved Alma Mater. It seems though, that one never learns; he still has Marines on the brain and we suppose that's where he will be found from now on.

Life here at the Academy has not dealt very severely with him. With the exception of a little set-to with steam Plebe Year, studies have caused work but not worry. The text books always got a rest when there was a "Cosmo" or a Liberty lying around the room.

And when it came to "snaking" very few hops went by without the presence of our hero. We don't know how he did it, but he always had a 4.0 drag at all the hops. Then there was the O.A.O. down in Old Virginny. She accounted for at least six or seven hours every week spent in letter-writing, which incidentally brought excellent results.

Guy also did well at shooting the rifle; both small and outdoor rifle teams had him in their midst. Of course it may be that getting out of drill on Mondays had something to do with it but if you don't think he can shoot take a look at his medals.

Rifle 4 2   2 Stripes

FRANK GLASGOW TINKER
DEWITT, ARKANSAS
"Hank" "Salty"

HANK comes from the far South where he acquired many of the mannerisms of that fair land. As is true of all mariners, he heard the call of the sea early, and by enlisting he fitted himself to become a Midshipman.

Hank is of a rather quiet nature, but he has a sparkle in his eyes that discloses a quickness of mind and a keen sense of humor. Girls in general or in particular, do not seem to interest him in the least.

Not confining his activities to academics, Hank early joined the ranks of the wrestlers and devoted all his spare time to the gym. In addition to this, he is a literary fiend, within the limits of Yachting and Collier's. Although not famous when it comes to working math probs and drawing Zeuner diagrams, he has managed to get by, and still keep up with the latest magazines.

It might be said that Hank has musical tendencies. At any rate he is the proud possessor of an old rheumatic accordian with which he is wont to divert his shipmates' thoughts from the cares and worries of this life.

Hank was "non-reg." But that doesn't count now. There are bigger things ahead, and the fact that you've bounced the rougher road and survived it, makes you stronger for it. Hank is no fair weather friend, and that's the best you can say of any man.

Class Swimming 3   Wrestling 4 3 2 1   2 P.O.

Tinker and his roommate, Morrow (*Courtesy of the Nimitz Library, U.S. Naval Academy*) hence; but it was the Army Air Corps that he really wanted. It was "the chance of a lifetime" and he "would rather go there than get a commission in the Navy."

Then it was June Week with its band concerts, parades, military rituals, and a whirl of parties and dances, culminating in the graduation ceremonies in Dahlgren Hall. Of the 602 midshipmen who entered four years earlier, 432 made it to graduation, an attrition of 28 percent; but of these only 244 received commissions. Tinker was not the class' "anchor man," but he ranked 393rd, which was close enough to the bottom. In the long run these class standings could be irrelevant. Two numbers below Tinker was John R. Bulkeley, who, as the commanding officer of the "expendable" Motor Torpedo Boat Squadron 3, distinguished himself during the grim withdrawal from the Philippines in 1942 and ended his career as a vice admiral.[14] Draper L. Kauffman, five numbers below Tinker, later served as an officer in the Royal Navy during the earliest years of World War II. Rejoining the U.S. Navy in 1942, he returned to the Naval Academy in the 1960s as Rear Admiral Kauffman and the Academy's superintendent. On the other hand, the midshipman who graduated at the head of the class resigned his commission in early 1934 and never returned to the service, not even during World War II.

Newly inaugurated President Franklin D. Roosevelt personally awarded the commissions and degrees that spring. He told the midshipmen that the first time he attended an Academy graduation was in 1917 when he was assistant secretary of the Navy. At that time, the United States had been in World War I only a few months, he had been working many late nights in his office, was dead tired, and fell asleep during the ceremonies. He solemnly assured them that he would remain awake this day, which produced a roar of laughter from his audience.

In his address to the graduates, the president cautioned them against elitism and clannishness; he urged them to cultivate the friendships of persons outside of their seagoing profession to obtain a broader view of the United States and the world. All hands present would have been amazed if they could have known how far Frank Tinker would go in this direction. In conclusion the president wished them all good luck and added, "I welcome you to the company of educated men." Then there was a great whoop and holler from the new officers as they hurled their midshipman hats into the overhead of Dahlgren Hall.[15] It was all over.

Just a few weeks shy of his twenty-fourth birthday, Tinker numbered among the happiest of midshipmen that day. He did not hold a commission in the regular Navy, his goal of seven long years, but in his pocket was a letter from the Army Air Corps that told him he had passed his second physical exam and should report to Randolph Field, Texas, in October.

This marked his first decisive step on a zigzag track over the next three years that would finally put him on the road to Port Bou.

3

ARMY, NAVY—AND OUT!

Being dumped into the streets of America in the summer of 1933 to join the millions of dispossessed and unemployed casualties of the Great Depression was an inauspicious way to begin one's adult life, but no graduate of the Naval Academy had to fear unemployment for long. Frank Tinker was not worried. During his four years at the Academy the Navy deducted $20 a month from a midshipman's pay, which it put in escrow to be returned on graduation so the young officer would have ready cash to buy new uniforms and meet other expenses. This amounted to $960, and Tinker did not have to spend it on uniforms. Moreover, he had his severance pay of $780 (less 15 percent for economy); the total was $1,623, and in 1933 its purchasing power was phenomenal.[1] Tinker had no plans beyond hunting and fishing in Arkansas until he had to report to the Army Air Corps.

When he finally cruised into Randolph Field in his Chevy convertible in mid-October, he was one of 176 new cadets. Ninety-four were recent graduates of West Point; seventy-four were a mixture of former Army enlisted men, Reserve officers, and civilian enlistees; there were two officers from the Mexican army and six ex-midshipmen (including Tinker).[2] At Randolph he found himself a plebe again, but here they were called "Dodos," the name of an extinct bird of the Indian Ocean islands that could not fly. But a cadet's life as a Dodo was mercifully short. It ended when he soloed—or when he washed out for lack of aptitude during dual instruction.

In 1933 Randolph Field was only two years old, and Tinker found it a magnificent layout. Sited on 2,618 acres 761 feet above sea level, about 20 miles northeast of San Antonio, Texas, it was the conception of Brigadier General Frank P. Lahm. One of the founders of Army aviation, Lahm had been taught to fly by the Wright brothers. He was unable to realize his plans for a centralized training base until the Air Corps Act of 1928. The Air Corps formally dedicated the base on 20 June 1930 and named it after Captain William M. Randolph, who had commanded the 25th Bombardment Squadron during World War I. He had died in the crash of a Curtiss AT-14 on 17 February 1928 at Gorman, Texas. As aviation training facilities went in the 1930s, Randolph Field ranked among the finest in the world.

The Air Corps used Randolph only for primary and basic training. After the cadets had logged 150 hours in training airplanes they transferred to Kelly Field, an old cavalry remount station that was part of Fort Sam Houston, a few miles southwest of San Antonio. Created on the eve of the United States entering World War I, it dated from February 1917. At Kelly the Air Corps introduced cadets to standard service aircraft, fighters, attack planes,[3] and bombers. They trained in radio navigation, gunnery, and bombing. On graduating from Kelly they received their silver wings, sometimes a 2nd lieutenant's commission in the Air Corps, but always a commission in the Air Corps Reserve. In the latter case, they were discharged to return to civilian life.

After Tinker drew his uniforms and bedded down in his barracks, he looked up his former classmates, thirty of whom had been at Randolph since July. Had it not been for his eye problem, Tinker would have been with this first draft. They had long since soloed and had just finished primary training. The ex-midshipmen were a curiosity at Randolph, where they became known as "the rich Navy bunch." They not only drew their $75-a-month Air Corps cadet pay (less 15 percent for economy), but their pockets bulged with their Navy severance pay and the return of their uniform funds. Most of them had new automobiles; and the bachelors among them were inclined to be big spenders, which made them popular in town.

From members of the first draft of ex-midshipmen, Tinker discovered that learning to fly was no bed of roses and could be extremely hazardous. A half-dozen of their group had already washed out, and only two months earlier William Pasch had died in a midair collision.

After two weeks in ground school, Tinker was marched out to the flight line and introduced to Form One, the standard flight report. Then his instructor told him to climb into the front cockpit of a blue-and-yellow Consolidated PT-3 trainer—a 2,400-pound biplane with a Wright J-5 engine of 220 horsepower. A docile machine unless it was bucking a headwind, it would fly at 100 mph. After takeoff the instructor climbed to eight thousand feet and, to Tinker's amazement, told him to take the controls. The instructor talked him through a half-hour of banks and turns that Tinker found to be "a lot of fun." Then the instructor took back the controls and ended the lesson by whip-stalling the airplane into a spin and holding the spin until they reached two thousand feet. A surprised Tinker regarded this as "the worst part of the lesson," but within a few weeks the same maneuver would be one of the great entertainments of his life.

After a week of dual instruction all of the cadets had to buy "crash tags." This was a metal identification tag worn on the wrist so that, according to Tinker, "in case you crash and the plane burns they can identify the remains." It was customary for a class to chip in ten cents a man and buy a fancy gold tag that was awarded by lottery. Tinker drew number thirteen and it won him the gold crash tag. He was not sure if that was lucky or not, but everyone told him to be careful of Porter Loring takeoffs and landings, and the luck would take care of itself. (Porter Loring was the man who operated San Antonio's largest funeral parlor.)

On 15 November 1933, after six and one-half hours of dual instruction, Tinker soloed and became the first of his class to escape the irksome label of Dodo. Garret S. Coleman, one of his Annapolis classmates, was next. Thereafter, Tinker did most of his flying alone, and it became great fun, especially after he moved into aerobatics. And when he was certain of no witnesses, there was entertainment to be had in diving on farmhouses, chasing herds of cattle, and racing railroad trains. In these experiments a cadet had to be careful to maneuver his airplane in a way that no one on the ground could get a good look at the big "buzz number" painted on his fuselage, just in case they became angry enough to phone Randolph Field with a complaint.

Although warned against flying in clouds, all cadets had to try it at least once before they had instruction in instrument flying. Flying in clouds fascinated Tinker, but twice he became badly lost, wholly disoriented, and had to spin his way out of it. In their solo practices, the cadets often paired off in some distant piece of airspace and played at dogfighting. Although against regulations, everyone knew it was done. Tinker took this much too seriously, and instead of breaking off his attacks at reasonable distances, he would roar by so close that the shadow of his airplane seemed to fill the other pilot's cockpit. When he broke away, the pilot of the other airplane could hear too clearly the roar of Tinker's engine above his own, and his next sensation was that of being rocked about by the turbulence of Tinker's slipstream. This was unnerving to the others; the word got around, and after a while no one would play dogfight with Frank Tinker.

Randolph Field was not all flying. Weekends in San Antonio, a city of 235,000 persons in 1933, offered diversions. The usual watering spots were the Gunter Cave, a rathskeller in the Gunter Hotel where there was dancing to "the lilting music of Chuck Woods," or the rooftop Coconut Grove of the St. Anthony Hotel, where Jimmy Joy and his "Brunswick Recording Orchestra" provided the music. There was also the Hollywood, a nightclub on Alamo Plaza, and the Alamo Nite Club out on Fredericksburg Road. Feminine companionship was always available from a corps of "cadet widows," young ladies of San Antonio anxious to make an enduring connection with one of the dashing air cadets. On the plains of Texas, Tinker took a definite interest in the company of ladies, in sharp contrast with the reservations he had expressed on the banks of the Severn.

Meanwhile, the United States' "noble experiment" was not yet wholly finished. Although beer and wine became legal in 1933, hard liquor still posed a problem. However, Barrelhouse John, a well-known and respected San Antonio bootlegger, was always prepared to supply some of his renowned "Sugar Whiskey" for an occasion; and for those who preferred sterner stuff, he also sold the fiery "Blanket Whiskey" turned out by the city's Mexican community. Years later, reflecting upon it from World War II, many a prewar pilot of the Army Air Corps remained convinced that napalm was nothing new. It had been invented ten years earlier by the Mexicans of San Antonio, but the Army Air Corps of the 1930s had not the wit to recognize its primary wartime use.

In November the cadets rented the largest suite in the St. Anthony Hotel for a "radio party" on the Saturday of the Army-Navy football game. If Army won the game, the ex-Navy cadets would pay for the party; if Navy won, then the Army cadets would foot the bill. The Army cadets outnumbered the ex-midshipmen by more than ten to one, but "the rich Navy bunch" had all the money. It was a great blast. Army won the game, and Navy paid for the party, which ended quite riotously at four o'clock the next morning. The survivors made their way out to the Sack & Witz Grill on Blanco Road for coffee and hamburgers before crawling through the dawn to their barracks. Indeed, the party proved so successful that the following Monday the Randolph Field command was inspired to launch an investigation of some of its aspects. But after the attending cadets paid the hotel for the torn draperies, smashed crockery, and broken furniture, the investigation was called off.

Beyond flying and after hours fun in San Antonio, there was also attrition. As 1933 became 1934, many faces that had begun training with Tinker no longer appeared to answer muster. Some washed out early in A-Stage for lack of aptitude; others washed out later. Two cadets crashed on landing; another stalled and landed in a tree; and yet another tried landing with one wing far too low, and instead of groundlooping he cartwheeled his airplane end over end down the runway. These airplanes washed out along with the cadets. In the realm of Randolph fun and games, one cadet literally lost his wings while trying to hedge-hop between a pair of trees, and another was reported for bouncing his wheels on the roof of a moving automobile; both received their walking papers.

Then two cadets had a midair collision. One died in the ambulance; the other died in the hospital without regaining consciousness. There were no witnesses, so exactly how the accident occurred remained a mystery. When word of this accident got back to the field, all the cadets were hustled out to their airplanes and told to log an hour in the air. This was standing procedure immediately after anyone died in training. Tinker was also having problems, but they were all on the ground. Returning to the field after a big night on the town, he ran his convertible into a ditch and put a deep part in his hair with the rearview mirror, which resulted in a dozen stitches in his scalp and thirteen days in the hospital.

The Chevrolet convertible, too, became a washout. Tinker replaced it with a 1928 Stutz coupe—a battleship of a car that was a delight on the open road. It guzzled gasoline, but on base fuel was only six cents a gallon.

In February 1934 Tinker passed all his stage checks and moved to B-Stage basic training. Consolidated PT-3s gave way to the heavier and more powerful Douglas BT-1s and BT-2s, but nevertheless these were "forgiving" airplanes. Both biplanes weighed in at 4,500 pounds; the BT-1 was powered by a 450-horsepower inline Liberty engine, the BT-2 by a more reliable and lighter 450-horsepower radial Pratt & Whitney Wasp. The BT-1 was representative of the Air Corps' fourteen-year effort to use up its vast stocks of Liberty engines left over from World War I, but their days were numbered. A few months earlier, in November 1933, a War Department order finally directed that all Liberty engines be retired from service. It was not until 13 September 1935, however, that this "Old Faithful," born of the requirements of 1917, powered its last flight for the Air Corps.

As Tinker moved into B-Stage his barracks began to look ominously empty. Two-thirds of his group had washed out. All the former midshipmen, however, still hung on. The washouts continued, and by March he remarked, "If they keep this up, there won't be enough left for a graduation formation over at Kelly."

Meanwhile, the first ex-midshipmen who had entered Randolph back in July 1933 finished their B-Stage and went on to advanced training at Kelly, but several of their number had fallen by the wayside. Their ranks were tragically reduced in March, when Nelson T. Samuels died in the crash of an observation plane. A few weeks later Francis R. "Fuzz" Drake, another of the Annapolis group, had a brush with fate when the D-12 engine of his vintage Curtiss P-1 fighter went to pieces during a cross-country flight, but he was able to bail out. As this group moved through advanced training toward the day they would receive their wings, the vexing question of commissions came up again.

The size of the U.S. Army, fixed by law at 125,000 officers and men, had within this small body—incredible as it may seem years later—the whole U.S. Army Air Corps. In 1934 the Air Corps consisted of 1,250 officers and 13,500 enlisted men, and it operated on a budget of $17 million, of which about $7 million was spent on new aircraft.[4] New officers could not be commissioned in the regular Army until billets were vacated by resignations, retirements, or death, all of which can be a tediously slow process. By the spring of 1934 it became clear that there would be no vacant billets. Upon graduation, the cadets would be given commissions in the Air Corps Reserve and discharged into civilian life. This proved a very expensive process, especially as regards the ex-midshipmen. The government had already spent a few hundred thousand dollars putting them through the Naval Academy, and then spent more thousands training them to be Army pilots. The crazy part of it was that after this heavy investment, the government refused to employ their services and justified it in the name of "economy." This training of pilots and dumping them back into civilian life, however, had the effect of a subsidy to American civil aviation. The airlines especially benefited, as it provided them with a well-trained labor force from which they could pick and choose. But for a young man trying to make his way through this muddled maze, it could be a personally frustrating experience indeed.

After February 1934, Randolph Field had felt a sudden squeeze on its staff as a result of President Roosevelt directing the Air Corps to fly the air mail. The president made this decision after air chief General Benjamin Foulois had assured him and Postmaster General James Farley that it could do so. Consequently, the service ordered many of its instructors to the air mail service. Despite Foulois' assurances, however, this was an operation for which the Air Corps had neither the training nor the equipment to execute well, and the initial results of the seventy-eight-day effort proved disastrous.[5] The Air Corps learned the hard way how much it did not know about radio communications, new radio navigation techniques, and all-weather flying. Tinker and his class felt the repercussions of this almost immediately, as there came to be a new emphasis in Randolph's B-Stage on instrument instruction and "blind flying." Also, a funny-looking gadget that "flew" without ever leaving the ground made its appearance at Randolph in these days and was put to increasing use. It was a Link trainer, the great-granddaddy of all modern aircraft simulators.

The scene brightened with spring, when staff members of *Popular Mechanics* magazine appeared at Randolph to do a big photo story on the school.[6] It became really exciting in May 1934 when a horde from Metro Goldwyn Mayer studios descended on the field with tons of camera and sound equipment to shoot scenes for the movie *West Point of the Air*. The film's script was authored by John Monk Saunders, who also wrote the script for *Wings*, the fabulous silent classic of 1927. Wallace Beery, himself an aviator, led the film company's entourage, accompanied by Robert Montgomery and Maureen O'Sullivan and a host of lesser lights.[7]

In the midst of the hubbub created by Hollywood's presence, a new mysterious airplane turned up at Randolph. It was a silver-painted biplane with the civil registration X-571Y. Upon investigation Tinker discovered it to be a Stearman.[8] The word going around the hangars was that it was being evaluated as a replacement for the venerable PT-3s. Unknown to anyone at the time, this strange airplane was the prototype of the PT-13, the soon-to-be-famous "Yellow Peril" that in a half-dozen variants trained thousands of Army and Navy aviators for World War II.

While Tinker busied himself with cross-country flights to San Marcos, Gonzales, Corpus Christi, and other points in Texas and practiced night takeoffs and landings, President Roosevelt found time to study the plight of the Naval

Academy class of '33. Roosevelt, always a "Big Navy" proponent, in 1934 planned to review and expand the Navy, which had been allowed to wither in the 1920s. Included in these plans was the retrieval of the services of the lower half of the class of '33. Thus, in the spring of 1934 Congress took action and the Navy invited its black sheep to return to the fold.[9]

The ex-midshipmen at Randolph and Kelly Fields received the Navy's invitation with great excitement. Then they had second thoughts. Most of them wanted to stay in the Air Corps, but this seemed hopeless.[10] And none of them liked a strange caveat in the legislation that provided for their commissioning. It said that they would be on probation for two years, and in the meantime their commissions could be revoked. The class of '32 was commissioned without such a qualification, and so were their seniors in the class of '31; why should they be singled out for probation? Another thing they didn't like was the Navy's policy that the ex-midshipmen have two years of sea duty before they could apply for flight training. It seemed ridiculous to be trained for aviation in the Army Air Corps, have to spend two years afloat in the Navy, and only then be able to apply for training as a naval aviator.

After some haggling late that spring of 1934, the Navy agreed to accept the group, then in advanced training at Kelly Field, as student aviators. They would be sent to Pensacola to finish their training. But Tinker and the five others in his group, who had not yet finished B-Stage at Randolph, would have to go the "black-shoes" route for two years before they could apply for naval aviation.[11]

This was to no one's liking. Indeed, it was absurd. Of course by this time these few ex-Navy Army Air Corps cadets, who were about to become "born again" Navy, had become experts on legislative and bureaucratic absurdities. The only thing that surprised them about this imbroglio is that no one claimed that their return to the Navy would serve the cause of "economy." Robert C. Hird, one of the ex-midshipmen at Kelly, came to the rescue by phoning his father, a captain on duty in the Navy Department in Washington. The elder Hird advised both groups to write a joint letter to Admiral Joseph M. Reeves, commander in chief of the U.S. Fleet, and explain the situation to him. Captain Hird had picked the right man; Admiral Reeves was not an aviator, but it was largely under his direction that the Navy's carrier aviation developed as dramatically as it did after 1929. With the new carrier USS *Ranger* commissioned in 1934, the Navy was feeling a shortage of pilots. The *Yorktown* and *Enterprise* were under construction, and Congress had recently authorized construction of the *Wasp*. The pilot situation promised to become even tighter, and Reeves was not about to let these "free" aviators slip through his fingers on a point of legalistic punctilio. He made arrangements for all fourteen of them to go directly into Navy flight training.

In July 1934 Tinker and his fellow veterans of the class of '33 Army Air Corps cycle arrived at Pensacola, and on 16 July he finally took the oath as officer of the U.S. Navy. A trifle more than nine years had passed since he enlisted at Little Rock with this commission as his goal. It had been his "heart's desire"; but eight years is a lot of time out of anyone's life, and in his case it had been too long—achieved through too many blind, anticlimatic passages—and too late to be cherished as it might have been in 1932 or 1933.

In the Air Corps Tinker and his friends had been known as the rich Navy bunch; but at Pensacola, where the tailors were taking all their money for new uniforms, they were known simply as "the Army bunch." Sic transit affluence.

Ordinarily Pensacola's flight curriculum took all of a year and included 160 flying hours in five "squadrons":

1. Primary seaplanes
2. Primary landplanes
3. Observation and torpedo planes, including level bombing and free-mounted gunnery.
4. Multi-engine flying boats
5. Fighter planes, dive bombing, and fixed gunnery.[12]

Each squadron was divided into left and right "wings"; while one wing was having flight training, the other was in ground school. Because each of the Army bunch brought more than one hundred hours of flight time from the Air Corps, they were an anomaly, treated as a special class, and crammed through the Navy regimen within seven months. They started in squadron 2 using Consolidated NY-1 landplanes, which were the Army's PT-3 with a Navy designation, and were immediately given solo status.

The Army bunch made fast work of squadron 2 and hurried on (or back) to squadron 1, in which they discovered that no black magic was required to fly NY-2 seaplanes. Here they found themselves in the company of a fifty-two-year-old captain, then in flight training. He had orders to take command of the carrier USS *Saratoga* the following year, 1935, and had been sent to Pensacola for a perfunctory aviation course to acquaint him with airplanes. But that wasn't enough for the middle-aged captain. He wanted the real thing and insisted on being put through the regular flight training regimen—and he got it. William F. Halsey Jr. would become a legendary commander of carrier task forces in World War II.

An old custom at Pensacola declared that the last man in the squadron to solo in seaplanes got thrown into the bay. As the result of a brief hospitalization, Halsey happened to be the last of his squadron to solo, but he did not regard his four stripes as immunity to this custom. The only favor he asked was to take off his shoes; they were new and it would be a shame to ruin them with salt water. With that favor granted, the Army bunch gleefully picked up Captain Halsey and tossed him into the harbor.

At first Tinker enjoyed Pensacola. Neither a midshipman nor a cadet, he was a commissioned officer—at last. But he soon became irritated at having to stooge around the sky simply to run up hours in the low-performance NY trainers. It seemed like a regression to A-Stage at Randolph, and he found it a bore. And there were money problems. He and most of the others now wished that they had not been so free and easy over the past year with their uniform refunds from the Academy. This may sound strange today, but in the 1920s and 1930s the naval establishment was small, its officer corps very small, and turnover in personnel was so slow as to be imperceptible. There was no "mass market" for officers' uniforms such as existed after World War II, along with ready-to-wear articles being available at reasonable prices from the "plain pipe racks" of the Navy exchanges. In the 1930s an officer's uniform had to be tailor made, and it was expensive.

Tinker's pay as an ensign was $125 a month plus $62.50 a month flight pay (less 15 percent for economy), a total of $159.38 a month, a trifle more than $1,900 a year.[13] Income tax was no problem because there was no withholding tax until after 1942, and in the 1930s a single taxpayer enjoyed a $1,000 exemption, married people a whopping $2,500. Out of his monthly pay, $25 went to the wardroom to pay his mess bill, whether he ate there or not. Tailors seemed to take the rest. A small bright spot appeared in August 1934, when one of the Army bunch popped into Tinker's room with the August issue of *Popular Mechanics*, in which Tinker's picture appeared in conjunction with the lead article, "West Point of the Air."

With a population of barely 25,000 souls, Pensacola seemed pretty dull after San Antonio. But there was good fishing in the bay—especially around the hulk of the old battleship *Massachusetts,* used as a target ship and sunk on 22 March 1923. And there were all kinds of boats available for sailing. By this time Tinker had turned in his gas-guzzling 1928 Stutz for an equally massive 1930 Cord coupe. Roaring around in this juggernaut, he soon discovered the night spots where aviators and available young ladies hung out, such as The Barn and the Half-Way House. He also discovered a local distillate known as "Pensacola Shinney." And one evening he was introduced to the local constabulary as a result of trying to gain flying speed in his Cord on Pensacola's main street. This was brought to the attention of the air station's commanding officer and Tinker was put in hack for ten days.[14]

However pleasant and plush Tinker at first regarded the bachelor officers' quarters on the naval station, they soon palled on him. He and his Naval

Academy classmate Elliott L. "Jesse" James pooled their resources to rent a cottage under the palms on the shore of the Gulf of Mexico. Many a good party was thrown in this "snake ranch," where Tinker played his accordion and, refining his sense of humor, liked to surprise overnight guests by putting live lobsters in the toilet bowl.

Flying became more interesting in September, when they moved into squadron 3, using Vought 02U Corsair observation planes and the big, boxy Martin T4M torpedo planes. These were regular service aircraft, but here they were introduced to intensive radio work. Radio was of vital importance to the 02Us' mission, which was scouting and spotting the fall of shot for battleships and cruisers.

In these practices they flew along in their Corsairs, taking turns at being pilot and radioman-observer, watching the "fall of shot" simulated on the ground by the detonation of powder charges relative to the outline of a ship whitewashed on the ground. Evaluating these detonations, they radioed back to the "gunnery officer" of a hypothetical ship, correcting his range and azimuth.

One day Tinker was leading a vee of three Corsairs over the spotting range and everyone was absorbed in watching the detonations below, working their radio keys, or laboring to hold formation, when another vee of Corsairs appeared almost dead ahead. Their crews were equally absorbed with their own problems. There was supposed to be a five-hundred-foot differential in altitude between the two flights, but someone had slipped up. The two flights saw each other only at the last minute; in the next instant Corsairs broke away at all kinds of angles in desperate efforts to avoid collisions. There were none but, as Tinker put it, "It was quite exciting while it lasted."

Their experiences with the 02U Corsair ended with an introduction to its seaplane variant that was ordinarily launched from a catapult. Tinker liked the catapult instruction and enjoyed being hurled into flight as if from a slingshot; but when he moved on to squadron 4 and its "big boats," he found them amusing at best but otherwise tiresome. These flying boats were Martin P3M-1s and P3M-2s—high-wing, twin-engine machines with a gross weight of 18,000 pounds. Powered by two 500-horsepower engines in nacelles under the wing, they did well to augur a passage through the air at 115 mph, assuming no headwind. With the pilots seated side by side in a spacious open cockpit, Tinker thought that flying these Martin boats was like driving an old Packard sedan across the endless plains of Texas.

While Tinker and the Army bunch plowed the skies over the Gulf of Mexico with their clumsy flying boats, Captain Halsey was having his problems with landplanes. Landing at an outlying practice airfield, he hit a soft spot in the turf; his Vought UO-1 dug in, nosed over, and flipped on its back. The captain undid his seatbelt, eased himself out of the inverted cockpit, and then insisted on a new airplane as soon as possible. Provided with a new machine, Halsey took off and spent the next hour shooting landings to make sure he would not become introspective about his accident. The "old boy's" performance favorably impressed the junior officers.

When the Army bunch returned from their Christmas leave at year's end, they found themselves in squadron 5 for sixty hours in fighter planes. They flew Boeing F3B-1s and F4B-2s. The latter had a gross weight of 2,750 pounds and was powered by a radial Pratt & Whitney R-1340 Wasp of 450 horsepower with a power-to-weight ratio of 1:6.1 and a top speed of about 175 mph. With its relatively low wing loading of 12 pounds per square foot, it was a nimble airplane and a good aerobatic machine. Armament was no different from the fighter planes of World War I: two .30-caliber machine guns. By 1935 the F4B was being replaced in the fleet with the Grumman F2F (power-to-weight ratio 1:5.4), which had a top speed in excess of 200 mph, but the F2Fs were too precious to risk at Pensacola.

As far as Tinker was concerned, squadron 5 was "what it was all about." No instructor could check ride with him in a single-seat fighter. The instructor sat in a chair in the middle of the field below, from where he crabbed about their approaches and landings—too high, too low, too fast, rollout too long. Unlike the Air Corps—which could always appeal to Congress to buy another hundred acres at the end of a runway and hire a contractor to pour a few thousand yards of cement—the Navy had to face bitter truth in the finite length of a carrier's flight deck. Naval aviators were drilled to put an airplane on the ground within a minimum distance, not because it was a virtue, much less "showy," but because some day it would probably make a difference between life and death—and these might not always be the pilot's.

As 1935 got under way, the ex-midshipmen trained in dive bombing and flew gunnery against towed-sleeve targets and targets on the ground, but it was the twelve hours of combat tactics that Tinker liked best. His fellow pilots found no love in their hearts for him during those hours. It always seemed that Tinker wanted to spit into their cockpits as he flashed past in a mock attack. His attacks against others not only were too close for comfort, but also for safety under peacetime conditions. One might wonder if this apparent rashness of flying technique owed something to the problem in depth perception that his first Air Corps physical exam detected in 1933. Whatever the case, Frank Tinker proved to be one of those go-get-'em and fill-the-gunsight types of fighter pilots—as at least eight Nationalist aviators would discover to their sorrow in Spain.

By the end of January 1935 it was all finished. The Army bunch received their golden wings (some of them already had a pair of Air Corps silver wings in their shirt pockets), and Tinker found himself Naval Aviator No. 4091 with orders to the heavy cruiser *San Francisco*. The entire Army bunch received orders to battleships or cruisers.[15] Most of them wanted carrier duty, but because they had no prior sea duty in the ordinary shipboard responsibilities of a junior officer, orders to a conventional surface ship made more sense for anyone who was committed to a naval career. They were naval officers first, aviators second; or at least this is what the Navy was forever telling its young and impatient aviators of the interwar years.

With Tinker, however, his commitment to the Navy was by no means the same as it had been that day when he first unpacked his gear in Bancroft Hall. He had found a new love and was inclined to make invidious comparisons between Randolph Field and Pensacola, to the expense of the latter. Although impressed by the Navy's instruction in aerial navigation

Tinker, Navy ensign, early 1935 (*Family photograph*)

and radio, he preferred to criticize the Navy for its perfunctory training in night flying. He wished that he was back in the Air Corps. So did some of the other members of the Army bunch, but they knew it was impossible and put it out of their minds. Tinker, to the contrary, became disgruntled. He was becoming bored all around. And in Frank Tinker this proved a dangerous condition.

Tinker and Jesse James drove out to the West Coast together. James got out at San Diego to join the light cruiser *Pensacola;* neither could know that their paths would not cross again. Tinker went on to Los Angeles, where he found the *San Francisco* riding to anchor in San Pedro Harbor. Placed in commission on 10 February 1934, the *San Francisco* was a brand-new ship. She was under the command of Captain Royal E. Ingersoll, one of the keenest minds in the interwar Navy. He believed in loyalty up and down and was respected by his officers and men as a model commanding officer. Ingersoll ran a tight but happy ship.

In the early evening of 18 February 1935, Tinker took a launch from the fleet landing out to the *San Francisco,* her pale gray paintwork aglow in the setting sun. The launch threaded its way among the hulls of the submarine tender *Argonne,* the battleship *Mississippi,* the old battleship *Utah,* now a radio-controlled target ship, and the transport *Chaumont.* Tinker looked up enviously as they rounded the long, sleek silhouette of the carrier *Lexington,* and then the launch finally drifted up to the foot of the *San Francisco*'s accommodation ladder. The officer of the deck logged Tinker on board, and a steward was called to show him to his quarters. When he unpacked his bags that evening, he clearly realized that he had finally achieved the goal of almost nine years of single-mindedness: "For the first time I find myself living in the Wardroom country aboard ship; it makes quite a difference."

But Tinker no longer valued the prize. Two years earlier, in the summer of 1933, there probably would have been a substantial difference in the value he now attached to it. But by 1935 "Wardroom country" was at discount. He would do his best to destroy it; and as with most things he set out to do, he would succeed.

The next day he met Lieutenant Frederick M. Trapnell, the *San Francisco*'s senior aviator. The ship's aviation unit was part of Squadron VS-11, whose airplanes were distributed among the *San Francisco* and three other cruisers of Cruiser Division Six (CruDivSix). Tinker and Trapnell's paths had crossed but not touched in 1928, during the *Lexington*'s passage to the West Coast; but in those days all he dared do was give Trapnell a smart salute. Trapnell, a raw-boned six-footer who graduated from the Naval Academy in 1923, had won his wings at Pensacola in 1927. He was one of the *Lexington*'s original complement of pilots and, as a member of Torpedo Squadron VT-1, he had flown extensive engineering development work on board the new carrier. Later he served as an engineering test pilot at the naval air station in Anacostia near Washington, D.C. (Until the Navy commissioned the air station at Patuxent River, Maryland, in 1942, Anacostia remained the Navy's only aviation testing facility.)

Trapnell came to the *San Francisco* after two years on board the Navy's airplane-carrying airships *Akron* and *Macon*, from which he operated the unique Curtiss F9C "skyhook" fighters.[16] A quiet but by no means taciturn man, he had a keen engineering mind, and what Trapnell didn't know about airplanes wasn't in anybody else's book in 1935. Tinker could not have asked for a better immediate superior.

Trapnell showed Tinker around the ship, with attention focused on the two powder-driven catapults elevated on turntables amidships, and the ship's four airplanes. The airplanes were Vought O3U-3 Corsairs, two-place centerline float, 4,500-pound biplanes, forty-eight of which the Navy had procured in 1932 and had taken delivery of them in June 1933. Like the *San Francisco*, her airplanes were practically brand-new. The O3U3's primary mission was scouting in search of enemy naval forces, and spotting for the cruiser's nine 8-inch guns and secondary batteries once contact was made with the enemy. The O3U had only one .30-caliber fixed machine gun synchronized to fire through the propeller; for defense astern it had two .30-caliber guns on a scarf ring in the rear cockpit, operated by the observer-radioman.[17] The Corsair's 550-horsepower Pratt & Whitney Wasp R-1340-2 engine provided a top speed of 160 mph; cruising at

110 mph, it had a range of 600 miles. The O3U was a good, solid airplane, equal in performance to its peers in foreign navies and superior to most. In Tinker's estimation, "They fly beautifully, however, they don't handle so well on the water."

Compared with carrier operations, flying from a cruiser consisted of a stolid routine. There were courier flights back and forth between San Pedro and San Diego, or to San Clemente Island when the ship was there, carrying guard mail. Then there were hours and hours of target towing for the benefit of the ship's gunners. But he had enjoyable flights, too. One day a machinist's mate needed some flight time, so Tinker took him up. They flew out to the islands of San Clemente and Catalina. On the north shore of Catalina, Tinker spotted some unusual activity and spiraled down for a better look. A large group of people had assembled on the beach and all of them were waving enthusiastically at his airplane. Tinker flew lower and the waving became even more intense. So he rolled the Vought into a dive, pulled out at wave-top level, and roared over the beach barely ten feet above its sands. Tinker waggled his wings for the crowd as he roared overhead, and from the rear cockpit his mechanic gave everyone a friendly wave. Unknown to Tinker, the crowd on the beach was a Hollywood motion picture company trying to shoot a scene. The noise of his engine loused up their sound track and they had been waving for him to get the hell away; the Navy received a stiff complaint about this incident, but no one was able to identify the offending naval aircraft.

On the other hand, seaplane operations from cruisers were fraught with more hazards than carrier operations and thus sported a higher accident rate. The problems did not occur with the catapulted launching of the airplanes but in their recovery from the sea. The Navy had long since developed a method for retrieving seaplanes on board known as the "cast system" ("cast" was the phonetic "c" of that day as "Charlie" would be later), which reduced the hazards. Before retrieving a seaplane the ship made a tight turn, its wake creating a broad slick on the ocean for the seaplane to alight upon. At the end of its turn the ship aligned across the wind, providing shelter for the plane while it taxied up to the cruiser. The serious problems occurred a few minutes later when the slick began to dissipate and the fragile seaplane bobbed alongside the ship's hard steel hull while the crew tried to hoist it on board.

The cast system used a "sled" trailed alongside the ship from the head of a boom. The seaplane taxied up onto the sled, where a hook in the bottom of its centerline float engaged a catch on the sled. When thus engaged, the ship towed the seaplane alongside, and both moved as one. Then it was relatively easy to attach a bridle to lifting points on the plane's upper wing and hoist it on board. This technique not only made retrievals easier and less hazardous for the aircrews, but it was of immeasurable value to the ship, which could keep moving at a relatively high rate of speed during recovery. But in spite of this engineering accomplishment, the sea is a capricious thing and accidents occurred.

In March 1935 the ships of CruDivSix resumed scouting exercises with the fleet that had been going on since mid-1934 in anticipation of the annual Fleet Problem. In 1935 it was Fleet Problem XVI, conducted over a vast area of the Pacific from the West Coast to Alaska, Midway Island, and Hawaii. During one of these practices Lieutenant (jg) Stanton Dunlop of the *San Francisco* landed crosswind in a heavy sea, put a wing in the ocean, and groundlooped across a trough into the hard face of an oncoming wave. He and his radioman climbed out of the wreck unhurt, a motor whaleboat retrieved the crumpled and water-filled Corsair, and that was the end of O3U No. A9320. An O3U from another cruiser simply disappeared during a scouting flight; its crew of two was never found. Seaplanes from two other cruisers made rough landings with damage. Another of the *San Francisco*'s Corsairs made a hard touch-down in a rough sea and smashed in its centerline float, which put the fuselage in the water and the sea breaking over it from astern mangled the tailgroup.

On one occasion Tinker made a rough landing. Heavy seas broke over the bow of his centerline float and splashed through the rotating propeller; the shock and resultant vibrations cracked the Corsair's engine mounts. The lot of a cruiser's "slingshot" pilot was not an easy one. At that time it was probably the most hazardous aviation duty in the Navy, resulting in considerable damage and waste of aircraft.

Meanwhile, on 11 March 1935 Tinker got into a serious scrape on The Pike, a lively amusement area of roller coasters, shooting galleries, hotdog stands, and sleazy bars that is strung out along the sandy oceanfront of Long Beach, California. An argument with some civilians occurred, ugly words were exchanged, a brawl ensued, and in its denouement the Long Beach police turned Tinker over to the Shore Patrol. An investigation resulted in charges, and in April Tinker found himself confined to the ship pending a court-martial.

The court convened on 18 April on board the cruiser *Louisville*. The charge: "drunkenness and conduct to the prejudice of good order and discipline." Tinker pleaded guilty and it was all over in a matter of minutes. The court sentenced him to the loss of eighty numbers in grade. This was a serious penalty to an officer of the regular Navy of the 1930s, but under the circumstances most of his fellow junior officers thought that he had gotten off lightly. The court recommended clemency to the reviewing authority, Rear Admiral Thomas C. Hart, who refused it, remarking that in view of Tinker serving on a revocable commission, "The sentence does not seem excessive."[18]

Tinker's social life ashore was suspended until the court's findings were published, and immediately after that the *San Francisco* sailed in company with the Black Fleet for Port Angeles, Washington, and Dutch Harbor in Alaska. Fleet Problem XVI was under way. The fleet steamed up the West Coast wholly blacked out at night against the possibility of being observed by "enemy" submarines, and at first daylight, airplanes were catapulted from the battleships and cruisers in relays to maintain a scouting screen against submarines. In the outline of the Fleet Problem, as put together by Admiral Reeves' staff, the "enemy" was Orange. On board the *San Francisco* and probably all other ships of the Black Fleet, that enemy was called "the Japs." The Japanese themselves were quite certain of this, and they lodged a diplomatic protest against the United States projecting its naval maneuvers so far west into the Pacific.

Port Angeles and Dutch Harbor came and went with their usual damp, foggy drizzles, and the fleet sallied out into the Pacific toward Midway and the ultimate battle situation of the Fleet Problem. There were several contacts and "combats" with Orange submarines, aircraft, and cruisers (performed by other units of the U.S. Fleet), but the real excitement on board the *San Francisco* did not occur until 15 May. Trapnell and Lieutenant (jg) Clifford S. Cooper were catapulted off in a pair of 03Us for antisubmarine patrols. In Cooper's rear cockpit, Frank Tinker served as radioman-observer.

The three-hour patrol was routine, with no enemy sighted. But the wind freshened while they were aloft, and when the airplanes returned to the *San Francisco* the sea ran with whitecaps. Trapnell alighted and the crew recovered him with some difficulty. In Cooper's landing, he porpoised across a crest, the nose of the plane's centerline float plunged into the oncoming wall of water on the other side of the wave's trough, and the Vought flipped onto its back. As soon as he got his head above water, Cooper popped the CO_2 cylinders to the flotation bags, which ensured the airplane staying afloat. Meanwhile, having released himself, Tinker bobbed to the surface. The *San Francisco* had her engines full astern, finally wallowing to a stop, and within a few minutes Ensign Morton Sunderland was alongside in a motor whaleboat to fish Cooper and Tinker out of the water. Sunderland's boat was followed by the salvage boat, and as Tinker remarked, "They finished the job of wrecking the plane in getting it aboard."

A few days later the Fleet Problem concluded. Black had won, Orange had lost; but then, Orange had a way of losing every year. By Tinker's account, the *San Francisco* was credited with getting away with only minor "damage" while "sinking" two Orange cruisers. But by his own observations his ship had also "shot down" one Black airplane, and it "sank" a Black submarine by mistake. Had they been using live ammunition, he went on, "*San Francisco*'s own Marine gun crews would have shot off their aft funnel."

On the evening of 25 May 1935 the fleet anchored in Pearl Harbor, dropped the steam on its boilers, and gave liberty to its officers and men to do the same in

Honolulu. Tinker played it slow. He had been in the islands before and thought that as a tourist attraction they were terribly overrated; on this visit he was most interested in seeing them from the air. One day he took up Ensign Sunderland for a spin in one of the Voughts, and they cruised around Oahu.

It was an easygoing joyride until Tinker spied a formation of Army planes that were engaged in a gunnery exercise. He dove upon them and, much to their consternation, swung up, over, and around them, taking various positions in their formation, simply to see if any of their pilots might be old friends from Randolph Field. With that finished, he flew on to the north shore of the island, where he saw a small picturesque cove and promptly alighted on its clear waters. This caused great excitement in a nearby school, from where a swarm of children came running down to the beach to look at the seaplane. Then he took off and headed back to Pearl Harbor, albeit taking time to buzz the flight line of the Air Corps base at Wheeler Field en route.

When Tinker finally paid a visit to Honolulu, it was his first day ashore in more than a month—and it would prove a disaster. Pearl Harbor's commander, Admiral Joseph M. Reeves, was a great proponent of Navy aviation, but he took exception to sloppily dressed officers whether aviators or not. He had recently noticed a tendency among younger officers to loosen the high collars of their dress whites in public as an evening wore on, and, prior to the fleet's arrival in Pearl Harbor, he had issued a special notice that this would cease immediately. There was a great floor show in Honolulu's Alexander Young Hotel. The star of the show was Hilo Hattie, by 1935 already on her way to becoming a legendary figure in Honolulu's entertainment world. On this evening of 30 May, who should become so overcome by the show that he felt impelled to join Hattie on the dance floor except Ensign Frank G. Tinker, the young man with all the fetishes about dancing. And, needless to say, the collar of his dress whites was quite undone. The audience, full of Navy officers, cheered him on, and Hilo Hattie made the most of the new member of her act. But one member of the audience, Admiral Reeves, definitely was not amused.

Tinker's evening celebration was hardly finished. Some hours later the Shore Patrol encountered him in Waikiki, swinging down the street barefooted, his blouse open and several leis around his neck, his uniform hat gone, replaced by a straw boater. He had his shoes in one hand and a jug of "oke" in the other. (Oke was Hawaii's counterpart to Pensacola Shinney and San Antone's Blanket Whiskey, but it was distilled from pineapple mash.) Tinker could not explain his costume and its accessories, and the Shore Patrol escorted him to the fleet landing, where they signaled for a launch from the *San Francisco* to carry him home.

This escapade on board the *San Francisco* was not a lone incident. He had a similar one from Pensacola in his service record. And there was another such incident at Randolph Field, although the Navy did not have immediate access to his Army file. The most telling aspect of these personal misadventures is that in each one he was alone; there was no buddy at hand who might have pulled him back from the brink of public disaster. A loner, he was his own best and worst consultant, and by 1935 he had been marching to the beat of a different drummer for some years, the tattoo becoming louder and faster since 1933.

A gloom settled on the junior officers of the *San Francisco*'s wardroom during the ship's return to the West Coast in early June 1935. All believed Tinker's Navy career was finished. But the most sobering thought among them was that he had done no worse than they had on occasion, but they had had the good luck not to get caught. As for the ship's commander, Captain Ingersoll, he had no choice but to recommend another court-martial.

Immediately informed of the captain's decision, Tinker also had no doubt that a second court-martial within sixty days of his first would result in his commission being revoked. He chose to offer his resignation out of the conviction that "the best interests of the Navy and myself will be served by permanent separation."

Then he got busy writing letters. In the spring and summer of 1935, Italy threatened war against Ethiopia, so he volunteered his services to the Ethiopian air force, such as it was. He also tried the governments of Colombia and Venezuela, as well as Pan American Airways, without replies. The Chinese Maritime Customs Service (which was staffed mostly by Westerners) offered him a second-officer's position on its coastal staff at 180 *haikun taels* a month. Unable to figure out how much that was in "real money," Tinker ended up accepting an offer from the Standard Oil Company of a job on board one of its tankers.

Meanwhile, after the *San Francisco* docked in San Diego there was a change in command; Captain Ingersoll was succeeded by a petty tyrant whom all hands, from wardroom officers to mess cooks, soon came to loathe. Then they were under way for the Pacific Northwest. On 12 July 1935, with the *San Francisco* anchored offshore of Seattle, Tinker took up one of the Corsairs for a radio test, flying a five-legged track around Puget Sound. His mind was not much on his work these days, and over Tacoma his engine sputtered and quit. He was out of fuel. As usual when in the air, luck was with him. The battleship *California* was directly below and Tinker spiraled down in a glide to alight alongside her. A launch towed him to a fueling connection, and the battleship's V Division officer gave him fifty gallons. This was more than enough to get back to the *San Francisco*, and he managed to get away from the *California* without having to sign for the fuel.

It would be the last flight he made in the Navy. Two days later it was 14 July, his birthday; he was twenty-six years old. Nine years had rattled through time's hawser pipe since he had enlisted at Little Rock. The next day the Navy

Department observed the anniversary with a letter that failed to say anything about his resignation—only that his commission had been revoked.

Tinker carried his gear off the *San Francisco* that same day and caught a train to Los Angeles, where a week later he shipped as a third mate on board the 8,155-ton tanker *Christy Payne*. She was loaded to her marks with 95,000 barrels of gasoline for the East Coast. With only a single quadruple-expansion reciprocating engine of 1,800 horsepower, the *Christy Payne* did well to cruise at 10 knots, and it was a leisurely voyage of three weeks via the Panama Canal. After arrival in the oil port of Constable Hook at Bayonne, New Jersey, Standard Oil transferred Tinker to the 9,640-ton tanker *E. J. Sadler*, then in the coastwise trade. During the next eleven months he wore a rut in the ocean between Bayonne and Baton Rouge, hauling fuels and lubricants from the Louisiana oil fields to the New York metropolitan area.

On 10 September 1935 on his first trip into Baton Rouge, while sitting in a restaurant, Tinker heard a wail of sirens accompanied by a great commotion in the street. Someone ran in to shout that Governor Huey Long had just been shot, gunned down on the steps of the capitol building. To the extent that he thought he had any politics, they were the politics of Huey Long, and this was the end of his hero. His calls at Baton Rouge also permitted frequent visits with his younger sister, Toodles, then attending Louisiana State University; and they provided her with opportunities to show off her aviator-seaman brother. The slow, coastwise voyages also inspired Tinker to his first writing. He bought a typewriter and began writing short stories for magazines, but his only result was a collection of rejection slips.

During layovers on the East Coast, between voyages on Standard Oil's *Sadler*, Tinker customarily stayed in Jersey City at the Journal Square's Plaza Hotel. While there, he dated various young ladies in New York and New Jersey. With one of them, as Thanksgiving neared, he became truly infatuated. Indeed, a young Russian Catholic, Nataschka Oberlensky, so captivated him that the two were wed in a Catholic ceremony on 31 December 1935. Tinker telephoned his parents shortly after the New Year with word of his marriage, and his mother, Effie, placed an announcement to that effect in the *DeWitt Era-Enterprise* early in January, which appeared in Martha Rothenhofer's "Social and Personal Column." It read:

Miss Nataschka Oberlensky of Greenwich Village, New York, and Ensign Frank Tinker of Washington, D.C., were married New Year's Eve in Greenwich Village by the Rev. Bryan McIntegart. Mrs. Tinker, daughter of Mr. and Mrs. N. V. Oberlensky of Russia, has only been in America eight months, and is . . . a beautiful brunette typically Russian, and speaks very little English. Ensign Tinker is the son of Mr. and Mrs. F. G. Tinker, having graduated from the U.S. Naval Academy at Annapolis with honors in 1933 and has recently been associated with the Marine Department of the Standard Oil Co.[19]

However infatuated Tinker may have been at the time of the nuptials, he and Nataschka soon parted ways, a parting made the easier by Frank's frequent voyages. Perhaps to distance himself from her and any associated unpleasantness, as the spring of 1936 came on the calendar, Tinker heard of a job flying for a mission hospital at Nipper's Harbour, Newfoundland. The mission had a twin-float seaplane and wanted an accomplished pilot who would also give its doctors flight instructions. So, on the strength of an acceptance letter, on 21 June he quit Standard Oil and the *Sadler*.[20] But the Newfoundland job fell through, and he had no desire to return to the tanker company and New Jersey. The coastwise trade, not to mention marriage, had proved too monotonous and confining for anyone as restless as was Frank Tinker. So he returned home to DeWitt, Arkansas, for some hunting and fishing and to think things over. If he discussed his separation from Nataschka at all, it was with his parents and sisters.

While Tinker traveled to Arkansas in mid-July, almost half a world away and at five thousand feet above the arid terrain of Morocco, a white twin-engine biplane droned across a cloudless sky, en route to Tétuan, Spanish Morocco, where the Spanish army had just risen in rebellion against the government. After this airplane disembarked its passengers at Tétuan, the rebellion took a direction that drew most of Europe into Spain's agony. Weeks would pass before it became clear to the world just what the Spanish turmoil portended; that November Frank Tinker would ask directions to the road to Port Bou.

4

OF PLANES AND SPAIN

Far from Arkansas, the twin-engine de Havilland D.H.89 Dragon Rapide G-ACYR¹ of Olley Air Services rolled out of its hangar at London's Croydon Airport for an extended charter flight. Captain James P. Olley, owner of the air service, struggled with a premonition that there was something extraordinary about this flight. Much cheaper and more comfortable ways existed to travel to Casablanca and the Canary Islands with two young eye-filling blondes than by chartering an expensive airplane for three weeks. He was especially apprehensive of the tall, smart-looking fellow named Luis Bolin who paid in cash for everything. He seemed too smooth; moreover, he was a foreigner.

But the chap named Pollard traveling with Bolin appeared to be a good, solid Englishman, and a glance at the girls made the trip seem self-explanatory. Jim Olley would have had second thoughts had he known that the girls were window dressing. One was Pollard's daughter, Diana, the other her friend, Dorothy Watson; their function: make this flight appear like the frivolous, self-indulgence of two middle-aged lechers. And Olley doubtless would have cancelled everything in an instant had he known that Bolin intended to deliver his airplane to the Canaries for the personal use of a quasi-exile from the stormy politics of Spain.

Business in early July 1936 was not so good, however, that Jim Olley could afford to permit his imagination to become fastidious about a £1,010 (about $5,000) charter. He nevertheless had Bolin sign a note that held him responsible for damages up to £10,000 if something happened to the airplane that its insurance would not cover. Olley and Bolin walked out to the tarmac where the Dragon Rapide's white paintwork sparkled in the morning sun, its two Gipsy Six engines gently ticking over. Bolin joined Pollard and the girls in the cabin. Olley wished them *bon voyage* and closed the cabin door. Then the pilot, Captain Cecil W. H. Bebb, revved up the engines and on the morning of 11 July taxied onto the field for takeoff. Four days later he arrived at the airport on the island of Las Palmas. On the eighteenth Captain Bebb flew from Las Palmas in the Canary

Islands via Agadir to Casablanca in French Morocco, but this time with three male passengers who looked uncomfortable in their civilian clothes.

One of the passengers, rather short, wore a small moustache and the other two invariably deferred to him. Bolin met the airplane in Casablanca. The Spaniards wanted to press on but that meant a night flight over mountainous terrain with which Captain Bebb was unfamiliar, and he would have none of it. The Spaniards spent an uneasy night in Casablanca. And as a precaution against the chance of his identification, the short man shaved off his moustache.

The next morning Captain Bebb had his passengers in the air again, on their way northeast to Tétuan in Spanish Morocco—on a flight that would change history. While he struggled with his controls against the airplane's changing trim, the short, rotund passenger got to his feet, peeled off his civilian clothes, and struggled into a khaki uniform. Finally he wrapped around his waist a scarlet sash with gold tassels at its ends that identified him as a general of the Spanish army.

After the Dragon Rapide landed at San Ramiel airfield on the outskirts of Tétuan early on the morning of 19 July, General Francisco Franco was the first passenger to disembark, on his way to take command of the Spanish army in Morocco (Ejército de África) in its revolt against the Republic.[2] The army's revolt, its seizure of Morocco and cities in Spain, unleashed civil strife throughout the country where other garrisons rose to join what Spaniards call the Alzamiento. Within a fortnight all of the fears, jealousies, and hatreds that had festered within the Spanish body politic for a generation transformed the many scattered elements of civil strife into a bloody civil war.

The focal point of the rebellion was the army, and most of its members subscribed to its cause. The navy divided on class lines; the officers were prepared to join the rebels, but the rank and file remained loyal to the Republic and demonstrated it by murdering most of the officers and taking control of most of the ships. The Spanish air force similarly divided, but most of its personnel remained loyal to the Republic; those in Morocco proved it by destroying many of their airplanes before the Franco-led insurgents could seize them.[3]

Relative to European aviation as a whole, Spain had become a rather somnolent backwater by 1936. Some of this was owed to Britain and France dumping war-surplus airplanes on the Spanish market after 1918, creating a glut that stunted domestic developments. Nevertheless, Spain's native sons made their marks among the world's records. In 1926 Ramón Franco with a crew of two made the first continuous flight from Europe across the South Atlantic to Brazil and Argentina; also in 1926, Eduardo Gallarza and Joaquín Loriga flew an aerial odyssey of 18,900 miles from Madrid to Manila, coincidentally making the first flight across the South China Sea; in 1933 Mariano Barberán and Joaquín Collar flew from Seville to Camagüey, Cuba, 4,906 miles nonstop and at that date the longest overwater flight ever made; and it was the genius of Juan de la Cierva that gave the world its first successful rotary-wing aircraft, the autogyro.

In the summer of 1936, Spain's air force consisted of about three thousand officers and men and about four hundred airplanes, not all of which were serviceable. They tended to be concentrated at Getafe, Los Alcázares, Barcelona, Seville, and in Morocco, where they were dispersed among a half-dozen airfields. There were flight training schools at Alcalá de Henares and Guadalajara, a school for mechanics at Quatro Vientos, and a gunnery and aircrew school at Los Alcázares. Small, combat-ready units were stationed at Tétuan, Larache, Nador, and Atalyou in Morocco, sites where they policed the Riff and the unruly desert tribes of the Spanish Sahara. With the exception of Morocco and the Cádiz-Seville area, all these facilities remained in the hands of the Republic at the beginning of the war, and only Getafe and Cuatro Vientos were lost during the first two years of the conflict.[4]

The aircraft on hand in July 1936 were for the most part of an average 1926 vintage. There were 120 CASA-built Breguet Br.19s of French design, and about one-third fell into the hands of the rebels. There were about fifty Hispano-built Nieuport fighters of French design, ten passing into the hands of the insurgents. Of multi-engine bombers there were a half-dozen Fokker F.7/3ms and a half-dozen de Havilland D.H.89A Dragon Rapides, both civil airliner conversions, and the Republic retained most of them.

The newest aircraft in any large numbers were twenty-seven CASA-built Vickers Vildebeests, massive single-engine biplanes conscripted as light bombers, whose British design dated from 1928. Based at San Javier near Valencia, practically all of the Vildebeests remained in the hands of the Republic. The navy had about a dozen CASA-built Dornier Wal twin-engine flying boats and a couple of dozen old, wooden-hulled Savoia SM.62 flying boats of dubious combat value; the Nationalists in Morocco seized a few of these seaplane types. There was also a civil air fleet of four new Douglas DC-2s, two Ford 4AT Tri Motors, three Fokker F.7/3m airliners, and a half-dozen smaller, single-engine machines of Líneas Aéreas Postales Españolas (LAPE), Spain's national airline. Except for one DC-2 seized by the Nationalists at Tablada-Seville, this fleet flew for the Republic; most of them were converted into crude bombers, the bombs being shoved out of their cabin doors.

During the 1920s Spain obtained most of its airplane designs from France, but by the mid-1930s it was looking to Britain and the United States. To replace its obsolescent Breguets and Nieuports, in 1935 the government studied the Boeing P-26 that was on strength with the U.S. Army Air Corps, and the Hawker Fury in service with the Royal Air Force. The Boeing was not only more expensive but inferior in performance to the Fury.[5] A license was purchased from Hawker to manufacture the Fury and the Hawker Osprey III single-engine scout bomber, to be built in Spain by CASA. Three Furys and one Osprey were delivered to Spain as pattern aircraft in early July 1936, just in time to be swept up in the war.

Neither the Fury nor the Osprey would be produced in Spain, however, because the British government's nonintervention policy kept Hawker from fulfilling its contract.[6] Similarly, a contract that the Republic negotiated with the Glenn L. Martin Company of Baltimore, Maryland, to manufacture the M-163W twin-engine bomber in Spain was even more abortive. The M-163W was an export version of the B-10 bomber, also then on strength with the Army Air Corps. No pattern aircraft had been delivered when the U.S. State Department pressured Martin into breaking off negotiations.[7]

One of the hypocrisies at large within Western democratic nations during the interwar years of 1919–39 held that the weapons business was a good business until a customer nation had to use them. Then weapons became sinful and were embargoed. This stemmed from a naïve belief that weapons were the root cause of conflict; if belligerents were deprived of weapons they would soon exhaust themselves, be forced to compromise their differences, the causes of conflict would be transcended, and "peace" would prevail. The totalitarian states believed just the opposite: that a war between third parties demanded their putting stakes on the table and wagering on one side or the other according to their own interests. The wagers took the form of weapons but could also include advisers, technicians, and organized "volunteers." The Spanish Civil War provides us a classic example.

At the beginning of the conflict the rebel forces—which soon adopted the name Nationalists—for all practical purposes had no air force at all, and their field forces suffered badly from harassment by Republican aircraft. Nationalist agents scoured the airplane markets of Europe and Great Britain for anything that could fly. They soon found themselves bidding in competition against agents from the Republic. The secondhand airplane market boomed and so did clandestine flights to Spain from all parts of Europe.

In England the well-known racing pilots Max Findley and Ken Waller were preparing a twin-engine Airspeed Viceroy for an air race from London to Johannesburg when a Spanish agent who wanted to buy their machine approached them. This Viceroy had a singular history; it was a civil airliner modified as a bomber for Haile Selassie's air force, but Ethiopia had collapsed under Italy's juggernaut before it could be delivered. Findley and Waller had no desire to sell it. The agent, however, knew that they had paid £5,500 for it and first prize in the race was £4,000, so he offered £9,500 (about $40,000). They took it, and this Viceroy disappeared across the Bay of Biscay toward Bilbao. Findley and Waller bought another airplane—the one in which they died during the race to South Africa.[8]

Also in the summer of 1936, Nevil Shute Norway, managing director of Airspeed, Ltd. (better known to the general public as the novelist Nevil Shute), pondered the precarious financial condition of his company. He had just repossessed six single-engine Couriers from an airline that had suspended operations, and he had four twin-engine Envoys parked in his hangars without a buyer in sight. Miraculously, an airplane broker appeared in his office and bought the whole lot! Shute excluded from the sale one Envoy, the prototype G-ACMT, because he was using it in important experimental work. Pressed to sell it, too, he quoted what he thought was an exorbitant price of £6,000. To his amazement it was paid immediately in cash, and G-ACMT flew off to Burgos to serve the Nationalist cause.[9]

More and more civil aircraft began to mysteriously disappear from British airfields. Some would be seen refueling at Bordeaux, Bayonne, or Toulouse, from where they would disappear over the Pyrenees. And for a moment the theft of airplanes became a lucrative business; the hard-pressed Spaniards were not inclined to fuss over titles. On 15 August the British government placed an embargo on the export of airplanes, aero engines, and their accessories as part of a policy of strict neutrality. Airplane smuggling continued, the Netherlands often serving as an entrepôt, or through a "paper" customer in France, but this traffic had to be conducted with great caution.

By September 1936 the Spanish airplane fever spread across the Atlantic to the United States, where the Americans had much to offer. The appearance of the Douglas DC-2 in 1934 and the fabulous DC-3 in early 1936 rendered all older airliners obsolescent, if not obsolete, and the airplane market was soon glutted with secondhand airline equipment. Although the Neutrality Acts of 1935 and 1936 applied only to wars between nations, not to internal commotions and civil wars, a few weeks earlier, on 8 August, the State Department declared a "moral embargo" on the sale of weapons to Spain. This put a wrench in the machinery of the Spanish ambassador in Washington, who sought sources of supply in the United States. But Félix Gordón Ordás, Spain's sagacious ambassador to Mexico, did not feel bound by a gringo's peculiar notions of morality. He had agents active in the United States buying up whatever they could find.[10] By the autumn of the year, dozens of American airplanes had cleared customs at Brownsville, Texas, while being ferried to the ports of Tampico and Veracruz for shipment to Spain. Some were flown directly to Mexico without paying any attention to the Rio Grande frontier. And some American entrepreneurs found it a simple matter to ship airplanes directly from American ports to "paper customers" created in the Netherlands or France.[11]

When Fernando de los Ríos, the Republic's new ambassador to the United States, pleaded a case for the recognized government of Spain to buy war matérials in the United States, Secretary of State Cordell Hull told him that there was no law against it, only a policy of "moral aloofness."[12] The "moral embargo" was openly challenged in late December when Robert Cuse, owner of the Vimalert Corporation, applied for a license to export 18 airplanes, 410 aero engines, and subassemblies for 150 engines—valued at $2.7 million. This matériel was not consigned to a "paper" customer, but overtly to Spain.

Robert Cuse was a Baltic German of Russian birth who immigrated to the United States in 1914. Although the news media of 1936 styled him as a Jersey City junk dealer, he was in truth a shrewd, innovative engineer. In the 1920s he did a thriving business with Amtorg, the Soviet Union's trading corporation, exporting American war-surplus matérials to Russia. Until the Russians became enamored of the air-cooled radial engine after 1927, he did a lucrative business in rebuilt Liberty engines. Concurrently, he reengineered the Liberty into a marine engine that proved to be a best-seller among rum runners to power the speed-boats they used to deliver cargoes of liquor into the United States from freight-ers that, during Prohibition, loitered beyond the three-mile limit. And, for good measure, he sold the same Liberty marine engines to the U.S. Coast Guard for its boats that chased the rum runners!

Likewise, after the U.S. Army rejected American Walter Christy's novel sus-pension system for tanks, Cuse handled the sale of its design and the export of one pattern chassis to the Soviet Union. He took care to see that it was exported as a "tractor," not as a tank chassis. And from that day to this, Russian tanks have employed the principles of the Christy suspension system,[13] perhaps the most famous of which is the T-34 used widely on the eastern front in World War II. In the case of airplanes for Spain, he acted for Amtorg, which in turn acted on behalf of the Republic.

Cuse's export license application, although legal, nonetheless was judged "immoral" by State Department officials. Its bureaucracy called in the news media and used them to publicly vilify Cuse by beating the drums of "pub-lic opinion"—the drumbeats intended to awaken Congress to the urgent need to close the loophole to civil wars. The department did not use dilatory tactics against Cuse's application because its analysis of available shipping indicated that he could not move his cargo before Congress acted to immunize the United States against civil wars. Airplanes of the 1930s did not weigh much, but they possessed considerable volume; even when dismantled they occupied a dispro-portionate amount of space relative to their weight. State Department function-aries did not believe that Cuse could find space for eighteen airplanes on any one ship and would have to divide his cargo among a half-dozen ships over a period of six to eight weeks.

But Cuse had an ace up his sleeve in the form of the freighter *Mar Cantá-brico*, whose name did not appear in the daily shipping news because she was in a Hoboken dry dock. Not only was she a Spanish ship but, on coming out of dry dock, her cargo holds would be empty. Word of this shocked State Department officials, then housed in the State, War, and Navy Department building on Seventeenth Avenue, and stimulated a hysterical effort to railroad an ad hoc Spanish embargo through Congress before the ship could sail. Meanwhile, the ship's loading was harassed by local police, customs officers, a parade of "inspectors," and the Coast Guard. The *Mar Cantábrico*'s "race against Congress" became front-page news. The ship sailed on 6 January 1937, a few hours before Congress enacted the Spanish embargo but days before the president could sign it into law.[14]

In an anticlimax to this imbroglio, because of having to depart in haste the ship sailed with only seven airplanes on board. From New York the *Mar Cantábrico* sailed to Veracruz, Mexico, where she loaded more matériel for the Republic. On 3 March, while attempting to run the Nationalist blockade of Bilbao, the *Mar Cantábrico* was intercepted and seized by the cruiser *Canarias*. The Nationalists subsequently put her cargo to use.[15]

At the outset of hostilities in 1936, the Republic exercised a rickety form of air superiority. But with the organization of the air force torn apart and in confusion, and its obsolescent equipment divided, it could not last. The Republic appealed to France, expecting enthusiastic assistance from the leftist Popular Front government of Léon Blum. But as usual with France of the Third Republic, its government was in confusion and divided against itself. To compound the confusion, Blum, an intellectual inclined to agonize over a question from this side and from that side, hoped that a decision could be avoided. Finally Blum decided to sell munitions to the recognized government of France's neighbor to the south, but to do so covertly. The intermediary, improbably, was the writer André Malraux, occasional aviator, opportunist par excellence, and at this moment playing the role of Lord Byron for the radical Left. He pulled together an organization that recruited French and other European aviators to ferry aircraft to Spain, to train Spanish pilots, and to enlist in a mercenary international squadron that would fly combat operations.

On 25 July, shortly after Francisco Franco landed in Morocco, spectators at Paris' Le Bourget Airport were intrigued by the sight of heavily armed guards meeting a bullet-holed Douglas DC-2 of LAPE, which touched down on the field with eighteen cases of Spanish gold valued at 18,865,000 francs (about $3.7 million). This was the first of twenty-eight similar bullion flights the Republic laid on to Le Bourget.[16] Meanwhile, at Étampes, twenty-five miles southwest of Paris, and at Toulouse-Francazal, sixty miles from the Iberian frontier, dozens of Dewoitine D.371 fighters and a few dozen Potez 54 twin-engine bombers were having their French air force markings painted over with a generic green camouflage before being ferried to the Republic.

These airplanes were as good as anything the Nationalists were able to muster during the war's first ninety days and, indeed, the Potez 54 was far superior to the Junkers Ju 52 as a bomber. But the homogeneity of the French-furnished machines was not matched by their personnel. European mercenaries flew these airplanes; most of them had never before flown together, did not know their compatriots, and had no reason to trust one another. Their performance tended to be uniformly good when it came to shooting up columns of troops strung out along a highway or strafing and bombing static targets in towns and villages undefended by antiaircraft batteries; but when challenged by Nationalist fighters, too many of them found a reason for returning to their base.

It was on this point of experienced personnel and standard training that the Republic was deficient. In the army's revolt, practically all the young company-grade pilot officers went over to the rebels. The Republic was left with sergeant pilots who had little flying experience, were rarely admitted to the elite ranks of fighter pilots, and were untrained to command. At the other extreme were senior officers whose cockpit skills had long since atrophied. In the midst of its national trauma, the Republic faced the problem of creating a new air force, and, during its first six months, it had to depend on a hodgepodge of mercenaries as a stopgap until the Soviets appeared with a homogeneous air force in November.

The covert but direct assistance from France did not last long. Spain's agony produced two fears that haunted French politicians. First, the Spanish conflict might expand into a general European war, for which France was not prepared. Second, they knew that the social and economic problems that exploded into civil war in Spain had counterparts at large within French society, and they feared that Spain might provide an example for a similar convulsion in France. The French government was desperate for any instrument that might isolate the "Spanish disease," and it seized on the idea of an international agreement for "non-intervention." The British had similar fears, and when they pressured France to terminate assistance to the Republic, the French were relieved to have an excuse to close their frontier to war matériel. On 9 August 1936, three weeks after the Spanish army's insurrection and eighteen days after their decision to assist the Republic, the French government did just that. It would not be opened again until March 1938, and then only for twelve weeks. Hereafter the Republic's military logistics were determined by the fraudulent politics of nonintervention, and they coincidentally dictated absolute Republican dependence on the Soviet Union. Influential elements within the French government, however, feared that a Nationalist victory would not be to the advantage of France, and they continued to assist the Republic, albeit clandestinely.

Meanwhile, back on the morning of 20 July at San Ramiel airfield, Tétuan, senior rebel air officers suggested moving the Ejército de África in Spanish

Morocco across the Strait of Gibraltar to Spain using three available Fokker F.7/3ms and two Dornier Wal seaplanes. This novel idea, an "airbridge" to Spain, was put before the Commanders' Board, chaired by General Franco, and was heartily endorsed. The airbridge ferrying flights began that same day to Seville, but each of these airplanes could carry barely a dozen men.[17] Franco realized he needed real transports to accomplish this crucial movement of forces, and he ordered contacts be made with the leaders of Germany and Italy requesting assistance.

Indeed, the Nationalists secured great success in treating with these two European dictatorships. Luis Bolin climbed back into the Dragon Rapide and Captain Bebb flew him to Marseilles, where he connected with an Air France flight to Rome. Through Count Galeazzo Ciano, the son-in-law of Italy's dictator Benito Mussolini, he obtained Italy's assistance. On 29 July Bolin was on board one of twelve Savoia-Marchetti S.81 trimotor bombers en route from Cagliari, Sardinia, to the air base at Nador, Spanish Morocco. They met headwinds; fuel consumption was excessive, and some fuel reserves proved insufficient. One bomber made a forced landing and another crashed in French Morocco, while a third ditched at sea with the loss of its crew. But the nine that arrived constituted a formidable force relative to the small volume of "airspace" across the Strait of Gibraltar.[18]

A Nationalist mission to Germany proved even more successful. On 26 July, after partaking of a performance of *Die Walküre* in Bayreuth's "Wagnerpalast," Adolf Hitler received a delegation sent by General Franco. The Nationalists had an army to transport from Morocco to Spain, but the Republic's navy commanded the Strait of Gibraltar. They were using three Fokker F.7/3m bombers and two Dornier Wal flying boats to fly troops across and needed a real airlift.

Deciding to assist the Nationalists, Hitler immediately dispatched twenty Junkers Ju 52/3m transports to Morocco. In airline service a Ju 52 carried sixteen passengers over a three-hundred-mile nonstop distance with ease; with its fuel reserves reduced, the weight of three dozen fully equipped soldiers was easily carried half this distance. Between 20–28 July the Fokkers and Dornier Wals, later assisted by the captured Douglas DC-2, lifted about 120 legionnaires each day from Spanish Morocco to Seville. During the nine days between 28 July and 5 August 1936, the Ju 52s lifted more than 1,500 soldiers over the 130 miles between Tétuan and Seville on the navigable Guadalquivir River; this served to consolidate the Nationalists' tenuous hold on this vital inland seaport. Moreover, the airlift did not have to terminate at a seaport but could deliver troops and munitions directly to inland points. Concurrently, the Italian S.81 bombers drove the Republican navy out of the Strait, and on 5 August the Nationalists managed to get a small convoy of ships carrying troops, vehicles, and heavy weapons across from Ceuta to Algeciras, Spain.

Map 4.1   The Provinces of Spain, 1936

From Seville and Cádiz, Nationalist forces spread out to control western Andalusia and to drive north through Estremadura to link up with the Nationalist army of General Emilio Mola, which was pushing south from the regions of León and Old Castille. By the end of September the Junkers trimotors had lifted more than 13,000 men and 270 tons of cargo from Morocco to Seville and diverse points in Andalusia.[19] The action marked a military milestone: the first time that large numbers of armed forces and equipment were airlifted into combat. Hitler later declared the Ju 52 to be key to the success of the Spanish Civil War, not Saint Isabella as Franco supposed.[20]

Incredibly, throughout the crucial period between 20 July and the end of September, the Republican air force command in Madrid failed to order its pursuit forces stationed nearby on the Mediterranean Coast to attack the vulnerable airbridge transports—this in spite of urgent messages dispatched to Madrid by Aurelio Villimar, the air base commander at El Rompedizo.[21] Other government air force commanders on the scene doubtless sent similar appeals. The strategic

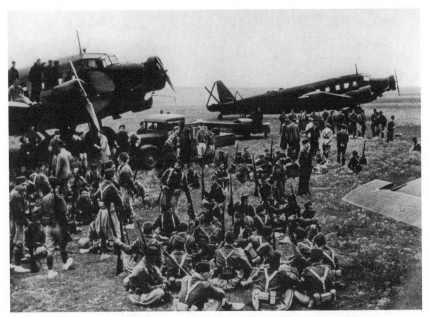

Nationalist troops waiting to board Ju 52 transports (*R. K. Smith Collection*)

blunder would not be the last made by the Republican government; this particular one, however, allowed the airlift to succeed and ensured the bloody civil war that followed.

Five days after Hitler's decision to assist the Nationalists, the German freighter *Usamero* steamed down the Elbe from Hamburg; among its cargo were twelve Heinkel He 51 fighter planes accompanied by eighty-six Luftwaffe personnel. On 6 August the airplanes were unloaded at Cádiz and transported to the airfield at Jerez de la Frontera for assembly. Thereafter, a ship sailed from Germany for Spain on an average of every five days, delivering aircraft, artillery, ammunition, motor vehicles, and other sinews of war. Technicians accompanied the equipment to supervise their assembly and instruct Spaniards in their operation and maintenance.

All the while an increasing number of Heer and Luftwaffe personnel began disappearing from Germany through the office of the War Ministry's Special Branch "W" in Berlin.[22] The only address given to their next of kin was c/o Max Winkler, Berlin S.W.68. About six months later they would reappear in Germany with souvenirs of Spain in their baggage. Inevitably, some failed to return; during 1936–39 some three hundred German military personnel died in the Spanish Civil War.

At first the Third Reich boldly pretended that these personnel were not in Spain; then it was claimed that they were "volunteers" in the simple sense of the word. This sham ended on 6 November 1936, after the Soviet Union's assistance to the Republic had become manifest, when German personnel in Spain organized under the command of Major General (Lieutenant General after April 1937) Hugo von Sperrle and were formally constituted as the Legion Condor. Colonel Lieutenant Wolfram Freiherr von Richthofen, son of the World War I German ace, served Sperrle as his chief of staff throughout most of the war. Although the Legion never had more than 5,000 men in Spain, as the result of a policy of rotation more than 14,000 officers and men passed through its ranks.[23]

At the same time Italian aid commenced. On 18 August the first fighter planes—a half-dozen Fiat CR.32s—arrived by freighter in Cádiz. In the course of the war Italy sent more than 2,000 aircraft to Spain[24] and rotated more than 72,000 men, most of them ground troops. The Italian aircraft were among the best in Spain, their pilots first rate. The same could not be said of the Italian ground forces, whose performance varied from disastrous to adequate.

While this German and Italian buildup was under way, the Republic's air forces began to decline. Airplanes lost in combat or in accidents, primarily because of inexperienced personnel, were no longer being replaced from France. And as the Republic's air superiority decayed, so did the performance of its mercenaries, who were usually more interested in surviving to payday than in taking risks for a cause in which they had no personal stake. By mid-August the Nationalists were already well on their way toward reshaping the political map of Spain.

The mountain range of the Sierra de Guadarrama, whose peaks reach up to almost eight thousand feet, provides a formidable barrier that divides the provinces of Old and New Castile, the city of Madrid being sited in the latter. In a series of small but bitterly fought battles for control of the Sierras' passes—the Somosierra, Navacerrada, and Alto de León—Republican forces stopped Nationalist columns from the north and prevented them from descending upon Madrid. By the end of July the Sierras were stabilized as a frontier between the Republic and Nationalist Spain and remained such until the end of the war.

Jumping off from Seville, a Nationalist column marched its way north through Estramadura to link up with Nationalist elements that controlled León and Old Castille. On 15 August, after a bitter fight, they took the city of Badajoz that controlled the railhead to Portugal and Lisbon. The Salazar dictatorship that ruled Portugal had no love for the turbulent Spanish Republic, and hereafter a substantial tonnage of German assistance to the Nationalists moved through the port of Lisbon, which was one day closer to Germany by steamship than Seville or Cádiz.

In the initial uprising the Nationalists seized control of the Balearic Islands of Majorca, Minorca, and Ibiza. On 9 August a Republican expeditionary force recaptured Ibiza. On the sixteenth another Republican force landed on Majorca.

Before it could move out of the beachhead, however, Italian bombers and fighter planes from Sardinia, operating from bases just set up on the island, threw the Spaniards into confusion and cut them to pieces in their enclave. On 3 September the Republicans retreated to their ships with heavy losses. The Italians developed a large bomber base near Palma on Majorca from which they bombed cities along Spain's Mediterranean shore from Barcelona in the north to Alicante in the south, all of which were within a radius of 175 miles, less than 90 minutes' flying time.

In the far north, army units from intensely Nationalist Navarre fought their way into the Basque province of Guipúzcoa and on 3 September took the city of Irún, where Spain's frontier with France reaches the Bay of Biscay. This cut off the industrialized Basque provinces, Santander and Asturias, from direct communications with France. Isolated in the "Cantabrian Pocket," these Republican provinces' sea communications with the outside world were sorely threatened by a Nationalist naval blockade.

By the end of August the Nationalist forces that took Badajoz had swung east and marched up the Tajo Valley for Talavera, Toledo, and Madrid. On 23 August Ju 52 bombers hit Getafe airfield south of Madrid; two days later they struck at the Cuatro Vientos airfield; and on the twenty-seventh they bombed Madrid itself. The air raid of 27 August marked the beginning of a series of bombardments of Madrid that went on for months. The world watched in horror the bombings of Madrid, but by 1945 that horror would seem quaint when compared with how far the science of "death from the skies" had progressed within nine years. In the sky over Madrid, techniques left suspended in 1918 resumed, marking the beginning of a worldwide process that worked its way through the streets of Guernica, Barcelona, Shanghai, Nanking, Warsaw, Rotterdam, London, and Coventry, to boomerang on Cologne, Hamburg, Tokyo, Dresden, and Berlin. Its logic culminated on 6 August 1945 at Hiroshima, coincidentally opening a new era of "air terror."

As the bombings of Madrid increased and the Nationalist columns moved inexorably closer to the capital, the Republic started organizing the city's defenses to withstand a siege. The Republic's forces in the field consisted of a mixture of militia, paramilitary groups from trade unions, and untrained volunteers who were leavened by a few officers and noncoms from the old regular army. They had little discipline and many were strangers to one another; they neither knew their officers nor were inclined to trust them, and there existed little sense of cohesion. They would be no match for the Nationalist regulars. Although they could stand and fight among the cover provided by towns and villages, they were unable to maneuver. Repeatedly outflanked and threatened by encirclement, they usually broke and ran, creating confusion in the rear. Nationalist air attacks and their own lack of air cover eroded morale. The only reason that the Nationalist advance proceeded so slowly was owed to its broad front, a desire to hold casualties to a minimum, thus conserving manpower for the assault on Madrid, and the fact that the closer they got to Madrid the further they moved from their sources of supply, which multiplied logistics problems.

The fall of the capital seemed certain. At this point, however, the Soviet Union's military assistance began to take effect. It is difficult to appreciate three-quarters of a century later, but in the 1930s, when Fascist dictatorships were on the ascendency throughout Europe, most liberal, leftist, and Socialist groups in Europe, England, and the United States—not to mention those persons who styled themselves "academics" or "intellectuals"—regarded Stalin's Russia as the only hope of "popular democracy" in Europe. Because of its self-styled "Socialist" homeland to the world, a "paradise of the worker and peasant," and self-proclaimed nemesis of Fascism, the Soviets had an important stake in maintaining their myth by acting aggressively in Spain, aside from any factors of realpolitik.

When Marcel Rosenberg, the new Soviet ambassador to the Republic, arrived in Madrid on 27 August 1936 he was accompanied by an unusually large staff. The Russians set up their headquarters in Gaylord's Hotel on the tree-shaded Calle de Alfonso XI behind the Prado Museum, and later expanded into the Hotel Nacional across the street from the Atocha railroad station. When Russian aviators arrived a few weeks later, they were temporarily billeted in the Hotel Alfonso. On 9 September the Soviet freighter *Neva* arrived in Alicante with a load of airplanes, tanks, artillery, and other munitions—the first of a stream of ships already at sea between Soviet ports in the Black Sea and those of Spain's Mediterranean Levante.[25]

While the Russians unloaded, assembled, and organized their equipment in the Levante, the Nationalists had four columns driving on Madrid with the Republican militiamen falling back before them. General Emilio Mola, who was coordinating the drive, boasted that besides these four columns there was a "fifth column" of Nationalist sympathizers concealed inside Madrid; when the Nationalist army appeared at the gates of the city they would rise up and fight in the streets. Mola's remark gave birth to the expression "fifth columnist"; its usage spread far beyond Spain and came to have a sinister meaning to the world of the late 1930s.[26]

As the Nationalists pushed past Talavera, their bombers, which had been based at Seville, moved to Cáceres, only 160 miles and less than 90 minutes' flying time from Madrid. From Cáceres the Ju 52s and S.81s began bombing the capital almost daily. Although these air attacks were widely interpreted as "terror raids," the German, Italian, and Spanish airmen actually were trying to hit what they perceived as military targets in a city then being transformed into

Savoia-Marchetti S.81 on a bomb run (*Courtesy of the National Museum of the U.S. Air Force ®*)

a fortress. But their equipment was primitive, their artificial peacetime training inadequate to the task, and, like the air leaders of bombing squadrons the world over, they tended to overestimate their capabilities. The Nationalists had no interest in reducing their prize of Madrid to rubble, but many bombs seemed to fall anywhere and everywhere among residential districts.

By military standards of only a few years later these attacks seem quaint. Not only was the equipment primitive, but the tactics seemed to hew slavishly to textbooks of 1917, and seldom did any attacking force number more than a dozen bombers. Few Republican fighters—a force that by now had degenerated into a mixed bag of equipment—rose to challenge the raiders. When they did they were usually driven off or shot down by disciplined elements of Fiats or Heinkels. At Cáceres the German airmen—billeted in the Hotel Alvarez—no longer took the precaution of wearing Spanish uniforms. They had good reason to believe that Madrid would be taken in a few weeks, the war would soon be over, and they would be home for Christmas.

The Spanish Civil War marked the rebirth of the manned bomber, and its palmiest moments occurred in the skies over Madrid in this autumn of 1936. No radar to detect the bomber's approach existed, no combat communication and information centers to track the raider and determine its target, nor were there ground controllers to vector defending fighters to an interception. At this date, detection of aircraft by electronic echo-ranging had only entered its "bread-board" stage of development and was being pursued in great secrecy by diverse national laboratories; even the word "radar" had not yet been invented.[27]

Hastily organized ground observers who might see or hear the bombers while they were en route and telephone word of their passing provided the only warning to Madrid of an incoming raid. Observers in the top of the Telefónica, the thirteen-story "skyscraper" headquarters of Spain's telephone company, provided the final warning. The Telefónica was not only the tallest building in Madrid, it was sited on the city's highest ground, from which the Gran Via runs downhill westward to the Plaza de España and downhill eastward to the Plaza de la Cibeles; it commanded a breathtaking view of the city's hinterland. During the siege of Madrid the Telefónica inevitably became a prized target and, inevitably, bombs and artillery fell everywhere in its vicinity—but without destroying the building.

By the time the alarm sounded from the Telefónica and fighters scrambled to make an interception, the bombers had usually dumped their loads and were speeding for home. And in the late 1930s the fighter plane's superiority in speed was so marginal that it had little chance of overtaking the bombers—even the slow Ju 52s if they had enough of a head start. In 1932 the British politician Stanley Baldwin, later prime minister of Great Britain, had moaned to Parliament and the world that "the bomber will always get through."[28] His words became a cliché, but the Spanish Civil War seemed to confirm the estimate.

By 4 November the Nationalist armies had overrun Madrid's Getafe airfield; the Cuatro Vientos airfield fell next. The Republic had already evacuated its air operations to Madrid's civil airport at Barajas, to Alcalá de Henares, and to recently created and well-camouflaged airfields north of the city. On this same day, and for the first time, Russian fighter planes challenged the Nationalist air forces over Madrid.[29] Colonel Petr Pumpur ("Colonel Julio") led the fighter contingent, assisted by Senior Lieutenant Georgiy Zakharov ("Rodriges Kromberg").[30] One Junkers bomber was shot down, and another was so badly shot up that it barely limped away and was wrecked in a crash-landing at Esquivias. The Russians' victory was spoiled, however, by two pilots losing their sense of direction and accidentally landing at Segovia, making the Nationalists a gift of two new Polikarpov I-15 fighters and themselves prisoners of war.[31]

On 7 November the Nationalist storm broke against Madrid with a frontal assault on the city.[32] They fought their way into the Casa de Campo, a sprawling parkland of some four thousand acres that is separated from the city by the Manzanares River. Where the Manzanares flows through Madrid, it is canalized between heavy masonry walls, is less than one hundred yards wide, and in the autumn can be at very low water. But it is a barrier, there are heights on the Madrid side, and there were only four bridges.

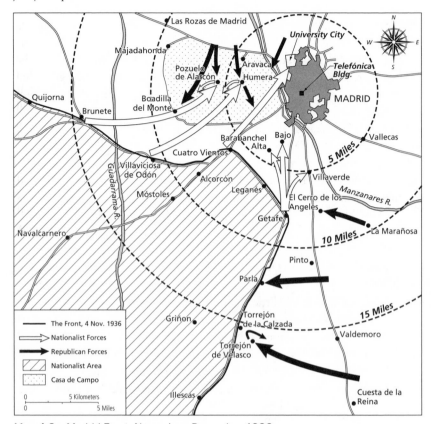

Map 4.2 Madrid Front, November–December 1936

By the thirteenth the Nationalists had beaten off a Republican counterattack on their southern flank at Cerro de los Ángeles east of Getafe and seized the commanding heights of Mount Garabitas in the Casa de Campo; two days later they reached the west end of the Franceses Bridge across the Manzanares. The fighting was bitter, the casualties on both sides unusually heavy, and the retreating Republicans blew up the bridge. But on the fourteenth, Nationalist patrols forded the river and during the night built a pontoon bridge. The next day a column poured into Madrid's suburb of University City. It was among the university's buildings that the Republican soldier who was often at a loss on open ground proved his mettle with the masonry shelter provided in urban street fighting. In the maze of University City the Nationalists paid dearly for every square meter of rubble they occupied, and within two weeks their casualties became unacceptable.

On 23 November the Nationalists suspended operations in the battered remains of University City to resume a war of maneuver in which they planned to encircle the city from the west. This operation, which came to be known as the Battle of the Coruña Road, jumped off on 14 December, pushing its way into the new year to become bogged down along the line of the road to Coruña. With the Republicans now well dug in northwest of the city, the Nationalists turned their attention to the area southeast of Madrid and a similar encircling movement—which eventually degenerated into the pitched battle of the Jarama.

To Americans of 1936, the Spanish army's revolt seemed to be just another European flare-up, but after the German and Italian intervention became manifest the conflict took on aspects of a morality play exploding with emotionalism. The tangled politics of Spain were incomprehensible to most Americans; the name "Republic" seemed to—or was made to—speak for itself; and the fact that the obscene, strutting Nazis and Fascists were helping a gang of generals overthrow an established parliamentary government was enough to put a majority of American opinion on the side of the Republic.

A substantial minority of Americans, however, viewed the Republic as the vehicle of bloodthirsty Bolsheviks who burned churches, shot priests, raped nuns, and functioned as a veritable engine of the Antichrist. Others found this less shocking than the Republic's lack of enthusiasm for the endeavors of free enterprise and its inclination to expropriate private property, especially that of foreign-owned corporations. In combination, these conservative American minorities acted as a check on the liberal enthusiasts who cheered and wept for the Republic, in effect exercising a veto over any U.S policy that might hurt the Nationalist cause; they became the enforcers of Secretary of State Cordell Hull's "moral aloofness."

Among those Americans who scoffed at Mr. Hull's sensibilities were Bert Acosta, Gordon Berry, Edward Schneider, and Frederick Lord; in November 1936 they turned up in Paris with a mercenary eye on the troubles in Spain. Acosta, a celebrated racing pilot of the early 1920s, had been one of Richard E. Byrd's pilots for Byrd's transatlantic flight of 1927, but he had fallen on hard times as a result of too many losing bouts with the bottle. Schneider was a well-known commercial aviator of the early 1930s, while Berry and Lord were veteran aviators of World War I who had made careers puffing up their alleged aerial accomplishments. A few days later they surfaced in Valencia, where the Republic's air ministry gave them contracts, bundled them into a Douglas DC-2, and flew them to Bilbao in the isolated Cantabrian Pocket on the Bay of Biscay.

Based at Sondica in the suburbs of Bilbao, they flew some of the old Breguet Br.19s, Miles Hawk Trainers, and Falcons—British-built sport planes equipped with bomb racks but no guns. A squadron of Russian I-15s at a base nearby provided their fighter cover. Thirty days in Spain's air war proved more than enough for Acosta and his friends, and they returned to the United States with all kinds of good stories, most of them far-fetched embellishments.[33]

In America, Frank Glasgow Tinker Jr. was an interested student of these events. He felt no "moral aloofness" toward the war in Spain; he saw a marvelous opportunity for an unemployed former naval aviator. On 27 November 1936 he dashed off letters to the Spanish consul in New York and to the embassies in Washington and Mexico City, offering his services. The embassy in Washington, taking care not to transgress American neutrality laws, replied that the Republic had no need of aviators; the consul in New York was noncommittal. But Félix Gordón Ordás did not pretend to be awed by Cordell Hull's fastidiousness. Mexico had just passed through a long, painful, but necessary revolution of its own, and in spite of much meddling by the United States, Mexico assumed that the Spanish situation was similar, and President Lázaro Cárdenas extended all possible assistance to the Republic. Thus the Spanish ambassador told Tinker to come to Mexico immediately for negotiation of a contract.

Tinker wrote to his sister Lucille to borrow a hundred dollars for the trip, warning her not to tell their parents, while assuring her that the stories she read in the newspapers were exaggerated and that the war in Spain held no extraordinary dangers. And he reminded her: "Just remember that this is what I've been trained to do." Lucille's money arrived promptly, and Tinker was soon rolling down the high iron of the Missouri Pacific Railroad for the Mexican border. On the evening of 18 December he got off the train in Mexico City's old Colonia Station to an awkward moment. He was in a foreign country and knew only three words of its language, "Si! Si!" and "Caramba!"—and he didn't know what the last word meant. He found a taxi driver who spoke English, and after a wild ride down the Paseo de la Reforma and past Alameda Park, he found himself at the Hotel Monte Carlo, an old but pleasant hotel of the colonial era on the Avenida Uruguay in the heart of the city.

The next morning he dashed out to La Embajada de España on the Calle Insurgentes, where he discovered that not only did he have a language problem, he was much too early. In the 1930s Latins had yet to conduct business early in the morning, and he was told to return in the evening. When Tinker returned after sundown, he was greeted by Colonel Roberto Fierro Villalobos, who spoke faultless English. Unbeknown to Tinker, Colonel Fierro was chief of the Air Corps and was advising Gordón Ordás on aircraft procurement in the United States and the recruitment of contract pilots from the Americas.

After examining Tinker's credentials, Fierro drew up a contract that provided for the rank of *alférez* (2nd lieutenant), $1,500 a month base pay, and a bonus of $1,000 for each enemy aircraft he destroyed. If hospitalized and unable to fly, his pay would be reduced to $500 a month, and $2,000 would be paid to his next of kin in the event of his death. The money would be paid in cash to his mother or father through the Spanish consul in New Orleans. Either party could terminate the contract with ten days' advance notice.

Four days later Tinker entered the office of the Spanish general consul at 515 Madison Avenue, New York City, where an American lawyer confirmed the contract made in Mexico. Tinker was told that he would be sailing on the *Normandie* the next day. After that, Tinker walked out into a snow-filled afternoon and took the subway to Thirty-Fourth Street, where he changed for the Hudson Tube to Jersey City's Journal Square and his old haunts from Standard Oil days. It was Christmas Eve; he spent it in his hotel room—alone. As far as we know, he made no attempt to contact his wife in Greenwich Village.

Christmas is a religious day among Latins, though their holiday festivities are reserved for 6 January, the Feast of the Three Kings; but how much any of this meant to a consul general of the violently anti-clerical Spanish Republic is debatable. Dr. Luis Careaga, the consul, personally greeted Tinker when he arrived Christmas day, suitcase in hand. Here he was introduced to his Spanish passport—a small but poisonous document that would contribute to his undoing in the years ahead. At this moment, however, he found the passport only amusing. Upon opening it, he discovered that he was now Francisco Gomez Trejo.

Careaga gave Tinker his new "life story": he had been born in the town of Oliveros in the province of Coruña, from which his parents had immigrated to Mexico when he was a child. They subsequently sneaked across the border into Texas, where they both inconsiderately died and left him to be reared by southern cotton farmers. This would explain Tinker's ignorance of Spanish and his pronounced southern accent. In these troubled times he was returning to Spain to look after the welfare of his aged grandparents, Señor and Señora Gomez and Señor and Señora Trejo. If inspectors of the Non-intervention Committee or French authorities at Cerbère asked him if he intended to fight in Spain, he should reply that he didn't know; after all, he might be conscripted. Careaga then made Tinker practice writing "Francisco Gomez Trejo" a few dozen times to develop a signature.

After this drill Careaga gave Tinker his steamship tickets, baggage stickers, and $100 in expense money that would be deducted from his first month's pay. With a "*buena suerte y próspero año nuevo*," he put Tinker in a taxi for the French Line piers at the foot of West Forty-Eighth Street.

When Tinker stepped aboard the *Normandie*, the ship was only nineteen months old and her marvelous draperies, carpeting, and furnishings had not yet had time to become even slightly soiled. The *Normandie* was not the most magnificent liner to ply the North Atlantic seaway, but she was one of the fastest and emphatically the most beautiful. After her maiden voyage to the United

States in June 1935, she steamed from New York to England in the breathtaking time of four days, three hours, and twenty-five minutes. In August 1936 the new *Queen Mary* had beaten this time, but by only a few hours. There were as yet no airplanes providing a transatlantic passenger service, but in 1936 the traveler in a hurry could book passage aboard the zeppelin *Hindenburg* that would speed to Europe in forty-eight hours. The Spanish Republic, however, was not about to buy passage for anyone on board a German airship.

Tinker thought the *Normandie* a fine ship, but she had a heavy roll in a following sea and vibrated too much in any sea condition—a criticism echoed by most of the *Normandie's* knowledgeable passengers. Few persons wanted to travel the North Atlantic in wintertime, fewer still during the Christmas holidays, and the ship's passenger list was accordingly small. Among his fellow passengers numbered Fritz Reiner, conductor of the Metropolitan Opera; the publisher Alfred Knopf; Lillian Hellman, author of *The Children's Hour* and mistress to the mystery writer Dashiell Hammett; the actor Otto Kruger; and Mme. Schiaparelli of cosmetics notoriety.

Because he was traveling under a phony name, on a phony passport, and with a very phony-sounding story, Tinker had no desire to meet anyone. Only about a hundred persons were booked in the tourist section in which he was traveling. Most of them were men and they seemed to know each other, some six dozen of them gathering in small, self-conscious knots. They were a strange bunch. Some were big, tough-looking mugs who appeared well acquainted with the harder side of life; others were skinny little bookish types who seemed to hide behind the lenses of their eyeglasses. What they all had in common was an obvious unease.

These seventy-six men represented the first American volunteers for the Abraham Lincoln Battalion of the Republic's International Brigades. Most of them had no military experience, and many of them were philosophically opposed to militarism. They were going to Spain to take up arms against "militarism," predatory capitalism, Fascism, and a host of other "isms." Their pay as foot soldiers would be ten pesetas a day, a trifle more than ten cents American. If they managed to survive three years of the war (and most of them did not), their total wages would not equal Frank Tinker's for one month. But they were the unskilled laborers of war; Tinker represented the skilled professional craftsman. What is more, as the expression went in Spain, these volunteers "had politics." Most of them were members of the Communist Party of the United States (CPUSA), and they sincerely believed that they would make Spain "the tomb of Fascism" and create a better world. Earl Browder, boss of the American Communist Party, had personally seen them off from party headquarters in New York City, giving each man a limp, sweaty handshake. At that moment Browder may well have been reflecting upon the words of the great American social philosopher Phineas T. Barnum: "There's a sucker born every minute!"[34]

By keeping to himself, however, Tinker became conspicuous. The Lincoln cadres noticed him, and they feared that he might be an FBI agent or some kind of undercover policeman. They noticed that he wore a large ring with its design always turned into his palm. One of the Lincolns sidled up to Tinker at the bar to get a close look at the ring; he managed to read "U.S. Naval Academy" in its design, and word flashed among their ranks that Tinker must be a naval intelligence agent. After this, Tinker was not about to bother with any one of these seventy-six "political" men.[35]

After disembarking from the *Normandie* in LeHavre, Tinker took the boat train to Paris. At a kiosk in the station he bought a copy of the Paris edition of the *Herald-Tribune*. One of its headlines read, "Neutrality Law To Be Applied to Civil Wars." Of course, Tinker could not imagine what this might portend for him. At 11 p.m. he arrived in the Gare St. Lazare, checked into a hotel, and promptly went out to sample the Paris nightlife. It was the evening of 31 December, so why not? The next morning, over a foggy cup of coffee, he dashed off a postcard to his sister Toodles: "Do these people know how to celebrate New Year's Eve!"

And so on this first day of 1937 he took a taxi to the Gare d'Orsay to board a train for the south that would carry him over the last five hundred miles of the road to Port Bou.

5

LA ESQUADRILLA DE LACALLE

By 1937 entry into Spain was no longer a simple matter. In early August 1936 France closed its frontiers to war matériel destined for Spain, and within four weeks the European states created the International Non-Intervention Committee with headquarters in London; it had the ostensible purpose of keeping the Spanish Civil War isolated from Europe's other political problems. But with Germany, Italy, and the Soviet Union among its members, the committee became a hollow joke inflated by platitudes from its British members, whom representatives of the U.S. State Department dutifully applauded.

Non-Intervention claimed to prevent foreign volunteers from entering Spain to take service with either of the belligerents. When the German and Italian governments began shipping military units to Nationalist Spain by the thousands, however, the French were inclined to be lax toward individuals who wanted to cross their frontier with the Republic—even when the Comintern[1] organized these "individuals" for service in the International Brigades. Much depended on the personal prejudices of the frontier officials. Those who sympathized with the Republic waved obvious volunteers (who always claimed to be "tourists") across the frontier without fuss; those inclined toward Fascism (a fast-growing force in French politics by 1937) proved difficult. Still a third category could be stalled—until a bribe was offered.

When Tinker explained the saga of the Gomez and Trejo families, the French were skeptical.[2] He made a conspicuous blunder when he gave his name as Francisco Trejo. In Spanish countries the last name is the mother's family name, the second is the father's and is usually cited as more important. He should have given his name as Francisco Gomez.[3]

Because the Spanish Embassy in Paris booked Tinker's train reservations, he was traveling in the company of a group of Catalonian political leaders who included the province's minister of external affairs.[4] This proved fortunate. The French border official was about to turn Tinker back when the Catalan minister intervened. Some quiet words were exchanged, probably accompanied by a hundred francs, and the border official was all smiles. The barrier rose and the Catalans escorted Tinker into the Spanish Republic, where they rolled out the red carpet.

On the Spanish side they boarded a shuttle train that chuffed them through a series of tunnels to Port Bou seven miles down the line. A change of trains at the Franco-Iberian frontier is necessary because the French railroads are standard gauge (4 feet, 8½ inches), whereas the trains of Spain roll on a five-foot gauge.[5] One of the transportation curiosities of Europe is that all of the Continent's railways are standard gauge except Spain at Europe's western extremity and Russia in the east, both using a five-foot gauge.[6]

The next train from Port Bou for Barcelona would not leave for five hours, so the Catalan minister took everyone to a restaurant for lunch. They were forking their way through a six-course repast when sirens sounded, followed by a great commotion in the street. Someone shouted *"Apparatos Fascistos!"* echoed by shouts of *"El refugio, dónde está el refugio?"* Everyone rushed out of the restaurant, leaving Tinker to wonder what was going on. In his sudden loneliness it occurred to him that something must be wrong.

Tinker put down his knife and fork and walked out into the street in time to see a hillside across the small harbor erupt in a ripple of brown earth; a second later the explosions reached his ears. Looking up he saw three multi-engine seaplanes speeding off toward the Mediterranean. They were bombers from the Nationalist bases on Majorca in the Balearic Islands, and he had just witnessed an attempt to bomb Port Bou's railroad terminal.

When the Catalans returned, they found Tinker at the table calmly working away at lunch. They praised his contempt for the air raid, and he was not about to volunteer an explanation. He later noticed that *"Refugio"* was painted on the walls of many public buildings. It had nothing to do with refugees. It meant air-raid shelter.

The Catalans and Tinker got away from Port Bou in the evening to arrive in Barcelona in the morning, and here he had to change trains for Valencia, which was yet another overnight crawl down the coast. Because Italian bombers based on Majorca liked to bomb trains, it was expedient to conduct most railroad traffic along Spain's Mediterranean shore between dusk and dawn. Upon arrival in Valencia's Estación de Norte, he learned that there was not a taxi to be had in the whole city; they had long since been requisitioned by the government and driven off to the front in Aragón. And as a result of the government being evacuated from Madrid to Valencia back in November, the city was frightfully overcrowded. He had been told to go to the Hotel Inglés, but it was full, as were others—filled with bureaucrats from Madrid. The Metropole served as the Russians' headquarters. It was with difficulty that he finally found a room in the

Regina. After a lunch that proved a successful experiment with the Mediterranean delicacy of fried squid, he hurried to the Ministerio de Marina y Aire, but a Canadian newspaperman he met assured him it would be a waste of time. War or no war, the government did not conduct business between noon and 4 p.m. When he finally went to the Air Ministry at four o'clock it was still too early; he was told to return at 7:30. It looked to him as if it were going to be a slow war.

The officer in charge at the Air Ministry tried to convince Tinker that the Republic had no need of contract aviators, but he was welcome to join the air force as a regular officer. What this man was trying to say was that they wanted no more expensive American mercenaries who were never sober enough to climb into a cockpit. Once Tinker produced his contract from Mexico, however, everything changed. He was given orders to the air base at Los Alcázares, a *salvo conducto*, and a railroad pass. A *salvo conducto* was a safe conduct pass; it was practically impossible to move around wartime Spain without one. This moment of difficulties in the Air Ministry would be the only occasion on which an agent of the Republic seemed to be trying to back out of the contract executed in Mexico City, and Tinker believed that this officer was acting on his own initiative. Thereafter the Republic honored the contract to its letter. Weeks later, after he had heard of the disgusting performances of Bert Acosta and his friends, and witnessed the antics of some other foreign pilots, he understood why the Republic had become skeptical of foreign mercenaries.

On the morning of 5 January 1937, when the conductor told Tinker to get off the train, he assumed that he had reached his destination. Instead, he found himself at the tiny village of Encina, a junction where one line swings west to Madrid and the other goes south to the port of Alicante and eventually winds its way to the port of Cartagena near Los Alcázares. Hopping on board the next train that came through, Tinker was certain that he now was on his way to Los Alcázares, but a few hours later the conductor put him off at a small station called Chinchilla.

He seemed to be in the middle of nowhere. Off to the south a single-track line disappeared across an undulating plain that faded into a horizon of hazy mountains. To the east the tracks ran off across another plain toward Valencia, and the view to the west was no more exciting. Tinker felt as if he were stranded somewhere in the wilds of Texas or New Mexico. Only after he walked around the lonely station and looked off to the north could he see the distant village of Chinchilla de Monte Aragón, huddled around the base of a dramatic mesa topped by a castle as old as the Arab occupation of Spain. After the train rattled away for Madrid, the stillness of Chinchilla enveloped him.

It would be a five-hour wait for the next train passing through for Alicante, Murcia, and Cartagena. Even a geologist would have been hard put to find five hours of entertainment within a mile of Chinchilla's railroad station. Tinker was dozing when the stillness was shattered by a series of rifle shots, followed by much shouting and people running in every direction. Through the commotion came the drone of airplane engines, lots of them. Hurrying to the station platform, Tinker looked up to see six trimotor bombers moving across the cloudless blue. Certain that each carried a ton of bombs, and that the railroad station and its sidings were the most probable target, Tinker decided to move elsewhere. Finding no signs that said "*Refugio*," he took cover in a ditch by the railroad tracks. Tinker counted six detonations, all big ones, but none of the bombs fell within two hundred yards of the railroad station. One hit the strategic target of a nearby winery, a four-story building of heavy stone construction; except for one corner left standing it was practically demolished. In his diary Tinker noted: "people panic stricken; destruction terrible."

About two hours later a pair of double-headed locomotives rolled through the station pulling a string of flat cars. Every other car carried a 10.5-ton Russian T-26 tank. Interspersed between the tanks were flat cars with sandbagged antiaircraft guns, the gun crews waving and giving the Loyalist clenched-fist salute as they passed the station. Fifteen minutes later a second trainload of tanks rolled through Chinchilla for Aranjuez and Madrid. Tinker assumed that these trains were the cause of the air raid. Perhaps. But Chinchilla is the junction of the main railway line from Madrid, where it branches off eastward to the seaports of Valencia and Alicante and due south to Murcia and the port of Cartagena. With or without trainloads of tanks en route to the Madrid front, the junction itself was a worthwhile strategic target.

At 8 p.m. Tinker's train to the south wheezed into Chinchilla. His coach was an obvious war veteran; its roof and sides were pocked with shrapnel scars and bullet holes, and many of its windows were broken. At 5 a.m. on the sixth of January he was awakened by the conductor and put off the train at the village of Torre Pacheco. At this hour the only life in town was a sleepy telegrapher at the station. After explaining that he was a *piloto Americano* on his way to *vuelo* for Spain—that is *España*—and *por la República*, and that he had to reach the airfield at Los Alcázares, the telegrapher got on the telephone and within the hour a small British Ford appeared and Tinker was finally delivered to Los Alcázares.

The airline distance from Valencia to Los Alcázares, near Cartagena, is about 130 miles; Tinker's odyssey by rail took almost thirty-six hours, the average speed being 3.6 mph. After shuffling papers with the military authorities, the next day he was driven to an airfield at nearby San Xavier. Here he was surprised to meet other aviators from North America. There was Harold E. "Whitey" Dahl, Orrin Dwight "O. D." Bell, and Derek "Dick" Dickinson from the United States, and Manuel Garcia Gomez, ostensibly from Mexico, but in truth a Guatemalan.

Back on 18 November 1936 Guatemala had become the first nation to extend diplomatic recognition to Nationalist Spain; perhaps because of this Garcia Gomez found it expedient to be a Mexican.

Bell and Dickinson seemed like "old timers" to Tinker; both claimed aviation experience from World War I eighteen years before, and Tinker estimated them to be about forty years old. Garcia seemed to be even older, and he claimed experience with the Paraguayan air force during the Chaco War with Bolivia in 1932. Dahl was the same age as Tinker, but an unruly head of blonde hair that was almost white, bushy white eyebrows, and a florid face not only made him appear much older than he was, but gave those he met the impression of a clean-shaven Santa Claus. The Spaniards called him "*el Rubio*," the blond one.

Born in Sydney, Illinois, on 29 June 1909, Whitey Dahl enlisted in the Army in 1932, went through pilot training at Randolph Field, and won his wings at Kelly in 1933. Commissioned a 2nd lieutenant, he was based at Mitchell Field, Long Island, and flew with the Air Corps during the air mail emergency of 1934, operating over Eastern Air Transport's route between New York and Florida. On 6 May 1934 he flew the Air Corps' last mail service into Atlanta, Georgia, where he told the press, "Just when our organization was functioning properly we found ourselves out of work."[7] Although the service judged him a skilled pilot, trouble with gambling and a civil court conviction caused the Air Corps to revoke his commission in early 1936, and Dahl found himself discharged to civilian life during economic hard times.

Always resourceful, Whitey drifted out to the West Coast where he flew odd jobs, fell in with show business people, and did some high flying among the Hollywood crowd. It was here that he met Edith Rogers, formerly a singer with Rudy Vallee's band, and charmed her into a companionship that lasted three years. Unfortunately, Dahl financed much of his California high life with rubber checks and in late 1936 found it urgent to explore the world south of the Rio Grande, taking la belle Edith with him. In Mexico he found employment ferrying airplanes from Brownsville, Texas, to the port of Vera Cruz for "the Spanish ambassador's collection."

In Mexico's small world of aviation, Dahl's connections inevitably led to a contract to fly for the Republic. He was supposed to have been in New York to sail on the *Normandie* on the voyage before Tinker's, but when he and Edith crossed the Texas border at Laredo, police greeted them and he learned that checks could bounce across state lines; they had a fugitive warrant from Los Angeles with Dahl's name on it. Released on his own recognizance, Whitey suddenly remembered that he had unfinished business in Mexico City. The Spanish Embassy booked passage for them on board the French freighter *Mexique* out of Vera Cruz. Its accommodations were not as plush as the *Normandie*'s, but they definitely were superior to those that awaited him in Los Angeles. On 21 December 1936 the two stepped ashore at St. Nazaire, France, celebrated Noël in Paris, and the day after Christmas hurried over the last miles of the road to Port Bou.

When Tinker met Dahl in Los Alcázares in January, Edith was living in Valencia. But the disordered world of wartime Iberia was not to her liking. After Whitey flew off to do battle on the Madrid front, she retreated to France. While her "husband" was anxiously trying to fill his gunsight with Nationalist airplanes to ring up a thousand-dollar jackpot, the comely Edith, with Whitey's monthly pay, luxuriated at the Hotel Miramar in the tony environment of Cannes on the French Riviera.[8]

Tinker and Whitey Dahl found much in common in terms of Randolph Field, the Army Air Corps, and their experiences in Mexico. Their ignorance of the Spanish language served to draw them together and they soon became good friends.

Driven to San Xavier airfield, nearby Los Alcázares, Tinker got his first look at the Russian airplanes used by the Republic. There were Tupolev SB-2 twin-engine "Katiushka" bombers that he believed to be copies of the Martin B-10s he had seen in the Army Air Corps. And there were Polikarpov I-15 biplane fighters that he regarded as improved replicas of the Boeing P-12 used by the Air Corps and its Navy equivalent, the Boeing F4B he had flown at Pensacola. He was wrong on both counts, but this was not unusual; in these estimates he had plenty of company in the 1930s, when most aviation "experts" in the West regarded the Russians as backward folk and their Bolshevik engineers incapable of designing modern high-performance aircraft.

Tinker had been apprehensive about being sent into combat in some aerial crate of ancient vintage and the sight of the SB-2s and I-15s proved reassuring. When taken out to the flight line on the morning of 8 January, however, he was turned over to a Spanish pilot who led him to a mild-mannered de Havilland D.H.60G Moth training plane for a check flight. Eighteen months had passed since Tinker had had his hands on an airplane's controls, but as he said: "Flying seems to be something like swimming—once you learn how, you never forget." In twenty-five minutes of flight he treated his check pilot to an exercise of memory in three dimensions that included loops, spins, and rolls, each maneuver snappier and better-executed than the last. After they landed, the Spaniard rated Tinker a *piloto de caza* (fighter pilot), and he received orders to the Manises air base near Valencia.

At this point Major Félix Sampill Fernández, the San Xavier base commander, intervened. He doubted that a fighter pilot could be checked out in so short a time and wanted to test Tinker himself. Sampill was nobody's fool. Before the war he was a captain commanding the Esquadrilla Colonial at Cape Juby in the Spanish Sahara; it consisted of four Fokker F.7/3m bombers. He had flown to Madrid just before the army's uprising. When his squadron was ordered from Cape Juby to Tablada-Seville, one pilot defected to the Nationalists by landing at Larache, Morocco; the other two Fokkers arrived at Tablada, where their pilots were bluffed into surrendering to the Nationalist insurgents.[9] Given the hysterical environment of July 1936, when the Republic's leadership was inclined to find "traitors" everywhere, Sampill was lucky not to have been shot according to the custom of those days. After this unpleasant experience he was not inclined to take anything for granted.

Sampill took Tinker out to a Koolhoven FK.51, a new single-engine, two-place Dutch biplane of 3,500 pounds with a Wright 450-horsepower engine. In late 1936 seventy-one of these airplanes were sold to France, and in early 1937 they suddenly turned up in Spain. Sampill told Tinker that the FK.51 could take anything, which Tinker understood to mean that he was expected to give the airplane a wringing-out. During his climb to five thousand feet Tinker felt out the FK.51 and found its handling characteristics similar to the O2U Corsair landplanes he had flown at Pensacola. At five thousand feet he shoved the plane's throttle wide open and whipped it into a tight loop with a snap roll at its top, the classic Immelmann turn. The professionalism displayed in this maneuver was enough for Sampill; he waved Tinker back to the ground, where he was pleased to endorse his orders to Manises.

Whitey Dahl checked out as a fighter pilot the same day. Derek Dickenson failed check-out as a fighter pilot but managed to get rated for observation planes and later served as a flight instructor. But O. D. Bell, who had served in the British Royal Flying Corps as a teenager in World War I, had so many problems with cognac and anis that he rarely got to the flight line before noon and was then in no shape to climb into a cockpit. Tinker discovered that Bell had been staggering around San Xavier for almost a month; he was still staggering around when Tinker and Dahl got on a bus back to Los Alcázares.

Tinker and Dahl felt lucky to have dealt with the embassy in Mexico. Dahl knew of three Americans—Charlie Koch, Jim Allison, and Albert Baumler—who had checked out as fighter pilots weeks ago. But they went through the Spanish Consulate in New York, which did not give them contracts, only letters of recommendation, and they did not yet have contracts. At Los Alcázares, Tinker and Whitey were told not to use their railroad passes for a thirty-hour junket via Chinchilla; instead, they were put on board a Fokker F.7/3 transport that flew them to Valencia in one hour. After checking into the Hotel Inglés, they went to the Air Ministry to have their orders endorsed and then retired to the Vodka Café, a popular Anglo-American hangout. Here they learned that the only airplanes at Manises were old Breguet bombers and some equally old Nieuport-Delage fighters. Having seen the sleek Russian I-15 biplanes at San

Xavier, this news disappointed Tinker; but his contract specified that he would fly any aircraft assigned to him, and he was not about to return to the United States.

Whatever encouragement Tinker may have felt in his resignation to fly anything drained away the next day after a close inspection of a Breguet Br.19. In his estimation they were "huge crates," and by 1937 that was precisely the sum of a Br.19—unless one wished to add that in combat it usually became a death trap. Designed in 1921, the single-engine, two-place Br.19 biplane began rolling out of Louis Breguet's works at Villacoublay the following year by the hundreds. In those days it was a phenomenal airplane. Its design was updated periodically during the 1920s, and the firm built several thousand Br.19s. The airplane enjoyed widespread sales among the lesser air forces of Europe, both as a direct export and by way of manufacturing licenses. Beneath its lower wings a Br.19 could carry two 550-pound bombs or an assortment of smaller bombs. These were released by means of a Rube Goldberg mechanical system of wires that often gave trouble. Nevertheless, a bomb load of more than half a ton was remarkable for a single-engine airplane of this vintage. Its protective armament varied; usually there was one 7.7-mm machine gun synchronized to fire through the propeller; in the rear cockpit there were two 7.7-mm guns on a scarf ring, and sometimes a fourth gun was installed that fired through a hatch in the floor.

A Br.19's pilot served as little more than a chauffeur who flew the machine to a given point while the man in the back seat did all the work. After the "backseater" had identified the target and determined that there was nothing more to be observed and no need of standing by his guns any longer, he got down on his hands and knees on the cockpit floor to hunch over a primitive bombsight and then release the bombs at what might be the correct moment. With luck the bombs hit within five hundred yards of the target. Functioning as the aircraft commander, observer, part-time navigator, top gunner, belly gunner, and bombardier, the gentleman in a Br.19's rear cockpit was probably the most overworked man in the history of aerial warfare.

At Manises airfield on 9 January, Walter Katz, an Austrian who volunteered for the Republic to fight Fascism in the skies over Spain, checked Tinker out in the Breguet.[10] It would have been a simple fifteen-minute flight except that the Br.19 had been used recently for dropping propaganda leaflets over Nationalist territory—three packages of leaflets had been left in the plane, and after Tinker got the sluggish machine into the air the leaflets began coming loose. One by one they fluttered off the cockpit floor, where the suction created by the open cockpit whipped them upward. As they flew through the cockpit they were caught by the slipstream, which plastered them against Tinker's face. Flying with his right hand and clawing away an endless flow of leaflets with his left, he managed to climb to altitude, circle the field a few times, and plop the machine's ungainly 4,800 pounds back on the field in a respectable landing.

Katz was satisfied, and Tinker found himself a duly qualified Br.19 pilot. Then he was assigned to a new Anglo-American squadron of Br.19s; there were three British pilots—Fairhead, Loverseed, and Papps—and two Americans besides Tinker: Eugene Finick and a man named "Nolde." And there was a "wild Irishman" whose name goes unrecorded.[11] They immediately began flying formation practices. Tinker thought Fairhead quite good, Loverseed excellent, but Papps was a real horror; he disrupted one flight with a near midair collision with Loverseed. Finick told Tinker that Papps' flying was mild when compared with some of the Wild Irishman's hair-raising performances.

Tinker discovered that Eugene Finick, already a veteran of four months in Spain, had flown during the Republic's desperate days in the autumn of 1936. Born in 1912 and a native of New York City, he had no military training to prepare him for combat. When Finick was an adolescent, his father died and he had to quit school and go to work as an automobile mechanic to help support his mother and the rest of the family. Crazy about aviation, Finick began hanging around Roosevelt Field on weekends; here Jimmy Collins took an interest in him. Collins was a freelance test pilot of the early 1930s and well known for an aviation column he wrote for the *New York Daily News* and an autobiographical book he wrote in 1935. Because of his interest in left-wing politics, which ultimately led him into the ranks of the Communist Party, he also became a controversial figure of the day.[12] As time permitted, Collins gave Finick flying lessons. Finick soloed, he got a student's license, and although his hours mounted, he never applied for a regular license because he could not justify the expense without knowing that a steady flying job awaited him.

One weekend in early September 1936 Finick happened to be at Floyd Bennett Field when an argument started about the war in Spain. Finick had no politics and was still young enough not to have voted in a national election; although a practicing Catholic, he found the Nationalists' claim to be the "defenders of the Faith" distasteful. Finick came out strongly for the Loyalists, as the government forces were often called. After the argument broke up, a man who had overheard the discussion asked if he might be interested in flying for the Spanish Republic. He put Finick in contact with Samuel Schacter, a New York lawyer who handled recruitments for the Republic. Three weeks later Finick was on the road to Port Bou—but he had a detour to Toulouse.

After reporting to the Spanish Embassy in Paris, its officials directed Finick to Toulouse in the south of France to ferry French airplanes to Barcelona. In the Toulouse locale not only were located the factories of the Latécoère and Dewoitine aircraft companies, there was a large military air base at nearby Francazal;

all three figured prominently in the muddy picture of French aviation assistance to the Republic during the Spanish Civil War.

In Toulouse Finick met Joseph Rosmarin, Arthur Vasnit, and Edward Lyons—other American aviators assigned to the Toulouse-Barcelona ferrying project. Because the French frontier had been closed to the export of war material since August, this was a clandestine operation. But the Toulouse area was well seeded with Nationalist spies. Lyons and Vasnit got away in an airplane and followed the silvery ribbon of the Canal du Midi to Narbonne, from where they would follow the Mediterranean coast to Barcelona, well offshore of the territorial airspace of France. But over Narbonne their propeller disintegrated. They glided down to a successful forced landing on a beach, where they were later arrested by French gendarmes. It was believed that sabotage caused their propeller problem.

Meanwhile, the airplanes that Rosmarin and Finick intended to fly to Spain were found to be sabotaged by French Fascists in sympathy with the Nationalists. When they finally did fly to Barcelona it was as passengers on board a LAPE DC-2. Some thirty years of age and regarded as too old for combat flying, Rosmarin, a native of Brooklyn, New York, was held at Barcelona to fly transports and communications aircraft. Finick proceeded to Madrid, where he was assigned to a squadron that included two Frenchmen, one Brit, and a Czech, the rest being Spaniards. Here he was introduced to the Breguet Br.19 "suicide basket."

This was October 1936, when Nationalist columns were swarming through Illescas and Navalcarnero for Madrid, only twenty miles away. The Republic's air force ordered Finick's squadron to strike at bridges in hopes of delaying the Nationalist advance. Their fighter escort was a curious mélange of three old Nieuport NiD.52s, three truly ancient de Havilland D.H.9s, one Dewoitine D.372, one Blériot-Spad 510, the one-and-only Boeing 281 purchased as an experimental prototype in 1935, and a Hawker Fury. This hodgepodge of airplanes dramatizes the desperate straits of the Republic's air force on the eve of the Russians' introducing large numbers of homogenous equipment. Leading this operational museum of military aviation in the Hawker Fury was Captain Andrés Lacalle, who would become the Republic's foremost fighter pilot. At this date he already had six victories to his credit, including one Ju 52 bomber.[13]

The clumsy Breguets had no sooner dropped their bombs and turned back to Getafe when a dozen Fiat CR.32s fell upon them. Six came after the Breguets; the others went after the fighter escort. The Breguets, cruising at a thousand feet, dove for the ground. By flying the nap of the earth it was impossible for the Fiats to attack their vulnerable undersides, and by holding a tight formation they could combine the firepower of twelve Vickers guns in their rear cockpits. Nevertheless, within a few minutes the Fiats sent two Breguets flaming to earth.

A few thousand feet above and behind Finick the fate of the fighter escort was not much better. Andrés Lacalle and a Frenchman named Jean Darry brought down three of the Fiats, but the other Italian fighters shot down all three of the Nieuports. The final score was five to three, with the Republic losing.

When Finick's squadron landed at Getafe, their Breguets were rearmed and they made two further efforts to strike at Nationalist road traffic south of Madrid. But they never managed to even see these targets. Patrols of CR.32s always stood between, and when the Fiats were sighted, most of the Breguets' fighter escort tended to develop "engine trouble" and run for Getafe. French mercenaries flew these escort airplanes. Finick liked to believe that their frustration was owed to poor equipment: "It wasn't bad piloting; we simply didn't have the planes." But he was also on the mark when he zeroed in on the mercenaries as "a bunch of racketeers and no more."[14] That evening a half-dozen Ju 52s and S.81s surprised Getafe, suddenly appearing out of the setting sun in a glide-bombing attack. When the bombers departed, Getafe's hangars were flaming ruins and most of its aircraft destroyed.

Finick and his fellow survivors were sent to Carmoli, an airfield near Cartagena on the Mediterranean where Russian ships were unloading the new equipment from the Soviet Union. By day they flew Breguets and Vickers Vildebeests on patrols of the coast north to Alicante or south toward Almería as a precaution against units of the Nationalist navy attempting a bombardment of Cartagena. By night they listened to the engines of Junkers Ju 52s groping through the darkness overhead in an effort to bomb the Russian ships in the port, and they watched dozens of searchlight beams from the port stab at the night in quest of the raiders while antiaircraft fire punctuated the night with orange flashes. No raiders were brought down; there were inevitable casualties caused by shrapnel among people on the ground, but serious material damage was minimal.

When Tinker met him in January 1937 at Manises, Finick was awaiting orders to Alcantarilla thirty miles northwest of Cartagena, where squadrons of new Russian R-Z "ground strafers" were being assembled. The R-Z was a Polikarpov design of 1927, a large, single-engine biplane similar to a Breguet Br.19, but its 750-horsepower engine gave it a cruising speed of 125 mph. It carried a half-ton of bombs—two 550-pound or four 220-pound—although in most ground attack work it carried eight 110-pound antipersonnel bombs. It had four ShKAS 7.62-mm machine guns in its lower wings, canted down at 30 degrees for ground strafing from level flight; for defense astern, a rear gunner had two 7.62-mm guns on a scarf ring. Although Spaniards nicknamed the R-Z "Natasha," it was usually known as a *Rasante* (strafer).[15]

Unaware that even better hardware would come his way, Tinker was eager to get his hands on one of these formidable-sounding Rasantes. Meanwhile, there was a patrol to be flown in one of the Breguets down the coast to Alicante and return. At the Br.19's cruising speed of 85 mph, this took three hours. On his return, Tinker discovered that the squadron had been ordered to undertake a formal organization. In those days the Republic still indulged in a variety of democratic military fetishes, and it was believed that the squadron leader had to be elected by popular vote. This did not make much sense to the Anglo-Americans, but they did it. Fairhead was elected leader, the American Nolde his executive, Loverseed the adjutant, and Tinker the squadron's navigator. As a former naval aviator, Tinker could not imagine why anyone needed a navigator to fly up and down a very distinct coastline.

The next day, 12 January 1937, there was no Mediterranean scenic route to be flown. The squadron was to make a bombing raid on a small town near Teruel, a Nationalist strongpoint in a salient only seventy-five miles northwest of Valencia. The Breguets formed up in two vees of three planes each. Vincent Schmidt, an American who was supposed to be familiar with the target, led the first vee. Fairhead led the second vee with Tinker and Papps as his wingmen. Fairhead was not briefed on the target; he and the others were supposed to bomb wherever Schmidt bombed. Their fighter escort consisted of three old Nieuports.

Older than the others, Vincent Schmidt had allegedly flown in World War I and was an expatriate living in Paris when the Spanish war started. He had just returned from Ethiopia, having arrived there too late to fly for the African nation's practically nonexistent air force during its disastrous war with Italy. Before that he had flown in China and claimed to have been a colonel in the Chinese air force—more likely the air force of some warlord. Radiating self-assurance and an oily charm, Schmidt usually disarmed his audiences; otherwise someone might have asked him if he had it so good in China, why was he in Spain?[16]

It was a routine flight until just short of the target, and then Tinker noticed a flurry of activity in the upper edges of his goggles. It was the three Nieuports diving for the ground with six Fiats on their tails. When he looked back through his windshield, Schmidt's formation had disappeared. Fairhead was equally distracted and did not see Schmidt dive for the treetops, and with the first formation gone he had no idea where the target might be.

Fairhead dove for the ground. Tinker and Papps followed, and for fifteen minutes they dodged hilltops, trees, and church spires around Teruel. Unable to locate the target at this altitude, Fairhead finally gave it up and signaled a return to Manises. All the while Tinker and his gunner were waiting for the Fiats to swoop down and blow them out of the sky, but the enemy fighters evidently lost track of the hedge-hopping Breguets in the ground clutter.

The worst was by no means finished. At Manises Papps went in for his landing downwind and almost collided head-on with a Nieuport whose pilot was landing correctly. In the tumult Papps lost control, his airplane flipped over on a wing and cartwheeled down the field end over end, bombs and all. None of the bombs came loose, nor did any explode. Papps crawled out of the wreck with a few scratches, his gunner with a broken nose.

As a spectator to this show Tinker was inspired to make the best landing he ever had in his "galloping Breguet." He was later told that Fairhead's patrol had been given up for lost when Schmidt returned and reported Teruel full of Fiats. When the three Nieuport fighters returned they were pretty-well riddled, with one of the pilots wounded. Tinker nevertheless was disgusted because the fighter cover fled so quickly, and he had angry words for Schmidt because he fled without a signal to the other formation he was supposed to have been leading.[17]

After a dawn patrol to Alicante and return the next day, there was nothing to do and everyone at Manises found themselves in the midst of an empty afternoon. Tinker introduced the American game of coin pitching. Instead of a silver dollar, he used a five-peseta piece of approximately the same size and weight. Two holes slightly larger than the coins were dug about twenty feet apart; a coin in the hole scored multiple points, the coin tossed nearest to the hole one point. The first player to score twenty points won the coins in the game. The Spaniards were intrigued by this *juego Americano* and became carried away by it when they discovered that the winner collected the other players' coins; soon little holes appeared all around the hangars' tarmacs.

For three days there was no flying and everyone sat around the hangars playing cards and dominos and pitching coins. On 18 January Tinker was sent out on coastal patrol to the south. Spotting an Italian freighter, he flew two low passes over it. After landing back at Manises, his mechanic took him by the arm, led him around to the front of the Breguet, and pointed at a bullet hole in one propeller blade. It had not been there at takeoff.

Two days later he was called to the Air Ministry in Valencia, where he was surprised to find Allison, Koch, and Dahl. Allison and Koch were still haggling over contracts. All were being assigned to a new fighter squadron at Los Alcázares. When they arrived at the railroad station that evening they met Manuel García Gómez, who was also en route south. From Valencia, it was a twenty-four hour crawl through the night and across the next day to Los Alcázares; while the battered train rattled, rocked, stopped, and started in an envelope of noisy darkness, the Americans played poker into the wee hours. Tinker summed it up: "A considerable number of pesetas changed hands, but not much real money."[18]

The new squadron's airplanes were not yet ready and *el jefe de campo* (chief of the airfield) at San Xavier could not bear the sight of the Americans lounging around, so he packed them off into the cockpits of some surviving Nieuport NiD.52s where they could become accustomed to "fighter planes." The Nieuport was a first-rate fighter when it first appeared in 1924, and even when Spain adopted the design variant in 1930. But against a gross takeoff weight of 3,975 pounds, its 500-horsepower engine produced a power-to-weight ratio of only 1:7.95 with a top speed of 160 mph, and its wingspan of 39.4 feet yielded a relatively slow rate of roll. With its almost kite-like wing loading of 7.9 pounds per square foot, it was reputed to be a pleasant airplane to fly, but Tinker found the NiD.52 to be a machine even worse than the Breguet.[19]

The Americans were finally loaded into a bus and driven to a new training airfield, one of several created in the vicinity of Los Alcázares for the reception of the new airplanes from Russia. The Russians introduced one novelty to Spain by creating numerous alternate airfields in any area where aircraft were to be concentrated, the airplanes being serviced by machine shops installed in trucks. This not only provided mobility but also injected uncertainty into any targeting by Nationalist bombers. When Tinker stepped out of the bus, he was pleasantly surprised to find five I-15 fighters parked on the flight line.

A very businesslike-looking little airplane, the I-15 bore a vague resemblance to Boeing's P-12 and F4B. But in fact its lines were more like Matty Laird's *Solution*, the racing plane in which Jimmy Doolittle won the first Bendix Trophy flying from Los Angeles to New York in eleven hours and sixteen minutes in the National Air Races of 1931. Doolittle's Laird racer, however, could do nothing except fly very fast; Nikolai Polikarpov's I-15 also could do that—and it could inflict an awful lot of damage as well.

At the *campo*'s headquarters the Americans met their squadron commander, the Captain Lacalle whom Finick had told Tinker about a few weeks earlier. A few months older than Tinker, Andrés García Lacalle was born on 4 February 1909 in the precinct of Sestau near the seaport and industrial center of Bilbao. He learned to fly in 1929, first as a civil pilot and then transferred to military aviation. His real matronym was simply Calle, not Lacalle, but when he first went into the air force a corporal in charge of recruits at Getafe insisted on calling him Lacalle, and the name stuck.

In the summer of 1936 Lacalle had finished a tour of duty at Larache in Morocco, and when the army's insurrection occurred he was a sergeant pilot stationed at Getafe. Here he participated in the fighting that suppressed the insurrection in Madrid. Flying one of the old Nieuports, he scored his first aerial victory over the Sierra de Guadarrama against another Nieuport.[20] Subsequently piloting one of the Hawker Furys, he flew in the increasingly desperate operations of September and October 1936 that sought to halt the Nationalist march on Madrid.

On 27 October he was co-opted by the Russians and made a member of an I-15 squadron commanded by Pavel Rychagov, who in Spain went by the nom de guerre "Palancar." Lacalle was assigned to a patrol led by a Russian named "José"; his real name was Ivan Kopéts, and he would eventually command all the aviation units in the Madrid area.[21] It was Rychagov's squadron that appeared so dramatically over Madrid on 6 November 1936, initiating a turn of the tide in the Republic's aviation fortunes. While Lacalle served with Rychagov, an increasing number of Russian fighter planes arrived in Spain, and he was ordered to Los Alcázares, where many of them were assembled, to organize his own squadron. Lacalle could not speak English and had little to say to the Americans. Through a Spanish interpreter he told them that all he wanted to see was results, and with that he turned the Americans over to a pair of foreign instructors.

They found themselves in the hands of two big, red-faced Russians who were doubtlessly equally Red in their politics. Stalinist Russia did not permit any but the most loyal of its Communist subjects to spend any time among the capitalist fleshpots of western Europe. The Russian aviators, tank and artillery specialists, and other technicians who served the Motherland in Spain nevertheless constituted a "security risk" to Stalin's empire after they had returned to the Soviet Union, and hundreds of them would be swept up in Stalin's bloody purges of 1937–40.[22]

Tinker was delighted to discover that the I-15 biplane fighter "handled almost exactly like the Navy fighter F4B," which was the last American fighter he had flown. But the Russian machine was not only a superior airplane, it was also a much superior weapon. Although of approximately the same gross weight, the F4B being 13 percent heavier, the I-15's 700-horsepower engine provided 21 percent more power, with a power-to-weight ratio of 1:4.47 against the F4B's 1:6.57. And the I-15 combined this superior power ratio with a 12 percent lighter wing loading: 13.9 pounds per square foot versus the 15.8 of an F4B.

The Boeing F4B had two .30-caliber (7.62-mm) machine guns; but neatly packed around the I-15's engine were four Nadasgkievich PV-1 7.62-mm guns synchronized to fire through the propeller at 780 rounds per minute. In one three-second burst an I-15 pilot could put 156 missiles into a target. With 750 rounds of ammunition each, the upper pair of guns provided two streams of fire that converged at 400 yards; each of the lower guns had 1,250 rounds, and their fire harmonized at 600 yards. This resulted in a devastating concentration of fire at 500 yards and served to compensate for a pilot's poor gunnery.

The sequence in loading ammunition belts was usually two incendiary, two explosive, and finally one tracer bullet, with ordinary bullets often substituted for the first two. The I-15 pilot fired his guns by pressing a pair of thumb triggers set in the "spade"-type yoke of his control column. It was practice to range and acquire the target with short bursts from the lower guns, and once their tracers were seen to tear into the target, the pilot cut in the upper guns to finish off the enemy.

Another aspect of the I-15 that impressed Tinker was its pilot's seat, protected beneath and in back by nine millimeters of armor. No fighter planes in the U.S. Army Air Corps nor the U.S. Navy had anything like this in 1937; five years would pass before American fighter pilots received similar protection. Under the I-15's lower wings were shackles for two 26.5-pound and four 11-pound bombs for ground attack missions. In 1937 the I-15 was superior to any fighter plane in the United States and most of those in Europe; in Spain it was matched only by the Italian Fiat CR.32.[23]

Tinker was surprised to discover that the engines of these I-15s bore the medallion of the Curtiss-Wright Aeronautical Corporation and that they had been manufactured in Paterson, New Jersey. Back in December 1933 the Soviet government had purchased a license from Curtiss-Wright to manufacture the R-1750 Cyclone engine in the Soviet Union.[24] The Russia variant of the R-1750 became known as the M-25.[25] The contract included not only the license and tooling but also a few hundred pattern engines made in the United States. Tinker's airplane had one of these. After the Nationalists seized two I-15s that landed mistakenly at Segovia, their Curtiss-Wright engines led the Nationalists, Germans, and Italians to misidentify the I-15 as a Curtiss fighter and an American export product.[26] Until the truth of the matter was untangled, much wringing of hands went on at the U.S. State Department.

Besides the Americans, six Spaniards served in the new squadron: Francisco Alarcón Rios, Luis Bercial Rubero, José Calderón Sánchez, Ramón Casteñeda Pardo, Gerrardo Gil, and Esteban Bueno Ortiz. Most of them had learned to fly only since the beginning of the war; however, Bercial, Calderón, and Gil had been mechanical officers before the war and had extensive experience with aircraft. The high-performance I-15 nevertheless had some unpleasant surprises for all of them.

Although by no means an unforgiving airplane, the I-15 could be intolerant of a pilot's more serious mistakes. Tinker found himself astonished by some of the extraordinarily rough landings the new Spanish pilots made; he was certain that they would have wiped out the landing gear of most American fighter planes. This doubtlessly was owed to Polikarpov overdesigning the structure to protect it from the thoughtless abuse by all but the most iron-headed peasants who made their way into the V-VS (Voenno-Vozdushnye Sily), the Soviet Union's Military Aviation Forces. The structural proofing of an airplane against abuses by "workers and peasants" counted among the foremost considerations of any Russian aircraft designer.

Initially dismayed by the Spanish pilots' treatment of their new fighters, Tinker found a wealth of respect for them after he learned that most of them had only fifty hours' flight time in their logbooks. Indeed, at the beginning of the war

Lacalle himself had logged only eighty-two hours. No Army Air Corps cadet was permitted to climb into the cockpit of a fighter until he had 130 hours' flight time; with the Navy it was much the same. Even then, Tinker recalled, the carefully trained American aviators managed to reduce more than a few airplanes to salvage, so the Spanish pilots didn't do so badly after all.

In the bus back to San Xavier, Tinker and the other Americans, secure in the belief that no one else could understand English, began discussing the performances of the Spanish pilots when a voice from a seat behind them said in English, "Before you start discussing me, I'd better tell you that I'm an American too!" The voice belonged to Ben Leider, alias "José Landon," his nom de guerre in Spain. Tinker recognized the name from Finick's telling of some of his experiences.

Ben Leider was born in Czarist Russia and in that part of the Jewish Pale of Settlement that faced the frontier with Rumania. Although brought to the United States as a child, he had memories of being hidden in cellars with other members of the family when the Russian pogroms ran amok in the village's Jewish community. He took to the world of journalism in the 1920s, learned to fly, bought a Cessna J-5, and became the *New York Evening Post*'s "flying reporter." Aviation and printer's ink proved insufficient for Leider; he also had some definite beliefs about social justice, and these led him to become one of the founders of New York City's Newspaper Guild and eventually to join the American Communist Party. This path was not unusual in the early 1930s, especially for a person of an eastern European background. At that time, the United States' political system offered precious little social justice by way of alleviating the corrosive effects of the Great Depression, and the CPUSA offered many proletarian panaceas.

When the commotion in Spain became recognizable as a civil war, and the German and Italian intervention obvious, Leider did what he felt compelled to do. Convinced of the righteousness of the Republic's cause, he sold his Cessna, said good-bye to his wife of less than a year, and sailed for Europe. Earl Browder did not see him off with a grand hurrah at the Party's headquarters; Leider's departure was without fanfare. But unlike Tinker, Dahl, Koch, and Allison, Leider "had politics." He was a sergeant pilot without a mercenary's contract, and his pay was only some six hundred pesetas a month.[27]

Being thirty-six years old and without military experience or training, he was originally assigned to ferrying airplanes from France and then to small transports and to communications aircraft—what the Spaniards call *avionetas*. But he desperately wanted to be a fighter pilot and at every opportunity begged Lacalle to recommend him for transition to them. Lacalle knew Leider to be a decent aviator, but this did not mean he had the makings of even a mediocre fighter pilot. He seemed too old; he had no military experience, and there was an emotional quality to him that Lacalle's sixth sense feared might be a liability. But Lacalle relented, took him into his own squadron, and, to keep an eye on him, made Leider one of his wingmen.[28]

Near the end of January 1937 the new Esquadrilla de Lacalle flew formation practices and dogfights between individual formations. There were three "patrols" in a squadron, each patrol consisting of three or four airplanes. The patrols usually flew in a vee formation of a patrol leader and two wingmen. The new pilots flying as wingmen experienced difficulties in holding formation on their leader during violent turning maneuvers until he might give them the signal—a violent waggling of his wings—to break up and find their own enemy for individual combat. All of these airplanes operated without radios; hand signals and wing waggling served as the only communication, the same as during World War I. Indeed, no radio communications would be found among any of the fighter planes of the Spanish Civil War until the Germans introduced it in their Messerschmitts during 1937–38.

As the month drew to a close, the Russians asked the Americans if they wanted to form their own patrol or be spread out among the Spaniards. None of them could speak much Spanish except Leider and Allison, and Leider was already one of Lacalle's wingmen, so they chose to stick together. Allison, a former naval aviator, owed his linguistic abilities to being a Texan, having a Mexican wife, and having turned a dollar or two flying liquor from Mexico to Texas during Prohibition. The "Patrulla Americano" formed around Charlie Koch as leader, with Allison and Tinker as wingmen, and Dahl taking a No. 4 position to the left or right of Allison or Tinker, depending on the sun gauge.

After the squadron finished its familiarity training and while packing its bags for a move to Murcia, Charlie Koch, the oldest of the American aviators at forty-two, took violently ill. All of the Americans were having trouble with Spanish cooking because of its heavy use of olive oil. Koch's ulcerated stomach finally gave up, and he had to be hospitalized. When he recovered, Lacalle's squadron already was in the Madrid area, and Koch was reassigned to a Russian squadron in eastern Andalusia. The Patrulla Americano was reduced from four to three, and Allison became its leader.

Before they left San Xavier, however, a small, slight Spaniard named José Sellés replaced Koch. The product of a Spanish father and Japanese mother, he had been born and reared in Japan, spoke Spanish, Japanese, and English with equal fluency, and because of his Asian background received the nickname "Chang." Tinker was fascinated by Chang's English; because he learned it from a British tutor, he spoke with a pronounced English accent. Perhaps Chang's unusual background harbored an omen of his future; he was destined to have a strange and rather ill-starred career with the Esquadrilla de Lacalle.

Standing, left to right: TINKER, A MECHANIC, RIVEROLA, GIL, CASTENEDA, CAPTAIN LACALLE, VELASCO
Seated: BASTIDO, WHITEY DAHL, CHANG SELLES, AND LECHA

Escadrilla de Lacalle, February–March 1937 (This photo was taken from Tinker's memoir, *Some Still Live*)

Lacalle awaited them at the Hotel Victoria in Murcia. It was month's end. He hustled everyone up to his room and, with Chang translating for the Americans, gave the squadron a rousing "fight talk." Tinker found Lacalle terribly impressive and marveled how he could inspire everyone, even when his words came through the halting filter of an interpreter. Lacalle finally produced a case of champagne, and the rest of the evening was spent drinking to the success of the new squadron.

The next morning, on 1 February, they were driven out to the airfield at Alcantrilla, five miles west of Murcia, where the pilots were introduced to the I-15s they would fly in combat. And they met the mechanics who would maintain their airplanes. Tinker's was a huge and very nearsighted Asturian named Chamorro. His I-15, No. 56, would serve him faithfully during the next sixty days and be the instrument of his first two aerial victories. When Tinker drew his parachute he was pleased to find that it bore the label of the Irving Air Chute Company of Troy, New York; but he was unaware that in the 1930s, directly or by license, the Irving parachute was the most widely manufactured parachute in the world.

On 2 February 1937 the squadron flew more formation and aerobatic practices and all went well except for Chang making a rough landing in which he stood his airplane on its nose. In the afternoon General Ignacio Hidalgo de Cisneros, nominally the chief of the Republic's air force, inspected the squadron. He commanded the patchy squadrons of prewar relics and what survived of the new French equipment, as well as Lacalle's new squadron, but he had no control over the several Russian squadrons in Spain. The de facto commander of the Republic's air forces was a Soviet, General "Douglas," one Jacob Smushkevich, whose headquarters were in Albacete. In politics a Communist, this arrangement did not offend Hidalgo Cisneros' sense of Spanish nationalism.[29]

That evening it occurred to Tinker that a month had passed since he had arrived in Port Bou. As a matter of fact, half a world away in New Orleans, Louisiana, Tinker's petite mother, Effie, was playing a role that, as far as she was concerned, could have been scripted by E. Philips Oppenheim.[30] In mid-January she received a letter from the Spanish consul in New Orleans with instructions for her to meet him in the lobby of the city's St. Charles Hotel on the first of February 1937. Her husband drove her to nearby Stuttgart, Arkansas, where she caught a train to Memphis and changed to the Illinois Central's Panama Limited for New Orleans. At the mysterious rendezvous among the potted palms of the St. Charles' lobby, the consul gave her an envelope that contained fourteen one-hundred-dollar bills. With a hundred dollars deducted for the advance he received in New York, this was Tinker's first month's pay.

Every month for the next seven months little Effie Tinker, who saved everything that Frank ever wrote, caught the train out of Stuttgart to keep her rendezvous in New Orleans. Sometimes the envelopes that the consul gave her contained substantially more, but they rarely held less than fifteen bills.

6

FIRST BLOOD OVER THE JARAMA

Tinker had been in Spain for all of a month with only twenty hours of flying time, twelve of which he had spent stooging around in Breguet suicide baskets. The only occasion on which he saw an enemy aircraft—except while being bombed on the ground—was over Teruel, and then he wanted for a gun to shoot back. He had yet to frame an enemy in a gunsight. Unlike Whitey Dahl, he was not eager to ring the cash register; his pressures came from within—to prove to himself that he was as good a fighter pilot as he thought he was. The opportunity for proof testing now seemed at hand.

On 3 February 1937, after a morning inspection at Alcantrilla concluded and the generals had departed, Lacalle put the I-15 squadron on alert, ready for takeoff on short notice. The minutes became hours, the sun was hot, and the wind created an endless tide of dust across the field. The Americans rigged a canvas cockpit cover as a windbreak, Dahl broke out a deck of cards, and they settled down to playing hearts for five pesetas a hand. A farmer appeared with a pitcher of cool wine. The vino proved so good that they bought three bottles from him. When relieved of their watch, Dahl wanted to dash into Murcia to phone his wife, who was still in Valencia. The others were hungry, so they went with him in quest of something to eat.

They had been gone only a few minutes when a motorcycle messenger sped onto the field with word that the squadron would take off for Albacete immediately. Lacalle roared into Murcia with a bus to round up the Americans and other members of the squadron, but after they returned to the airfield it was the old story of "hurry up and wait." What no one knew (except possibly Lacalle) was that they would be flying from one inspection to another. They waited at Alcantrilla, about an hour's flying time from Albacete, for word that an assembly of generals and political leaders at the airfield in Albacete was imminent.

The Americans resumed their card game and their patronage of the farmer's wine. While uncorking their third bottle, a dull thud sounded in the sky where a red Very flare punctuated the blue.[1] This was their takeoff signal. They clambered into their cockpits, the starting trucks were backed up to their nose spinners, and engines were started.

The Esquadrilla de Lacalle consisted of twelve airplanes divided into three patrols of four each.[2] After takeoff each patrol formed into a vee of three airplanes, with the fourth usually taking position on the "down-sun" leg of the vee and slightly above it to serve as a lookout. Before 1938 it was standard practice to fly in a "vee of vees," Lacalle's vee leading with the other patrols formed up to rearward on the wings of his patrol and at a slightly higher altitude. This gave the other patrol leaders a clear view of Lacalle and his hand signals.

When Lacalle taxied his squadron up to the tarmac of Albacete's hangars on this third day of February, a huge crowd of military and political leaders was on hand to welcome them. To the Americans, their I-15s represented a great improvement over the miscellaneous junk they had been flying; but to the Spaniards, this was the first squadron of the Republic's air forces to be equipped with the new Russian fighters. The Esquadrilla de Lacalle was a powerful symbol of the Republic resurgent, a harbinger of better things to come—the crushing of the Nationalist *sublevados*.

If the Americans had been made aware of this, their performance probably would have been much better, but when they climbed out of their cockpits they hoped to find some beds to flop into. Instead, they discovered that they had to line up in front of their airplanes while generals, colonels, and sundry politicos took turns at making speeches in Spanish and Russian. None of these worthies could speak his mind in less than twenty minutes, and the pilots' heads soon swam in a sea of fiery Spanish and Muscovite political rhetoric. Unable to understand a word being said, Tinker felt reprieved; otherwise he had nothing but evil thoughts for people who kept tired, hungry, and half-drunken aviators standing in the hot sun after flying hours. An occasional hiccup or belch from the ranks of the Patrulla Americano punctuated the tangent of speechmaking, which brought dark looks from Lacalle. He did not take exception to the Americans' behavior at Alcantrilla, although annoyed and seriously worried by their antics en route to Albacete; but he was absolutely furious at their behavior during the reception and its speechmaking. Lacalle, however, was one of those persons who have a talent for making the best out of a bad situation. He appreciated the Americans' demonstrated superiority at aerobatics, and the next day he made them redeem themselves by flying an exhibition for the same delegation of VIPs. It was a great show, everyone went away slightly awed, and Lacalle was genuinely pleased.

Tinker, however, was disturbed by the reaction to their aerial display among the squadron's mechanics. Although his vocabulary was still inadequate to understand exactly what was being said, his ear had become sufficiently attuned to the language that he had a good idea of the meaning. The mechanics of the Patrulla Americano were lording it over the other mechanics: their Spanish pilots could not fly as well. Tinker feared that this would create hard feelings among the Spanish pilots; instead, he was surprised to discover that they felt that the Americans' expertise reflected to the credit of the whole squadron. In early 1937 the word "*camarada*" was an everyday form of address in Republican Spain, the Communist influence reducing it to a cliché. In the Esquadrilla de Lacalle, Tinker discovered, it was not an empty expression.

On 5 February, Lacalle took the squadron up for mock combat with a Russian squadron of I-15s that had just returned from the Madrid front. They met in head-on attacks, broke up in individual combats, and for the next fifty minutes corkscrewed around the sky in pursuit of one another. Whitey Dahl managed to grab on to the tail of his Russian and stay with him, but Tinker and Allison were theoretically "shot down." After they landed, the Russians got together with Lacalle and his pilots to brief them on their mistakes and to give them evaluations of the Nationalists' fighter planes and their tactics.

Tinker's Russian adversary did not speak English, Tinker knew hardly a word of Russian, and the two conversed in incredibly bad Spanish. But fighter pilots speak less with their tongues than with their hands; it is a universal language. An interpreter sat in on their "conversation," and he explained the fine points that otherwise might not have been clear.

The Russian told Tinker that his "fatal" mistake occurred when he attempted to escape in a dive instead of turning into a climb, and he warned him against ever trying to dive away from a Heinkel or a Fiat. Both enemy airplanes not only were better streamlined than an I-15, they were also heavier and could always overtake an I-15 in a dive. The I-15, however, had a more powerful engine than the Fiat and could climb away from it; and, although the Heinkel's engine power was practically the same as an I-15's, the Russian airplane was lighter and could outclimb a Heinkel. In level combat the I-15 had an advantage in its ability to turn inside the He 51 and CR.32, but because of the short coupling of its fuselage it was inclined to skid; here, much depended on the skill of the individual pilot. Although the Russian did not spell it out precisely, what he told Tinker was that with all other things being approximately equal, power-to-weight ratios establish the baseline from which the margins of superior performance among fighter planes are measured and, relative to the Nationalist machines, the I-15 possessed most of the advantages—if a pilot learned how to exploit them.

With either of the Fascist fighters on one's tail, the thing to do was to lead them through tight climbing turns; somewhere in these maneuvers the advantage should eventually rebound to the I-15. The Russian warned Tinker that

	I-15	He 51	CR.32
Gross Weight, lb.	3,030	4,180	4,120
Horsepower	720	750	600
Power to Weight Ratio	1:4.2	1:5.5	1:6.8
Wing Area, sq. ft.	242.0	292.6	237.8
Wing loading lb./sq. ft.	12.5	14.2	17.3

the Heinkel had to be respected, but it was not very maneuverable and carried only two 7.9-mm guns served by only five hundred rounds per gun. But the Fiat CR.32 was an enemy best kept in front of you; it was not only a nimble airplane but some of them—the newer CR.32 bis—carried not only the usual pair of 7.7-mm guns but also two 12.7-mm guns (equivalent to the American .50 caliber). One good burst from this battery of four inflicted incredible damage.[3]

When this session of hangar flying concluded, the Russians, Spaniards, and Americans piled into buses for an inspection of Albacete's nightlife. While they celebrated on this evening of 5 February, both the Nationalists and the Republic prepared to launch offensives across the Jarama Valley twenty miles south of Madrid, and each was aware of the other's preparations. The Republic vacillated. The Nationalist attack jumped off the next day, in the dawn of the sixth. There had been talk of the Esquadrilla de Lacalle being sent to Tabernas in eastern Andalusia for operations on the Málaga front where Italian forces were on the eve of overrunning the seaport of Málaga. The Jarama offensive decided otherwise.[4]

Back in mid-December the Nationalists had attempted an encirclement of Madrid from the northwest but were stopped in January by the bloody battles of the Coruña Road. Now, in February 1937, they attempted a similar operation from the southeast. Even if not wholly successful, it promised to cut the railway between Madrid and Aranjuez that would terminate all direct rail logistics from the Mediterranean seaports and the Madrid front, and the Nationalists also expected to cut the Madrid-Valencia highway. With these communications severed, all supplies to besieged Madrid would have to be routed by road through Guadalajara in the northeast—and the Nationalists already had plans to take care of Guadalajara. The Jarama River represented the greatest obstacle to this offensive. The Jarama rises out of the Sierra de Guadarrama, absorbs the Henares near Alcalá, the Manzanares a few miles west of Arganda, and continues south to flow into the Tajo at Aranjuez. Both sides of the Jarama are rimmed by heights, and the river had begun to rise toward its flood stage at this time of year, as heavy rains had saturated its hinterland. During 6–10 February the

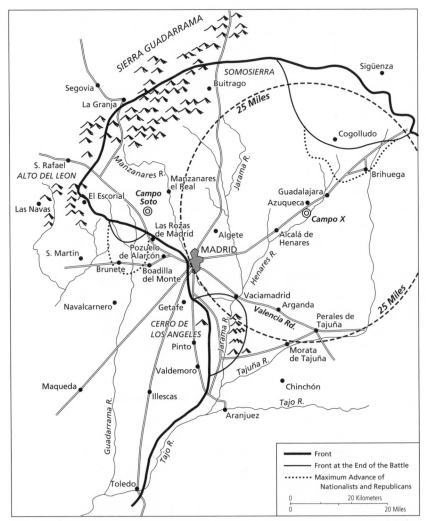

Map 6.1   Three 1937 Battles for Madrid: Jarama (February), Guadalajara (March), and Brunete (July)

Nationalists broke through the Republic's defenses to command the west bank of the river and seized a railroad bridge intact at Pindoque. The Madrid-Valencia road was only a few miles away.

The day after the Nationalist offensive jumped off, Lacalle's squadron appeared on the Madrid front. The squadron's mechanics, tools, baggage, and some spare parts were loaded on board a Douglas DC-2 of LAPE's, which the fighters escorted to their new base on the outskirts of Guadalajara. It is only 130 miles from Albacete to Guadalajara—about forty-five minutes' flying time at the cruising speed of a DC-2. After they crossed the Tajo River with Guadalajara coming into view on the horizon, Lacalle signaled the squadron to break up its vee formations and regroup into a right echelon to enter a landing circle.

Lacalle's right wingman, Ben Leider, was already in the correct position, but Casteñeda on Lacalle's left had to swing down underneath Lacalle's and Leider's airplanes and then climb to his new position off Leider's right rear quarter. As Casteñeda swung under Leider's plane they flew into turbulence and the two machines brushed in collision. Casteñeda's propeller chopped off Leider's right wheel, mangled his landing gear strut, chewed up part of his lower fuselage, and sawed on across the underside of his right wing, cutting its fabric to ribbons. The only damage to Casteñeda's airplane was slightly damaged propeller tips, but Leider's airborne I-15 was an obvious mess.

After the DC-2 landed, Lacalle led his squadron to land in Guadalajara. Meanwhile, Ben Leider had slipped out of the formation to orbit the airfield. Everyone thought that Leider would choose to use his parachute, but the easy way was not his habit. When the field was clear, Leider dove down and made a few landing approaches for practice, each time gingerly touching down with his one good wheel. Then he came in to land, making a two-point landing on his left wheel and tailskid and keeping his right wing high. When he felt himself losing speed he pushed the rudder and ailerons hard over and threw the airplane into a controlled groundloop to the left. The centrifugal forces created in this maneuver balanced the airplane on its left wheel as long as possible, so when the shattered leg of his right landing gear crunched into the earth, the airplane had little forward motion. There was a small noise and slight cloud of dust; the I-15 stood up on its nose briefly and then fell back on its tailskid. A large crowd had gathered on the field to watch Leider's travail, and all were impressed by his surgical pilot skill. Moreover, he had saved one of the precious I-15s to fly again.

Lacalle's squadron was supposed to have its own airfield, but it was soaked with rain and they had to use another one in Guadalajara temporarily. Lacalle didn't like this at all. The Guadalajara airfield was too well known, located near the Hispano-Suiza factory, and sited between the Henares River and the Madrid-Zaragoza railway—both convenient navigation aids for Nationalist bombers. Although the Hispano factory had long since been bombed out of business and its tooling removed to La Rabasa, the Nationalists did not seem to know this and periodically returned to bomb it again and again. Lacalle did not want to lose his new fighters through the happenstance of a casual air attack.

What took Tinker's eye was the sight of ten stubby but sleek Russian monoplane fighters dispersed around the field. On board the bus to headquarters he asked Lacalle about them and the Spaniard read his mind. He told Tinker that if he behaved himself for the rest of the war he might be permitted to fly one of those monoplanes—after the peace was signed. Tinker assumed these Russian I-16s to be "almost exact copies" of the U.S. Army Air Corps' Boeing P-26. He was wrong, but in 1937 he had lots of company among those supposed to be far more knowledgeable than he. Just as the "experts" liked to refer to the SB-2s as Martin bombers and to the I-15s as Curtiss fighters, so they chose to compound their ignorance by calling Polikarpov's I-16 a Boeing fighter. Many in the Western world simply refused to believe that the "primitive Bolsheviks" could design and build a high-performance airplane such as these ten that Tinker found at Guadalajara.

In Spain it was customary to billet aircrews away from the airfield. After the sun went down it made no difference to flight operations, because even when Nationalist bombers made night raids it had no means of directing fighters to an interception. And if the bombers managed to drop their bombs on the airfield—which seems to have been rather seldom—it was better to have the pilots elsewhere. Until they could get quarters near their own field, Lacalle's squadron was billeted with the Russians in Guadalajara's Palace Hotel; from there they commuted by bus to their daily air war.

The next few days were long ones. The ceiling hung at less than a thousand feet, and the rain fell in sheets, varying its beat on the roof of the pilots' field house with an occasional clatter of hailstones. The pilots and ground crew played cards and dominos or pitched coins across the rug. And while the rain fell in the valley of the Henares, it also fell in the Jarama Valley thirty-five miles away to the south, where more than 100,000 men struggled through the mud in determined efforts to kill one another.

The rain stopped on 10 February, the ceiling lifted slightly, and when the squadron arrived at the field they found armorers shackling twenty-five-pound bombs to the lower wings of their I-15s. Lacalle briefed them on the target, a chemical and explosives factory at La Marañosa on the west bank of the Jarama. A single red Very flare burst in the gray overhead and, one by one, the squadron's planes squished across the field's rain-soaked sod and roared into the air. After crossing the Jarama Lacalle led the squadron around to the far side of their target, where they rolled into almost vertical dives. The air around them was suddenly filled with white puffs. Because the sky was overcast and otherwise filled with broken clouds, not until later in the mission did Tinker appreciate that these first puffs were antiaircraft bursts.

During World War I antiaircraft fire developed its own national signatures. As a result of the chemistry of their respective bursting charges, Anglo-French antiaircraft bursts were white, whereas German ammunition exploded black. The ammunition being fired at Lacalle's airplanes this day clearly owed its origins to the old Anglo-French chemistry.

Lacalle's patrol attacked the antiaircraft batteries sited between a pair of the factory buildings; Allison led Tinker and Dahl against one building while

Bercial led his patrol against the other. Dust churned up by the airplanes' forty-four streams of machine-gun fire seemed to fill the target area; the ground beneath them swarmed with men running in every direction. After releasing their bombs, Lacalle held the squadron in its dive until they were almost on top of the buildings; they pulled out at rooftop height and sped back across the Jarama at treetop level.

Rearmed on their return to Guadalajara, the planes returned for a second strike. The pilots complained about their bomb-releasing mechanisms. The electric releases on the pilots' control columns did not activate. Evidently, when the airplanes were shipped from the Soviet Union, someone had left the batteries that energized the solenoids on a pier in Odessa. They had to use a backup manual release. Set too low on the cockpit's floor, in reaching for its handle a pilot had to stoop and this meant removing his eye from his gunsight, which doubled as the bombsight—an unsatisfactory arrangement at best.

On their second strike they found the antiaircraft fire more concentrated, but their attacks nevertheless went well. The tightly held formations tended to break up after each pass because the pilot twisted around in his cockpit trying to see the results of the bombing. Tinker had wondered why they were not challenged by enemy aircraft, but en route back to Guadalajara he understood when he saw numerous SB-2s and I-15s returning from strikes against Nationalist airfields. They were flying under a top cover of I-16s. In this battle of the Jarama the Republic seized control of the air at its outset and held it throughout the two-week struggle that followed.

That night after dinner downtown, the sound of rifle shots and sirens interrupted the squadron's coffee and cognac. The Americans looked at Lacalle, who remarked with a shrug, "*Yoonkers—los apparatos Fascistos.*" After the appearance of large numbers of Russian fighter planes, the Nationalists had restricted the lumbering Ju 52s' operations to night bombing, and they now flew in daylight only under escorts. Lacalle added that they should go to the *refugio*, but there was no hurry; they could wait until the city turned off the lights. To make certain the city blacked out, the main switches were pulled at the power plant.

An old wine cellar served as the *refugio*, one in which several new side tunnels had been dug; candles set in niches dug out of the walls provided illumination. The civilian population of the neighborhood also took refuge there, and some brought animals with them. The Spaniards produced the inevitable goatskins of wine; some played cards and dominos while the women chatted. Instead of a moment of possible life or death, it struck Tinker as an ordinary social gathering. The Americans took advantage of the opportunity to practice their Spanish with some of the señoritas they had seen around the neighborhood. It became a pleasant two hours. After the "all clear" sounded, they returned to their quarters.

Later it was discovered that all of the bombs had fallen in a field outside the city. Whatever the Junkers had been trying to hit remained a mystery.

On the next day, 11 February, Lacalle had the squadron in the air to bomb and strafe artillery positions near Aranjuez and then to strafe the Nationalist forces attacking the vitally important highway bridge west of Arganda. After they entered their dives, a thick box of flak filled the air directly in front of Lacalle's patrol. This flak burst black, the trademark of I. G. Farben and Krupp, and it suggested the presence of units from the Legion Condor's flak battalion. The next flak pattern burst in their midst with a terrific explosion. One airplane disappeared in a ball of fire and smoke. Allison's and Bercial's patrols following about four hundred yards behind were able to jink their airplanes around the Nationalist flak box and dive on their targets.

After landing back at Guadalajara, they learned that the I-15 that took the direct hit was José Calderón's, an old friend of Lacalle's from the prewar air force. He was the squadron's first loss, and the Americans seemed to take it the hardest. The Spaniards concealed their feelings behind a shrug and the remark "*Está la Guerra!*" After all, no one can live forever, but all the fine words in the world would not bring Calderón back.

While they were discussing the loss of Calderón, Chang Sellés flew in from Albacete with his newly repaired I-15. Then Lacalle appeared with orders for them to fly to their new permanent airfield. Situated midway between Guadalajara and Alcalá de Henares, it was about a mile south of the village of Azuqueca and would be known as "Campo X."[5] Campo X was formerly the *finca* (country estate) of the Marqués del Valle de la Colina of the old Spanish nobility. A simple Old World miniature of the great haciendas that the descendants of Spain's conquistadores created in Mexico and California during the eighteenth and early nineteenth centuries, it was by no means a lavish establishment. Even in 1937 it would have been considered primitive relative to the facilities of most farms in Wisconsin or Iowa, but its simplicity radiated charm. Although Tinker would experience fancier accommodations in Spain, he always regarded Campo X as the most pleasant.

The airfield, sited on a floodplain between the Madrid-Guadalajara highway and the Henares River, was about thirty feet above the river. It was somewhat more than one-half-mile square with a substantial addition off its southeast corner. The prevailing wind was from the north so there was more than enough of a north-south run for an I-15, which required no more than 820 feet to become airborne. The building in which the pilots stood their alerts—the *caseta de mando*—was a comfortable little house nearly concealed by a grove of pine trees near the field's northeast corner and not far from the *finca*'s main buildings. A small stream nearby to this field house flowed off to the Henares and served to drain the landing ground.

About two hundred yards away from the field house stood a walled-in complex of whitewashed buildings with red-tiled roofs that included the former living quarters of the *marqués*, his family, and a small staff of servants. The main house—an unpretentious two-story building of rectangular floor plan—was hardly luxurious. Its thick-walled rooms with low ceilings of exposed beams were relatively small and boxy, cool in the summer and easily heated by their fireplaces in winter. The attached buildings that made up the other two sides of the courtyard contained kitchens, servants' quarters, and stables. The *finca's* sole claim to anything ornate was a large, arched gateway attached to the carriage house. The roofline of the carriage house was decorated with small spires that reminded Tinker of the minarets on a mosque. From the gateway, a road ran through a straight corridor of silvery poplar-like trees toward the west and the main highway a half-mile away.

The *finca* was not large enough to provide living accommodations for the squadron and its logistics staff. The only local persons who lived on the premises were a few elderly militiamen who served as caretakers and occupied the servants' quarters; everyone else commuted from accommodations in Azuqueca.

Although Tinker regarded his occupation of the *marqués' finca* with equanimity, it is likely that he would have felt differently had he known some of the details of its most recent history. The anarchy that reigned in Spain during the ninety days after the army's July 1936 uprising was used by tens of thousands of individuals to settle ancient grievances against their personal enemies and the enemies of their forefathers. Folklore was transformed into a terrible engine of revenge. Between 17 July and 31 December, Republicans executed some 5,200 priests and clergy alone.[6] The violence and bloodletting was extensive, often ghastly, and reminiscent of the French Revolution; it was by no means limited to the Republic's territory.

During the last days of July, an armed mob appeared at the *finca* of the Marqués de la Valle. Acting in the name of "the people," they rudely seized the thirty-year-old *marqués* and hauled him off to prison, from which he would not emerge alive. His offense: having been born a *marqués*. Fearing for her own life and that of her ten-month-old son, the young *marquésa* fled to Madrid where relatives gave her and the infant refuge. She and her son had a precarious and invisible underground existence until the war ended, and she emerged as a widow in the spring of 1939.[7] Frank Tinker never learned of this.

In 1937 two sisters, Maria and Christina, managed the *finca*. They were Madrileñas of a white-collar family whose children had been pointed toward better stations in life. When the war started, Christina, then twenty years old, was on the eve of entering the University of Madrid; twenty-two-year-old Maria had already finished two years at the university. The war had destroyed their home in Madrid. Their father and two brothers served in the militia somewhere among the trenches around Madrid, and a third brother had been killed earlier in December's fighting.

The sisters managed the staff of cooks, laundresses, housemaids, and handymen needed for support of the squadron while it was at the airfield. Their headquarters was in a sewing room on the second floor; here, with the assistance of a new Singer sewing machine, they mended the establishment's linens, the uniforms and personal effects of the military personnel, and occasionally they repaired parachutes. They were attractive girls, cheerful, charming, and intelligent, and their sewing room became Tinker's favorite hangout when his patrol did not have alert duty. Tinker established a rapport with Maria, while Chang Sellés attached himself to Christina. Although the other pilots teased Tinker about Maria being his *novia* (sweetheart), from what he wrote about these sisters they are more easily understood as Iberian surrogates for his own sisters, Lucille and Toodles.

Like most squadron civilian personnel, the girls did not live at the *finca*. At the end of a day they retired to Azuqueca, where they lived in the home of an elderly woman. After flight operations stood down at sunset, Tinker and Sellés usually walked with the sisters over the mile to Azuqueca. Each patrol had an automobile and driver at the disposal of its pilots. They could ride, but except on days when it was raining the walk proved more satisfying.

On its first evening at Campo X, the squadron had dinner in the *marqués'* dining room. A relatively small room, the pilots and members of the mechanical staff overcrowded it. Like the rest of the house, the dining room still had its original furnishings, even to its crockery and silverware. Although the *finca* would be vandalized later in the war, during the months that the Esquadrilla de LaCalle occupied the premises it seems to have had good care.

After dinner, a violent argument broke out between Lacalle and the mechanics. With Chang translating, the Americans discovered that it occurred because Lacalle asked the mechanics to eat in another room; and out of all this noise, they learned that most of the mechanics were commissioned officers. The Americans, accustomed to the American practice in which pilots are officers and mechanics are enlisted men, did not know that in the Republic's air force rank and promotion differed. Here it depended on seniority, unusual devotion to service, or both, regardless of a man's function. Chang Sellés was a sergeant pilot while his mechanic was a *teniente*, and even Tinker was only an *alférez* while Chamorro was a *teniente*.[8] The mechanics were understandably outraged by Lacalle's inference that they were not good enough to eat with the pilots, most of whom were their juniors in rank.

A telephone call with word that enemy bombers had crossed the Sierras and appeared to be heading for Campo X interrupted the argument. Everyone clambered into a bus that waited to take them back to Azuqueca, but they only reached the main highway when the sound of many aero engines could be heard overhead. The driver hit the brakes, opened the door, and everyone dove for the ditches alongside the highway. Although a bright moonlit night, there were clouds and the raiders could not be seen.

As Tinker listened to the deep thrumming that filled the night sky, he could reflect on the fact that American-designed Hornet engines powered each of those German Ju 52 bombers. Pratt & Whitney had sold a license for the Hornet's manufacture to the Bayerische Motorwerke (BMW) some years earlier.[9] Here in Spain the Russians flew with Curtiss-Wright engines, the Germans with Pratt & Whitney. Did that make Curtiss-Wright "Communist" or Pratt & Whitney "Fascist"? It was a crazy world. And it would have seemed crazier yet if he had known that the Ju 52s flying overhead used Texaco gasoline and lubricating oils that the Texas Company supplied to the Nationalists—on credit![10]

The whistling of bombs in mid-passage interrupted Tinker's thoughts. After what seemed to be an eternity, a chain of blinding orange flashes rippled along the airfield's eastern perimeter. An instant later the ear-splitting detonations of dozens of 110-pound bombs beat upon his eardrums. It occurred to him that only six hours had passed since the squadron had arrived at Campo X. The *finca* had never before been used as an air base, and already the *apparatos Fascistos* had found them. It bespoke a well-established Nationalist espionage system.

Thinking that the attack had finished, Tinker got to his feet and started for the bus. But the Junkers turned around and came back to lay down another line of bombs. This one rippled along the field's western perimeter and only a hundred yards from where the squadron huddled in the roadside ditch. Tinker jumped back into the ditch so hurriedly that two false teeth in his lower jaw popped out and disappeared in the muddy darkness.

Without antiaircraft fire to harass them or night fighters to interrupt their proceedings, night bombing was usually a very leisurely affair, and the Junkers came back for yet a third pass, carefully planting their final line of bombs across the center of the field. Only after this did the baritone choruses of Hornets fade away toward the Sierras. And then everyone got into the bus for Azuqueca, where the squadron had its living quarters.

En route to the airfield the next morning, Tinker stopped at the ditch of the night before in quest of his dental plate, but without success. Thereafter, he had a smile like a picket fence, what the Spaniards call a *sonrisa serrado*, and it added a slight lisp to his Southern drawl. At Campo X, Lacalle showed everyone the advantage of scattering the airplanes all over the field instead of lining them up along the airfield's perimeters. The bomb lines ran up and down the perimeters with Teutonic precision, but only one plane had been destroyed, coincidentally

Andres Lacalle with his prescription goggles (*R. K. Smith Collection*)

boxed in by three bombs. Ironically, this airplane was Chang's.

By this time, Tinker had noticed that Lacalle had the peculiar habit of clapping his flying helmet and goggles on his head as soon as he arrived at the airfield, and that he never removed them until ready to leave at sundown. Lacalle was nearsighted and had special corrective lenses in his goggles that accounted for the practice. During an alarm early in the war he had got his helmet and goggles mixed up with another pilot's. In the excitement, he did not discover this until after takeoff and, once in the air, he was practically useless, even to himself. Moreover, he had trouble finding his way back to the airfield. Meanwhile, the pilot who was flying with Lacalle's goggles couldn't figure out what had happened to his eyesight; shortly after landing his eyes crossed temporarily from the strain. After this accident Lacalle took no chances; when his helmet and goggles were on his head, he knew their whereabouts with certainty.

The rain kept the squadron grounded until noon of the twelfth, when it took off to bomb and strafe railway targets south of the Jarama. After the first strike Lacalle returned the squadron to Guadalajara because he thought the field at Campo X too soft from the rain. Takeoffs were one thing, but landings could tear up its thin sod. On their second strike the pilots found a troop train near Ciempozuelos, and, in shooting it up, the squadron had a great time.

While making his strafing runs, Tinker felt a new and ominous vibration in his airplane. Suspecting that it came from his upper pair of guns, he switched them off and continued his strafing with only the lower pair. Back at Guadalajara he discovered that the upper-right gun had slipped out of synchronization; there were nine bullet nicks and holes in one propeller blade and seven in the other to prove it. A few more bursts from that gun and he would have sawed the blades in two—and from the low altitudes at which strafing is conducted, his parachute would have been useless. He heaped many unkind words on the squadron's Russian chief armorer.

That night Lacalle's pilots bunked in Guadalajara's Palace Hotel with a squadron of Russians who were flying I-16 monoplanes. The Russians were celebrating. They claimed to have shot down seven Heinkel He 51s over the Jarama on this day.

The next morning Chamorro had a new propeller on Tinker's plane, but nothing about it was right. Shortly after takeoff for an attack south of the Jarama, his plane began vibrating so badly that it shook all four of his bombs out of their shackles and Tinker had to abort the mission. He gave the mechanics a lecture on the alignment and proper balancing of propellers and their blades. Although they labored mightily, they still could not set it right. Tinker had to abort a second attack in the afternoon, and this caused him to miss the squadron's first contact with Nationalist fighters.

A double-rocket alarm sent the squadron scrambling for the Jarama. Near Arganda they intercepted a half-dozen Heinkel He 51s. Lacalle charged upon them with a head-on attack, but being outnumbered the Heinkels turned and dived away toward their side of the river. There was no point in attempting a chase, and Lacalle turned his squadron parallel to the Jarama, patrolling its boundary to determine if the Nationalist fighters might be covering for another operation. Coming out of his turn, he noticed that Ben Leider was no longer flying wing on him.

Leider had left the formation and dived after one of the Heinkels. Perhaps unknown to him, another Heinkel jumped on his tail. To protect Leider, Lacalle had to commit the squadron to a useless chase. He and his wingman Casteñeda went after the Heinkel on Leider's tail. As he closed with the He 51 he fired a stream of tracers after it and, seeing them, the Nationalist pilot broke away. Lacalle signaled Casteñeda to follow him while he continued to cover Leider's tail.

The three entered a long dive to the ground that ended just above the treetops, where the three airplanes chased one another less than a hundred feet above the hilly terrain, the hapless Heinkel leading. Leider was practically on top of the He 51 but Lacalle couldn't see any tracers; Leider wasn't firing. The Heinkel tried to break to the left. Lacalle fired a burst across its path, which made the Nationalist pilot jink back under Leider's guns, but a frozen Leider still wasn't firing. The Nationalist tried to break to the right and Lacalle fired with the same result, but he still couldn't see any tracers issuing from Leider's airplane. Flying barely twenty feet above the ground, the Heinkel went out of control and hit the earth at almost 200 mph, spreading wreckage over a hundred yards. Lacalle closed on Leider, took the lead, and signaled a return to the squadron.

After landing at Guadalajara, Lacalle took Leider to the field house and ordered everyone else out. He was furious. Leider did not have a satisfactory explanation for leaving the formation, nor could he explain why he failed to fire on an enemy who was fat in his gunsight. Lacalle told him that he had had misgivings about him from the first; now, he intended to transfer him out of the squadron, out of fighters, and send him back to flying transports. Leider broke down and started sobbing.

Lacalle found this response hard to take. He personally liked Leider, and the Republic was still short of fighter pilots. Leider was a good aviator gaining in combat experience, and he would probably learn something worthwhile from this unhappy episode. Lacalle relented and, to rebuild Leider's confidence, he told the American that he would be credited with the destruction of the Nationalist fighter. Exactly what caused the Heinkel's pilot to fly into the ground Lacalle never determined to his satisfaction. Perhaps one of his own bursts wounded him; more likely, the pilot became disoriented and accidentally flew into the ground. The squadron was told none of this.[11] When Lacalle led Leider out of the field house, he announced Leider's victory. Everyone cheered. Tinker noted in his diary: "first aerial victory for Esquadrilla de Lacalle—and so to vino."

With benefit of hindsight, Lacalle's generosity was a tragic mistake. If he had sacked Ben Leider as he first intended, it probably would have given the other Americans second thoughts about chasing off to fight their own wars—as they would try five days later. And Leider would not have died in the way he did, providing material for a legend.

The next morning, the fourteenth, the squadron flew back to Campo X, but Tinker was left at Guadalajara with his temperamental propeller. It was still vibrating when he finally flew to Campo X, and by the time he landed he was furious. Several large ponds of water still stood on the field. Tinker knew that they weren't very deep but forgot that their bottoms were soft mud, and, in his anger, he taxied right through them. He was halfway across the largest when his wheels sank into two feet of goo. With his airplane almost up to its belly in water, he began to feel very foolish, a sentiment magnified when he deplaned before onlookers and sloshed to solid ground.

Lacalle stomped out of the field house shouting, "You damned fool; why didn't you go around that *laguna?*" Tinker decided that this was a moment not to understand Spanish, but Chang appeared on scene to serve as interpreter while a large crowd gathered. Tinker explained that he was trained as a naval aviator, was accustomed to flying seaplanes, and simply forgot himself. Chang was laughing even before he started translating, and when he finished the Spanish pilots roared. This shattered the seriousness of the moment, and Lacalle stalked angrily back to the field house, leaving Tinker to figure out how to get his "seaplane" out of the pond.

A team of horses pulled the I-15 out of the mud, but the problem of its propeller vibrations remained. Tinker remembered that when the mechanics replaced the propeller they replaced only the blades and did not remove the hub. If dirt or grit lay inside the hub, the blade roots would not seat properly, and

Ben Leider giving the Republic's right-arm, clenched-fist salute (*R. K. Smith Collection*)

the whole unit would be out of balance. The mechanics were skeptical, but with all other possibilities exhausted, off came the whole propeller. Enough grit was found inside one of the hub seats to throw a steam locomotive out of balance.

In the midst of this propeller job, a bitter political argument developed among the mechanics. Tinker's Chamorro was a Communist; Juanas, who usually serviced Dahl's airplane, was a Socialist; and those who serviced Allison's and Chang's airplanes were Anarchists. Ordinarily they always helped one another, but not on this day. The two Anarchists became so infuriated during the argument that they stomped off, shouting that they would have nothing more to do with Communists and Socialists. Not to be outdone, the Socialist announced that he wouldn't help anyone anymore, either. So Tinker rolled up his sleeves to help Chamorro. They were not making much progress when Tinker had a brainstorm.

Tinker rounded up Allison, Dahl, and Chang and explained the plan. Then they walked over to Tinker's plane, where the Americans began a fierce argument in English. By the time it reached its red-faced shouting stage, all the mechanics had gathered, baffled by what was troubling the Americanos. Finally the Americans sneered at one another and stalked off separately, each cursing the other in English and Spanish. The perplexed mechanics asked Chang "*Que pasa?*" He solemnly explained that Trejo was a Democrat, El Rubio was a Republican, and "Allee-sohn" was an Independent; they had just had a political argument and hereafter would not cooperate with one another on the ground or in the air. The mechanics were shocked. This would mean the end of the formation flying of which they were so proud. It could also mean that two of the pilots would flit about the sky idly while the other was shot down by a Fascisto. An inconceivable outcome; it would mean the end of their Patrulla Americano.

The mechanics sought out each of the sulking pilots and appealed to him to make peace with the others. The Americanos agreed, but reluctantly; it was, after all, a point of honor. But it would make no difference what they did in the air, they asserted, if political squabbling among the mechanics failed to keep the airplanes in flying condition. At this point the mechanics realized that they had been hoaxed, but they grasped the moral and sheepishly went off to work on Tinker's propeller. Before sundown, the propeller was reassembled, driven down the splines of the engine's shaft, and locked up. When Tinker took No. 56 up for a test hop, she was perfect.

In mid-afternoon of 16 February, two red Very flares popped over the field, signaling enemy aircraft approaching. All hands scrambled to their planes and took off for the Jarama. In this Republican alarm system, each squadron based in the Madrid area was assigned a sector of the front, with each sector divided into quadrants. Ground observers at the front alerted headquarters in Alcalá, reporting the number of approaching airplanes, their type, direction, and approximate altitude, and headquarters alerted the various squadrons. Lacalle was always standing by the field house where the calls came in; his airplane, No. 60, was parked outside and hooked up to a starter truck.

When the alarm came over the phone the Very flares were fired, the number of the quadrant to be defended was hoisted on a signal mast, and Lacalle ran for his airplane. Meanwhile, the patrol on alert duty had already started its engines and was rolling for the downwind end of the field. After turning into the wind, they waited for a takeoff signal given by an Aldis lamp[12] or the wave of a flag. If any changes in the situation occurred while the squadron formed up over the field, they were conveyed (in absence of radio) by means of cloth panels laid out on the ground. Whenever Lacalle's squadron, or any other squadron of I-15s, was scrambled to the front, they could usually count on a squadron of I-16 monoplanes being scrambled from some other airfield to provide them with a top cover.

This day's alarm was caused by a dozen Ju 52s headed toward Morata de Tajuña, a village about halfway between Arganda and Chinchón; it commanded a road up the Tajuña Valley that crossed the Madrid-Valencia highway less than three miles away at Perales de Tajuña. Lacalle's squadron flew between two thick layers of cumulus at 4,800 and 13,000 feet; as they approached the river, he began flying a roller-coaster track, up and down, checking the tops of the upper cloud layer and then diving to see what might be under the ceiling of the lower one. Upon breaking through the lower layer, they were confronted by six Ju 52s in a double vee formation.

Within a few months a double vee of already obsolete Ju 52 bombers operating by daylight would be less an instrument of warfare than a ready-made cliché for a dreadful Hollywood aviation film, but in this instant Tinker found the sight awesome. And he remarked in his diary: "Most impressive sight of war is a perfect formation of Junkers even when under fire."[13]

The Junkers also saw Lacalle's fighters and immediately began turning back toward their territory. Lacalle signaled the squadron out of its formation of a vee of vees into a right echelon of vees, and finally into a right echelon. With the squadron now stacked up in 1-2-3 order, he led everyone into a dive off to the left and away from the fleeing bombers. Tinker was at first puzzled. But over his shoulder and below them, Lacalle had spotted yet another half-dozen Ju 52s that were going after the village of Morata. Having deterred one group from attacking, Lacalle intended to break up the other in the midst of its attack.

One by one the I-15s rolled out of their echelon and fell upon the hapless Junkers like a swarm of angry bees, hosing them with four streams of fire. As Tinker pulled out of his dive he looked back to see the leading bomber roll over drunkenly on its back before starting its plunge to earth, its cockpit a raging inferno. The other bombers had turned back toward Nationalist territory, but with the I-15's superior speed, Lacalle was able to whip around and meet them with a head-on attack.[14] As Lacalle's airplanes sliced through their ranks, a second Junkers staggered out of the formation, its center engine pouring black smoke. Its pilot struggled to nurse his cripple back to Nationalist territory but succeeded only in ditching the airplane in the Jarama River, where the unfortunate machine became a target for Republican artillery.

Unknown to Tinker, among the spectators to this aerial drama were some of his fellow passengers from the *Normandie*. By coincidence, the Abraham Lincoln Battalion had just arrived in Morata de Tajuña, on the eve of its baptism of fire. The Junkers had just treated its members to their first experience of aerial bombardment, and they were thrilled by the spectacular destruction of two bombers.[15]

After this second pass Lacalle broke off his attack. The Junkers were now across the river, and he had no intention of pursuing them into a "Heinkel trap" that might be hiding in the glare of the afternoon sun. The Jarama ran north and south; the Nationalists to the west always had the "sun gauge" in the afternoon.

At Campo X, Lacalle found his telephone ringing off the wall with congratulatory calls from all over the Republic. If the squadron had destroyed a dozen Heinkel fighters, it would not have created as much popular excitement as the destruction of the two Ju 52s. The angular Junkers trimotor had long since become the hated and feared symbol of Nationalist air power.

The squadron discovered that the reason they had such free play with the bombers was that between the cloud layers a squadron of Russian I-16s overhead had met the Ju 52s' escort of He 51 fighters. The Russians shot down one and scattered the rest. Further intelligence brought word that a day earlier, on 15 February, the Russians encountered large numbers of Fiat CR.32 fighters. Fiats were known to be operating in the south but had not been seen around Madrid for months. This was unwelcome news because the Fiat was superior to the German Heinkel.

During a patrol of the Jarama on 17 February, Lacalle and his airplanes spied a dozen Fiats loitering over the river's western shore. He crossed the river to attack but the Fiats dove away to escape. This seemed unusual, but these were Italian units and at this moment they operated under restrictions from Rome, where its politicians feared repercussions if Italian airmen fell in Republican territory. In response, the local Italian air commander was inclined to take this too literally.

A double-rocket alarm signaled action on the eighteenth, but when the squadron neared the Jarama no bombers were to be seen. Instead, Lacalle began waggling his wings violently—the danger signal. Then he signaled the squadron into a Lufbery circle, a defensive formation whose World War I origins are attributed to Raoul Lufbery, a Franco-American who flew with the Lafayette Escadrille. Each plane followed Lacalle to form up in a flat circle that rotated to the left; in this formation no enemy could attack the circle from any quarter without one or two planes in the circle being able to bring their guns to bear in defense. Lacalle had warned the squadron that this would be his tactic if they were ever greatly outnumbered, and only after twisting his neck could Tinker see why. Six thousand feet above them the sky seemed black with Heinkels, seventy-some by Tinker's excited estimate.[16]

In fact there were twenty-seven, two Italian squadrons led by Guido Nobili and one patrol (three airplanes) of Spanish Nationalists led by Joaquín Morato. Although they had Lacalle outnumbered two to one, Nobili felt bound by his orders to defend the west bank but not to engage in combat over Republican territory. Morato and his Spaniards were not bound by the rules of Rome, and these dove to attack. One of them came directly at Tinker. This was his first combat, and it took more than a few seconds for him to realize that this airplane was really shooting at him. He finally jinked away, rolling steeply into the circle and fired a burst at the Fiat as it flashed past. Then he returned to the circle.

Having dove past Lacalle's circle without results, there was nothing more Morato's Fiats could do unless Lacalle chose to come down after them, and they loitered in the river valley. From the altitude of the Lufbery circle, it seemed easy to select one of these Fiats, dive on it, and score an easy kill using the energy developed in the dive to escape on the deck before any of the others could do anything. Allison could not resist this temptation, and he rolled out of the circle in a dive.[17] A few seconds later Nobili led a patrol of Fiats out of the upper formation, and they dove on Allison's tail. Allison was intently firing at one of Morato's Fiats when Nobili's threesome caught up with him, and Tinker saw Allison's plane shudder on the impact of their fire. Allison broke off his attack, jinked away, flew off toward the north, and disappeared.

Within a minute of Allison diving out of the circle, Whitey Dahl decided that he, too, would not be denied a kill and a thousand dollars in the bank. He rolled out of the circle and fared far worse than Allison. He drew down another vee of Fiats from the upper formation. The Italians' gunnery was good, and they gave Dahl a good hosing. Tinker was amazed to see Dahl's I-15 suddenly tear apart aft of its cockpit. The whole tail assembly came off, and the rest of the airplane spun away crazily to earth.

Having been chewed out and almost cashiered by Lacalle a few days earlier, Ben Leider was disinclined to imitate Allison and Dahl. So was Frank Tinker. Although Tinker could exercise incredibly bad judgment on the ground, once he climbed into an airplane he seemed to become a different person and operated as very much the professional. In this instance it was a matter of survival. Lacalle's circle, now reduced to ten airplanes, viewed the nine Fiats cruising around in the valley below as no threat, but there were still eighteen of the enemy loitering overhead. If he broke up the circle and attempted to run, they would be diving on his tail in a flash. At just that moment a dozen I-15s flew in from the northeast and joined Lacalle's circle. This was Ivan Kopéts' squadron of Russians.

With twenty-two I-15s now in the circle, they could break out in a climbing attack against the Fiats above them. But now a squadron of I-16s sped in from a higher altitude still and broke up the high formation of Fiats. Lacalle and his I-15s now dove out of the circle to attack the Fiats in the valley. It was in this brief firefight that Ben Leider disappeared. Exactly what happened to him nobody knows. He was flying wing on Lacalle when they dived out of the circle. When Lacalle next looked around to check his tail, Leider was nowhere to be seen.

While Lacalle's squadron went after the enemy in the valley, Kopéts and his Russians maintained the Lufbery circle, waiting to intercept any Fiats that might try to dive away to escape the I-16s. According to Tinker, "From [this] time on everything went our way." Or so it seemed to him. The Republicans claimed seven enemy destroyed for the loss of five fighters; the Nationalists claimed eight for the loss of one.[18]

No matter how these pathetically small figures are examined, the Nationalists clearly came out winners because the abstract numbers are less important than how men felt about them in 1937. For the Republic this was just another air battle. But since November the Nationalists knew that they had been losing control of the air, and by the time of the Jarama they knew that they had lost it. With this air battle, a quaint fracas by the standards of August–September 1940 but a big fight for February 1937, the Nationalists began to sense that the balance was tilting back to them.[19] The Republic had superior numbers of machines but its high command tended to use them unimaginatively, and after February 1937 the Nationalists regained the aerial initiative they had lost in November.

After Lacalle's squadron landed at Campo X, he told his pilots to report to him at his automobile, which was parked out in the middle of the airfield and well out of the hearing of ground personnel. He had a case of beer in its back seat. Without saying a word he started opening bottles and passing them around. When the first round was gone, he passed around a second, his only command being "*Bebaselo!*"—drink it down!

Only then did Lacalle bring up the obvious: "*Camaradas*, we lost three pilots and airplanes today, and it was entirely unnecessary!" He reminded them of his previous words about the effectiveness of the Lufbery circle; those pilots who chose to ignore his words and his explicit orders no longer numbered among them. They had all been warned that a Fiat could outdive their I-15s. After the expensive demonstration they had just had, he hoped that they believed it. He gave a short lecture on aerial tactics, ending with remarks on the glory of dying for "The Cause," and then distributed a final round of beer. Episodes such as this made clear to Tinker why Lacalle was so effective as a leader and why, aside from his piloting skill, he had been chosen to command the Republic's first wartime fighter squadron.

Meanwhile, Tinker had to face the squadron's mechanics, who brooded over their missing pilots and airplanes. At the sound of an airplane engine they would run out to study the sodden overcast, then shuffle back dejected when an airplane failed to land. And Tinker became grimly aware that he alone remained the only American in the squadron.

Late in the afternoon of 18 February a double-rocket alarm interrupted the brooding and sent the decimated squadron streaking for the Jarama. A few miles west of Arganda they intercepted three Junkers Ju 52s. The bombers had a high escort of Fiats that were intercepted by a squadron of I-16s. The bombers spotted Lacalle's fighters and before the I-15s could close to gun range, the Ju 52s turned back toward the peak of Marañosa. This mountain rises more than three hundred feet above the river valley, and it commanded this sector of the Jarama. Lacalle was not inclined to chase them, but neither would he be denied a contact, and he initiated a 200-mph game of cat and mouse.

After the Ju 52s turned for home, Lacalle conspicuously abandoned the interception by making a broad climbing turn in the direction of Madrid. But once out of sight of the Jarama he dove for the ground, made a 180-degree turn and led the squadron back up a valley at treetop height. They sped cross country to another valley that Lacalle used to sneak back to the Jarama. When they arrived at the river, the Ju 52s were making their way across. But his interception was too soon; the bombers saw him and again retreated toward the west. Lacalle again made a show of giving up the chase, again sneaked back among the hills over a roundabout track on the deck, which brought them back to the Jarama, where they caught the bombers attempting a third penetration. And, again, the Ju 52s beat a retreat to the west. The squadron could not stay around to see if there was a fourth attempt; low fuel reserves dictated a return to Campo X where the Esquadrilla de Lacalle could lick its wounds.

7

HOT BATHS, HEMINGWAY, AND HE 111s

When sunset terminated flight operations at Campo X on 18 February 1937, the squadron's pilots returned to Azuqueca with cold anger because they had been unable to avenge the day's losses. There, Lacalle received a phone call from Alcalá de Henares that said a wounded American pilot had landed, but the caller did not know his name. In the midst of dinner the phone rang again. The Spanish pilot who answered it could not understand the voice on the other end of the wire. Assuming it to be a Russian, he called Chang, who served as the squadron's linguist. When Chang exclaimed "Whee-tee!" everyone realized that Whitey Dahl had survived. There were cheers, a banging of mugs on tables, and a series of toasts were drunk to the *buena suerte* of the Patrulla Americano.

With Dahl alive, the wounded American who had landed in Alcalá could be either Allison or Leider. Lacalle loaded his pilots into a bus and they took off to Alcalá, where they learned that the American had been transferred to the *hospital de sangre* in Madrid. The hospital was in what had been Madrid's once-luxurious Palace Hotel, just off the Prado on the fashionable Plaza de las Cortes. Americans serving in the Abraham Lincoln Battalion had a saying: although life at the front was hell, a man always had a chance of dying in the Palace. In Spanish, *sangre* means blood, and Tinker found the Palace a bloody place, indeed, remarking: "They had evidently a very busy time of it that day."[1] But the hospital knew nothing about a wounded American aviator. The squadron trekked back to Azuqueca without any further word on Allison or Leider.

The next day was an easy one. In the morning the squadron rushed to the Jarama, where they intercepted a half-dozen Ju 52s near the heights of Marañosa. At the sight of the I-15s, the bombers executed a 180-degree turn and returned to their own territory. A similar alarm followed in the afternoon. The squadron expected to find the same Ju 52s attempting another penetration, but when they reached the river the sky was empty.

Meanwhile, searchers located Ben Leider's airplane, and he was still in it, dead. The airplane was not shot up; he had wrecked it attempting to land in rough terrain. Engine trouble, presumably, caused the forced landing. Leider died by puncturing his skull on the eyepiece of his collimator gunsight.[2] His remains were buried in a cemetery near the village of Colmenar de Oreja, to be exhumed and moved eighteen months later for service as the centerpiece of a Communist Party extravaganza in New York City. With Leider accounted for, the wounded American in Alcalá had to be Jim Allison.

That evening the pilots drove to the hospital in Alcalá, where "Tex" Allison had been ever since he landed. He told them that he had set fire to one Fiat, when three others were suddenly all over him. Some of their bullets carved up his leg, but damage to his airplane was negligible. It was a painful flight to Alcalá, but at least he didn't have to struggle with the machine. He had lost a lot of blood, and the wound was infected, but he expected to be back with the squadron in a few weeks. They left Allison a bottle of cognac and some cigarettes and then returned to Azuqueca where the indestructible Whitey Dahl awaited them.

Dahl explained that simple impulse caused him to leave the Lufberry circle; those three Fiats fiddling around below seemed like such easy targets that he couldn't resist. He did not mention that one Fiat represented an extra $1,000 in his pay account at the end of a month, and that he always felt pressure to ring the cash register. He had one Fiat square in his sights and was firing on it when he felt bullets smashing into his plane. Then a gray mass—the attacking Fiats from the upper formations—flashed through a corner of his eye. He was about to break off his attack and climb back to the circle when he discovered his controls to be useless. And—was he ever surprised—when he looked around and saw his entire tail empennage had been shot away.

There was nothing left to do except determine how well his parachute worked; and this wasn't easy. At first the two doors that served to streamline his cockpit refused to open, but he burst through them. Then his foot caught on something and, as he told Tinker, "Believe me, I did some foot-shaking—that plane finally came off like a rubber boot when you kick it off!" He couldn't recall pulling his ripcord, but the chute popped at 1,500 feet. After that he was harried by a couple of Fiats' pilots who seemed to be determined not to let him reach the ground alive. They made a couple of firing passes at him before being driven off by three Russian I-16s.

Unhurt, Dahl came down among a bunch of olive trees where he was quickly surrounded by a crowd of soldiers and farmers. This was a bad moment for him. German and Italian aviators who parachuted into friendly Nationalist territory were often mistaken for Russians and were badly beaten or shot outright by angry Spaniards.[3] Sergei Tarjov, a Russian squadron commander shot down over Madrid in November, parachuted into an ostensibly friendly part of the city where he was mistaken for a German and a mob beat him to death.[4] This incident resulted in the Republic's high command forbidding anyone to shoot at parachutists or maltreat them after they landed. Even if they were of the enemy, they were valuable sources of information and useful in trading for persons held by the Nationalists.

When the Spaniards discovered the poverty of Dahl's Spanish they thought him to be a German, but they were satisfied to take away his automatic pistol and march him off to a nearby command post. En route they met a soldier who spoke English. Dahl showed him papers he had from the Air Ministry, after which there was a round of voluble apologies and his captors became his hosts. They even hustled up a donkey so El Americano could ride to a headquarters, which was across the river from Nationalist-held San Martin de la Vega. But after a few minutes atop this hard-spined beast, Dahl wondered if this honor was such a nice idea after all.

Since 8 February the Nationalists had driven a large salient into the east bank of the Jarama, seizing the heights of Pajares-Pingarrón that overlooked the Madrid-Valencia highway. Before being driven back they had succeeded in cutting the vital artery near Vaciamadrid, but thereafter kept the highway under artillery fire. On the twentieth the Republic unleashed its counteroffensive, and Lacalle's squadron had orders to bomb and strafe artillery positions on the east bank. With Allison out of action, Lacalle asked Tinker to lead the Patrulla Americano, but he declined the responsibility. Whitey Dahl, meanwhile, had managed to convince Lacalle that he was now a true Member of the Faith, so Lacalle made him the patrol leader.

Their attacks went well. Arrangements were made with Republican ground forces—for the most part irregulars unaccustomed to working with aircraft—to lay out white canvas triangles on the ground behind their positions for identification. Too many times the Republic's aviation had bombed and strafed its own entrenchments because the inexperienced ground forces had failed to identify their positions. In these operations Lacalle's squadron silenced at least two artillery positions and strafed Nationalist trenches again and again. Meanwhile, patrols of Russian I-16s flew lazy zigzag tracks overhead in anticipation of Heinkels or Fiats attempting to interrupt the proceedings, but Nationalist fighters failed to show.

While the airplanes at Campo X were being rearmed for a second strike, a double-rocket alarm burst over the field. As quickly as their bombs could be removed, the squadron was off to the Jarama, where they caught three Ju 52s well inside Republican airspace. Overhead, a swarm of Russian I-16s met some dozen Fiats escorting the bombers. Lacalle signaled his planes into an echelon and they began rolling off to hit the bombers, now hurriedly turning for home. This was a bad moment for the I-15 fighters because the bombers were now banked in steep turns and able to bring their top and belly guns to bear on the narrow stream of attackers. According to Tinker, they flew into a "veritable hail of bullets."[5] Tinker followed Dahl into the attack so closely that for a few seconds he was actually flying a tight wing position, leaving Chang to straggle behind. They fired until within a hundred yards of one of the Junkers, and then half rolled into a dive beneath. Tinker saw one of the bombers stagger out of the formation.

As Tinker climbed for altitude to make a second attack, an I-15 of the third patrol went whirling off toward the ground. There was no smoke. It did not appear to be damaged but it was completely out of control. The fighter hit the earth and disappeared in a flash of fire and a ball of smoke.

By the time Lacalle's fighters had reformed for a second attack, two of the Junkers had fled across the river; the third was losing altitude and limped across the Jarama, where it was seen to make a crash landing on the western shore.[6] With the bombers gone, Lacalle led everyone to higher altitudes, where I-16s still-grappled with the Junkers' fighter escort. This put the Fiats in a vise because, although they could outmaneuver the faster I-16s, they could not escape them in a dive, and although they could outdive the I-15s now climbing toward them, they were at a distinct disadvantage with the nimble Russian biplane at close quarters. Seeing this threat, the Fiats started working their way westward, finally diving away into their own airspace.

Tinker was flying a close-in wing position on Dahl throughout their climb, and by the time the Fiats had run back across the Jarama they were flying in a corner of the sky all by themselves. Then a third I-15 flew in and took position off Dahl's left wing. It was Chang Sellés. Always pleasant, always useful on the ground, in the air Chang seemed always subject to constant hard luck. From his nose-over at Albacete to this moment, separated during the violent combat maneuvers, he appeared to have experienced more of the same. But his arrival in this instant assured Tinker and Dahl that the I-15 that spun in was not Chang's.

At Campo X they discovered that the squadron's casualty was Luis Bercial, leader of the third patrol and Lacalle's executive officer. This was a hard blow. Bercial was a good pilot and popular among members of the whole squadron, including ground personnel. Within nine days Calderón, Leider, and Bercial were dead and Allison so badly wounded that he wouldn't be back for a month. Of the squadron's original eleven pilots, eight remained. (Indeed, if casualties continued at this rate—this was not a subject that Tinker would pursue too far. But it was on his mind; that night he scribbled in his diary, "Bercial shot down— leaving seven of original eleven." He wasn't counting Lacalle. Tinker assumed that Lacalle was immortal.)

Squadron members were relaxing into their after dinner coffee and cognac in the Casa de Pilotos in Azuqueca, when the phone rang with a warning of *apparatos Fascistos* having just crossed the lines. The women of the household—cooks, laundresses, cleaning women—were warned, the word passed to the townspeople, and everyone headed off to one of Azuqueca's three *refugios*, all of them substantially enlarged wine cellars.

The pilots regarded an evening in the *refugio* as less of a nuisance than an opportunity for a pleasant social hour, and everyone did his best to turn it into a party. As in Guadalajara, an air raid was about the only occasion they had to get acquainted with the local girls. In spite of a coterie of leftist "intellectuals" in Valencia who promulgated all kinds of wild theories about "free love," which were supposed to "revolutionize" society, boy-girl relationships in the Republic continued to be locked in the old Iberian formalities. Air raid shelters provided happy exceptions. Chang brought along his ukulele, Tinker his accordion, and the others brought plenty of wine. No bombs fell within a mile of Azuqueca, and in the bomb shelter a good time was had by all.

The next morning, 21 February, the squadron again rushed into the air for an interception west of Arganda, but when they arrived at the Jarama the skies were empty. The rest of the day passed slowly until just before sundown when Lacalle rushed in with an order for takeoff. Ivan Kopéts' squadron of I-15s had orders to bomb an isolated Nationalist salient on the east side of the river near Vaciamadrid, and they were to provide top cover during the bombing. This was unusual because fighter operations rarely took place at dusk, and on this occasion Kopéts' squadron did not finish bombing until after darkness had fallen. Then, with assistance of starshells fired from the ground, Lacalle took his squadron down to expend its ammunition on the Nationalist positions. Its pilots returned for landings at Campo X by the light of flares, a new experience for them.

This surprise operation paid off because the Republic's ground forces succeeded in clearing this Nationalist pocket that had threatened the Madrid-Valencia road. Along other parts of the line, the Republic's offensive ground on to the end of the month with terrible casualties and small results. Nationalist air forces were relatively quiescent; after 21 February Lacalle's squadron was not called to operate again until 6 March. By that time the Jarama front had settled down into its positions for the next twenty-five months.

The three-week battle of the Jarama had gained the Nationalists less than 58 square miles of relatively useless territory. They had cut the railroad between Madrid and Aranjuez, transforming the latter into Madrid's rail terminal; but they had failed to cut the Madrid-Valencia highway. The Republic saved Madrid's communications to the Levante[7] but failed to expel the enemy from its salient on the east bank of the Jarama. The Republic's air superiority was useful, but if the airplane had not yet been invented by the spring of 1937, the results probably would have been the same. The Jarama campaign cost the Nationalists some seven thousand casualties; the Republic paid with about ten thousand. The Abraham Lincoln Battalion, beset with mutinies and desertions, performed poorly and took heavy losses. Afterward, with both sides well dug in and provided with defenses in depth, static "caretaker" warfare prevailed in the valley of the Jarama until the Republic's collapse in the spring of 1939.

Bad weather put a brake on air operations in the Madrid area during the last week of February. One evening some Russians from a new squadron at Alcalá paid a visit to Campo X and stayed for dinner. These Russians had been operating in eastern Andalusia. One of them remarked that they had a blond American named Alberto in their squadron. Tinker guessed that he must be Albert Baumler, about whom he had heard. It would be weeks, however, before Tinker and Baumler managed to get together.

On 25 February, Tinker, Whitey, and Chang wangled a pass out of Lacalle for a visit to Madrid. On the way they stopped off to see Allison. He was getting along, but the infected leg wound refused to heal and the doctors were sending him to Valencia. In 1937 not even sulfa drugs, much less antibiotics, were available; the military medicine of the Spanish Civil War had more in common with that of the American Civil War seventy years earlier than with World War II, only a few years away. Five years later a few syringes of penicillin would stabilize an infected wound within forty-eight hours, but in 1937 the same wound could remain septic for weeks, accompanied by the ever-present threat of gangrene, amputation, and death. Meanwhile, the draining wound smelled bad, and a hospital ward full of such wounds smelled awful. The evil smell was an inspiration to cut hospital visits short, and the airmen did not tarry long with Allison.

The trio finally arrived in the besieged capital after dark and crept through the blacked-out streets from one set of sandbagged street barricades to the next. Armed *milicianos* (militia) manned each barricade, and each was a checkpoint at which papers had to be produced. Only after the documents were duly scrutinized were the pilots permitted to snake their car through a narrow zigzag passage—and speed on to the next barricade.

Once they had penetrated to the heart of the city everything seemed normal. Street cars were running, theaters were operating, and the bars and nightclubs were jammed with *milicianos* from the front (which was only a few blocks away in University City), or with soldiers from the International Brigades on leave from the Jarama. Huge posters that exclaimed *"Viva los Rusos!"* and *"Viva Mejico!"* and *"Viva la Republica!"* plastered the walls of most buildings. The slogan *"No Pasarán!"* (They shall not pass!)—the battle cry of Madrid's defenders—seemed to be painted everywhere.

When they finally arrived in the Plaza de Callao and checked into the ten-story Hotel Florida, following a few hours of inspecting Madrid's nightclubs, no one was feeling any pain. Tinker and Chang attended to formalities at the desk while Whitey headed for the elevator. The elevator was one of those venerable wrought-iron cages that stuttered up and down between floors within the security of a shaft of lace-like wrought iron around its four sides. In such a machine a person did not "go up," they "ascended!" And, indeed, in Spain an elevator is called an *ascensora.*

The Florida's elevator was a self-service unit equipped with the best Edwardian controls. But once Whitey got inside its cage and the door slid shut behind him, he discovered that with five bottles of champagne in his arms he could neither reach the start button nor open the door again. While Whitey fumbled around inside the cage, a large, barrel-chested man with a moustache entered the hotel and went directly to the elevator. The man wanted to go up, but seeing Whitey inside the cage he waited, expecting Whitey to go up or get out. By this time Whitey had decided to wait for Tinker and Chang, so he did neither. The big man became impatient, slid open the door, and asked Whitey in Spanish what the hell he thought he was doing. Dahl could not understand the man's Spanish, but there was no mistaking his tone of voice. In English he asked the stranger why he hadn't opened the door before, instead of standing there like a damned fool.

The big stranger laughed and replied in clear American English that people shouldn't get into strange elevators when they didn't know how to operate them. Whitey, stunned by being answered in English, though only for a moment, told the man that he was an aviator; he could fly an airplane—any airplane—and he could fly this goddamned elevator, once he'd been checked out. The big American had a sense of humor. He stepped into the cage and checked out Whitey on the controls of this quaint apparatus. Full of confidence, Whitey asked the man if he wanted a few snap rolls on the way with a chandelle at the top, or if he simply wanted to go straight up. The American only wanted to go up, so Whitey took the controls and their cage clattered upward and out of sight of those in the lobby.

Tinker watched all this in amusement. After the cage had started its deliberate climb toward the first floor, he asked the hotel clerk about the American. The deskman, amazed at Tinker's ignorance, replied, "Why, he is the great American *autor,* Señor Ernesto Hemingway." Hemingway had arrived in Madrid only the week before and was in Spain to cover the war for the North American Newspaper Alliance.[8] It paid well: five dollars a word for everything he wrote. This was a good rate even a half-century later, but in 1937 it transcended the fantastic. But, what is more, for him it was a pleasant assignment. Hemingway had a sentimental attachment to Spain that dated from the 1920s, and a romantic, he-man macho attachment to war in general ever since his experiences in Italy during World War I. The former attachment had inspired his *Death in the Afternoon* (1932), the latter his *Farewell to Arms* (1929), while both were featured in *The Sun Also Rises* (1926). The Spanish Civil War prompted him to write an undistinguished play, *The Fifth Column*, a series of short stories, the novel *For Whom the Bell Tolls* (1940) that became a contemporary motion picture (1943), and a rarely remembered propaganda film on which he worked called *The Spanish Earth* (1937).

Warned of the matériel shortages in Madrid, Hemingway brought with him a complete expeditionary kit from the outfitters Abercrombie & Fitch, plus several hundred pounds of coffee, dozens of cases of the best liquor, a formidable supply of other groceries, and his own supply of gasoline. These precautions served him well. His first-floor rooms in the Florida became the off-duty headquarters for hundreds of men from the International Brigades' battalions, American and otherwise. Many colorful and sinister personalities of the Republic's armed forces regularly enjoyed Hemingway's hospitality. They drank his whiskey, ate his canned hams, and relaxed to his collection of American phonograph records played on a wind-up gramophone. Inside the door to his rooms was a hand-printed sign that read: "Straight Through To The Bathroom"; his visitors also used his bathtub and the Florida's marvelous hot water. They talked with him, to one another, and he listened; his suite was their clubroom. He reigned as "Papa Hemingway," and the intellectual copulation produced the grist for many a five-dollar word.

Among the aviators who frequented the Florida were Antoine de Saint-Exupéry, who came to Spain as a journalist, André Malraux, Ramón LaValle, and Abel Guide. Hemingway liked Saint-Exupéry because he wrote about what he knew best: flying. But Malraux he regarded as a phony, possessed of a marvelous publicity apparatus. Malraux knew how to fly an airplane in a vague sort of way but usually required a "copilot" to serve as chauffeur; he was not a real aviator. To be sure, he served as front man in organizing the "International Squadron" of mercenaries recruited in France, which operated for a short time in Spain, but when matters became grim for the Republic in the autumn of 1936, he skipped off to do other things. In February 1937 he was back in France writing a book called *Man's Hope*. A jaded claque of effete leftist intellectuals acclaimed it as a masterpiece; Hemingway called it a "masterpiss."[9]

Hemingway enjoyed the company of the American contract aviators, especially Whitey Dahl and Frank Tinker.[10] Their conversation did not degenerate into a jungle of abstractions about this or that "ism," empty words about fighting for "The People," or any of the claptrap then à la mode among politicoes and self-proclaimed intellectuals. They were in Spain for excitement, to prove something to themselves, for the contract money, and maybe all three, and Hemingway respected them for this. He became perhaps closer to Frank Tinker because Frank was from DeWitt, not too far from Piggott, Arkansas, which was his first wife's hometown. It turned out that he and Tinker had fished many of the same creeks and streams, hunted the same territory, and knew most of the same hangouts and local characters. He subsequently worked Tinker into *Night Before Battle*, one of his short stories of the Spanish Civil War. But the "Tinker" in this story is like "Lefty" in Clifford Odets' play *Waiting For Lefty*; he is frequently mentioned, his presence is anticipated, but he never appears. Whitey Dahl, however, appears as a conspicuous character, thinly disguised as "Baldy," who tells about shooting down a Junkers Ju 52, getting his own tail shot off, and there is an oblique reference to his ability to "fly" an elevator.[11]

The Hotel Florida was on the Plaza de Callao, where the Gran Vía almost finishes its long climb up from the Plaza de España and makes a slight dogleg in its charming passage to the Plaza de la Cibeles. By this February of 1937, however, the Gran Vía was a battered alley filled with broken masonry, its pavement glittering with millions of tiny bits of glass blown out of the windows of buildings along the street. The beautiful fountain of the Cibeles was safely hidden beneath tons of sandbags covered by masonry, while the Plaza de España had long since been dug up for artillery positions. Beyond the Plaza was the shell of North Station, the Paseo de Rosales, and the Parque del Oeste (West Park), which was in the front lines.

Life in the Florida had become quite precarious ever since October 1936 when the Nationalists seized the heights west of the Manzanares River and brought the city under artillery bombardment. From Mount Garabitas in the Casa de Campo the Nationalists practically looked down the throat of Madrid. The news media seized upon the novelty of the few aerial bombings of October and November to sensationalize their effects well beyond reality, but the damage they inflicted was nothing when compared with that done by the daily labors of old-fashioned artillery.

The daily hazard was not only from artillery fire; random small-arms fire could be equally dangerous. Martha Gellhorn, a correspondent for *Collier's* magazine who had developed a cozy relationship with Hemingway (and would become his third wife), returned to her room in the Florida one evening to find a bullet hole in her bathroom mirror. Only a few hours earlier she had been studiously applying lip rouge in front of that hole. Foreign newsmen nevertheless found the Florida attractive because it was directly across the Gran Vía from the Press Association Building and only a few blocks away from the Republic's censorship office on the fourth floor of the Telefónica. A number of prostitutes had rooms at the Florida, "whores de combat," as Hemingway called them, but this hotel's attraction for Americans turned on its excellent plumbing and a water heater of seemingly infinite capacity. As one of the characters in Hemingway's play *The Fifth Column* assessed the Florida: "The only reason we live in this damn death

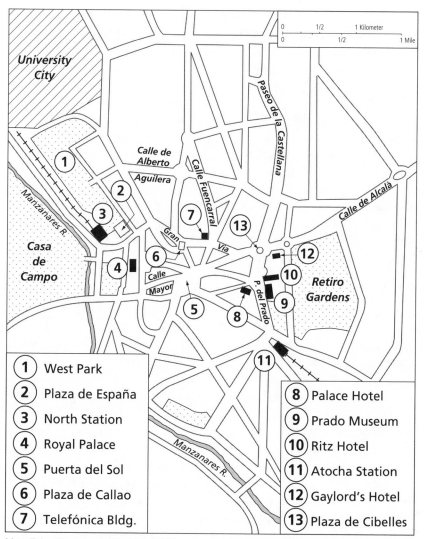

Map 7.1   Downtown Madrid, 1937

The legend entries on the map:

1. West Park
2. Plaza de España
3. North Station
4. Royal Palace
5. Puerta del Sol
6. Plaza de Callao
7. Telefónica Bldg.
8. Palace Hotel
9. Prado Museum
10. Ritz Hotel
11. Atocha Station
12. Gaylord's Hotel
13. Plaza de Cibelles

trap is for the hot water."[12] Indeed, it was the prospect of steaming out their pores that brought Tinker, Whitey, and Chang to the Florida this particular evening.

The Florida's hazards met Tinker directly when he joined Dahl on the seventh floor. Outside Whitey's door a huge hole bridged by some heavy planks looked down into the hallways of the sixth and fifth floors. The maid in charge of the floor explained that it was "only" a shell hole and casually pointed to where the projectile had entered at the end of the corridor. Tinker recognized her narrative as the familiar Spanish story of *está la guerra*. He only hoped that *la guerra* would not manifest itself in the same place during the next few hours.

Once in his room, Tinker set the hot water running. Whitey and Chang were indulging similar rituals in rooms down the hall. A nicety of life that Spanish airfields and small-town hotel facilities, such as those in Azuqueca, wanted for was hot water from a tap. In the hinterlands, washing was done in a big china bowl filled with cold water from a pitcher. When a pilot could hustle a kettle of hot water from the kitchen, it was something of a luxury. Neither Tinker nor Whitey had luxuriated in a hot bath since they left Valencia a month ago, and tonight they were really living it up.

After an hour of testing the capacity of the Florida's water heater, the three pilots met in the hotel's tea room. A waiter was paid to bring ice and glasses, and they eased into their chairs for some serious champagne drinking. When they finally found their way back to their car and hurtled through the night over the highway to Azuqueca, it was with the feeling that it wasn't such a bad war after all.

The Florida's hot baths proved addictive, and a few days later Tinker, Whitey, and Chang again sped into Madrid. Lacalle warned them to be back by 11 p.m. The next day's flying weather looked bad, but the enemy west and north of the Sierras would know what the weather was while Madrid was still trying to work out a forecast. In the event of an alarm, Lacalle didn't want any groggy pilots groping around the field.

On this evening, however, the Patrulla Americano chanced upon a big party in Hemingway's rooms. It included Herbert Matthews, the romantic leftist who propagandized readers of the *New York Times*, Henry Gorrell of the United Press, James Minifie of the *New York Herald-Tribune*, and Sefton Delmar of the British *Daily Mail*. Unknown to his contemporaries of this date, Delmar doubled as an agent for British Intelligence.[13] There was Martha Gellhorn,[14] of course, and some men from the Abraham Lincoln Battalion and others from similar units of the International Brigades. Hemingway supplied an abundance of Scotch, and everyone made the most of it. Hours slipped by before the aviators made their ways to the rooms that spewed forth the marvelous hot water, and by that time a hot soak did them no harm whatever.[15]

When the pilots finally rendezvoused in the Florida's tea room, Tinker discovered that Whitey had not trusted him to bring the champagne, so each showed up with two bottles. This created a problem of volume versus time. By 1:30 a.m. only three bottles had been drained. They nevertheless decided it was time to head back. The fourth bottle they consumed while speeding along the blacked-out, narrow, two-lane highway to Azuqueca.

Entering the Casa de Pilotos they were careful not to turn on any lights, but while tiptoeing through the parlor and dining room they found themselves

Martha Gellhorn and Ernest Hemingway (*Archive Photos/Getty Images*)

bumping into furniture in all kinds of strange places. A great clatter was made, but it awakened no one.

The next day was a dark one on more counts than just meteorology. Lacalle wanted to know what time they returned. Tinker said it might have been as late as midnight, but he wasn't sure. Whitey had not been looking at his watch either, but he thought it might have been as late as one o'clock. Chang said his watch had stopped earlier in the evening, so he had no idea. Lacalle expressed his confidence in their ability to tell time by restricting them to Azuqueca for a week.

It was during these forays into Madrid that Tinker finally met Albert Baumler, of whom he had heard so much since January. Baumler was with a Russian squadron led by a Senior Lieutenant Kosenkov based near the village of Algete northwest of Madrid. He had been flying with the Russians since January and had seen some bitter fights.

Albert J. "Ajax" Baumler was born on 17 April 1914 in Bayonne, New Jersey, "in the shade of the Statue of Liberty," as he liked to put it. As an adolescent he logged a few hundred hours on his bicycle pedaling out to Miller Field on nearby Staten Island, or hitchhiking to Floyd T. Bennett Field in Brooklyn and the more distant Curtiss and Roosevelt Fields in the hinterland of Long Island to witness the takeoffs or landings of the great transcontinental or transatlantic flights. Lindbergh, Wiley Post, Kingsford-Smith, Tinker Hawks, Roscoe Turner; he had seen most of them. It would have been remarkable if Baumler had sought a livelihood in anything else except aviation.

In July 1933 Baumler joined the Army and was assigned to the Signal Corps at Fort Monmouth, New Jersey. Two years later he passed the Air Corps examinations and was sent to Randolph Field as an air cadet; by February 1936 he was in advanced training at Kelly Field. Baumler was finishing familiarization with multi-engine bombers when he had an accident with a Keystone LB-5A. This big, clumsy twin-engine biplane bomber should have been in a museum by 1936. It was widely said that the LB-5A took off at 65 mph, cruised at 65 mph, and landed at 65 mph; its greatest hazard to a pilot was his falling out of its cockpit while parked on the ground.

Baumler took off with one fuel tank empty, but there was enough gasoline standing in the fuel lines to get the big crate into the air and over the hangars—and that's when one carburetor went dry and that engine quit. The old Keystone would not fly on one engine, but Baumler managed to set her down in a nearby farm field without even scratching her paintwork. A "washout board" convened, negligence was determined, it "outweighed" the pilot's skill in safely landing, and Baumler received his walking papers. Only a few weeks away from winning his prized silver wings and a 2nd lieutenant's commission in the Air Corps Reserve, it was a bitter experience.

Returning to New Jersey, Baumler obtained a civil pilot's license and did some commercial flying out of the Somerset Hills Airport at Basking Ridge, but he found it a precarious living. Although he obtained a transport license in October, in the environment of the Great Depression unless a pilot had at least five hundred hours in his logbook, a transport license was simply a ticket to starvation. Then he heard about the opportunities in Spain, presented himself for recruitment, and in early December 1936 sailed for Europe on board the *Queen Mary*, accompanied by Jim Allison and Charlie Koch.[16] They all traveled under the care of a pleasant little Spanish aviator named Sanz Sáinz.

Augustín Sanz Sáinz is a curious and somewhat tragic victim of the Spanish Civil War. In December 1930, when King Alfonso XIII nominally ruled Spain, Republican military officers, many of whom were of the air force, staged an abortive uprising. One of them, Ramon Franco, coincidentally the brother of Francisco Franco, was a national hero as a result of his transatlantic flight of 1926; he flew over Madrid in a Breguet Br.19, tossing out leaflets that urged the public to rise against the monarchy and establish a republic. Sanz Sáinz, a fighter pilot, refused orders to take off and shoot down Franco's plane.[17] Other pilots, too, refused. After the uprising failed, the government imprisoned Sanz Sáinz. Released by an amnesty in 1934, he immigrated to Venezuela, where he worked as a flight instructor. Later he moved to Puerto Rico and in the summer of 1936 was in the United States, where he volunteered his services to the Republic through the embassy in Washington. On board the *Queen Mary*, later in Paris, and on the train to Port Bou and Valencia, Baumler and the other Americans traveling under Sanz Sáinz's care found him to be engaging and most agreeable. And he proved to be quite the ladies' man. No matter where they went, or how short the time, the little Spaniard always seemed to turn up with a charming woman on his arm.

In Spain Baumler was sent to San Xavier, where Félix Sampil checked him out in a Caudron trainer. Later checks were flown in a variety of Miles Hawks, Koolhovens, and Fleet trainers. On the first day of 1937, while Frank Tinker was leaving Paris, Baumler was rated a *piloto de caza* and assigned to an Esquadrilla de Extranjera (literally, squadron of foreigners), flying Nieuports out of the Las Rabasas base near Alicante. Flying the more-than-venerable NiD.52s, Baumler had the good fortune not to encounter any Fiats. At the end of the month he was sent to Carmoli, an air base near Los Alcázares on the Mediterranean. This air base had grown in importance since the arrival of the Russians, especially since the I-15s off-loaded at Cartagena were assembled at Los Alcázares and then moved to Carmoli. At Carmoli, Tinker first saw the I-15, and met Charlie Koch again. Koch had just recovered from the stomach problems that caused his separation from Lacalle's squadron.

After a week of familiarization with the I-15, Baumler and Koch were sent to Albacete, where they joined a mixed squadron led by the Russian Ivan Kosenkov. Its personnel included nine Spaniards, including Alfonso Jiménez Bruguet, Alfonso Cabo, and Guasa Marin, all of whom would become notable later; Russians by the names of Ukov, Pietchka, Zucarov, Beliakov, Lakeev, and Lasnikov; and the two Americans. Neither Baumler nor Alessandrov Zucarov could speak a word of the other's language, but as a result of their experiences in the air, and working through their Anglo-Russian pidgin Spanish, they soon became the best of friends. On 10 February their squadron flew to the Málaga front, where they operated from an airfield near Tabernas.

Baumler and Koch's first combat occurred while escorting two twin-engine Potez 54 bombers against targets in Málaga. The Potez, a big, slab-sided, high-winged French crate with a crew of five, carried one ton of bombs; its two 690-horsepower Hispano engines sent it racing through the air at 120 mph. Although a better bomber than the German Junkers, much depended on how an air force chose to use these machines, and the Republic had a tendency to throw them away in penny packets. Homogeneity of aircrew also made a difference. German and Spanish crews, all of whom knew one another, flew the Junkers; the Potezes were flown by French mercenaries from diverse backgrounds, who seldom knew one another until they met on the airfield.

The first attack on Málaga proved to be a milk run, the second a disaster. A horde of Fiats dove through the screen of I-15s to engage the Potezes, and before the Republican fighter pilots could swing their heads around, both bombers were badly shot up and smoking. The Potezes staggered back to Republican territory, where one crashed on a beach and the other flopped into a farm field. In this fight Baumler never managed to frame a Fiat within his propeller arc, much less his gunsight. He was too busy dodging the deadly Breda tracers that the Fiats seemed to be spewing everywhere. Charlie Koch did better; he was credited with shooting down one Fiat, and a Russian named Kromberg got another.

From Tabernas, Kosenkov's squadron moved to Almería where they did a lot of dive-bombing and strafing along the Málaga-Motril road, shooting up Italian truck convoys. But this failed to prevent the Italians from taking Málaga, which fell on 8 February. After that they provided a combat air patrol to protect the old Republican battleship *Jaime Primero* in the port of Almería. German Ju 52s had bombed the ship in August and now tried to hit it again. When events overtook this threat—the fall of Málaga, stabilization of the front a few miles east of Motril, and the withdrawal of Italian units to the north for an assault on Guadalajara—Kosokov's squadron moved to the front in Toledo.

Based at Tembleque and Madridejos, the squadron operated against Toledo, where it encountered little air opposition but terrible flak. Later, the squadron provided fighter cover for Aranjuez during the Jarama battles, and on 24 February it moved to Alcalá and finally to Algete, and had not done much since. Meanwhile, Charlie Koch's ulcerated stomach went bad again. He had to be hospitalized and decided to get out of Spain before the olive oil killed him. This left Baumler the only English-speaking member of the squadron.

Though a bit lonely among the Russians, Baumler was learning to speak both Russian and Spanish, and he had plenty to do on the ground. He nevertheless wondered if he and Tinker couldn't manage to get together in the same squadron. He invited Tinker to come up to see their base near Algete, a former duke's country estate that wanted for nothing. In loyalty to the Esquadrilla de Lacalle, Tinker assured Baumler that the *marqués' finca* at Campo X, combined with the social whirl of Azuqueca, was more than satisfactory. But he hoped that they could join forces some day.

Back at Campo X, wet clouds continued to press upon the treetops, and the airplanes parked under their camouflage nettings sat idle for days on end. Every day the pilots and ground crews rode out from Azuqueca to lounge around the *marqués'* parlor, playing cards, dominos, or chess, and every night they rode back to Azuqueca. The miserable February weather made for miserable days that passed slowly and, without an air raid to send them to the *refugio*, the evenings became even more of a bore. Tinker became desperate for diversion in Madrid and finally complained to Lacalle of *un dolor de diente muy formidable*—a terrible toothache. Tinker always had dental problems; the squadron knew of his missing front plate, so his complaint had credibility. Lacalle muttered, "*Muy bien*," called an automobile, and gave Tinker an escort to a dentist in Madrid with whom he was acquainted. Tinker failed to anticipate this, and the dentist turned out to be a great bear of a man who proved quite capable of holding anyone in his chair with one hand while manipulating his pliers with the other, and he could not understand a word of Tinker's primitive Spanish. Within a few minutes Tinker had two of his molars yanked out. However, the ruse did not completely backfire. The dentist, disturbed by Tinker's *sonrisa serrada*, began making casts for a new plate. This was all to the good; if nothing else it provided excuses for more trips to Madrid.

When Tinker returned to Azuqueca he found that the first replacement pilot had arrived, a tall, dark Spaniard named Eusebio Fernandez Velasco. He arrived without an airplane, the squadron had no spares, and the new pilot quickly made himself unpopular by making the rounds of the field and trying on cockpits for size. Each pilot had his own numbered airplane, it was practically his private property, and Velasco soon learned to leave them alone.

The wreckage of Leider's, Dahl's, and Bercial's airplanes had been salvaged and trucked back from the front to be cannibalized for spare parts. Velasco gave careful study to these carcasses. Tinker remarked that maybe Velasco was going to build his own airplane. Whitey Dahl guessed that the new man was simply anxious to fly and would prove to be a good fighter pilot. A month later Lacalle made Velasco leader of the squadron's newly created fourth patrol.

Shortly after Tinker's visit to the dentist, the airfields in the Henares Valley began to receive nightly visits from Nationalist Ju 52s and S.81s.[18] The bombers sought to damage the Republic's air forces on the ground in advance of yet another offensive, but their aim at night was incredibly bad, and the bombs fell anywhere within a mile or so of the airfields.

Tinker, Chang, and the other pilots did not mind their hours in Azuqueca's *refugios* because they enhanced their acquaintanceships with the local girls. With a wife in Valencia, Whitey Dahl professed no interest in the *refugios'* nightlife, and when the air raid alarms sounded he rolled over and went back to sleep— until one night four 220-pound bombs fell within two hundred yards of the Casa de Pilotos. The concussions bounced him out of bed and sent him running for the *refugio,* where he arrived clad only in his shorts and his fright transformed into embarrassment.

The air raids proved more of a nuisance than a menace, but they had some collateral benefits. The villagers along the Henares River learned to spread nets across the river every evening, certain that *los Fascistos* would drop a few bombs in it; in the mornings they harvested a catch of bomb-killed fish. The farmers around Azuqueca had refused to sell the pilots chickens for their kitchen because as poultry they could be sold only once, whereas eggs could be sold every day. One night a Nationalist bomb fell among the local henhouses, and the pilots ate nothing but chicken for more than a week.

On 6 March 1937 the weather cleared slightly, and if the pilots were uncertain of it, that fact was announced by two red Very flares bursting over the field. They arrived over their sector of the Jarama just in time to intercept two strange bombers that seemed to be headed for the town of Chinchón.

When first sighted, the bombers were about two thousand feet above them. As Lacalle led the squadron in a climbing attack, the enemy saw them and started turning. The bombers split, each turning away from one another in smoothly executed 180-degree turns. They reformed at the ends of their turns and sped back into Nationalist airspace—performing just like an air show display. These strange airplanes were twin-engine machines, finely streamlined and almost as fast as the fighters. Lacalle's squadron tried some long-distance deflection shots at them while they were in the predictable courses of their turns, but with no apparent hits. Recognizing them as the new German high-speed bombers he had been told about, Lacalle did not waste time in pursuit. After a slow patrol of the Jarama, the squadron returned to the valley of the Henares. Lacalle decided that Campo X was too soft from the rain for landings, so they put down at Guadalajara.

The talk at Guadalajara turned to the new enemy bombers. Known to be in Spain, this was the first time they had been seen to cross the lines. Rumor had it that they were a new type of Junkers, the Ju 86.[19] In fact, they were twin-engine Heinkel He 111Bs of the Legion Condor's Kampfgruppe 88, and during February thirty of them had flown to Spain via Italy. Equipped with retractable landing gear, the low-wing Heinkel He 111B monoplane could deliver 3,300 pounds of bombs against a target within a 500-mile radius, but its defensive armament was only a trifle better than the old trimotor Ju 52s. It had only three 7.9-mm guns in flexible mounts: one in the nose, one in the top of the fuselage, and one in a retractable "dustbin" position on its underside. The He 111's primary defense was its speed. With a crew of four and a full load of bombs, its two 950-horsepower, liquid-cooled Daimler Benz engines provided a cruising speed of 200 mph; and, once rid of the weight of its bombs, an He 111 could run away at 230 mph.[20]

The maximum speed of an I-15 was only 230 mph. Although the I-16 monoplanes could speed up to almost 300 mph at full throttle, even they were hard put to intercept a bomber as fast as the He 111. Without radar to provide early

He 111B on a bomb run (*R. K. Smith Collection*)

warning and constant tracking, and without even radio communication with ground controllers, too much depended on crude information received before takeoff and on chance after that. Lacalle and his handful of I-15s had frustrated the He 111Bs this morning, but that was simply the bombers' bad luck. More noteworthy, he regarded making contact as hopeless.

At breakfast the next morning there was a double-rocket alarm. Lacalle and the alert patrol started their engines and got rolling; the other pilots clambered into starting trucks, and there was a noisy drive across the field to get to their dispersed airplanes. The I-15s did not have electric starters for their engines and depended on trucks rigged with a mechanical Hucks starter—or else their propellers had to be pulled through by hand. The Hucks starter was a Rube Goldberg apparatus developed by the British in World War I; at the time, it was judged a remarkable device. Mounted on the front of a truck, it connected the power from the truck's transmission via a flexible connection to the airplane's propeller hub. Through this connection the truck's engine got the airplane's engine turning to build up compression for a start. Once the airplane's engine had fired and turned over, the truck driver engaged a clutch that disconnected the transmission linkage; he then drove clear of that airplane and went to the next one. Although a primitive system, it worked well, and in the hands of well-drilled ground personnel it was not as clumsy as it may sound. Its shortcoming: for quickest response

Hucks starter attached to an I-15 (*Courtesy of Sergei Abrosov*)

each airplane required its own truck. As a rule, only the three airplanes of the patrol in alert status stood parked with the "dogs" of their propeller hubs connected to the starting trucks. Once they were started, the trucks went on to the other planes.

On this morning of 7 March Lacalle and his alert patrol were ready for take-off when the *caseta de mando* signaled them to stay on the ground. The enemy was a lone Heinkel He 70F, a fast, single-engine, photo-reconnaissance airplane. A military variant of the Heinkel Blitz Lightning,[21] it was used in commercial service as a mail carrier; stripped for photo-recon work, it had a speed in excess of 230 mph. No I-15 stood a chance of overtaking it, and only one patrol of I-16 monoplanes was scrambled without result. The He 70, doubtless touring the Henares Valley to collect targeting information, simply dissolved among the thick clouds over Guadalajara.

The next day Lacalle moved the squadron back to Campo X, which was fairly well dried out now. Two new pilots reported for duty: Augusto Lecha, who had very little flying time and even less in fighters; and Antonio Blanch, a veteran of the prewar air force. Blanch had been caught in Morocco when the generals launched their revolt. His sympathies were with the Republic, but he judged discretion the better part of valor, and for the next six months he flew for the Nationalists. Finally assigned to a twin-engine Dornier Wal flying boat, he possessed an airplane that had the range to fly from Morocco to Republican territory. The Wal had a crew of five and Blanch waited until he found a fellow sympathizer; together they planned their escape. Back on 5 December 1936, their Wal took off from Ceuta on a routine patrol. Once in the air, Blanch signaled his own miniature revolt by shooting the pilot and taking the controls. His partner overpowered the other two crewmen, and they flew to Málaga, at that time still held by the Republic.[22]

Since the loss of Bercial, Lacalle had been trying to select a leader for the third patrol and judged Tinker a likely candidate. Like Naval Academy classmates, he would later remember Tinker in Spain to have "a fine sense of humor and [he] was a rapid study. He was tall, quick, with a large mustache and always wore a beret. If he didn't speak, he could pass for a native. He was an excellent pilot, calm and most disciplined. Many times, because it was hard to decipher his terrible Spanish, we couldn't tell if he was serious or joking."[23] The latter practice was one that Tinker, throughout his life, especially enjoyed. Lacalle asked Tinker to lead the patrol, but he declined; Tinker wanted to stay with Whitey and Chang, and Lacalle understood. After seeing Blanch perform with the squadron Lacalle made him leader of the third patrol, and everyone agreed it was a good choice. While Lacalle and his pilots sorted out squadron administrative problems, fifty miles to the northeast the Nationalists prepared to launch another major offensive. This time it would be down the Zaragoza-Madrid highway, toward Guadalajara, Alcalá, and Madrid.

On the night of 8 March 1937 the air raid alarms sounded again and again throughout the valley of the Henares, while Ju 52s and He 111Bs from Cáceres and Avila, and S.81s from Soria, prowled the darkness overhead trying to bomb the many airfields sited between Madrid and Guadalajara. Alarms at Azuqueca sent Tinker and his comrades to the *refugios* three times, but the bombers did not hit Azuqueca and environs until 11:30 p.m., and then their bombs fell all over the hinterland, hitting nothing of consequence. The next evening two dozen He 111Bs sped in from the west and distributed some thirty tons of bombs among the airfields at Barajas, Madrid, and Alcalá de Henares. This action introduced He 111s on their first combat operation anywhere, and it provided a dramatic demonstration of their breathtaking capabilities in 1937.

During the previous thirty days, in the struggle for the Jarama, everyone had become well acquainted with the triangle of topography framed by Alcalá, Arganda, and Aranjuez. Now their attentions were about to swing 150 degrees to the north—to the corridor of the Zaragoza-Madrid highway. Although no one could be certain of it yet—not even the Nationalists launching the offensive—what would become known as the Battle of Guadalajara was already under way.

8

THE DEBACLE
OF GUADALAJARA

ecause the capture of a capital in a civil war has transcendental political value, the Nationalists remained determined to take Madrid. Nevertheless, in November 1936 their frontal assaults on the city failed. December's battles of the Coruña Road stopped their attempt to encircle the city by means of a breakthrough northwest of Madrid; the attempt to encircle the city from the south ended in February's stalemate on the Jarama (see map at page 102).

The Jarama might have been a smashing success for the Nationalists if its execution had even approximated the scope of its original plan, which called for a simultaneous push from the north by the Italian Corpo Truppe Volontarie (CTV), or the Voluntary Army Corps. But the Italians, late mopping up Málaga in the south, moved their 32,000-man corps later still on a semicircular track of some 600 miles from Málaga on the Mediterranean over Spain's rickety rail system and poor roads to Sigüenza and environs in the highlands of Old Castille. While enroute, the Italians learned that the Republic had massed forces for its own offensive in the vicinity of the Jarama. On 6 February 1937, Nationalist forces in the south mounted an attack to preempt the Republic's offensive, and they acted without the Italians.

During the Jarama struggle the Nationalists repeatedly asked the CTV for a diversion from the north, but its leaders always claimed to be not yet ready. In truth, the clique around Mussolini in Rome and the dictator himself wanted its army to act alone, to be victorious alone, and to storm into Madrid as the liberators of Spain. It is only sixty miles from the CTV's jumping-off point near Algora to Madrid's Gran Vía. With some justice, it could be assumed that the Republic's proletarian rabble was exhausted after the Jarama and that a drive from the north should be a walkover. Not one of the CTV's high command anticipated a Battle of Guadalajara, much less a battle so named, which failed even to occur within ten miles of that city.[1]

The Republic had ample warning of the Italians' conspicuous buildup along the rail line of Almazán-Medinaceli-Sigüenza. Both sides enjoyed reasonably good espionage services in the other's territory; in any case, it was impossible to keep secret a weeks-long conspicuous movement of an army of 32,000 foreigners. By the first week of March 1937, the Republic had reinforced its units along an irregular line between Cogolludo in the west and Algora to the east, but when the blow fell on the eighth, they had something less than 10,000 men in position behind amateurish defense works, and desertion was endemic. Against these the Italians had four divisions totaling more than 32,000 men, albeit most of them without combat experience, but by the standards of the day they were unusually well armed.

In the predawn of D-day on 8 March a steady, icy rain enveloped the region, rain that could easily turn to sleet and, as the Spaniards well knew, would probably become wet snow after sundown. The Nationalists advised the Italians to postpone their attack. The Italians refused to counsel delay. At 7 a.m. the artillery barrage opened up, and at 7:30 the troops started moving out. The CTV achieved complete surprise. Its artillery punched holes in the ramshackle Republican defenses, and by midmorning tanks, troops, and trucks were moving down the Zaragoza-Madrid highway toward Guadalajara, Alcalá, and Madrid—but at a snail's pace.

By evening the CTV had advanced but five miles to the outskirts of the village of Almadrones. Although only two hundred Republican irregulars held the village, the Italian commander suspended operations for the night. His troops bivouacked in the rain when, for a small firefight, they could have slept in the shelter of Almadrones. This decision, which precluded anything that might be described as an "incident," proved to be typical of the mindlessness that afflicted the *Guerra Celere* (war with speed—the Italian synonym for "Blitzkrieg") as it was ineptly executed along the Zaragoza-Madrid highway.

At Campo X double-rocket alarms sent the pilots running to their airplanes three times during the eighth, but each was cancelled. Shortly after dawn on the ninth an alarm chased them into the air. The squadron was barely off the ground and had not yet formed up when three Heinkel He 111s popped out of the clouds north of the field. When the German aircrews saw the swarm of fighters clawing the air in their direction, they dropped their bombs in the Henares and fled off into the gloom to the west. Lacalle's fighters rattled off a few bursts at long range, but the bombers were too far away to be hit and had too much of a lead to be overtaken. The squadron returned to Campo X.

At the same time, two dozen He 111 bombers struck at other airfields in the Henares area, Barajas-Madrid and Alcalá being hit especially hard. Shortly after Lacalle's squadron landed, and while the planes were being refueled, a Heinkel He 70 photo-reconnaissance airplane materialized out of the overcast and overflew Campo X, presumably to photograph the "damage" done by the He 111s.

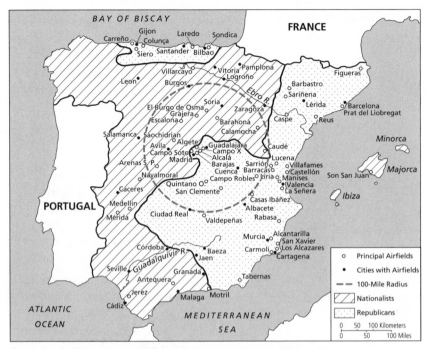

Map 8.1   Principle Spanish Airfields, March–April 1937

Two patrols scrambled into the air, but before they could gain five hundred feet of altitude the He 70 had dissolved into the thick ceiling.

Meanwhile, the Italians continued to move south under curtains of rain, sleet, and wet snow. The wretched weather made their slow advance even slower, and it rendered their air forces useless, but it also protected them from the Republic's aerial reconnaissance and air attacks.[2]

As the rain fell into the second day of the offensive, the aircraft on these airfields slowly sank into the sod; the least bit of activity transformed the sod to mud; and as the mud became worse, their operations came to focus on Soria. This not only created congestion, it did nothing to stabilize the characteristics of its sod. While the Nationalist air force tried to cope with these dilemmas of a natural environment that refused to support all-weather operations, the Republican air force deployed its airplanes from the well-drained airfields at Barajas, Alcalá, and Guadalajara, and sod fields in the Madrid area that enjoyed good natural drainage into the valleys of the Henares, Manzanares, and Jarama. In the Battle of Guadalajara, well-drained airfields had as much and possibly more to do with "control of the air" as did airplanes.[3]

With both air forces practically grounded by weather and the Republic's ground forces in disarray, the CTV continued to move southward. Late in the evening of 9 March, an Italian column of armored cars roared into the key side-road town of Brihuega, with some three thousand inhabitants, and took possession of it before the local Republican commander knew what had happened. A rare display of audacity, this represented the way the *Guerra Celere* was supposed to be executed. On the main Zaragoza-Madrid highway, however, the advance moved with painful cautiousness. This slowness was owed to traffic congestion in the rear and the high command's obsession with textbook orderliness, rather than the objective beyond their fore. Nevertheless, on the evening of the ninth, it appeared as if the CTV would be swarming into Guadalajara the next day. But the Nationalist forces on the Jarama, under General Franco, failed to join in the attack on Guadalajara.

That night Nationalist bombers climbed into the cloud-filled darkness to strike with their usual blindness at roads, rail points, and airfields in the Henares Valley. There were three alarms in Azuqueca, sending its population to the *refugios*. Tinker noticed an absence of the usual good cheer. The villagers, tense and silent, no doubt wondered what would happen to them if the Nationalists overran Guadalajara and Azuqueca on the morrow. Those persons who had conspicuously associated themselves with the mélange of leftist politics that made up the Republic had special cause for concern; political officers who moved in the wake of the Nationalist armies had ways of seeking them out and seeing to their "re-education." And those villagers who had joined the mob that had dispossessed the Marqués de la Valle of his *finca*, terrorized his wife, and hauled the *marqués* off to die in prison, could expect at least similar treatment if the Nationalists occupied Azuqueca.

Only a hint of dawn could be seen on the tenth; the day was dark and full of rain. Lacalle sent Dahl out on a reconnaissance flight to the north. He returned with word of Italian tanks, armored cars, and trucks swarming over the roads. Lacalle ordered the planes bombed-up, but just as they were ready to take off the opaque ceiling dropped into the treetops, and the attack had to be cancelled. The pilots returned to the *marqués'* parlor, their frayed cards, dominoes with increasingly rounded sides, and well-polished chessmen until the day's gray dissolved into darkness. At that time, armorers removed the bombs from the airplanes, and everyone stood down for the day. When the pilots boarded their bus for Azuqueca, the rumble of artillery could be distinctly heard off to the north where the armies had finally begun to grapple.

That evening Lacalle gave Tinker, Whitey, and Chang permission to go into Madrid. The Florida's hot water was good, Hemingway's hospitality even better. The aviators became the center of attention. Everyone wanted to know what was going on in the north. They could only answer with a shrug of the shoulders and a "*Quién sabe?*" (Who knows?).

En route back to Azuqueca, they were speeding through the village of Torrejón de Ardoz when air raid sirens hailed their passage. Tinker hit the brakes, stopped the engine, and they listened. The distinctive snarl of the Ju 52's Hornet engines filled the night. Piling out of the car, they made for the ditches alongside the road.

Two airfields existed near Torrejón, but the bombers seemed to be trying to hit the local railroad station and its sidings—a relatively fruitless target even in the best daylight conditions. Their bombs fell in a two-hundred-yard strip between the railroad tracks and the highway, much too close for the three airmen's comfort. Lacalle was waiting for them at Azuqueca, ready to dress them down for being twenty minutes late—until he saw their automobile, its roof and sides slashed by bomb fragments.

Daylight on the eleventh appeared reluctantly, and when it finally arrived it put its feeble light on another damp day of low ceilings. Then the telephone rang. Lacalle shouted for the airplanes to be bombed up. They took off between rain squalls. The front now only fifteen miles away, the ceiling at less than two thousand feet, they had barely finished their climb-outs when they reached the target area. The whole valley was blanketed by low clouds, but the squadron found a few holes around the assigned target. They made glide-bombing attacks against buildings in the village of Trijueque, believed to be the CTV's forward headquarters; they released their bombs from six hundred feet and then flew on along the highway toward Torija, strafing troops and vehicles on the road.

No antiaircraft fire harassed their passage, and everything on the ground appeared to be a mess. The off-road terrain had been transformed into a sea of mud, and what trenches had been dug appeared to be full of water. The soldiers had no place to take cover without diving into the mud, which they obviously preferred not to do. Troops scurried everywhere, pulling mud-laden feet with them through the vast quagmire as the airplanes roared by overhead.

Lacalle broke off the strafing after one pass because he wanted to return to base before another low ceiling blanketed the field. They returned none too soon; the last plane was squishing its way across the field when the clouds dropped into the treetops. Everyone was certain that this ended the day's flying, but just before sundown the weather cleared and Lacalle ordered another attack.

This proved to be a mistake, but it might have taken a first-rate meteorologist to advise otherwise. While the squadron formed up over Guadalajara, a black wall came rushing out of the north, and they found themselves in the midst of an awful thunderstorm. Lightning filled the sky. Instead of rain there was hail, and in an instant the air was full of big white stones, each a distinct threat to any fabric-covered airplane. All eyes turned to Lacalle's cockpit. He signaled for everyone to dump their bombs in the river and head for home.

The Patrulla Americano managed to hold formation until its bombs were jettisoned. But when Chang bent down to pull his bomb release he momentarily lost control of his airplane, and it went skidding across the vee formation, sliding under Tinker's plane and missing it by only a foot or two. To compound the confusion of this moment, a whole formation of strange airplanes suddenly appeared out of the stormy gloom to the north. It was a squadron of Rasante attack airplanes returning from the front. In the next instant, the gathering darkness seemed filled with airplanes, each breaking away in its own unpredictable direction in an effort to avoid collisions. Remarkably enough, there were none. But in this confusion Chang's airplane vanished into the murk. Tinker held tight on Whitey's wing, and they made their way back to the airfield.

The thunderstorm had worsened. Although the hail had stopped, heavy rain now filled the air. Elements of Lacalle's scattered squadron created confusion in the landing pattern over the field, and in a few minutes the last dregs of daylight would be gone. Whitey signaled Tinker a dive to the left; they headed for the deck and for Albacete about 130 miles away to the southeast. At Aranjuez they picked up the main railway line, an "iron beam" that took them almost directly to Albacete. An hour later they landed at the Los Llanos airfield. A car took them to the Casa de Pilotos, a palatial establishment about two miles from the field. Spanish pilots informed Tinker that it was the hunting lodge of the Duke of Albacete, but he thought it was more like a royal palace.

Here they met some Russian pilots whom they knew from Alcalá and who introduced the Americans to "General Douglas," commander of the Soviet air forces in Spain and the de facto commander of the Republic's air force. As was the case with most Russians in Spain, "Douglas" was a nom de guerre; his real name was Jacob Smushkevich. About six feet in height with short, black curly hair, Smushkevich was one of those men so heavily bearded that no matter how close he shaved, his face had a perpetual bluish cast. A handsome man of great charm, with a ready smile from which

Jacob Smushkevich (*Courtesy of Andrey Simonov*)

he flashed a jaw full of gold crowns, in March 1937 he was but thirty-five years old. Recalling the graying generals of the U.S. Army Air Corps and the seemingly ancient admirals of the U.S. Navy, Tinker was fascinated by Smushkevich's relative youth. But in the 1930s the Red Army Air Force was a very young service relative to its counterparts in the West, and men in their thirties and forties led most of its high commands.[4]

After Tinker telephoned air force headquarters in Alcalá, reported their safe arrival, and learned of an impending squadron move, he and Dahl joined General Smushkevich for dinner. Other Russians were present, and Mrs. Miriam Rosmarin, the wife of Joseph Rosmarin, the American pilot flying transport planes for the Republic, also attended. Although an English-Russian interpreter assisted the gathering, Mrs. Rosmarin, who served as an interpreter for General Smushkevich, spoke Russian, Spanish, French and English, which made for an easy flow of conversation. The dinner was excellent and lasted well into the night.

The next morning, on 12 March, Tinker and Whitey arrived at Los Llanos shortly after dawn and were told to wait; they would fly escort on General Smushkevich to Alcalá. Tinker assumed that this meant flying lazy Ss back and forth across the track of some slow transport plane, but to his surprise the general appeared on the flight line in a fleece-lined leather flying suit and climbed into the cockpit of an I-15. After takeoff Tinker and Whitey formed up on the general's airplane as wingmen; this may well be the only instance in the history of the Red Army Air Force where two American aviators provided a military escort for one of its generals. When the Henares appeared over their engine cowlings, the Russian waggled his wings to signal breakup, and he rolled out of the formation to land at Alcalá. Tinker climbed to bleed off speed and fell back to take a wing position on Whitey, and they turned north for Guadalajara, where Lacalle had moved the squadron early that morning.

After they landed, the mechanics Chamorro and Juanas welcomed them as if they had returned from the dead. Although Lacalle had told the mechanics that their pilots were safe in Albacete, they knew that Lacalle had a technique of indulging in "little lies" by way of softening the blow for inevitable bad news. Lacalle professed irritation with Tinker and Dahl for having diverted to Albacete so soon; but Tinker later heard that he had bragged to the Russians about how his two Americanos had been able to find their way out of the thunderstorm and to Albacete without any maps.

The rest of the squadron pilots had given up trying to land at Campo X in the storm. They climbed above it and circled the valley until the storm had passed. By that time darkness had fallen, and they had to land by the light of flares. The exception was Chang. Bad luck continued to dog him. He became lost, landed in a freshly plowed field, and nosed over. Although uninjured, his airplane could

Tupolev SB-2 twin-engine bomber (*National Air and Space Museum, Smithsonian Institution*)

not be flown out. Some days' labor was required to dismantle the machine, haul it back to the field, and restore it to flying condition. Meanwhile, Chang was assigned another I-15.

Lacalle had already taken the squadron on one mission on the twelfth that included dropping propaganda leaflets on the Italians. Tinker and Dahl returned in time to have their airplanes bombed up for a second strike. After takeoff they climbed to 8,000 feet and orbited the field until a dozen SB-2 Katiuska twin-engine bombers from Barajas appeared at 3,200 feet. A Tupolev-designed light bomber that reached Soviet service in 1936, the midwing SB-2 monoplane featured retractable main landing gear, an enclosed cockpit, and stressed-skin all-metal construction. At a gross weight of 13,500 pounds, its two 800-horsepower M-100 radial engines gave the SB-2 a cruising speed over 230 mph while carrying a bomb load of 1,102 pounds.[5] The SB-2 also reflected the bomber design philosophy that prevailed in the 1930s: speed was its primary defense.

After the SB-2s passed below, Lacalle led his planes down to 6,500 feet and fell in behind the bombers as their top cover. Crossing the lines near the town of Torija, which the Italians sought to take, Tinker could see even from his

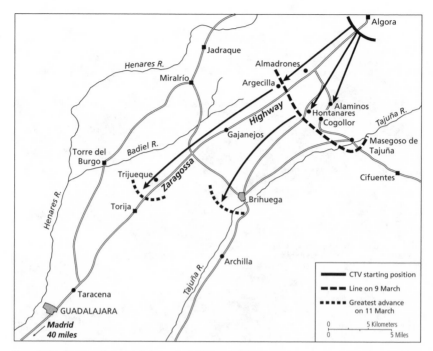

Map 8.2   Battle of Guadalajara, 8–18 March 1937

relatively high cruising altitude that a great battle was raging below. Artillery flashes appeared almost continuously along the front; smoke, punctuated by geysers of earth that erupted in clusters, appeared everywhere. As they flew farther north, the zigzagged tangle of vehicles along the highway made the Italians' situation obvious.

The SB-2s' target was a crossroads on the main highway between Trijueque and Gajanejos, where a secondary road came in from Brihuega in the east and ran off to the village of Miralrío in the west, with the railhead of Jadraque a few miles beyond. CTV troops and their vehicles poured into this junction. The traffic jam was fantastic; bumper-to-bumper vehicles filled the roads for miles. General Confusion commanded the highway, with his authority enforced by General Mud, who commanded the treacherous hinterland.

Three SB-2s dropped their loads of 220-pound bombs directly into the crossroads. There was no question of their hitting something. Men, mud, and motor trucks suddenly churned upward by the dozen detonations of high explosive. The other nine bombers flew up the highway toward Gajanejos, leisurely cutting loose their bombs over the distance of a mile. On the terrain below, vehicles were jammed up, often two or three abreast, with dozens of others shoved off or overturned on the shoulders, and the entire area was thick with men. The bombs passed through their ranks like so many muddy flowers suddenly popping out of the earth, tossing men and vehicles skyward in their rush. It amazed Tinker to see trucks and automobiles hurled into the air and turn end over end before falling back into the mud.

After the SB-2s finished their labors and turned away for Barajas, Lacalle took his squadron down to attack. The function of the SB-2s had been to spread destruction and confusion. Lacalle's squadron now would compound this with more personal forms of disorganization: reinforcing the havoc and spreading panic in the ranks. Although motorized, the four divisions of the CTV were not mechanized divisions as such would come to be understood after 1940. Horse-drawn wagons had been replaced by trucks, and trucks and tractors had displaced horses for pulling artillery. Armored cars and motorcycles had replaced horsed cavalry for scouting.[6] Most of the CTV's infantry, however, moved in the same mode as that used by the legions of ancient Rome: on foot. Most significant in the wetness of Guadalajara, the Italian vehicles were wheeled and not tracked. The CTV's only tracked vehicles were its pathetically small 3.5-ton Fiat-Ansaldo tanks; not much larger than a Volkswagen and armed only with machine guns, their tracks were not wide enough to navigate the mud of Guadalajara. Thus road bound, an aerial attack against the struggling CTV truly was like shooting fish in a barrel.

Diving to attack the Italians, Lacalle's squadron sought out targets of opportunity—clusters of men and vehicles that had survived the bombers. Although the four bombs carried by an I-15 totaled only 100 pounds, any one of them bursting among a group of men could slaughter the lot, and even a near-miss on a truck could put it out of action. But the I-15's most deadly weapon was its battery of four 7.2-mm guns; a few seconds' burst of these four streams of fire could tear a motor truck to shreds.

The Italians did not march along the sides of the road in single files, ready to disperse against an aerial attack, and they gave no indication of having been trained to bring their rifles to bear on low-flying airplanes. Instead, they displayed a fatal tendency for togetherness, bunching around their vehicles, which only provided a pilot with a better target. Tinker spotted an unusually large group marching in company with a pair of Fiat-Ansaldo tanks. He sped downwind, rolled his I-15 through a tight 180-degree turn and nosed over into a 60-degree dive. By making his attack upwind he would not overfly the target too quickly.

Passing through seven hundred feet, he opened fire with one upper and one lower gun to range the target, watching where his tracers struck. The two yellow streams churned up the road short of the fleeing group, so he pulled up his nose a bit to drop his fire directly into their midst and then flicked on the other two guns. Instead of running for cover at right angles to the attack, the panic-stricken troops did the worst thing possible—they attempted to run forward away from the airplane, which only served to give Tinker a longer target. None of the soldiers attempted to fire at his plane; they simply ran, throwing away their rifles, bandoliers, and shaking off the burdens of their backpacks. A few had the good sense to dive into the water-filled ditches alongside the road or run into the fields beyond, running with great clumps of mud dragging on their boots; but most chose to stay on the road's solid asphalt, and most of them died on its rain- and blood-slickened black surface.

Gently working his rudder from left to right and back again, Tinker's guns followed the movement to sweep their fire back and forth across the road in a zigzag of macadam chips, smoke, and broken flesh. As he overflew the groups clustered around the tanks, he eased back on his stick to bring up the nose a bit, which stretched the range of his four fingers of fire to drop a rain of missiles into a knot of stragglers farther down the road. Pulling out of the attack barely twenty feet above the ground, Tinker zoomed back to altitude where the rest of the squadron circled in search of targets, and then dove after them.

So it went, again and again, until their ammunition was exhausted, and then Lacalle waved everyone for home, now the better-drained airfield at Guadalajara.

After rearming at Guadalajara the squadron took off for still another strike at the crossroads. Over the target, they had just shifted into an echelon for dive-bombing when Tinker spotted a cloud of enemy fighters—fifteen Fiats headed in their direction. Intent on identifying a ground target, Lacalle did not see the Fiats; he rolled into a dive and took the squadron down with him to hit the tangle of vehicles and men in the road junction. By this time, the crossroads on the Zaragoza-Madrid highway encompassed utter disaster. Vehicles pointed in every direction, going nowhere, and most of them were burning; hundreds of figures scurried among the fires, smoke, and confusion.

After landing at Guadalajara, Chang's mechanic showed him some four dozen bullet holes in his tail. Being the last of the second patrol to roll into the attack, Chang thought he had been holed through the carelessness of the third patrol coming down behind him, and he was furious. But then it turned out that an airplane of the third patrol had been similarly holed. The guessing was that the Fiats had made one attack on the squadron while it was rolling into its dive-bombing, yet no one had been aware of it. Everyone wondered why the Fiats had not followed up while the squadron was engrossed in its ground attacks. But the Italians had an eighty-mile flight from their bases near Soria, and it was possible that their fuel reserves were too low to risk a fight.[7]

That evening word came through that the Republican ground forces had fought their way into the crossroads, occupied the area, and captured scores of stalled Italian vehicles. Next morning, the thirteenth, Lacalle sent Tinker and Whitey off on a reconnaissance of the north. They spotted several truck convoys on the Zaragoza-Madrid highway, and between the railhead at Jadraque and the CTV's logistics center at Sigüenza three long freight trains—all headed north. Lacalle ordered the planes bombed up, but just as the squadron taxied out for takeoff, two red rockets popped over the field signaling an imminent attack. No one wasted any time getting into the air, especially when other squadrons based at Guadalajara were also scrambling to get off so they would not be caught on the ground.

As Whitey led Tinker and Chang into their first turn after takeoff, they spotted three He 111s sliding out of the clouds at about five thousand feet and directly above them. The bomber crews saw them at the same time, and their gunners sent streams of tracers arcing down toward the fighters. One bomber suddenly broke away, executed a steep 180-degree turn, and sped back toward the north. Perhaps he was in difficulty; more likely this was a ruse to divide the fighters.

The rest of the squadron went after the lone bomber; Dahl kept the Patrulla Americano climbing for the other two. Meanwhile, the bombers crossed Guadalajara's airfield and loosed their loads among the ruins of the Hispano-Suiza factory. As the fighters closed the altitude and distance, the bombers started diving away into the thick clouds. A few second later one slipped out of the clouds, and the fighters got off some shots at it. For a moment there was a duel of sorts between them and the Heinkel's rear gunner. When the bomber's gun suddenly stopped spewing tracers, Tinker assumed that they had scored some hits. This was the moment to close for a kill, but the bomber again vanished into the low cloud base.

Meanwhile, only Blanch, leader of the third patrol, managed to close with one bomber that had turned away from its target. He got off a few shots, but as he rolled away from his attack in a predictable textbook-coordinated turn, the He 111's gunners pumped two streams of bullets into his aft fuselage. Thus weakened, the I-15's whole tail section broke away.[8] Blanch bailed out. The squadron saw his parachute open and stream out behind him, but its canopy failed to open. Blanch plummeted through 6,500 feet to the earth below with the useless silk of his parachute trailing after him like a pennant.

Lacalle swept in among his scattered planes, re-formed them, and led them off to the north for strikes at the rail targets near Jadraque and to strafe the CTV ground forces retreating along the highway between Gajanejos and Almadrones.

Chang did not fly north with the squadron. When he saw Blanch plunge to earth, he dove after the Spaniard, took note of the impact point, and landed back at the field to make a search for him. A remote chance existed that he might barely be alive, and he summoned a car. But when Chang returned to the field, it was with Blanch's corpse. Lacalle carefully inspected the parachute; it had failed to open because it was wet. This doubtless was owed to it having been sat upon for too long in an open cockpit that had been rained into for too many days, but Lacalle suspected sabotage. He ordered an immediate repacking of all parachutes. This was a wise move, if only to determine how much dampness was in them and open their folds to the air. Thereafter, the squadron had a grim reminder of this day in the form of a large bloodstain on the rear seat of the car that Chang had used to retrieve Blanch's body.

That evening after dinner Tinker, Whitey, and Chang made a run into Madrid. In the Florida, they met most of their newspaper friends assembled there, all of whom had hundreds of questions about what was going on at the front. Herbert Matthews assumed the role of a self-styled Clausewitz, proclaiming Guadalajara to be "the battle of the century" and probably one of fifteen decisive battles in the history of the world![9] With only a little more modesty, Hemingway compared it to the Italian military disaster at Caporetto in October 1917.[10] Neither Tinker nor Whitey was so sure about any of these high-flown analyses, but this evening they had more to say than "*Quién sabe?*"

Lacalle was waiting for their return, not to deliver a scolding but to tell Tinker that he was now the leader of the third patrol—whether he liked it or not. Fortunately, Tinker was not superstitious or he might have been inclined to regard the third as the Hoodoo Patrol; the loss of two leaders in less than four weeks was not a confidence-inspiring record. Both Bercial and Blanch had been shot down while attacking bombers. Tinker knew that Blanch led all of the others, practically alone, when he went in for his attack, and Tinker felt that Blanch would have survived had he been covered by a wingman. Tinker suspected timidity among the third patrol's wingmen. This was not cowardice, only a reluctance to hold close formations and a failure to appreciate how important it was for one to cover the other's tail. With his own life more than ever on the line, he now determined to have an end to this.

Low clouds oozed down from the Sierras on the morning of 14 March, creating a ceiling that varied from zero to 1,600 feet. Tinker was out early to inspect his third patrol when Lacalle stalked out of the *caseta de mando* shouting for the armorers to start shackling bombs. The target was more rail traffic near Jadraque. By this date the rains had slackened, the Nationalist airfields were drying out, and the squadron barely had crossed the lines when Fiats, charging in from the west, challenged it. There was an echelon of seven that had an altitude advantage of about one thousand feet and another echelon of five stacked up at a still higher altitude.

Lacalle waggled his wings furiously, jettisoned his bombs, and everyone followed suit. After signaling the squadron into a right echelon, he started a climbing turn into the west for a head-on meeting with the Fiats, now diving toward them. Lacalle's and Dahl's patrols tangled with the lower seven Fiats. Flying at the rear, Tinker's patrol climbed into the fight just as the five Fiats of the top cover dove into the melee. Suddenly the sky filled with airplanes wheeling around on all kinds of crazy and at such close quarters they dissolved into fleeting shapes that came and went so fast that there was no time for gunsights. All Tinker could do was fire random bursts as one of the mustard-colored Fiats flashed across his propeller arc.

In this close combat, the Fiats were at a slight disadvantage because the more maneuverable I-15s would turn inside them, especially if one combined the turn with climb. Finally one of them made a mistake on this point, and Tinker corkscrewed around behind him and held the enemy in the circle of his gunsight for fifteen seconds of firing. The Fiat began trailing a gray ribbon of water from the radiator of its twelve-cylinder liquid-cooled engine, which was followed by black smoke; the enemy rolled over on one wing, slipped into a spin, and went out of control, plunging earthward.

Breaking away from this target, Tinker found another Fiat dead ahead. Its pilot displayed great skill in evasive action, leading Tinker across the sky in a zigzag chase, which the Italian terminated by diving away. Knowing the futility of attempting a diving chase after a Fiat, Tinker turned away and scanned the sky for the rest of his squadron. As he feared, none of his wingmen had managed to stay with him. He was alone. A mile or two off to the south were some specks in the sky, which he took to be Lacalle re-forming the squadron. If so, he was deeper into enemy territory than he had imagined. Then he glanced up and saw, about two thousand feet above him, an echelon of five Fiats whose leader was already diving to attack.

A few thousand feet below, Tinker spotted the comfortable refuge of a huge cloud bank. Clouds do not come in standard sizes, and its exact distance was hard to gauge. But with the Fiat's superior performance in a dive he knew that they would blow him out of the sky before he was halfway to his vaporous objective. The moment called for wit, and he decided to try subterfuge.

Starting a slow dive for the cloud, Tinker watched the Fiats in his rearview mirror as they rolled out of their echelon. When its leader appeared to be lining up to fire, he whipped his I-15 around in a tight vertical bank to the left. A Fiat with its higher wing loading would have been hard put to follow this maneuver in any circumstances, but with the speed built up in its dive, this one found it impossible. All the Italian pilot could do was flash past. Tinker held his controls hard over to come around 360 degrees, bringing himself in astern of the Fiat, and fired a burst after it while the next attacker loomed up in his mirror. He repeated this maneuver twice with the same results. With every second he was getting lower, and by the time the fourth Fiat closed up on him Tinker vanished into the cloud's damp protection.

When he popped out of the cloud a few minutes later, he found himself fly-ing through a dark valley bounded by mountains whose tops were shrouded in clouds. The Fiats were gone, but now he was lost. None of the terrain speeding by below revealed a familiar landmark that might give him a course for Guada-lajara, and he had no maps. So he rolled into a turn that put the lubberline of his compass on 160 degrees. The Republic's air force imposed this general rule shortly after the two Russian pilots got lost in November 1936 and made the Nationalists a gift of their I-15s by landing in Segovia. The rule decreed that when a pilot got lost in the Madrid area, he should fly a compass course of 160 degrees, and sooner or later he would find himself somewhere in the vicinity of Albacete.

But Tinker's point of departure was farther east than he reckoned, and an hour came and went with no sight of Albacete. This might have been owed to compass error because of a lack of care in their installation in the airplanes; Rus-sian compasses were notoriously inaccurate. An I-15's fuel tank held 68.6 gallons; its normal endurance at 160 mph was about two and one-half hours. Tinker had been flying for more than two hours since takeoff, and it included almost fifteen minutes of combat flying at full throttle that ran up fuel consumption. He knew that he was fast approaching a dry tank; he also knew that all of Spain was not as large as the state of Texas, but the Republic's territory alone was beginning to seem incredibly large.[11] Then he climbed over a range of mountains to see the Mediterranean spread across the horizon.

The Mediterranean was more gray than blue on this afternoon of the four-teenth, and its ordinarily pleasant surface was whipped up into miles of whitecaps. From his Breguet days operating out of Manises, he recognized the conspicuous headland of Cape Antonio framed between his starboard wings, realized that he was closer to Valencia than Albacete, and rolled into a turn for the north and for the airfield at Manises less than fifty miles away.

When he flew into Manises a few minutes later, the field was in the clutches of a fierce windstorm, part of a Mediterranean mistral. Circling the field, he saw dozens of soldiers struggling with the awkward bulk of a Fokker F.VIIb3m transport-bomber, trying to prevent it from being blown backward across the field and secure it with tie-downs. Tinker wished that he could circle until the storm blew itself out, but his fuel was almost gone and to attempt a dead-stick landing in the face of such winds would be the height of insanity.

As his wheels touched down on Manises' turf, a terrific gust slammed into his 2,500-pound airplane, bouncing it back into the air at a crazy nose-up angle. Fifty feet above the ground, he felt himself teetering on the edge of a stall, instinctively shoved the throttle wide open, regained control, and finally got three points on the ground. The wind was so strong that his rollout after touchdown was barely thirty feet. Even then he had to keep his engine at half throttle and his stick full forward to prevent the plane from being blown backward or flipped over on its back. A dozen militiamen struggled through the wind to put their weight on his wingtips, which permitted him to taxi to the security of a hangar.

The wind was too high to attempt takeoff for a return to Guadalajara, so Tinker went into Valencia and booked a room at the Hotel Inglés. Then he hiked down the street to see who might be hanging out in the Vodka Café. To his great surprise, he found Jim Allison and Charlie Koch lounging at one of the tables. The infection in Allison's leg had become worse; he had terminated his contract and was returning to the United States. Charlie Koch was still having his stomach troubles; he never again wanted to hear of garlic or olive oil. Allison figured that he would eventually find some flying back in Texas, and Koch hoped that he still had a job with Seversky.

This chance meeting was not only the occasion of a bon voyage party for Allison and Koch, it was also a celebration of Tinker's first victory. And a noisy time was made of it into the wee hours. Tinker nevertheless rose early the next morning, the fifteenth of March, somewhat the worse for wear, to catch a bus to Manises. He expected to get away immediately, but he may as well have slept. He had to wait for a Douglas DC-2 bound for Alcalá that required a fighter escort, and it did not get away until noontime. He and a Russian in another I-15 flew the escort. He never found out who was on board this DC-2, but its passenger manifest probably consisted of a dozen VIPs of the Republic's government en route to the Madrid area to mark the victory of Guadalajara. It was an hour's flight; over Alcalá, Tinker waggled his wings in good-bye to the Russian and the DC-2 and rolled out of the formation for Guadalajara.

Lacalle and his squadron had just returned to Guadalajara from a morning's dive-bombing and shoot-up of Italian motor convoys north of Brihuega and were circling to land when Tinker flew in from Alcalá. So Tinker simply fell in with the landing pattern, taking his place at its end. Consternation ensued among the *caseta de mando*'s ground staff when they discovered that one more airplane had returned than had taken off for the attack. This was most extraordinary! But the squadron recognized Tinker's No. 56 and were delighted at having their American prodigal returned to the fold.

That evening in the Casa de Pilotos the squadron met a new draft of replacement pilots. One of them was Manuel Gomez García, the Guatemalan Tinker had known at Los Alcázares, and there was Hipolito Barbeito, a lively little transport pilot he had met in January at Manises. Another, Justo García Esteban, came without much combat experience, but Tinker instinctively sized him up to be a good fighter pilot. When Lacalle reshuffled the squadron personnel a few days later, Tinker quickly grabbed Justo García for his patrol.

The new pilots arrived in time for an introduction to the nightlife of the Henares Valley, orchestrated by Nationalist bombers. The air raid alarms sounded shortly after dinner, from 9:30 to 11:30 p.m., while Ju 52s, S.81s, and He 111s prowled the darkness overhead. One of their first attacks occurred against Campo X, where they dropped hundreds of small incendiary bombs. But Lacalle still had the squadron based at Guadalajara, and Campo X was empty of airplanes; fortunately, none of the bombs fell among the *finca*'s buildings. Otherwise, they fell all over the countryside without rhyme or reason. The last attacks were against Alcalá and environs, probably in attempt to hit the SB-2 and Polikarpov R-5 Rasante squadrons temporarily based on airfields in that area, but they produced negligible results.

The hours in the *refugio* would prove a nuisance, but they created time for Tinker and Whitey to swap stories with Gomez and Barbeito about what had happened since they had last seen one another back in January. It seemed a long time ago.

The next morning, the sixteenth, Lacalle rushed the squadron into the air at the first blur of dawn with their wings weighted with bombs. They orbited the valley until several squadrons of single-engine Russian ground-attack planes appeared from their bases around Alcalá. These "new" open cockpit biplanes with fixed landing gear, R-5s, were not really new at all because their design dated from 1927. To Tinker they were "huge crates," the same words he used to describe the Breguet 19, and that is pretty much what they were. But with a more powerful inline engine and more imaginative and far superior armament, the two-place R-5 was at least a "Super Breguet 19." The R-5 Rasante, an earlier version of the R-Z Rasante, was the airplane that Gene Finick had told Tinker about sixty days earlier at Manises. In a day when ground troops possessed few rapid-fire antiaircraft weapons and none of any great accuracy, and when the R-5s had a fighter escort to cap their operations, they served effectively as ground-attack airplanes.[12] On this morning the two dozen Rasantes that spiraled up to rendezvous with Lacalle's squadron north of Alcalá not only had his fighters for an escort but also Ivan Kopéts' squadron of I-15s, plus a squadron of I-16 monoplanes as topmost cover.

Their target was a road junction near the small town of Brihuega that commanded a network of secondary roads east of the main Zaragoza-Madrid highway, including one that ran south along the east bank of the Tajuña River. The CTV had planned to use this latter road to outflank Guadalajara and attack Alcalá from the east, but they were stopped by determined Republican resistance south of Brihuega. The CTV had managed to unlimber a respectable number of small-caliber antiaircraft guns in this sector, and the Republican aviators did not have the "free ride" they did along the main highway.

The Rasante biplanes, nevertheless, dove down among the webs of ascending tracers and delivered their attacks with mechanical precision, lumbering over the length of the trench systems. Each Rasante had four fixed 7.62-mm guns under its lower wings and canted downward at 30 degrees so the airplane could strafe from level flight, and each carried twenty-four 55-pound antipersonnel fragmentation bombs. Sweeping the trenches with their guns and cutting loose their bombs at intervals, they reduced about a mile and one-half of trench works to a chain of small craters obscured by a curtain of smoke.

After the Rasantes had cleared the target, Kopéts and his Russians jumped in for a few minutes of dive-bombing and strafing while Lacalle's squadron provided the fighter cap for the Rasantes as they climbed, turned, and plodded off toward Alcalá. When Kopéts and his I-15s had finished, they climbed back to altitude and provided the fighter cap while Lacalle's squadron dived down against the trenches. No enemy aircraft interrupted these extended proceedings.

As Tinker rolled into his dive, he saw dozens of lumpy Russian T-26 light tanks start to squish their way out of the Republican lines toward the CTV positions. Unlike their Italian counterparts, the T-26 mounted a 37-mm cannon and 7.72-mm machine guns. As he released his bombs he saw the Italians, panicked by the sight of the Russian tanks, scramble out of their battered trenchworks and in spite of the bombing and strafing start running for the rear.

At the road junction near Brihuega, chaos ruled supreme in the form of almost a hundred vehicles. Six SB-2s flew in to plant their loads in the midst of it; then Lacalle led his planes down for a series of strafing attacks that increased the confusion. In the midst of his strafing runs, Tinker saw an I-15 fall out of the sky in a ball of fire. Only later did he learn that the Fiats' attempt at penetrating the area was beaten off by Kopéts' squadron—at the cost of this one airplane. At about the same time, Kosenkov's squadron of I-15s swarmed in from the south to assist Kopéts, and two Fiats were shot down before the rest of them retired to the north. Albert Baumler shot down one of the Fiats, but he shared this victory with Alexandrov Zuitov.

On the ground this day, behind the Republican lines, stood *New York Times* correspondent Herbert Matthews. He absolutely salivated over the aerial action that swirled around almost directly above him. A "big dogfight," he cried; it was "a correspondent's dream come true!"[13] In his ecstasy he exclaimed that "surely this world of ours can offer few more thrilling sights." Perhaps so, if the observer knows what he is watching. Matthews did not, and he provided a childishly romanticized picture for his readers, the oddly garbled stuff that still passes for "history" with regard to the Spanish Civil War.

By the time Lacalle and his squadron landed back at Guadalajara, the cloud-filled day was degenerating into drizzle, and everyone figured that their flying day was finished. It was time for lunch and an afternoon of watching the rain. But at 1:30 two red Very flares popped overhead, sending everyone running to their airplanes. The squadron arrived over its sector of the front north of Brihuega in time to intercept five Savoia-Marchetti S.81s. The big trimotored bombers spotted them at the same time and promptly turned away into a shallow dive, speeding away toward their base near Soria. Lacalle rolled the squadron up on its wingtips and turned back for Guadalajara where, again, everyone assumed the day's work had finished.

Just before sundown, however, another double-rocket alarm burst over the field. The squadron sped off northeast to Brihuega where they found the same five S.81s trying to sneak across the lines again. Once again the bombers turned tail, but this time Lacalle gave them a long chase back into their own territory.

While over the Nationalist territory the squadron flew through a few pockets of intense flak. After landing, Tinker discovered that he had a flak hole in each propeller blade. One was about six inches from the blade tip, the other about ten inches; but because of their different sizes they counterbalanced one another.

The day's drizzle finally became rain that shut down flight operations, and the next day, 17 March, a zero ceiling kept operations suspended. In the afternoon General José Miaja, commander in chief of the Ejército Popular (People's Army), visited the squadron. Miaja, a man of sixty-some years, seems to have had no strong initial convictions toward either side of the Spanish conflict, but he had given his oath to the Republic, and that was that. When the war started he led militiamen against Córdoba, where the Nationalists defeated his force. This led extreme leftists to doubt his loyalty, but instead of shooting him (the custom of the hour), they retired him to Valencia. When the Nationalists threatened to take Madrid in October 1936, however, old Miaja was hustled out of retirement and named supreme commander of the defenders with orders to "save the city."

The panic-stricken government under Largo Caballero then abandoned poor old Miaja to his fate and decamped to Valencia.[14] Back in the capital, Miaja could not even obtain an automobile and had to tour the city's defenses on a bicycle. In truth, he had a very able chief of staff in Colonel Vicente Rojo, who possessed the support of the Russians, their equipment, and their International Brigades. Very soon thereafter, the Russians possessed him and Miaja. Now, in March 1937, in the midst of the Guadalajara battle, Miaja was practically a puppet of General Vladimir Goriev, who commanded all Soviet forces in Spain from his suite in Gaylord's Hotel. Goriev's T-26 tanks operated under General Dimitri Pavlov; Jacob Smushkevich in Albacete commanded his air forces; and the gray eminence behind them all: Major Aleksandr Orlov, who directed the NKVD,[15] headquartered in an old monastery in Alcalá de Henares. Without the Soviet Union's tanks, aircraft, other weapons and technical assistance, and the Comintern's timely creation and deployment of the International Brigades, it is likely that the Republic would have collapsed back in November without the drama of the "Battle of Madrid," now in its last phase.[16]

Even if he had been aware of all this, Frank Tinker had no interest in the Byzantinepolitik of the Spanish Republic. On this day the brevity of Miaja's speech to the pilots, and that the general kept Lacalle's squadron standing at attention for the least possible time, most impressed him.

On the spur of the moment, Lacalle decided to show the visiting general just how quickly the squadron could respond to an alarm, and he quietly picked up a Very pistol and fired two flares. Dahl and members of his second patrol had the alert duty. They did not know it was "for show" and they ran to their planes, had the engines ticking over, and taxied out to a downwind position on the field where they waited for the "go" signal to take off. All this executed within twenty seconds. General Miaja was suitably impressed, but the weather remained bad and no flying took place.

On the eve of the Republic's counteroffensive, Miaja's visit was meant as a morale booster for the Republic's first and only all-Spanish fighter squadron. But when Lacalle's pilots arrived at the field on the dawn of 18 March, it was not to join in the Republican counteroffensive but to fly a defensive mission. A double-rocket alarm sent them scrambling off to Brihuega where they intercepted five S.81s. Most probably they were the same five as two days before; if so, they were a persistent fivesome but no more determined. As before, when they saw the I-15s' stubby silhouettes flying toward them, they turned tail and fled back toward Soria. The I-15s returned to Guadalajara.

While the Republican counteroffensive rolled into the morning against CTV forces, Lacalle's squadron was held on the ground as standby fighter cover. Finally, in the afternoon, Lacalle broke out a large military chart and, with a great air of secrecy, showed the patrol leaders their targets. The Italians still held Brihuega, and the counteroffensive would push against this town in particular. Their part in the aerial attack was one of several and had to be coordinated with other squadrons. This would not be the same as shooting up trucks and trenches, and Lacalle wanted to be sure that everyone understood.

After takeoff the squadron rendezvoused with four dozen Rasantes from Alcalá and its satellite airfields, escorted them to Brihuega, and covered their attacks. After the Rasantes finished their work and returned to Alcalá for rearming, Lacalle took his planes down for a dive-bombing attack, but no strafing. Instead, they made a quick climb-out and orbited the area just under the cloud base to provide a fighter cap. Somewhere above the clouds there circled a squadron of I-16 monoplanes. This remained standard tactics: I-15s flew escort on the slow Rasantes or provided a cap for the fast SB-2 twin-engine bombers to prevent enemy fighters from interrupting their bomb runs, while the high performance I-16s provided top cover for the whole operation.

While Lacalle's squadron circled Brihuega, a half-dozen SB-2s sped in low to drop their bombs on Italian artillery positions. Then the four dozen Rasantes, which had bombed earlier, returned with new loads from Alcalá, dropped down to treetop height, and distributed their bombs along the Italian trenches. A few minutes later another squadron of SB-2s roared in for a second strike against the artillery positions. Then the Republican T-26 tanks lurched out of their concealments and crawled across the battlefield. The time for fighter cover had ended, and the moment for ground support had arrived; Lacalle waggled his wings and waved the attack signal. He rolled into his strafing run and everyone followed. And so it went, again and again, until their ammunition was exhausted and they had to return to Guadalajara.[17]

Back at the airfield, which was adjacent to the railway and main highway from the north, the pilots found that their mechanics had been amusing themselves by chalking up counts of captured Italian motor vehicles moving down the highway toward Guadalajara. According to Tinker, they had counted more than eight hundred thus far. This number is terribly exaggerated; one hundred would have been more likely. It is possible, however, that the mechanics actually saw something like eight hundred Italian vehicles pass by—driven around and around again by circuitous routes devised by the genius of Communist propagandists—for credulous spectators who would enthusiastically spread the word.

By sundown on 18 March, the first day of the Republic's counteroffensive, the Battle of Guadalajara was practically finished. The Italians broke and ran, but not very far. The Republic's army did not pursue the CTV back to Soria, or to Sigüenza, or even to their jumping-off point of Algora. For lack of the Republic's dynamics, the Italians managed to stabilize a line between Argecilla in the west and Masegoso de Tajuña in the east, which was ten miles south of the line from which they launched their offensive three weeks earlier.

In 1937 most western newspapers trumpeted Guadalajara as a "great victory" for the Republic and a Nationalist disaster. To be sure, it was a political disaster for the Italian intervention in Spain. Although the Republic's Loyalists had succeeded in preserving Madrid, they had achieved little else; moreover, they could not know that this would be the "only actual battle" they would clearly win in the entire civil war.[18] Few appreciated in 1937 or thereafter that the Republic's forces failed to drive the Italians back to their original lines of 8 March, much less beyond them. When the lines stabilized, the Nationalists held more than a hundred square miles of hitherto Republican territory, although it was neither a great gain for them nor an important loss to the Republic. Perhaps the most significant aspect of this battle was that the CTV's offensive—the first executed by a relatively modern army—initially had been brought to a standstill by air attacks alone.[19]

Ernest Hemingway liked to compare the Italian defeat at Guadalajara to Italy's military disaster at Caporetto in World War I. His assessment, picked up and widely disseminated, has echoed across the twentieth century. But the two are hardly comparable. At Caporetto, Italy lost some 300,000 men and the whole province of Venezia-Giulia; relative to this, Guadalajara was simply a massive firefight conducted within an arena not as large as metropolitan Los Angeles at the cost of 2,000 dead and about 3,000 wounded.[20] Guadalajara became the Nationalists' fourth act in the bloody battle for Madrid that had started in the Casa de Campo five months earlier. In a sense, it can be regarded as another Bull Run. And just as the outcome of the American Civil War was not decided by any "Battle of Washington, D.C.," neither was the Spanish Civil War determined by any of the battles for Madrid. Actions far away from their respective capital cities ultimately decided both conflicts.

9

RAIL TARGETS
AND RURAL RELAXATION

With the Battle of Guadalajara grinding down, the Nationalist forces falling back, and the weather turning bad again, everyone lounged around the field house at Guadalajara playing cards or dominoes. By midmorning of 19 March 1937, a small patch of brightness appeared in the low gray ceiling, suggesting that it might be about to break up, and Lacalle told Tinker to take advantage of the first hole in the overcast to make a reconnaissance flight to the north. Tinker chose Justo Garcia for his wingman. Garcia had been born and reared near Guadalajara and knew well its surrounding terrain. It was afternoon before the weather let them off the ground, and they sped away to Cogolludo, a small town the Spanish Nationalist columns under General Moscardo had seized early in the offensive. Unlike the Italians, the Nationalists were falling back slowly, in good order, and they never did give up Cogolludo.

East of Cogolludo they picked up the railway line near Jadraque and flew on north to Sigüenza, where they cut across to the Zaragoza-Madrid highway, which was the main avenue of the Italians' retreat. Here they turned south and followed the highway back to Guadalajara. The ceiling had risen to 1,600 feet, but they found it expedient to fly at 300 feet, where they were too close to the ground for heavy antiaircraft weapons to be used against them. Nevertheless, the air on occasion became thick with small arms fire, which sent them jinking. As they returned across the front lines and roared over the Republican trenches, hundreds of soldiers recognized the airplanes' red striping and stood up to give its pilots the Republic's right-arm, clenched-fist salute.

Tinker and Garcia had little to report. A lot of small truck convoys, a couple of trains—all headed north. But the weather clamped down again; it was pointless to organize an attack. Lacalle busied himself with a reorganization of the squadron, in anticipation of a draft of new pilots when the old squadron would be divided in half to create cadres for two squadrons. As a first step, he created a fourth patrol and made Manuel Gomez its leader.

The reorganized squadron got off to an early start on 20 March with a double-rocket alarm at dawn, which sent them off to their sector near Brihuega. Tinker fully expected to see the familiar five S.81s sneaking across the lines again, but the sky was empty. Hidden among the muddy clouds off to the southeast, however, Kosenkov's squadron had intercepted the enemy—three S.81s and five Fiats. The bombers promptly turned and ran while the Fiats covered them. In the ensuing dogfight, Albert Baumler shot down one Fiat and sent it spinning into the Republic's side of the lines.

As soon as they returned to Guadalajara, Lacalle had the planes bombed up for an afternoon cooperating with Rasantes and escorting a squadron of SB-2 light bombers against targets near the village of Masegoso. Here the Italians held a small salient on the east bank of the Tajuña River to protect the left flank of their offensive, and it was now covering their retreat. The first attack went well, but when they returned for a second strike, they ran head-on into an enemy attack under way by three S.81s escorted by a dozen Fiats. These probably were the same S.81s Kosenkov had driven off a few hours earlier; meanwhile, they had taken the precaution of increasing their escort numbers.

While the Rasantes plodded on to their targets, Lacalle's squadron jettisoned its bombs and climbed for the enemy. Lacalle led his patrol against the bombers, which also jettisoned their loads and fled back toward Soria. Dahl led his patrol to the left against the Fiats, which sought cover in the heavy clouds. Tinker took the Fiats on the right, but while flying through a cloud Garcia became lost, and Tinker emerged with only Rafael Magriña on his wing. They found only three Fiats, and two of them promptly dove away into the clouds.

The third Fiat very gamely turned to meet his attackers and attempted to out-maneuver them. It was a fatal error. Tinker managed to swing around behind the Fiat and hold him in his gunsight for thirty seconds of firing. There was no fire, but the four streams of tracers chopped the Fiat's after fuselage into shreds; it rolled over into a downward spin that ended on the earth five thousand feet below.

Meanwhile, Gomez led his new fourth patrol against the uppermost formation of Fiats. Or at least he thought he was leading his patrol. Upon closing with the enemy, he discovered that in his climb he had lost his wingmen in the clouds. He was alone, and the five Fiats made fast work of him. A few days later Lacalle told squadron members that Gomez had crash-landed in Republican territory and was hospitalized with serious wounds; later yet they had word that Gomez had died.

As the Nationalists fell back, their lines finally hardened; each side dug in, and the pace of war between the Henares and Tajuña gradually stagnated. On 21 March heavy rains kept everyone grounded, and the next day the field was too wet for use. The next five days were punctuated by double-rocket alarms, sometimes twice a day, sending the squadron north to Brihuega and occasionally south to the Jarama. When they arrived over their sector the bombers inevitably spotted them and turned away, or else the sky was empty. And there was more rain, more mud, and more bad field conditions.

Whitey Dahl had never managed to get his stomach adjusted to Spanish cooking, and he suddenly became seized by severe abdominal cramps. A doctor put him on a diet of goat's milk and eggs, but he got no better. Captain Agustín Sanz Sáinz, now chief of the headquarters air base at Alcalá, who still handled the affairs of the American aviators in the Madrid area, visited the field with mail for Whitey and Tinker. He was shocked at Whitey's condition and took him off to a hospital in Madrid. That was the last Tinker saw of Whitey for almost three months.

Shortly after Whitey Dahl had gone off to Madrid, a staff car from Kopéts' headquarters in Alcalá arrived at the field looking for Chang Sellés. His linguistic abilities were needed at Alcalá to assist with interpreting and translation work. Or at least that is how it was explained. After Chang left, Tinker suddenly felt very much alone: he was the only one left of the old Patrulla Americano.

On 23 March, three of the Legion Condor's He 111s sped through the Republic's air defense system to drop four tons of bombs on Alcalá. The only casualty was the *jefe del aeródromo*, Augustín Sanz Sáinz; a few days later the little Spaniard who had returned from across the ocean to assist the Republic died in a Madrid hospital.[1]

Ivan Kopéts (*Courtesy of Andrey Simonov*)

Then Lacalle called the squadron together and announced that he had been promoted to commandante (major) and would be transferred to headquarters to take command of the fighter group formerly headed by Senior Lieutenant Ivan Kopéts (aka "José"). This fighter group included Kopéts' and Kosenkov's squadrons of Russians, and Lacalle's old squadron. Another Russian was taking over Kopéts' squadron, while Kopéts moved up to command all aerial operations in the Madrid area. Everyone was pleased with Lacalle's promotion, but everything else came as a shock. The realignment ended La Esquadrilla de Lacalle.

Lacalle's first choice for a new squadron leader was Whitey Dahl, whom he regarded as an outstanding combat pilot. But aside from Whitey being hospitalized, Lacalle had to discount him as being too irresponsible. His second choice was Frank Tinker. Lacalle regarded Tinker as not only an extraordinary pilot, but, remarkably enough, quite sober and responsible, a true unit member who did not charge off on his own. But Lacalle had to face the fact that Tinker's Spanish was inadequate; he might do a brilliant job of leading the squadron in the air, but he was not up to handling the administrative and political duties of command on the ground.[2]

Lacalle finally selected José Riverola, a relatively new pilot but one whose aggressive flying and sober military character created great confidence. This decision had hardly been reached, however, when the old squadron was essentially divided in half to create two; Riverola's half was assigned to a flight in the north to relieve Bilbao, while the other part was given to the command of Alfonso Jiménez Bruguet, and this was the squadron in which Tinker remained. Like Lacalle, Jiménez had been a sergeant pilot before the war, and since December he had been flying with Kosenkov's squadron of five Russians, nine Spaniards, and one American—Albert Baumler. Jiménez was a good pilot, but, as events would prove, he possessed neither the innate personal qualities needed for leadership, nor the tactful diplomacy of his predecessor, Lacalle. But any new commander would have been hard put to fill the shoes of someone as versatile and popular as Andrés García Lacalle.

Indeed, Jiménez quickly got off on the wrong foot with his new squadron. He posted an order that rotated the pilots' alert duties in numerical order, two hours at a stretch; and while on alert they not only had to be fully dressed in flying clothes, with parachutes, but also seated in their airplanes instead of standing ready in the alert facility. This was absurd. Even after thirty minutes of sitting in a cramped cockpit on the ground, working up a sweat inside a fleece-lined flying suit, a pilot was certain to be less effective than if he climbed into his plane fresh, his muscles loose. Lacalle had permitted each of the patrols to work out their own watch lists; Jiménez's rigid rules suggested that he did not trust his pilots. This matter of trust would soon become a serious issue, the squadron members losing whatever trust they initially had in Jiménez—and it would have its consequences.

Meanwhile, the Ju 52s, S.81s, and He 111s visited the Henares Valley nightly, seldom hitting anything of importance but interrupting a lot of sleep. The Russians, however, had been busy for several weeks installing searchlight batteries around the valley, and on the night of 25 March the Nationalist bombers were surprised when hundreds of thin fingers of milky-white light stabbed through the darkness to illuminate their passage for the benefit of the antiaircraft guns. The bomber crews evidently required some time to think about this new development, because for the next few nights they stayed on their own side of the Sierras.

At the end of March two new pilots joined the squadron, Mariano Palacios and Manuel Zarauza Clavero, and Jiménez ordered Tinker to break them in with three flights. Each was an "emergency" running start from their starter trucks. In the air Tinker found them both a bit timid about holding a tight formation, and he landed with a stiff arm as a result of waving to them, again and again, to close up. Starting out gently, he worked them into more complex and violent maneuvers; and when he considered that neither of the new pilots had a hundred hours in their flight logs, he thought they had done exceptionally well. Tinker was most impressed with Zarauza, who seemed to anticipate all of his maneuvers, followed through beautifully, and displayed all the characteristics of a born fighter pilot.

That evening Tinker recommended to Jiménez that Zarauza be given leadership of the fourth patrol. This resulted in a bitter argument; Jiménez thought Zarauza too new, but Tinker finally won his point. A few months later, after being transferred out of the squadron, Zarauza distinguished himself on the beleaguered northern front around Bilbao and Santander; he later commanded a squadron of I-16s and in 1938 became a group commander.[3]

With the constant rain continuing into early April, flying gave way to too much sitting around the field house and too many arguments over which of the squadron's automobiles the pilots could use for their forays into Madrid. As a result of Jiménez's intervention, Tinker, Garcia, and Magriña tended to lose out in these arguments, while Elias, the Russian interpreter, always won. Tempers were not cooled by a series of violent hailstorms that left the airfield covered with an inch of ice.

One cold, stormy evening Tinker visited the house in Azuqueca where Maria and Christina lived with the old woman who functioned as landlady and *dueña* (chaperone). He brought his accordion with him, and while the rain beat on the roof and the wind rattled the windows, they all sat around the fireplace with Tinker playing and everyone singing. One number he had added to his repertoire, recovered from memory, was "In a Little Spanish Town"—which thereafter always reminded him of Azuqueca.

A loud knock at the door interrupted the pleasant evening. It was Justo Garcia. Everyone in the squadron was scouring the village for Tinker. A couple of Russians from Alcalá had come to dinner and they had brought an American with them: Albert Baumler. Tinker made his good-byes to the girls and the señora and joined Garcia in the icy rain for the walk to the Casa de Pilotos.

Tinker and Baumler considered driving into Madrid for a small celebration but decided the night was too nasty. This was a pity. They missed meeting Errol

Flynn, the Hollywood hero of so many picaresque films. Flynn had hung his fencing foil in the Hotel Florida for two days as one of a growing number of American celebrity "war tourists" who simply *had* to put war-torn Madrid on their European itinerary. A day later, while Flynn viewed a bombardment of Madrid from the hulk of a building in the Parque del Oeste, a Nationalist shell burst nearby and jarred loose a big piece of plaster that clobbered him on the head, allegedly knocking him cold. Thus having been "wounded" on the Madrid front, Flynn hurried back to Paris.[4]

As it turned out, the evening was pleasant enough in the Casa de Pilotos. The Russians had brought a dozen bottles of champagne, and it was a lively dinner. Christina had been curious about Chang, so Tinker asked Baumler if he had seen him. Baumler didn't even know that Chang was supposed to be in his unit. A Russian general of the secret police operated a prison in Alcalá; perhaps they had Chang interrogating captured aviators there. But Baumler had seen Whitey Dahl, who looked terrible; Lacalle had given him leave to go to Paris for medical attention.

Baumler had heard rumors from Alcalá that there might be a new offensive in the south against Extremadura, but other rumors pointed to the Madrid front. Both Americans wondered how they could get assigned to the same squadron. Baumler thought that Kosenkov might be able to swing it—with a few words to Ivan Kopéts. When the party finally broke up, Tinker felt much better, and the champagne had nothing to do with it.

On the morning of 3 April, Tinker and Garcia took off under a low ceiling for a reconnaissance of the north. This was not an easy flight for Tinker; his engine was overdue for overhaul, was leaking oil badly, and after thirty minutes in the air, his windshield was obscured by an oil film. To keep his gunsight clean he flew with a cap over its front lens; he could poke it off when combat appeared imminent. But the most ominous aspect of his faithful No. 56 these days were the vibrations created by the two flak holes in his propeller. As yet no spare propellers had been received.

Speeding north beneath a cloud layer that hung at three hundred feet, Tinker and Garcia spotted several small concentrations of trucks. But the most interesting sight occurred near the village of Baides, where they found three trains standing in the station. All three pointed north, which indicated that the enemy was still pulling out of the area in a big way.

They hurried back to Guadalajara, where Jiménez ordered all the planes bombed up; but then the leaden ceiling descended into the treetops, a thick drizzle filled the air, and everyone returned to the field house and their cards and dominoes. Daylight, such as it was, dissolved into darkness, the attack was cancelled, and everyone imagined that their fat targets had steamed away unscathed to Sigüenza and safety.

Dawn arrived on 4 April with broken clouds and patches of blue sky, and Jiménez hurried the squadron into the air with the hope that one of the trains might still be standing in Baides. To their great surprise they found all three still there; two of them were in sidings, the third was on the main line preparing to pull out for Sigüenza. Tinker was certain that his reconnaissance of yesterday must have raised an alarm, but Baides was so far behind Nationalist lines, and they had been flying so low, the enemy must have confused them with their own aircraft operating out of fields at nearby Almaluez. So much the worse for them.

As the alarm spread on the ground, the train on the main line immediately started chuffing away. This was a mistake because its motion made for a relatively longer target. Jiménez's first patrol went down after it, planting their bombs around the locomotive, whose boiler disappeared in a great cloud of steam. The rest of the train tended to crumple up in a zigzag of cars. The other patrols dived on the trains in the sidings, trying to put their bombs between the two so that even if they missed, one or the other train would be straddled.

The bombs were only twenty-five pounds, but any one of them was enough to derail one of the small European freight cars. But as it happened, some bomb fragments punctured tank cars spliced into the trains, and some of them contained gasoline that exploded in high order, showering the area with flaming fuel. And what the bombing missed, fifteen minutes of strafing finished, turning Baides into a burning shambles. Tinker cheerfully estimated that this was the most destructive flight the squadron had ever made. The nicest part: there was not an antiaircraft gun anywhere in the neighborhood. All in all, it proved to be a very good day.

Shortly after the squadron's return to Guadalajara, the weather deteriorated once more, and a bitter wind came screaming down the snow-covered slopes of the Sierras, filling the valley with a bone-chilling cold. But cold as it was for the pilots huddled around their stove in the field house, they were living in the lap of luxury compared with the miserable foot soldiers in their trenches and dugouts in the lines around Utande, Ledanca, and Masegoso de Tajuña only twenty miles to the north. And when the sun went down, the pilots clambered on board their bus that took them back to the Casa de Pilotos in Azuqueca, to a warm dinner and a dry bed.

A fierce thunderstorm lashed Guadalajara the next day, dumping tons of wet snow and icy slush on the airfield. Flying was out of the question, so Tinker asked permission for his patrol to make a quick run into Madrid. Jiménez wouldn't hear of it; everyone had to remain on the field until sundown. Tinker and Garcia argued that the weather was so thick no one could guess when the sun went down, much less get into the air in the meantime. But Jiménez was one of those who found refuge in a rulebook, and he simply dug in his heels.

Jiménez's unreasonableness irritated Velasco, a pilot of the fourth patrol noted for his short temper. He jumped into the argument to support Tinker. It became hot and heavy, and when Tinker realized Jiménez was not about to change his mind, he suddenly accused Elias, the Russian interpreter, of having appropriated the third patrol's automobile. Then Garcia and Magriña jumped in. A great shouting match ensued. Jiménez finally shouted down everybody by ordering all of them out of the field house and back to their airplanes. And a day of bad weather ended with equally bad feelings.

The morning of 6 April dawned with promising weather, but dark clouds remained in the minds of the squadron members as a result of the previous evening's arguments. Jiménez ordered Tinker to fly another reconnaissance to the north, but this time as far as El Burgo de Osma, which was considerably beyond the territory with which they were familiar. When Tinker asked for a map, Jiménez gave him a tattered old Michelin road map that was virtually useless. He was able to convince Jiménez that his old No. 56 was not trustworthy for so long a flight, especially deep into enemy territory, so he was given No. 60, an airplane in better mechanical condition.

After takeoff Tinker and Garcia sped north to Cogolludo, scouting the back roads to its north for any activity, and then began climbing to top the five-thousand-foot crests of the Sierra de las Cabras. The weather had been poor when they took off, but once north of the Sierras it turned bad. The cloud cover became so thick Tinker decided that they would be unable to see anything, so he signaled Justo to turn for home. But Tinker had waited too long. The clouds behind them had completely closed in on the mountains. To the west and north lay enemy territory, and they were cut off from the south, so Tinker swung east and dove for the deck where he picked up a highway. Then he began studying his wretched map for a village, river, or crossroads that would provide some idea of where they were. At this point, in the open cockpit, the tired old map tore in half and the draft across the open cockpit sucked half of it out into the slipstream— the eastern half, of course.

Following the highway along the northern slope of the Sierras, the ceiling continued to lower until it seemed as if they were in a race with zero-zero visibility. Finally the ground began to fall away and the path between the mountain slopes widened; they found themselves in a valley somewhere around the rail junction of Ariza. This was still Nationalist territory. Although Tinker had only the vaguest idea of where they were, he sensed it was time to turn south. A few minutes later they were streaking over the forested ridges of the Serranía de Cuenca, the clouds suddenly began to break up, and they flew out into the broad, sun-filled valley of the Júcar.

Tinker thought he recognized the valley as part of the plain on which Albacete was situated, but he could not be sure. They had been flying for two hours and, though uncertain about his position, he was quite certain of one thing: in a few minutes his Cyclone engine would be protesting a lack of fuel. While keeping his eyes peeled for any promising stretch of landing ground, he spotted a small emergency landing field on which he and Garcia wasted no time in setting down.

The airfield had not been used in many months, and it had no facilities whatever, not even a fuel cache. A peasant who lived nearby and served as the field's caretaker told them that they were about three miles east of Villanueva de la Jara. Albacete was only about thirty miles away to the south, but neither pilot believed that they had enough fuel to fly even that short distance. What is more, neither felt like "dipping" the fuel tanks to find out. They were exhausted, and no doubt it would be pleasant to be "out" for a day. There seemed no point in hurrying back to Guadalajara for another argument with the irascible Jiménez.

Unlike the chilled valley of the Henares, spring came early to the Júcar Valley, and Tinker and Garcia had a long, hot walk into town, sweating profusely in their fleece-lined flying clothes. The military commander of the local hospital had the only telephone in town, and here Garcia took charge and phoned Jiménez, who promised immediate assistance from Albacete. After that there was nothing to do but wait—and enjoy the hospitality of Villanueva de la Jara.

It was sundown before a starter truck with gasoline and oil arrived from Albacete, chaperoned by a Russian, and by the time the airplanes had been serviced it was too late to attempt a takeoff. Furthermore, by this time Tinker and Justo were really tired, not only from their flight and hike into the village, but as a result of an afternoon of entertainment by its leading citizens. The *alcalde*, the town's mayor, felt most honored by their presence. It had been a long time since airplanes had operated from Villanueva de la Jara; moreover, he treated the appearance of Tinker and Garcia, the first fighter pilots, as a great occasion.

They had dinner in the *alcalde*'s home, and Tinker found himself fascinated by the building's ancient structure of heavy stone masonry. The house did not have a dining room and kitchen, but rather a large combination cooking and eating room distinguished by a huge open hearth in the center of its floor with a conical ceiling overhead, like an inverted funnel, whose flue served to keep the room free of smoke.

Because the *alcalde* had invited the head of each house that Tinker and Garcia had visited, his cooking room was quite crowded. While the men sat in a circle around the hearth drinking wine and talking, the women laid a slow fire in the middle of the hearth. One of the *alcalde*'s daughters brought in a large iron skillet and a freshly butchered kid. Known as *cabrito*, it is considered a luxury in Spain and in most Latin American countries. Not only is the meat tender and tasty, but in a rural world there is the all-important economic fact that by eating the *cabrito* one necessarily sacrifices the animal's future services as a goat.

Tinker watched with great interest as the *alcalde*'s wife and two daughters greased the skillet and carefully wiped it with garlic, onion, and other season-ings, and then began cutting up the *cabrito* into small pieces. The skillet was then placed on the hearth, and those pieces of the *cabrito* that had been cut off were tossed onto the grill while the women proceeded to cut up the rest.

While Justo, Tinker, and the *alcalde* were talking over their wine, the *alcalde* suddenly produced a clasp knife. Opening the knife, he reached out and grabbed up the *cabrito*'s carcass by its hindquarters and neatly cut off its scrotum. The *alcalde* surgically extracted the testicles, split them open, and wrapped them in some damp leaves; then he placed them in the hot embers beneath the skillet. Puzzled, Tinker gave this peculiar procedure no further thought.

About twenty minutes later the *alcalde* raked the testicles out of the fire, removed their charred wrappings, and told Tinker and Justo that because they were the guests of honor, these choicest parts were theirs! Tinker had done a lot of hunting in his youth, had dressed many an animal carcass, and was not squeamish, but in this moment he felt his stomach do a snap roll. Justo sensed his distress and called for some special condiments to give his companion a few minutes in which to readjust his ideas of what constituted *hors d'oeuvres*. Tinker finally wolfed down his tidbit, licking his chops with a big smile, as if he had been doing it all his life, much to the pleasure of the *alcalde* and his other guests.

Another hour passed before dinner was served, at which time the skillet was removed from the hearth and placed before the semicircle of guests. The women of the household gave each person a round, flat loaf of bread about six inches in diameter and a sharp knife. Tinker was wondering what to do for a plate when Justo again intervened, this time to play Emily Post. The bread was held in one's lap and served as the plate. Pieces of meat and vegetables were speared from the pan and cut up on the bread and eaten, with pieces of bread carved from the rim of the loaf. Meanwhile, the loaf soaked up all the juices, and by the time the diner had reduced the loaf to its center, he had an unusually tasty piece of bread to eat. Tinker would remember this meal as one of the most satisfying he had ever had. Afterward, the *alcalde* took Tinker and Garcia to visit a few homes overlooked previously in the afternoon before showing them their quarters for the night. For the two aviators, the unexpected rural day off proved a marvelous, relaxing interlude in the grim business of aerial combat operations.

They arose early the next morning to find a Russian pilot awaiting them with a car. He had brought some mechanics up from Albacete and had dropped them off with the I-15s en route to the *alcalde*'s home, so when they arrived at the field they found the airplane engines already ticking over, all warmed up. This was service! But that was not all. Once in the cockpit, the Russian gave Tinker a nine-by-five-inch red-bound volume entitled *Mapa de la Peninsula Iberica* that contained an excellent set of 1:1,000,000 meter charts of Spain and Portugal, artfully bound with internal folds for use in the cramped space of an airplane's cockpit. For the rest of his time in Spain, Tinker guarded this book of maps with great jealousy.[5]

Now equipped with a real aviation map, Tinker and Garcia departed the warm Júcar Valley to return quickly to the cold weather in Guadalajara. Sure enough, Jiménez met them on landing and publicly chastised them for losing their way and causing concern all around, but Tinker and Justo would have none of it. They admonished him for sending them out on a deep reconnaissance mission in bad weather and without a proper map. Tinker pulled out the Russian's book of charts and with a wry smile waved it at Jimenez, and that closed the subject. Tinker's mechanic, Chamorro, who was present for the exchange, had become accustomed to his periodic evenings away. He shrugged his shoulders and declared for all to hear: "*Un centime malo siempre volvera*" (A bad penny always returns).

The next day, 8 April, Jiménez ordered Tinker and Garcia out on another reconnaissance mission, but this time equipped with an excellent aviation map of the region to be surveilled. The two scouted behind the Guadalajara front and found nothing of note. No Nationalist troops, trucks, or trains were to be seen. The Italians appeared to have completely evacuated the area. Hearing this finding on their return to Guadalajara, Ivan Kopéts seemed well pleased; he intimated that their squadron might soon have more interesting things to do.

On the morning of the ninth the whole squadron roared off into the dawn to make dive-bombing and strafing attacks on the Nationalist positions in the Casa de Campo, the high ground that overlooked the Manzanares River and Madrid. It was in the Casa de Campo that the Republic first stopped the Nationalists back in November and prevented them from overrunning Madrid. Static trench warfare had prevailed since then, but when Jiménez led the squadron down against the Nationalist trenches this morning, it signaled the opening of a Republican offensive. Or at least it was supposed to appear that way. In fact, this "offensive" was a feint intended to distract the Nationalists from their mounting pressure on Bilbao and the north.

Except for sniping and occasional artillery duels, the war in the Casa de Campo had settled into fixed routines on both sides of the lines, and this morning's dive-bombing attack took the Nationalists completely by surprise. There was no antiaircraft fire whatever. After releasing their bombs, Jiménez led his I-15s low over Madrid's red-tiled rooftops to re-form the squadron over the Plaza de Toros—the conspicuous circle of the bull ring providing an excellent rendezvous point—for a strafing attack. A total of four aerial attacks were made, each one awakening more antiaircraft gun crews, and by their final pass the air had become unpleasantly thick with flak. The roar of their engines so low overhead also awakened Madrid, and as Tinker flew back from his attacks at rooftop height he saw the roofs, balconies, and windows filled with hundreds of Madrileños waving scarves and obviously cheering. This was the first time in more than two months that the Madrileños had seen a large force of the Republic's airplanes active over the city. They enjoyed the moment, certain that the hated Nationalist artillery batteries in the Casa de Campo finally were receiving a small dose of their own bitter medicine.

After landing back at Guadalajara Tinker determined that the four strenuous attacks had taken the last life out of his I-15. But only after much complaining was he given another one—and it was not really new. But at least its propeller didn't have any flak holes in it, and the fabric of its wings and fuselage had fewer patches than old No. 56, which was turned in for a complete overhaul. Although unaware of it, he would not fly that airplane again. His mount for the next thirty days would be No. 58.

The squadron returned to Madrid for a second round of attacks in the late afternoon. But without top cover, no one in the squadron liked the assignment. All kinds of Heinkel and Fiat fighters could be hiding in the glare of the late afternoon sun behind the Casa de Campo. Moreover, some of the pilots thought Jiménez careless in his choice of approaches to the targets. Fortunately, no fighters appeared, but the Nationalists had brought in more than a few new flak batteries, and the air was full of the deadly stuff, plus much heavier small arms fire. Remarkably, none of the I-15s was shot down, but their mechanics in Guadalajara would work overtime repairing the numerous airplanes that sustained battle damage from enemy gunfire.

For this "matinee" performance, more spectators than ever crowded the rooftops of Madrid. At that time Madrid's population numbered just over one million inhabitants, and Tinker guessed that during the aerial attacks, "At least half of them were on housetops, in the windows of the taller buildings, and out in the open streets. The fact that the air was full of shrapnel and bullets didn't seem to bother them at all. . . . We could see [them] jumping up and down and waving everything they could lay hands on."

As suddenly as it started, this decoy offensive against the Casa de Campo abruptly concluded. Perhaps this was owed to the heavy rains that filled the next two days keeping all airplanes grounded. But when the sun finally reappeared and the airfields dried out, the attacks were not resumed. On one of those rainy days Tinker and his patrol managed to slip into Madrid for an evening. He had the first fitting of his new dental plate and then met the others for the ritual hot bath and champagne at the Hotel Florida.

On 13 April Tinker and Justo flew a reconnaissance of the north, which by now had become a familiar track. The only extraordinary sight was six Italian tanks clattering down the road toward Guadalajara. This was something new, and when it was reported to Kopéts in Alcalá he immediately ordered an attack against them. Meanwhile, the tanks had found a camouflaged shelter somewhere, because when Jiménez's squadron scouted the area they were not to be seen. But a truck convoy had the bad luck to blunder down the road at just that moment, so the flight did not go to waste. The squadron spent a half-hour bombing and strafing the hapless convoy.

During his first attack on this convoy, after he pulled his bomb release, Tinker felt his airplane shudder with a terrible jolt. At first he thought it a result of antiaircraft fire, but no flak was to be seen. After that there were too many things to be done and no time to brood over it. He pulled the airplane out of its dive and climbed for altitude to begin his strafing attacks.

After Tinker landed, taxied his airplane to its dispersal point, and cut its engine, Chamorro took him by the hand and led him around to the I-15's tail. Chamorro pointed out that one of the two struts that supported the right horizontal stabilizer had carried away. Now Tinker understood the "jolt." He had entered his dive too steeply and skidded slightly to the right when he released his bombs. One bomb from the right wing must have struck the stabilizer's supporting struts; the impact broke the forward one, but the after one held fast. Of such things fatal accidents are made, and when they don't occur it's called "luck." Tinker reflected upon the terrific elevator forces he had put on the stabilizer during his dives and pullouts from the strafing attacks, and was surprised—most pleasantly surprised—that the weakened tailplane had not completely failed and sent him spinning to earth.

That afternoon a beautiful red Lockheed Orion transport materialized out of the low ceiling and landed at Guadalajara to refuel. This was one of "*Der Rotte Orions*," with which Swissair introduced American speed to the European airways in late 1931, and which had an electric effect upon European airlines.[6] Like so many of Europe's civil airplanes, in late 1936 it "disappeared" into the clandestine secondhand airplane market to reappear south of the Pyrenees. So colorful an airplane was a rare bird at Guadalajara, but Tinker was even more surprised to discover that its pilot was an American—Joseph Rosmarin, whose wife he and Whitey had met in Albacete.

Both Tinker and Rosmarin enjoyed their providential meeting, however brief, if only for the opportunity to speak English for awhile. Because of his age and lack of military flying experience Rosmarin had been rejected as a fighter pilot, but the Republic had been pleased to accept his services as a ferry and transport pilot. During his first month he was kept busy ferrying French airplanes from

Toulouse to Barcelona and Valencia. Flying transports in wartime Spain was interesting work; a man got around and saw a bit of everything. He and his Orion had had more than a few close scrapes.

On one flight he almost wiped out during a landing at Linares, the Rasante base on the Cordoba front. Unknown to Rosmarin, the airfield had been hit by Nationalist bombers only a few hours earlier. Demolition personnel had stacked some unexploded bombs near one boundary of the airfield and laid out cloth panels to warn pilots away from the area. Rosmarin had failed to see the panels; he flared out for his landing and brought the Orion over the fence when the demolition crew detonated the bombs almost directly beneath him. The Orion was tossed violently upward, but he managed to regain control and bring her down to a three-point landing. An ambulance greeted him when he taxied up to the field house; everyone was concerned for the well-being of his passengers. They were shocked to discover that Rosmarin's only "passengers" were several thousand rounds of machine gun ammunition.

Within the hour Rosmarin's Orion was serviced. He and Tinker said their good-byes, and Rosmarin took off for Albacete. They had met by chance; they never saw each other again.

Everything at Guadalajara seemed to have quieted down. The next day, 15 April, there would be no dawn reconnaissance to the north. Nor would there be any alarms sending the squadron to Brihuega or to the Jarama. And the Nationalist night bomber remained strangely inactive. Rumor had it that they had all been moved north for the Nationalist offensive against Bilbao. And there were rumors of a Republican offensive against Huesca; a few squadrons from Alcalá already had flown to Lérida.

The rains had stopped, and Tinker wondered how long it would be before the airfield at Campo X would be dry enough to support airplanes at Azuqueca again. Then, at noon, Jiménez issued surprise orders to the squadron assembled in the field house: Pack a small bag with toiletries and clothing that could be stowed in an I-15, and report to the airfield. They would be gone for a week.

Where?

Jiménez wouldn't say. At that moment, perhaps even he didn't know. But the time for the much-rumored aerial move was at hand.

10

ACTION AT TERUEL
AND ON THE GRAN VÍA

When the pilots arrived with their gear at the Guadalajara airfield on the afternoon of 15 April 1937, they still did not know where they were going. The new pilots were excited; they speculated about being sent to Don Benito in the west for a long-rumored offensive against Merida in Extremadura. (One of them, Juan Comas Barrás, would command his own squadron of I-15s by September and have a distinguished combat flying career, becoming an ace and group commander before a serious wound grounded him in late 1938.) After all the rumors, the veterans stoically suggested that most likely they would fly to Barajas, all of thirty miles away, to temporarily relieve another squadron. Only after they had stowed their small bags on board the planes and had started turning over their engines did Jiménez announce their destination: Sarrión on the Teruel front.

After takeoff, Jiménez led the squadron to a rendezvous point south of Alcalá where a dozen I-15s spiraled up to meet them. Roberto Alonso Santamaría commanded this squadron, and, after Lacalle's, it was the second squadron of I-15s to be organized and commanded by a Spaniard. Alonso Santamaría was a corporal pilot at the beginning of hostilities, and he fought hard for the Republic in those days of confusion, flying old Nieuports and French Dewoitines when they became available. Back in September 1936 he was promoted to an *alférez*, quickly became a *teniente*, and in February 1937 was promoted to captain in command of his own squadron of I-15s on the Aragon front (although often it was based in Lerida). In the months that followed, he and his pilots had fought over the Jarama and at Guadalajara.[1]

After some jockeying around, Jiménez got his squadron formed up on Alonso Santamaría's, and the latter led the group eastward toward the highlands of Aragon, a territory with which he was most familiar. An hour and thirty minutes later, the two squadrons sped across the plains of Castille and broke into a landing pattern over Sarrión. Even today, Sarrión is hardly more than a village; in 1937 it hosted fewer than one thousand souls. Set among the pine forests of the

Sierra de Javalambre some three thousand feet above sea level, on a map Sarrión is only one of several little beads on the steel thread of the Zaragoza-Valencia railway. The airfield, sited on a plateau northeast of the town, was large, hard and dry, and an excellent field for the operations of two or three squadrons. Its only shortcomings stemmed from the very nature of this part of Aragon in late spring: it was hot with variable winds, which tended to blow curtains of dust in all directions.

When Alonso Santamaría and Jiménez brought their airplanes into Sarrión, they found a squadron of I-15s already dispersed around the field. It was Kosenkov's, and because he was senior to the two Spanish leaders, they would be operating under his command. When Tinker squirmed out of his cockpit and jumped into the dust of Aragon, a running and waving figure who spoke American English hailed him. It was Albert Baumler, a charter member of Kosenkov's squadron.

This was a surprise because Tinker knew Baumler's unit was based in the highlands northeast of Madrid. Baumler explained that they had left El Soto more than a week ago for Lérida and had spent a week escorting bombers in an offensive against Huesca. Kosenkov had told him that the offensive against Huesca and the short-lived offensive by Tinker's squadron against the Casa de Campo were intended to divert the Nationalists' attention away from the Republican buildup against Teruel.

What neither of the Americans knew, and what probably no one at Sarrión knew that day, was that the offensive against Teruel was also a diversion of sorts. If the Republic succeeded in taking the city, well and good; but the primary purpose of this operation was the same as the others: to relieve the Nationalists' pressure on the isolated Cantabrian pocket, with its important centers of Bilbao and Santander.

Tinker asked Baumler if he had heard anything further about Chang. More than two weeks had passed since Chang was called to Alcalá. Baumler had talked with Lacalle just before his squadron left El Soto, and he suggested that Chang may have gone back to Japan for a rest, but he couldn't be sure. Japan seemed a long way to go for a rest; it was all rather strange.

That evening in Sarrión, members of the three squadrons discovered that supplies only provided enough to meet the needs of Kosenkov's pilots; the evening's meal was skimpy. Then they discovered that they didn't even have a roof to sleep under, much less beds. Someone muttered something about cots arriving from Valencia around midnight. Tinker and Baumler refused to fret about this; they celebrated their reunion with three bottles of wine, and when these were drained, Tinker scrounged around the town until he found an empty automobile whose back seat he pressed into service as a barracks for the night.

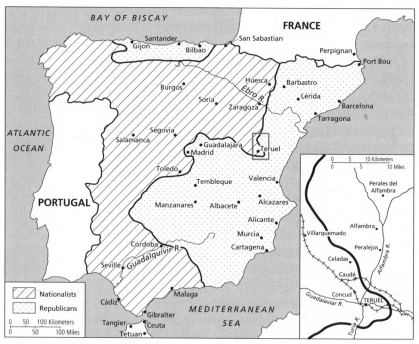

Map 10.1   The Teruel Salient, April 1937

It was a grumpy bunch of pilots that rolled out of their makeshift beds at 4:30 on the morning of 16 April and clambered on board trucks that took them out to the airfield, where they found themselves lucky to get a cup of coffee. While the airplanes were being armed with bombs, Jiménez spread out a large map of the area to acquaint his pilots with the lay of the land. Teruel (pronounced Tair-yoo-el) was a city, a province, and, as far as the war was concerned, also represented a major salient. About twenty miles long and ten miles wide, the salient lunged out of the northwest into Republican territory and seemed to be pointed like a pistol at Valencia only seventy miles away on the Mediterranean. Teruel is the ancient capital of the province of the same name that is the southernmost province of Aragon, and it had been in the hands of the Nationalists since the beginning of the war. Situated high above the junction of the Turia and Alfambra Rivers, this historic fortress city of about 30,000 persons also straddled the Zaragoza-Valencia railway and commanded the junctions of five important roads.

On an ordinary map, Teruel and its extended salient would appear to be easily pinched off by any determined army, especially if they had control of the air. But any topographic map immediately dispelled such notions. Men had been fighting over Teruel for thousands of years—the ancient Iberians, the Romans, and the Arabs and Spaniards, in their several dynastic and fratricidal wars; Teruel always proved a tough nut to crack. A bastion sited on the cutting point of a wedge, it was protected on both sides by its rivers and steep mountains of jagged rock that combined to provide formidable natural defenses.

In this battle the three squadrons of I-15s based at Sarrión would provide fighter cover for the squadrons of Rasantes and SB-2s that were dispersed among bases at Castellón and Sagunto along the coast, and at Barracas, Segorbe, Lucena and Vistabella in the hinterland between Teruel and the Mediterranean. After the attack planes and bombers had done their work, then the I-15s would make their own contribution, dive-bombing and strafing the enemy in the confusion created on the ground.

Shortly after dawn a swarm of Rasantes showed up on schedule, the three squadrons of I-15s stormed into the air and escorted them up to Teruel, covered their attack and withdrawal, and then the fighters went in to do their own work. When the squadrons got back to the dusty field at Sarrión, they fully expected that the commissary department would have a real breakfast ready for them. Dive-bombing and strafing and pulling all kinds of G's on one's system is no fun at all on an empty stomach, especially after a bad night's sleep. But after touch-down, rollout, and dispersal, they discovered they had nothing to eat. Even the coffee was gone. The Spaniards grumbled that what the fat Aragonians and Valencianos needed was a taste of war as it was fought around Madrid; then they would get off their *colas* and stop mumbling *otra dia*.

While the aircraft were being rearmed there was nothing to do except sit around in the shade of their wings, drink lukewarm water—and gripe. The griping was conducted in four languages: Spanish, Russian, English, and a unique combination of all three. At 10:30 the Rasantes reappeared, and the fighters rushed into the air once again to cover the day's second strike on Teruel. Shortly after takeoff, however, Jimenez's plane fell out of the formation with a broken fuel line and, as next-senior man, Tinker climbed into Jimenez's slot and led the squadron to its attack. Whereas the first attack had met no opposition—not even antiaircraft fire—this time there was ground fire and some token opposition in the air.

Kosenkov's squadron ran into a patrol of Heinkel He 51s based in Zaragoza that had been chasing an SB-2 but could not overtake it. Seven of Kosenkov's pilots went after three He 51s. In spite of the odds against them, the Heinkels managed to shoot down one of the I-15s. The Loyalist pilot, Luis Tuya, was said to have been a volunteer from Argentina. (Originally assigned to Lacalle's squadron in March, shortly thereafter he had been ordered to Kosenkov's.) In any case, this was the end of Tuya, and small wonder: he had made the mistake of tangling with Ángel Salas Larrazábal, who led this patrol and who would end the war as one of Nationalist Spain's ranking aces.[2]

Kosenkov subsequently claimed that his planes bagged one of the Heinkels, but the record does not seem to confirm this. Many such "little lies" were told, no doubt on both sides, simply to keep up morale. And when any squadron lost a pilot, such fabrications probably seemed more necessary than ever.[3]

Kosenkov's squadron flew four escorts on 17 April, scrambled off to one false alarm, and scrambled off again late in the day to intercept a dozen or more Heinkel He 51s that had sped in to dive-bomb the Republican trenches around Teruel.[4] By this date the Nationalists and their German allies had recognized the He 51 to be inadequate to tangle with the Russian I-15s and I-16s, and they now employed it primarily as a ground-attack airplane that would be able to fight its way out of an interception and make its way home. Its operators no longer expected the He 51 to stand and fight. On this same day, in contrast with Kosenkov's pilots, Jiménez's squadron made only three flights, and these escorted Rasantes. Exactly what Alonso Santamaría's squadron did is not known, but it doubtless performed at least as many missions as Jiménez's. This pattern of aerial activity clearly suggests that the Russians still functioned as the backbone of the Republic's air forces.

At three o'clock in the afternoon the pilots finally got something to eat, and this consisted of a few hard rolls, some tough ham, two hard-boiled eggs, and two bottles of wine per man. Combat flying consumes an awful lot of nervous energy, not to mention calories, and this was by no means enough; after this repast everyone remained hungry. The Spanish pilots familiar with the climate of Aragon and the environs of Teruel could console themselves with the fact that it was the spring of the year. During any winter Teruel accumulates three or four feet of snow and records some of the coldest temperatures in Spain; the combination of a disgruntled stomach with the heat and dust of spring was ever so much better than a growling stomach in the Arctic cold of December. When the pilots reconvened at the field in Sarrión that evening, they were prepared to draw and quarter their commissary officers; instead, they found themselves pleasantly surprised: the situation had been rectified. Dinner was excellent, and, addressing their exhaustion, more than enough real beds had been provided.

Meanwhile, all was not well with the old Esquadrilla de Lacalle, for the express reason that Lacalle, whom the pilots liked and trusted, was no longer its leader. Although many of them had come to dislike Jiménez for various reasons, dislike is one thing and distrust is something else. A squadron cannot function effectively when a majority of its members both dislike *and* distrust their commander. That poisonous combination now called Jiménez's leadership into question. Too many of its pilots believed that on too many occasions he had jeopardized the squadron, leading it into dangerous situations where, if attacked, it would have faced a tough fight at a disadvantage and probably would have emerged with heavy losses. The fact that the squadron had not been attacked in these situations made no difference. That was a matter of *buena suerte*, and luck does not last forever.

On this special evening at Sarrión, the fiery Velasco made a formal protest to Kosenkov on behalf of his comrades to ask for the return of Lacalle. Tinker was well aware of the turmoil among the Spaniards, but as a foreigner he chose to stay out of the contention. Kosenkov consulted all of the other squadron pilots before he made his decision. Hereafter, Jiménez would command the squadron on the ground; Tinker, being the squadron's senior pilot, would lead it in the air. For a Russian of the Soviet Union at this moment in time, it was not an unusual solution. Since their revolution, the Soviets had divided the direction of all military commands—divisions, brigades, and battalions of the army, squadrons of the air force, and ships of the navy—between political commissars and actual commanders.

When his wingmen told him of Kosenkov's decision, a surprised Frank Tinker, upon reflection, decided it made sense; it resolved the morale problem that was eating at the squadron from within, and, if he could perform, might well eliminate the issue of distrust in the air. But only after he determined that Jiménez and the other pilots found it agreeable was he pleased to accept the Russian's decision.

The I-15 squadrons would be based at Sarrión for ten days during this diversionary offensive against Teruel.[5] Each day was a busy one, but the most active was the second day after their arrival. The first escorts and strikes flown during the morning of the eighteenth were routine; there was antiaircraft fire, but no enemy aircraft to be seen. At noontime the pilots ate sandwiches and drank wine under the shade of their airplanes while awaiting the Rasantes to return after being bombed up at their bases to the south, when two red Very flares exploded with thuds over the field. In an instant everyone was pulling on their parachutes, clambering into their airplanes, and shouting for their starter trucks. In a few minutes, only a great cloud of dust remained where before thirty fighter planes had stood parked.

Tinker and his wingmen, Justo García and Rafael Magriña, were first off the ground. They circled the field once to give Esteban Ortiz and his patrol time to get into the air, but because of mechanical problems, Jiménez and his three airplanes would not get airborne during this event. On other parts of the field, Kosenkov's and Alonso Santamaría's patrols stirred up huge clouds of dust as they hurried into the air.

Tinker's six fighters arrived over Teruel at 13,000 feet to find nothing unusual. But a few miles north of the city, he spotted an airplane streaming a trail of smoke. It was an SB-2, speeding toward them in a shallow dive, black smoke

I-15 refueled for another mission (*National Air and Space Museum, Smithsonian Institution*)

pouring from both engines. The bomber obviously had run into trouble up the line, and the enemy were probably still around, so Tinker wheeled his two patrols around to follow the bomber and cover its retreat. Then he saw the enemy Heinkel He 51s—three echelons of them that he took to have seven planes each, which meant he was outnumbered twenty-one to six. In fact, two of the Nationalist echelons had only six airplanes and the other one five. But his reaction of the moment is typical of fighter pilots who have to make their estimates in an instant and tend to overestimate the number of specks they see in the sky toward which they may be closing at combined speeds of 400 to 500 mph.[6]

For an instant, Tinker believed that he and his two patrols were about to be overwhelmed. Then he saw three I-15s of another patrol closing on the lower formation of Heinkels and others heading for the middle echelon. Tinker took his two patrols toward the highest formation of Heinkels, against which they had the advantage of altitude and the sun over their tailplanes. He was certain that because of the sun the enemy would not see them, and he was confident that a slow buildup in speed gained in his shallow dive gave him and his pilots an even greater advantage.

Frank Tinker would not live to hear the word "energy" applied to aerial combat; how the "kinetic energy" generated in a dive can be traded for the advantage of a zoom to altitude for another attack, which will build up even more kinetic energy for another attack from altitude. Yet this was exactly what he and the Russians were doing in the Spanish Civil War, especially with the I-16 monoplanes. And this is exactly what tens of thousands of aviators in all the major air forces would shortly be doing during World War II.

As Tinker's six I-15s closed with their targets, a wild dogfight already was under way with the two lower echelons of Heinkels. Two He 51s lurched out of the confused tangle of airplanes and went spinning toward the earth below. Then an I-15 fell out of the dogfight, its wings waggling uncertainly; it suddenly zoomed upward in a steep chandelle to the left and collided head-on with one of the Heinkels. Even on this cloudless day filled with bright sunlight, the explosion of the midair collision seemed blinding in its intensity. An instant later only a pall of black smoke remained, sputtering with a shower of flaming objects that arced across the sky before falling to earth; the bits and pieces fluttered down lazily as if they were leaves off a ten-thousand-foot tree on a still autumn day.

As the orange tracer bullets from Tinker's two patrols reached in among the half-dozen He 51s, their neatly stacked echelon formation quickly came apart. Tinker waggled his wings for his own pilots to break up and seek their own targets of opportunity. Everything became a mad swirl of sharp-nosed green airplanes with black roundels mixing it up with flat-nosed airplanes of mottled brown colors sporting bright-red fuselage bands and red wingtips. The pilots of the highly maneuverable I-15s had to be careful making very tight turns at combat speeds. The airplane would respond, but it posed a serious question for the pilot: could he make it without blacking out or "graying away" as a result of the severe centrifugal forces imposed upon his body—the g-forces of a tight turn or pullout draining blood away from his brain into his lower extremities?

Although U.S. Navy dive-bomber pilots in their regular dive-bombing exercises had become acquainted with the unfortunate effects of g-forces as early as 1930, the Spanish Civil War is the first time that this condition became recognized as a hazard in "normal" aerial combat. But in Spain, given the primitive circumstances of aeromedicine worldwide and the circumstances in which this war was fought, nothing could be done about it except to warn the pilots that under certain turn and pullout conditions it would occur. More than a few pilots in the Spanish Civil War, especially those flying the maneuverable Russian I-15s and the Italian Fiat CR.32s, found themselves in narrow squeaks as a result of the phenomena of "blackout" and "grayout." And it is suspected that a number of them flew unconsciously to their deaths as a result—shot down while they were slowly "graying back" to consciousness.

Off to the right, Tinker spotted a Heinkel turning toward him; there was no getting away, so he immediately whipped around to meet him. He could see the He 51's two guns winking at him from behind its propeller; but out of the corner of his eye he could see its tracer bullets streaming by well off his left wing. Meanwhile, his own four streams of tracers were pouring into the Heinkel's engine. Black chunks of metal began flying off, the enemy airplane appeared to shudder, rolling off on its right wing, which allowed Tinker's concentration of tracers to chop neatly down the left side of the He 51's finely streamlined fuselage from nose to tail. The He 51 rolled over completely and fell away. Tinker flashed past his adversary, now diving toward the ground at the head of a long column of greasy black smoke.

Swinging back into the whirl of airplanes, Tinker caught several He 51s in his gunsight, but only for brief deflection shots. Then one of the enemy made the mistake of pulling out of its dive almost directly in front of him, and Tinker fell on its tail. He had a habit—learned at Pensacola—of not squinting through his telescopic gunsight with one eye. Instead, while he acquired and lined up his target in the gunsight, he always kept his other eye open to observe what else might be going on around him. This was a generally known practice; but it was more usual for pilots to squint with one eye and thus lose contact with the world outside its narrow scope—risking the loss of their life.

Just as Tinker brought this He 51 into the center of his gunsight, his free eye was distracted by a bright light twinkling off to his right. Tracer bullets! And some of them were chopping into his right wing. He forgot the He 51 ahead of him as he threw his controls hard over out of instinct for survival and rolled the little I-15 into a tight vertical bank to the left. Out of the corner of his goggles he saw the dark shape of his attacker flash on past him.

By this time the fight had followed the rule of "lower and lower." Aerial combat usually starts at high altitudes and at high speeds, and degenerates when airplanes under attack seek escape by diving away, thereby taking the fight to lower altitudes. Speed and altitude decay concurrently. Circling around in search of a new target, it appeared to Tinker that all of the Heinkels had now dived away to escape. Little wonder, given the known liabilities of the He 51 against the more nimble I-15. Indeed, it was surprising that these Nationalist pilots, outnumbered as they came to be, did not run from the first.

Tinker waggled his wings to re-form the squadron and one by one they straggled in. He was pleased to see that none were missing. By this time they had descended to five thousand feet, with only about a thousand feet between them and the inhospitable mountains below. The only enemy aircraft left in the area were two He 51s that five of Kosenkov's pilots had cornered in a small valley hemmed in by mountains. The climbing characteristics of an He 51 were miserable compared with an I-15's; the Spanish pilots of the German aircraft had completely run out of luck. Trapped in the valley, they could only jink around in its restricted airspace until shot down or attempt to crash-land on the wretched terrain.

The dispatch of these two He 51s proved clinically interesting to watch, but as it reached its end it was not pleasant to think about. As Tinker remarked, "They didn't have a chance." On the other hand, "You can't even surrender in an airplane; your opponent wouldn't know whether you were joking or not." But he expected no different an ending were he similarly cornered.

The day's work was by no means finished. After landing at Sarrión, each of the squadrons was refueled and rearmed for further escorts of Rasantes against Teruel and for their own attacks on the city's trench works, which went on throughout the afternoon. Tinker and Baumler had time to exchange notes between attacks. During the noontime melee Baumler claimed two victories. He nailed one Heinkel early in the fight, sending him down trailing thick black smoke, but did not see if he hit the ground—he was too busy dodging the other Heinkels. Then he found another one exposed, pounced on his tail, and really riddled him. The Nationalist pilot tried desperately to get away, and their fight corkscrewed around the sky—lower and lower until they were less than two hundred feet above the ground, where maneuvering gave way to a chase across the trenches. Finally Baumler's guns torched the Heinkel's fuel tank, and the enemy flew into the ground between the lines, hurtling end over end across the pockmarked terrain.

That evening, reports from front-line observation posts said that five He 51s had fallen on the Republican side of the lines and that three others were seen to crash on the Nationalist side. One of these, however, was the He 51 lost in the midair collision, and unknown to the pilots at Sarrión, an He 51 flown by Javier Allende succeeded in making a forced landing among the incredibly bad terrain north of Teruel.[7]

In any case, the pilots at Sarrión were certain that they had destroyed eight enemy aircraft, and eight out of seventeen was a score that called for a celebration. That the Nationalist fighters had been outnumbered almost three to one made no difference; after all, it was war, not a football game. All the nonsense scribbled about "chivalry of the air" meant nothing in the Spanish Civil War, assuming, outside of pulp magazines, that it had ever meant anything since men first put guns on airplanes and began hunting each other across the skies.

The I-15 squadrons' own losses consisted of the sole airplane in the midair collision. The wreckage of these two aircraft fell in Republican territory, and after-action reports determined that the pilot of the I-15 was a young Spaniard named Calvo. When his body was recovered, examination ascertained that a bullet had passed through his neck, severing the jugular, and the medical authorities assured Kosenkov that Calvo would have bled to death before he could have even crash-landed his airplane. Was Calvo's violent chandelle that brought him into collision with his enemy a deliberate act of desperation? Or was it simply

Albert Baumler in Spain, 1937 (*Courtesy of the National Museum of the U.S. Air Force ®*)

an accident, resulting from his clutching the control column back to himself in reaction to the shock of the enemy's bullet? Everyone liked to believe that it was a final heroic gesture; it may well have been.

The victim of Calvo's last act was Jaime Palmero, who had a long service in flying the Breguet "suicide basket" bombers possessed by the Nationalists; he had only recently become a fighter pilot. Finding such documentation in the wreckage of his airplane, the Republic's propagandists extrapolated Palmero's lack of experience in fighters to the whole Nationalist squadron. This may have been good propaganda, but it was by no means the truth. Most of the Nationalist pilots in this fracas were in fact veterans; and when all is considered, they fought valiantly in their wretched Heinkels.

The pilots at Sarrión were determined to celebrate their victories, and well before midnight all the champagne in the village had disappeared. A headache-filled bunch made their way out to the airfield early on the morning of 19 April. Fortunately, there was little to do until ten o'clock when a rocket alarm sent Tinker's squadron dashing up to Teruel. But the sky was empty. The rest of the day was spent escorting Rasantes to targets in and around the salient.

Only five miles up the road from Villarquemado was a Nationalist airfield at Torremocha, and within thirty miles of Villarquemado other Nationalist airfields could be found at Ojos Negros, Bello, as well as a relatively large base at Calamocha. The Republic's fighters and bombers neither made any serious effort to strike at these airfields, nor, after 18 April, did Nationalist fighters rise from these bases in any further attempts to interrupt the daily bombings of Teruel and environs.

Air strikes in company with Rasantes and SB-2s continued for the next few days, and as there was no air opposition by the Nationalists, these operations settled down to routine. Kosenkov rationed the escort duties among the three squadrons so that only six fighters were employed to escort the bombers to their targets around Teruel and the villages of Celadas, Villarquemado, and Caudé within the salient.

Meanwhile, at Sarrión, fighter planes were taking off and landing during all hours of the day between dawn and dusk, rushing to and from their escort duties in the relentless bombing of Teruel. Most of the pilots not flying sat around the field under the shade of their airplanes playing chess and dominoes, sipping wine, and cursing the dust in their teeth and the wind for blowing away their playing cards. So it went, from 4:30 every morning to 7:00 every evening. It was becoming monotonous, until Tinker introduced a new entertainment after he found a peculiarly large and vicious species of centipede that lived under the rocks around the field. Two centipedes were teased into fighting rages and then put in a glass jar to fight it out while pilots and mechanics wagered on which would win. It seemed like a cockfight in miniature, but far more quiet—except for the cheering among spectators. These were tough and bitter fights, sometimes lasting as long as a half-hour. The only problem involved maintaining a sufficiently large stable of centipedes to keep the battles going from day to day.

During the morning of 22 April, a few days before the squadron departed Sarrión, a lone I-15 appeared over the field. It was a brand-new airplane recently delivered from Russia and fresh from the assembly works near Alicante. But

most important, it was the first replacement that Jiménez's squadron was scheduled to receive. Unfortunately, its pilot turned out to be very green and everyone
on the ground was perplexed to see him attempt a downwind landing in a very
strong wind. The plane shot across the field, its wings rocking violently as its nervous pilot tried to work his way down to a three-point landing. He was fast running out of airfield, and everyone thought he would hit a stone wall that rimmed
one boundary. But he managed to pop up over it and climb out for another try.

The primitive field did not have a landing tee, but it did have a windsock, and
there was always enough dust blowing that any fool could see the wind's direction. Everyone on the ground had long since begun to wonder what this idiot
thought he was trying to do. The pilot made two more downwind passes with
the same precarious results; but on his third attempt, he lost control and came
lurching drunkenly across the field and careened head-on into Magriña's parked
airplane.

Tinker breathed a sigh of relief; his own plane was parked only a few yards
away. Magriña could see that his airplane was an obvious write-off, as was the
brand-new I-15 that hit it. The only good thing about the accident was that there
had been no fire; the carcasses of both aircraft could be cannibalized for parts.
And as is usually the case in accidents like this, the unaccomplished pilot who
caused it climbed smiling out of the wreckage completely unscathed.

The whole squadron was furious. Pilots and mechanics had been nursing
their patched-up planes for so long and crying for new ones, that to see this
one, along with Magriña's, destroyed by such mindlessness was simply too much.
Magriña, beside himself, pulled his automatic out of its holster and shouted, "That
cabrón, I'm going to shoot him!" "Go ahead," Tinker said—as patrol leader, he
gave Magriña his official permission. But Justo Garcia jumped forward, grabbed
Magriña, and relieved him of his weapon. A very red-faced Kosenkov stomped
across the field uttering ugly oaths in Russian. Then he grabbed the hapless pilot
by the neck and cursed him roundly in Spanish and Russian. At that moment the
pilot may well have wished that Magriña had been kind enough to shoot him.

The ill wind that had felled the *cabrón* was not yet finished. Later that afternoon among squadron airplanes returning from escorting Rasantes in an attack
against Caude, pilots Velasco and Lecha got caught in a wind shift during their
landings. When they touched down in a crosswind, the impact wiped out their
landing gear. Two more aircraft demolished and two put out of commission in
one day, all as a result of pilot error. It was too much for Kosenkov. For the rest
of the day no one dared approach the angry Russian without risking his fury.
Baumler told Tinker that the Nationalists were foolish trying to fight them in
the air. If simply permitted to go on making landings, the Republic's air force
would eventually put itself out of business!

That night proved to be a bad one in the Casa de Pilotos. Dinner started with an ominous silence, and when conversation did develop it soon degenerated into a series of arguments. Kosenkov and two of his Russian pilots debated among themselves at the head of the table. Jiménez hurled accusations at Lecha and Velasco across the center of the table, while the other Spanish pilots managed to throw in their *dos centimos* when the contention died down for a moment. The other Russians grumbled loudly among themselves.

From another table, Tinker could hear his former mechanic, Chamorro, now the squadron's chief mechanic, booming away in his Asturian dialect that no pilot of *his* patrol had ever crashed one of his airplanes. And if it weren't for that *cabrón* from Los Alcazares, his record would be perfect! Tinker noted that Chamorro took pains to ignore Chang's earlier misfortunes.

After a while, even Tinker and Baumler found something to argue about. Tinker thought the whole phenomenon similar to that which occurs among seamen after a ship has been riding out a storm for too many days. Everyone becomes introspective and irritable. Though he hadn't any nautical experience, Baumler disagreed. As it was, the three squadrons had been flying steadily from dawn to dusk for seven days. No one liked the heat, the dust, and the capricious winds at this airfield, and no one liked the uncertain living conditions in Sarrión; nevertheless, to Tinker's mind, it approximated the conditions of a ship long-buttoned-up by a storm.

Whatever the cause, their commissary officer sensed the growing malaise among the squadron members. He suddenly stepped into the uproar with a case of champagne that he set on the table with great fanfare. He changed the subject to the Heinkels shot down a few days before; that occasion, he asserted, had not been adequately celebrated. Thereafter the attentions of the pilots turned to the popping of corks and the lifting of glasses.

After the next day's operations, Kosenkov announced that their work at Teruel was finished. Although no one cheered, everyone was relieved. More than a few wished they could fly back to the Madrid area that night, but they had to wait for tomorrow, and its dawn could not come soon enough.

At 6 a.m. on the twenty-fourth the three squadrons climbed out of Sarrión's dust and headed westward; Kosenkov's squadron home to El Soto; Alonso Santamaría's to Alcalá; and Tinker's to its old homestead at Campo X, where they touched down some two hours later. Tinker immediately arranged for a major overhaul of his airplane and then hurried across the field to the *marqués'* villa, where Maria and Christina remained in command as housekeepers.

The girls had heard that an American pilot had been killed at Teruel so they were pleased to see Tinker. He told them that the gossip they had heard probably related to Tuya, because the American killed at Teruel was a Latin American.

Christina asked about Chang, but Tinker could tell her nothing. When he finally got back to the Casa de Pilotos in nearby Azuqueca that evening, he noticed that Chang's personal effects were still there. Wherever he had gone, he evidently didn't feel the need of his toothbrush and razor.

The next day, on Sunday, a car whipped in off the Madrid-Guadalajara highway, charged down the road between the handsome corridor of poplars, and came to a screeching halt in front of the villa. Only one man drove like that, and Tinker knew the driver had to be Lacalle. Tinker asked Lacalle about Chang; Lacalle claimed he knew nothing and quickly changed the subject. He observed that only four pilots of the squadron's original twelve remained: Casteñeda, Ortiz, Gil, and Tinker. He thought they all looked exhausted and announced that they should have a week's leave. This represented one of those intuitive estimates of a situation and quick action to it that endeared Lacalle to his men. Perhaps Lacalle's years as a sergeant provided the key to his sense of leadership, but the fact remains: some men have it and others do not.

Casteñeda had a girlfriend in Azuqueca so he chose to stay there. Tinker, Ortiz, and Gil quickly packed their bags, piled into a car, and within the hour were speeding down the highway toward Madrid. They all booked rooms in the Florida, where they found pleasure spending an hour testing that establishment's marvelous hot water while scrubbing the dust and crust of Aragon off their hides. They would not check out until the next Sunday morning, on 2 May 1937.

Tinker had not been in Madrid since 30 March, and then only for a bath followed by some hurried drinking, so he wasted no time in looking up the Americans homesteading the Florida. As usual, they were gathered in Hemingway's rooms on the first floor. Hemingway planned to leave Madrid for other parts of Spain the next morning, the twenty-sixth, and then head on to Paris and New York. He had been in Spain for more than two months. Though not yet bored by the war, he had business to attend to back in the States that involved a documentary movie about the war, called *The Spanish Earth*. On this afternoon a noisy farewell party was in progress. Among those present, the usual crawl of newspaper people: Martha Gellhorn, Herbert Matthews of the *New York Times*, Henry Gorrell of the United Press, and Sefton Delmar of the London's *Daily Mail*; plus the American author John Dos Pasos,[8] Robert Merriman, commanding officer of the Abraham Lincoln Battalion, and several other Lincolns. Actually, Merriman, whom Hemingway used as his model for Robert Jordan, the hero of *For Whom The Bell Tolls*, was esteemed by few in the Lincoln Battalion; most of the rank and file referred to him as "Captain Murderman."[9]

The whiskey was flowing fast while a boisterous craps game rattled on in one corner of the room. No one could hear the phonograph record playing above the buzz of conversation. Suddenly, a shrill scream filled the street outside, followed by an explosion that shook the room and the sound of falling masonry. Tinker jumped up and ran to a window. The shell had struck the top of the Paramount Building, whose tower of "1930 modern" architecture stood directly across the Plaza de Callao from the hotel.

Tinker was about to exclaim, "My God!" when he noticed that no one else appeared excited; all of them continued talking, drinking, rolling dice, and making sandwiches as before. The only other person in the room who took an interest in the explosion was a newsreel cameraman who grabbed up his camera and ran out with hopes of getting some good footage of the bombardment. As a result of his rush to the window, it dawned on the Lincolns that Tinker had not spent much time in Madrid, so they explained that this was simply the beginning of the usual afternoon bombardment. Merriman told him that the shells usually arrived in salvoes of three in a series of four; after these twelve it seemed that the Nationalists had to reload, which offered a few minutes of quiet. They called this representative cannonade the "unholy trinity" and the "twelve apostles."

The Lincolns warned Tinker that if he got caught outside during a bombardment he should always stay on the west side of the street and be ready to duck into a doorway. Most of the big buildings in Madrid were of heavy stone construction and no single shell could bring one down, but flying glass and masonry were distinct hazards. They also cautioned him to be very careful while walking along the main thoroughfares, especially the north–south streets like the Gran Vía, the Calle de Atocha, and most of the streets leading out of the Puerta del Sol. And it would be especially bad to be caught on these streets during the siesta period between noon and four o'clock. Tinker wondered about this last warning; it sounded so odd that he suspected he was being led into a joke, and he refused to bite. A few days later he would wish that he had pursued the subject further.

Tinker soon became accustomed to the triads of shells that came screaming into the city from the Nationalist batteries on Garabitas Hill beyond the Casa de Campo. When in Rome you do as the Romans do, and on the streets of Madrid the visitor took his cues from the Madrileños. When the scream of the first shell was heard and they casually stepped into a doorway like a citizen of Little Rock would step under the portico of the McGehee Hotel to avoid a spring shower, then you looked around for your doorway, too. It was as simple as that; at least most of it was. Some of the rest, however, could be hair-raising.

At the end of April 1937, there was not much one could do in Madrid. The treasures of the ancient palaces, museums, and art galleries had long since been removed to safe storage in the hinterland. The monuments and sculpture that decorated the once attractive parks and plazas were hidden behind tons of protective sandbags and masonry. The animals in the zoo had long since been slaughtered as liabilities, and the Madrileños had a joke that a few days after the elephants were killed a strange meat appeared in Madrid's butcher shops. The charming Plaza de España sat almost in the middle of no-man's-land, the parks along the Manzanares River were the battle line, and the beautiful Retiro Gardens had been turned into an artillery park, its elegant lagoon drained for fear of its reflection providing a navigation aid to night bombers.

Tinker busied himself with trips to the dentist, where his lower plate was nearly finished. He was glad of this because the dentist appeared increasingly nervous as a result of the bombardments and spoke about moving to Valencia.

One day he made a visit to the front lines where the militiamen extended every courtesy to foreign visitors. And when they discovered that Tinker was an aviator in the Republic's service, they couldn't do enough for him. Protocol made it customary to offer a visitor a rifle and let him try his luck at picking off a Nationalist soldier on the other side of the lines. Tinker tried his hand at it but with uncertain results. The militia officers thanked him for his visit and urged him to drop around again, but next time with his airplane!

Food had become a dull affair in Madrid even for those who could afford the best, and it was a sometime thing for those who could not. Cut off from the cattle lands of Andalusia and Extramadura and the grain country of Leon and Galicia, all of which were in Nationalist territory, the Republic had to pull in its belt and in Madrid the squeeze proved tightest. Instead of being at the geographical center of the national economy as it had been before the war, Madrid was now a beleaguered outpost on the Republic's western front, surviving at the end of an interdicted single-track railroad and a primitive road network. The Republican government's leaders, who had fled Madrid the preceding November to wax fat in Valencia, knew that they had to send guns to Madrid, but they were inclined to forget about butter. The Madrileños' diet consisted mostly of rice, beans, lentils, and potatoes. Meat was a rarity, although fish was often available. By this date most of the prewar restaurants were closed. Those that still operated offered only mundane bills of fare, and then the chances were that what stood in print on the menu no longer stood on the shelves in the kitchen. The foreigners in Madrid, for most of whom cost was no object, usually ate in the rathskeller of the Hotel Gran Vía, where the food, although substantial, varied from mediocre to bad.

If Madrid's restaurants were moribund, the city's bars and nightclubs remained as lively as ever. There was Chicote's on the Gran Vía, the Café de Lisboa on the Puerto del Sol, and a host of lesser places such as the Miami Bar, Molinero's, and the Aquarium. The bars in the Hotels Florida and Gran Vía and The Ritz and Palace Hotels on the shaded Paseo del Prado had furnished posh watering spots before the war swept their bar shelves clear of Scotch, cognac, and anis, to have them replaced by bottles of medicinal alcohol and morphine to serve their new battered and bloodied clientele.

Chicote's was Madrid's most fashionable prewar bar, most popular among those young men now fighting on the Nationalist side. When the hostilities broke out in July 1936, Pedro Chicote was attending the Olympic Games in Berlin, and he subsequently decided it the better part of wisdom not to return to Madrid but to devote his attentions to another bar he operated in San Sebastian, in Nationalist territory. Chicote's waiters had their own special form of loyalty, however, and they continued to operate the bar as if it were their own, doing their best to maintain its prewar dignity. While on leave, Frank Tinker always spent a few hours of his day at Chicote's; it also served as one of Hemingway's favorite meeting places and listening posts. He used its environment in some of his short stories of the Spanish Civil War, such as *The Denunciation*, *The Butterfly and the Tank*, and *Night Before Battle*.[10]

Further on down the Gran Vía the Miami Bar could be found, a pleasant place that almost equaled Chicote's in its ability to obtain foreign liquor, but the waiters did not have the same sense of tradition and it could not match Chicote's atmosphere. Both numbered among the Lincolns' favorite hangouts when they were in Madrid, but they favored the Miami because of its wheezy phonograph and the bar's selection of American records.

When it came to eating and drinking, however, Tinker's late-April visit to Madrid enjoyed excellent timing. Shortly after his arrival at the Florida, he received invitations to be a guest at two magnificent banquets, one in honor of General Miaja in the Hotel Nacional, which the Russians had taken over for the lesser functionaries of their staffs, and the other in the Russians' headquarters in Gaylord's Hotel to honor the Fuerzas Aereas of the Ejército Popular.

Gaylord's was variously regarded as sinister, an example of Communist cynicism, or as a status symbol to which an invitation was highly prized, all depending upon who provided the estimate. It had been a three-star hotel in *Baedeker's* of 1936, but after the Russian high command moved in, it became Spain's No. 1 Red Star hostelry. Through its lobby, guarded by heavily armed NKVD men, walked not only the great names of the Spanish Republic but many formidable personalities of Soviet politics and the Red Army, most of whose real names will never be known with certainty.[11]

The Madrileños joked that the Russians had chosen Gaylord's as the headquarters of their high command not only because of its isolation on the quiet Calle de Alfonso XI, but mostly because of its proximity to the Prado Museum. Not that *los Rusos* were so fond of Spanish art and culture, but they were confident that the Nationalist artillerymen in the Casa de Campo would not attempt zeroing in on Gaylord's for fear of a near miss hitting the precious museum. They also joked about the Russians' collateral headquarters in the Hotel Nacional because it was so close to the Atocha railroad station. If things went bad in Madrid, the Russians had only to dash across the street to catch a train for Valencia.

The Comintern's Lords of Gaylord's, like the lords of any great political apparatus, hardly shared the tastes enforced upon their proletarian cannon fodder at the front. The ships that slipped through the Bosporus and sneaked across the Mediterranean to run the Nationalist naval blockade with airplanes, tanks, artillery, and trucks from Russia also carried a tonnage of vodka, champagne, caviar, and other tasty canned goods. Tinker ate well at Gaylord's and at the Nacional, and the after-dinner musical entertainment proved excellent. His only complaint: all the speechmaking was in Spanish and Russian, and while his Spanish had become more than adequate for ordinary conversation, it was not up to coping with long sentences packed with fiery political rhetoric.

On the third day of his leave, Tinker left a session with some of the Lincolns at Chicote's and walked up the hill to the Florida, where he discovered that a 75-mm shell had scored a direct hit on his quarters. The room was a shambles, and the adjacent bathroom looked only a little better. His suitcase had been slashed by shell fragments, and inside it he found only the remains of his electric razor and Graflex camera. His most shocking discovery came after rooting around through all of the fallen plaster in the bathroom. Two bottles of Johnny Walker that he had hidden behind the bathtub had been shattered by the blast. Scotch was a scarce commodity in Madrid, and when one found a source of it he paid an outrageous price. The shelling of his room was one thing, the destruction of his bathroom too much of another, but vandalism that destroyed his Johnny Walker was an outrage beyond forgiveness. In this moment Tinker felt his first personal dislike of the Nationalists. During the rest of his stay in Madrid, Tinker came to feel that the artillerymen on Garabitas Hill knew as much about his daily life as did he, that they were tracking his footsteps, determined not to let him return to Alcalá.

While in Madrid Tinker met a girl named Dolores, whom he found to be most pleasant company. She found the handsome aviator equally charming, and the two kept company during his leave. One afternoon he and Dolores went to the Capital Theater to catch the matinée showing of Charlie Chaplin's toils in the over-mechanized world of *Tiempos Modernos* (*Modern Times*). It is said that *Modern Times* enjoyed the longest continuous run of any film in Madrid during the civil war.

Everyone was enjoying the film when three shells came whistling out of the Casa de Campo. Two struck the upper works of the Paramount Building; the theater shuddered under each detonation and plaster dust fell from the ceiling. Tinker tensed, gripping the arms of his seat; any second he expected the audience to dissolve into panic and stampede for the exits. But few heads even turned to look at the ceiling and the only sounds heard were some angry voices that exclaimed, "*Criminal Fasciosos!*" Though favorably impressed by the audience's calm, Tinker wondered how much of their indifference was owed to the stoicism developed in their daily life under bombardment and how much to the thrall of Charlie Chaplin's production.

At those times when the movies ended and the audiences departed the matinée and evening showings, the Nationalist artillery had a practice of raining a series of random shells into the Plaza de Callao that housed Madrid's theater district. Theatre managers could have rescheduled their showings, but these were published in Madrid's newspapers and the Nationalists across the line also subscribed to them. This was one of several strange aspects of the siege of Madrid and the Spanish Civil War in general. Another one involved the telephone system, owned and operated by the American syndicate IT&T that threatened to withdraw its technicians and cut off the supply of spare parts if either side tampered with it. Neither side could function without telephones—nor did they have the expertise to operate a truncated telephone system—so both respected this caveat and phone service in Spain continued much as it had before the war. If Tinker had known this he could have picked up a telephone and put through a call to General Franco's headquarters in Burgos to protest the destruction of his Johnny Walker. Only the intervention of a government censor in the Telefonica's main exchange would have stopped such a call.

When the movie ended, Tinker and Dolores walked out into the Plaza de Callao. He was expressing his admiration at the ability of Popeye and Mickey Mouse to speak Spanish when he saw where the third shell—the one that missed the theater—had struck. Right in front of the Florida Hotel. It had hit the sidewalk directly outside a window where Tinker had a habit of sitting each afternoon, drinking coffee and reading his newspaper, or simply watching the world go by on the Gran Vía. Fortunately the shell was a dud, which saved the life of an old man who sold newspapers outside the hotel. He had been standing five feet away when the projectile showered the area with glass and masonry, but he escaped with minor cuts and bruises. The hotel was not as fortunate. It lost four huge windows, and plate glass had become a scarce commodity in Madrid. More than ever, Tinker felt that the artillerymen were dogging his tracks.

On Tinker's last day in Madrid, he and Dolores had lunch in the Hotel Gran Vía, where he managed to buy two bottles of champagne from the head waiter. The waiters in the Gran Vía were all Anarchists in their politics, and they did a thriving under-the-counter business in fine wines and champagne, most of which was said to have been looted from the homes of wealthy Madrileños who had fled to Nationalist territory. They also trafficked in dubiously labeled whiskey and gin that Tinker believed to be unfit for human consumption.

Madrileños customarily ate at one place and had coffee at another, so Tinker and Dolores started up the Gran Vía for the Florida only four blocks away. They had covered about half the distance when the first shell came whistling out of the Casa de Campo. Tinker looked around for a doorway to duck into, but there was none. All the stores along the Gran Vía had steel shutters rolled down over their store fronts. It was the siesta period! He and Dolores were standing in a deserted canyon of vertical masonry with no place to hide, and *now* he realized why the Lincolns had warned him to avoid the Gran Vía between noon and four o'clock.

The first shell hit the Paramount Building about a hundred yards ahead, showering the Plaza de Callao with chunks of masonry, steel fragments, and dust. The next shell exploded against the fourteen-story Telefónica almost across the street from them, pelting them with bits of stonework. Poison gas was the great bogeyman of the 1930s, and so much dust enveloped the street that for moment Tinker feared that the Telfónica had been hit by a gas shell.

Dolores relieved Tinker of one bottle of champagne, and together they hurried up the street, hugging the walls, when the third shell screamed overhead to explode behind them against the front of the Hotel Gran Vía three floors above street level. The detonation threw stone and glass all over the street, and Tinker saw a huge cornice hurled into the hotel's front door, through which they had walked only a few minutes before.

Then the air became still. So went the peculiar "rule of three" that governed the bombardments. The other nine of the "twelve apostles" would soon be on their way, so without saying a word Tinker grabbed Dolores and they sprinted through the rubble and glass that cluttered the sidewalk to the relative safety of the Florida. Once inside, they immediately sought out the bar for a couple of double cognacs.

The next morning, 2 May, Lacalle appeared at the Florida and led Tinker down to a brand-new Plymouth sedan. Tinker tossed his suitcase into the car's rear seat with some relief. Flying, he was certain, had to be less hazardous than a leave in Madrid. The battle for that city was not Frank Tinker's brand of war; he had found this visit an unnerving experience. While Lacalle sped up the highway toward Azuqueca, they talked about what had happened to the other pilots. Tinker again asked about Chang, but Lacalle still had no information. Rumors, however, held that the squadrons of Jiménez and Alonso Santamaría were going to be stripped of their most experienced pilots, and that these would form a new squadron that would fly up to Bilbao and Santander. Still other rumors circulated of an offensive against Extramadura. Rumors, always rumors, and no one could know for sure what to believe.

It was good to be heading back to Azuqueca, returning to the certainties of wartime flying, where man and machine functioned as one, the hazards were known, and a man had a definite measure of control over the moments of truth that he had to face. It made far more sense to Tinker than the casual lottery of mayhem and death that ruled life in Madrid.

11

KOSENKOV & CO.

As the new week began at Campo X on 3 May 1937, Tinker discovered that Chamorro had his old No. 56 in the midst of a complete overhaul. The little fighter's wings and fuselage had been entirely recovered with new fabric, and the taut surfaces gleamed under fresh coats of dope. Chamorro proudly showed Tinker the new cylinders, pistons, and connecting rods that he was about to install in the engine block and the new valves and rocker arms to be installed later. He had also foraged new magnetos and had completely overhauled the carburetor.

As Tinker ran his fingers over the oily parts, he was every bit as pleased as Chamorro. These shiny bits of strangely shaped metal were vital constituents of his life. When Chamorro finished his work, Tinker virtually would have a new airplane. But in their shared pleasure of the moment, neither man knew that Tinker would never have the opportunity to fly No. 56 again.

After checking in with Chamorro, Tinker walked over to the *marqués'* villa to pay his respects to Maria. There he found a distinct Castilian chill in the air. Some of the other pilots had managed to get evening passes to Madrid, and they had witnessed Tinker's antics in certain nightclubs of the city. Maria had overheard their uproarious appreciations of these performances. And she had heard about Dolores. A former Madrileña, Maria was aware of these nightclubs by reputation, and it embarrassed her even to mention their names.

Tinker hurried to assure her that the war had changed all that. She had not been in Madrid for several months, and since then these nightclubs had become paragons of Republican virtue. If he had been seen in such places with a girl, it was only to do a favor for a friend—without saying that the friend was Justo, who thought he was doing a favor for Tinker by introducing him to Dolores. In any case, he said, the girl in Madrid was not nearly as attractive as Maria, and perhaps this was all she wanted to hear. After that, she opened the sewing room to him again. But as soon as he could, Tinker returned to the Casa de Pilotos to fill in Justo and the others on his story so that their stories would square with it.

The next day Chamorro knocked on the sewing room's door to tell Tinker that his No. 56 was ready for its test flight. With Chamorro at his side, he was about to climb into the cockpit when an automobile rushed out onto the field, braked to a stop next to them, and a messenger from Alcalá got out. Tinker learned that he had just been transferred to Kosenkov's squadron, effective immediately. As for the airplane, he should turn it over to someone else; the important thing now was to pack his bags. This news shattered Chamorro's proud moment, and, upon leaving Campo X, Tinker never saw his fiercely partisan Asturian Communist mechanic again.

A few hours later Baumler drove into Azuqueca to provide Tinker a lift with his luggage. He explained that Ivan Kopéts ("José") thought that since he and Tinker were the only Americans still flying fighters, it would be best if both served in the same squadron. From Azuqueca they drove down the valley to Alcalá, where they turned off into the highlands north of Madrid, speeding past the airfields at Daganzo, Cobeña, and Algete. Finally Baumler swung the car off onto a side road and stopped in the former country estate of the Duke of Albuquerque, which featured a sumptuous manor house. Located about thirty miles from the town of Soto del Real, the estate was known to the pilots as "Campo Soto." The establishment favorably impressed Tinker. He was moving up in the world, from a *marqués' finca* to the country estate of a duke. None of the Army airfields or naval air stations in the United States had class like this!

The Russians created Campo Soto as their first airfield when they began moving their aircraft into the Madrid area during October 1936. The site was only some fifteen miles from the center of Madrid, and at that time no other fields were closer except the well-known ones at Barajas and Alcalá, which the Nationalist bombers struck daily. A week or two later, on 4 November, the Russians surprised friend and foe alike by rushing a swarm of fighters into the air to confront the bombers. After that the Nationalists no longer owned the sky over Madrid.[1]

By the spring of 1937, the Nationalists knew that a dozen new airfields existed in the Madrid area, but they had not yet pinpointed Campo Soto. The Russians can be geniuses at camouflage, but most important, they enforced the discipline among ground personnel that made the camouflage effective. And at Campo Soto they had made the most of the area's natural cover. The airfield itself was so narrow that it could be landed upon only from the east or west, and from the air it did not look like it could be an airfield. A false winding road crossed the runway area, along with two or three false ditches. Along the runway's south boundary a creek flowed into the upper course of the Jarama, and on the far side of the creek stood a tall grove of dense oak trees. Two carefully camouflaged bridges spanned the creek, and as soon as an airplane landed it taxied across a bridge into the concealment provided by the oaks.

Among the same oaks stood the duke's manor and miscellaneous outbuildings that housed the pilots and ground crews and served the maintenance of the airplanes. It was a far more sophisticated setup than Tinker had known at Campo X, to be sure, and far more sumptuous than the *marqués' finca* into the bargain. Despite the prestige that attached to flying with the Soviets, Tinker still did not think his new setting had the same homeliness. Perhaps the missing elements were the *marqués'* sewing room with the sisters Maria and Christina.

Baumler showed Tinker to their quarters in the duke's home on the second floor, which they shared with two Spanish pilots. Their room had been the duke's nursery, and it appeared that at least one generation of little Albuquerques had been reared within its walls. Murals of various fairy tale characters from Grimm, Anderson, and Mother Goose, which Tinker recalled from his own childhood, decorated the walls.

Few introductions were necessary with the pilots of this I-15 squadron, led by another young Soviet aviator named Ivan Kosenkov.[2] Except for a few recent replacements, Tinker knew them all from their operation at Sarrión. The only formal introductions that had to be observed were with the señoras and señoritas who kept house for the pilots. Tinker had little to say about them, so we can assume that none compared favorably with Maria and Christina.

Squadron members were briefed on a target and next morning, shortly before sunup on 5 May, Kosenkov led his I-15s into the air. The objective of this, Tinker's first mission with the Russians, was a collection of Fiat fighters detected the day before parked on an airfield behind the Guadalajara front. When the squadron found the airfield, however, the Fiats were gone, doubtless having departed in response to the observation plane that had overflown them the day before. Having been joined by an SB-2 bomber, Kosenkov signaled a turn toward their secondary objective, a railroad station in the small town of Espinoza de Henares. This time luck was with them, for they found a Nationalist freight train taking on water at the station.

The SB-2 went over the target first, and being a level bomber its bombs fell wide of the narrow train; but the fighters that dived to deliver their bombs directly on the target practically demolished it. The bombs from the first three I-15s scored near misses, but Tinker and Baumler bracketed the locomotive, which suddenly began blowing steam in all directions.

After climbing out of their dives, the fighters returned to the destructive work of strafing, the effectiveness of which tends to be underrated. But with each airplane chopping away at the train with four streams of 7.62-mm slugs, and 520 bullets arriving on target with each ten-second burst, the damage was terrific. When they finally ran out of ammunition and turned back for Campo Soto, the train was cocked across the tracks like a drunken snake, burning furiously in three places. Tinker guessed that it would take at least a week to straighten out the mess, but flying over the same area a month later, he was surprised to find the wreck still sprawled in the station, blocking the tracks.

On this first mission, Tinker's newly assigned I-15 fighter made him most unhappy. En route to the target its engine had quit four times, and on the way back it had ceased operating five times. Each time it had either reluctantly coughed back to life or Tinker had to choke it back with a dive to keep the propeller windmilling while he conducted some angry handwork with his wobble pump and mixture control. He suspected that his airplane, No. 28, was the twenty-eighth I-15 to have arrived in Spain, and that the Russians had been flying the guts out of it ever since last November without once removing its cowling to inspect the engine's remains.

On the flight back Tinker contemplated the possible outcome had the engine conked out at low altitude during their attack on the train, and he became furious. After landing, he stomped into the field house and told Kosenkov that the piece of junk in which he had risked his neck this morning was worse than his old one before it went to overhaul, and he demanded a new airplane. Surprisingly, the Russian did not blow up in response to newcomer Tinker's angry demand. He promised him the first new airplane that the squadron received, and, in the meantime, No. 28 would get a new engine. Now Tinker was all smiles. Good old Kosenkov! And the American and the Russian walked over to the duke's *residencia* for a second breakfast.

A few hours later Tinker went out to check on the engine situation. The offensive hunk of iron that might have killed him had just been removed from the airplane. It was an early Curtiss-Wright Model C Cyclone. Type-tested at 500 horsepower in the late 1920s, the R-1750 carried the embossed marks of Paterson, New Jersey, U.S.A., on its nameplate. He noticed the new engine that the mechanics were preparing to install looked exactly the same except that it had Cyrillic lettering on the nameplate. It was a Russian engine manufactured in the Soviet Union under a license from Curtiss; but the Russians had worked in a few improvements, besides providing it with a new carburetor of their own design, which raised its horsepower to about 715. This turn, Tinker thought, was all for the best.

Because of his own experiences in the life-or-death aspects of everyday combat flying operations, Tinker had developed an unusual interest in engine reliability. That interest intensified on rumors that the squadron would fly to Santander in the Cantabrian Pocket on the north coast of Spain. The continuing Nationalist offensive against the pocket, with its important industrial centers of Bilbao and Santander, had Republican defenders in near extremis. Squeezed into a small mountainous area with few good airfields for dispersal, and with most of the Nationalist air forces—including the Italian Legionaria and the German Legion Condor—concentrated against the area, the Republic's air force had been decimated, and reinforcements were desperately needed.

From Guadalajara to Bilbao is some 180 miles, to Santander about 200 miles, with the 5,000-foot Cordillera and its uncertain weather in between, not to mention lesser mountain ranges and the fact that the Nationalists held most of the territory. A range of mountains five thousand feet high does not sound like much of an aerial "barrier," but one must recall that I-15s were open cockpit airplanes. Adding to the risk, neither electrically heated flying suits nor oxygen masks existed, and clouds moving in from the Atlantic can pile up against the Cordillera to heights of 10,000 and even 15,000 feet. In sum, unless the weather was unusually good, the flight would have to be made *through* the mountains, snaking along their valleys, any one of which could be plugged with clouds. Moreover, if the science of meteorology in the 1930s was crude at best world-wide, in Spain it was truly primitive. Considering contemporary pilots, Tinker and Baumler shared extraordinary credentials, having had extensive training in instrument flying, thanks to the Navy and Army Air Corps. But neither the Spanish pilots nor even most of the Russians possessed instrument training remotely like that.

If a flight to Santander posed formidable natural obstacles, at this moment Tinker was most concerned that his engine not have tantrums anywhere in the vicinity of the Nationalist air bases at Escalona, Aranda, Burgos, and Calahorra if the Fiats swarmed up to greet him.

Meanwhile, Tinker and Baumler dealt with an awkward incident in the nursery where they bunked with the two Spanish pilots. All winter long Baumler had slept in this room with it carefully buttoned up against the chill outside air, but as spring crept down the slopes of the Sierras the room became increasingly stuffy. The Spanish pilots expressed shock at the suggestion that some windows be opened. The nursery had wide French doors that opened out onto a porch above the building's main veranda, which Tinker and Baumler habitually opened, only to have the Spaniards habitually close them at some time during the night.

Complaints and argument got the Americans no results, so they finally moved their beds out onto the porch. The Spaniards and Russians were horrified at such a drastic move. They were certain that the night air would have deleterious effects on the health of the Americans, and no one in the squadron wanted that to happen. Kosenkov himself came up to inspect the strange sleeping arrangements, stalking around the area scratching his chin and mumbling to himself. Tinker and Baumler explained that sleeping in an airless, stuffy room was unhealthy. Kosenkov had never heard of anything like this before and thought it nonsense. He consulted the squadron's physician, who assured him that the Americans were correct. This diagnosis, however, did not change the sleeping habits of the other pilots, and they always seemed amazed when Tinker and Baumler arose each morning and entered through the French doors in the best of sorts after sleeping all night in the fresh air.

Tinker and Baumler had fewer difficulties with the señoras and señoritas who ran the house, and within a few days their "new room" on the porch had a table and several chairs, the table soon equipped with pitchers of fresh water, glasses, and even a couple of siphon bottles. The secret of this was Tinker's "soap system," wherein one devotes special attention to the ladies, a technique that he had honed during Army Air Corps training in San Antonio. It still worked wonders.

On 8 May Tinker drove down the hill and up the valley to Campo X to see his old squadronmates and tell them how it was living like a duke. He was surprised to discover that Jiménez and the squadron had flown east to Reus, near the port of Tarragona, only a few days before. Jiménez, he learned, was moving the squadron to the Bilbao front. This puzzled Tinker. He wondered how anyone flew to Bilbao, which was directly to the north, by flying east to Reus. Only the paper pushers in the Air Ministry could have figured this out, and, as Tinker soon learned, it was a badly bungled affair.

At the very moment Tinker visited Campo X, Jiménez and Gil were guiding a squadron of nine I-15s and six R-5 Rasantes over the Pyrenees, following a Douglas DC-2 that not only provided navigation for them but carried the squadron's logistics. At about 9:30 that morning, this formidable cloud of Spanish airplanes swarmed out of the French sky and landed at the airfield in Toulouse, France. Here arrangements had been made to have the airplanes clandestinely serviced by the Compagnie Latécoère, a French aircraft manufacturer, and then they would speed on to Pau, France, be refueled again, and finally fly to their Spanish destinations around Bilbao and Santander.

Unfortunately, it is difficult to be clandestine when crossing an international border with fifteen Russian fighter planes and a Douglas DC-2 in the middle of the morning—especially in France at that time, which swarmed with Fascist spies, sympathizers, and informers. Members of the international Non-Intervention Committee, that fatuous body created to "neutralize" the Spanish Civil War, promptly arrived at the airfield and raised a great political storm. This "non-intervention" committee would not prevent German bombers from flying to Spain via Italy, but it was determined to do its utmost to prevent the Republic's fighters from flying to another part of the Republic via ostensibly neutral France.

The next day Jiménez and Gil were obliged to lead their airplanes back across the Pyrenees, following the DC-2 to Catalonia, leaving behind one I-15 that had been damaged in landing. Although furious, the Spanish pilots were thankful that they had not been interned by the perfidious French.[3]

After leaving Campo X, Tinker drove to the old Casa de Pilotos in Azuqueca where he had dinner with those few mechanics still there. Here he noticed that Chang's personal effects remained in his room. But when he asked for word on Chang's whereabouts, the answer was "*nada.*" No one knew any more than did Tinker.

When he got back to Campo Soto, he discovered that the new engine was now installed in his I-15, but that a new pilot named Javier Jover Rovivre had already test-hopped the machine. Tinker didn't like this last bit of news at all. That airplane was *his* airplane, and he didn't want strangers fooling with it. Although it was dark, he nevertheless climbed into the cockpit and tried out the engine. The old clunker had done well to idle at 1,500 rpm and then only with some teasing; the rebuilt engine idled nicely at 1,600 rpm. She sounded more than good enough to get him across the Cordillera to Santander.

On 10 May Kosenkov assigned Tinker two wingmen and sent them out to make a reconnaissance west of Segovia, which was west of the Sierras and all new territory for him. After takeoff they flew northwest following the Burgos-Madrid highway to Somosierra, where they crossed Nationalist lines and then swung south to follow the highway along the western slope of the Sierras, thus approaching Segovia through the "back door." The only sign of enemy activity was a convoy of about fifteen trucks winding its way down through the mountains toward the village of Villarejo. Around Segovia and the nearby town of La Granja, they found nothing; everything on the ground looked to be incredibly quiet.

Determined not to let the flight go to waste, Tinker wheeled his I-15s around and pushed on his throttle for the north, hoping to catch these trucks coming down through the Somosierra Pass. Sure enough, there they were—still snaking their way through the mountains. Tinker signaled for an attack and down they went. Although the I-15s carried no bombs, in this geography guns were better. If the truck drivers had had any sense, they would have stopped and pulled over into the cover provided by the canyon walls, where they could have jumped out and taken refuge in the ditches alongside the road. Instead, they panicked at the sight of the Republican airplanes, stepped on the gas, and tried to hurry their passage through the pass. That proved to be a fatal mistake.

The attack's first pass shot up most of the trucks, torching their fuel tanks, and the second nailed the rest. Tinker roared down through and around the narrow canyon with his four PV-1s spitting bursts of fifty-two rounds per second while he sang to himself, "She'll be comin' round the mountain when she comes . . ." Another three-second squeeze on his triggers and another four streams of 156 finger-sized missiles were launched to tear up his target. Behind him his two wingmen lined up in their gunsights whatever he had missed. Down below the trucks burst into flame, collided with one another, smashed into the canyon wall to go spinning down the road swapping end for end, or hurtled through the railings and tumbled into the canyon.

All in all, it was a very satisfactory five minutes out of a flight that otherwise amounted to an hour and forty minutes of boredom. The trucks made for a worthwhile day, and the results much pleased Kosenkov. In Madrid, the high command was equally pleased to learn of the absence of activity in the area because it was planning an offensive against Segovia.

The next day, the eleventh, Kosenkov sent Tinker, Baumler, and a new Spanish pilot named José Bastida Parres on a mission over the Casa de Campo nearby Madrid to locate a recently installed artillery battery that had begun to harass the city. The Republicans knew the azimuth of the new guns in a general way, but not their exact positions. This appealed to Tinker; it promised a small measure of retaliation against the artillerymen that had turned his leave in Madrid into such a hair-raising ordeal.

The three took off from Campo Soto shortly after noon so as to be over the city when the guns usually started their daily interruption of Madrid's siesta. But the new battery proved to be well camouflaged and very coy about performing with airplanes overhead. On their first pass they saw nothing. Circling back over the city to the conspicuous circular landmark of the Plaza de Toros, Tinker lowered their altitude from six thousand to three thousand feet and dove across the Manzanares for a second look-see. This time it seemed as if every gun in the Casa de Campo was zeroed in on them; tracers and flak bursts filled the air around the patrol. The enemy's aim proved almost too good, because every which way they turned they found themselves among ugly, black flak bursts. When Tinker made his next turn over the bull ring, he looked back and could follow his path across the city traced in the sky by a sinuous trail of black smudges lingering in the air. It suggested that a flak battery or two of the Germans' Legion Condor, with its deadly 88-mm guns, recently had moved into the Casa de Campo; their fire control system was excellent, and even though they missed they were never far behind.

The three stubby biplane fighters rolled through a tight turn that pointed one set of wingtips straight at the ground, the other set directly skyward, and Tinker led them down in a dive that brought them back directly over Madrid's carpet of red-tiled roofs, well beneath the sandbagged parapets of the fourteen-story Telefónica, from which a dozen men with binoculars waved their hats and gave them the clenched-fist salute as they streaked past. Crossing the Manzanares for a third time, they dropped to treetop level and headed directly for the area marked on their maps and confirmed by their recent experience. The concentrated flashes of heavy small-arms fire greeted them from a discolored patch on the hillside and, sure enough, there lay the gun battery carefully shrouded under camouflage netting.

Upon landing back at Campo Soto, they taxied their airplanes across the southernmost of the two bridges and parked in a glade under the oak trees. After reporting the location of the Casa de Campo gun site to Kosenkov, Tinker walked back to the glade to relax. He had found it a great place to unwind while watching the fish and small water snakes that inhabited the creek and its pools. Previously, he had amused himself trying to catch the large green lizards that homesteaded the area. Although the Spaniards had warned him that the lizards were poisonous, he doubted it. In any case, on a warm day it was just good to lean back beneath the leafy canopy of the duke's splendid oak trees, doze, and think how much this location resembled the hardwood timber country back in Arkansas.

On this afternoon, Baumler picked up a bit of news about some new Nationalist airplanes spotted near Madrid. One was a high-speed bomber quite different from the Heinkel He 111s, the other a sleek-looking monoplane fighter. There had long been reports of German monoplane fighters operating in the north around Bilbao and Santander, and their performance was said to be very good. If the new machines appeared on the Madrid front now, they definitely would be something to reckon with.

When he returned to the duke's *residencia*, Tinker brought with him one of the small snakes that he'd grabbed out of the creek with which to surprise the señoritas. After he sent them off screaming, he released the snake into the garden but quietly let it be known that he had hidden it in Kosenkov's room. On hearing of it Kosenkov said nothing, but that night he and the three Russian airmen who shared his room decided that they too required some fresh air, and they hauled their beds out onto the porch with Tinker and Baumler.

On the morning of 13 May the whole squadron took off on a flight that mystified Tinker and Baumler. They flew three circuits of a rectangular track bounded by Campo Soto, Madrid, Alcalá, and Guadalajara—a total of about 217 miles. When they touched down at Campo Soto an hour and fifty minutes later, everyone was baffled. Kosenkov told the mechanics to drain all of the airplanes' fuel tanks and carefully measure the residue. Finally, responding to queries, Kosenkov explained that he ordered this flight to prove that the I-15s had enough fuel capacity to reach Santander. The fuel tank of an I-15 held about 68.5 gallons, and after this flight most of them still had about 13 gallons remaining. Their fuel consumption worked out to about 0.255 gallons per mile; it was only a little more than 186 miles to Santander, so it was clear that under ordinary circumstances the flight could be made there with a nominal fuel reserve. Nevertheless, if they met headwinds, had to spend fuel to climb above high clouds over the Cordillera, became temporarily lost for too many minutes, or had to expend fuel in combat en route, they risked a forced landing in enemy territory.

This test made sense to Tinker and Baumler, but they wondered privately why the whole squadron had to make this flight; might not one airplane have accomplished it? Perhaps the Russians wanted to be certain that no single one of the I-15s had extraordinary fuel consumption. Kosenkov and his Russian aviators were solid fellows with whom to fight side by side, but more often than not they proved to be close-mouthed and damned mysterious regarding flight operations. One received only the information needed to accomplish a mission and no more.

While Tinker and Baumler conducted I-15 flight distance checks for Kosenkov, the Republic's government in Valencia unraveled. Incessant political infighting within the government among Socialists, Communists, and Anarchists turned into armed fighting between adherents of the latter two in the streets of Barcelona during 3–6 May, with considerable loss of life. At a cabinet meeting on 13 May, a majority of his ministers walked out, and the Socialist and anti-Communist Prime Minister Largo Caballero, the head of government, turned in his resignation to the head of state, President Manuel Azaña.

Early on 14 May, Kosenkov's squadron members were driven from Campo Soto to the airfield from which they would take off for the north. It was high on the slopes of the Guadarrama near the tiny village of Manzanares el Real, which is located on the shore of the Embalse de Santillana, a great reservoir that supplies Madrid its drinking water. The airfield—the smallest Tinker had seen in Spain—was situated at four thousand feet altitude, so takeoffs would not be easy. Although it was pretty to look at, nothing else appeared attractive. But the field at Manzanares el Real was twenty miles closer to Santander than the airfield in Guadalajara. If the squadron ran into fuel consumption difficulties en route, every extra mile counted.

Upon their return that evening Tinker discovered that his new Russian engine performed too well. Javier Jover, who had first test-flown it, wanted Frank's airplane. Jover had been selected to lead the flight to Santander because he had flown on the Cantabrian front earlier in the war and was familiar with its territory. A prewar pilot with an excellent record, Jover had paid his dues flying the old Nieuports during the first few months of the war and had served with Lacalle in the confused defense of Madrid in the autumn of 1936. That October he accidentally flew a Hawker Fury into transmission lines and, in the resulting crash, the airplane burned. He was lucky to get out alive and was hospitalized for months. Now, with Jover as flight leader, Tinker did not blame him for wanting a reliable machine. But if it meant taking away his airplane, that was too much.

A bitter argument ensued between Tinker and Jover, with the rest of the squadron siding with Tinker. Kosenkov finally intervened and offered Tinker his airplane, and as Kosenkov flew one of the best I-15s, Tinker agreed to the swap. But it turned out to be all for naught. Next day, on 15 May, word came up from headquarters at Alcalá that no Russian or American pilots would make the flight north.

This word arrived a week after the fiasco in Toulouse in which Jiménez and his pilots became international victims. The Republican government in Valencia had learned nothing from that tonic experience and now planned to send Jover's flight to Bilbao via France, this time stopping only at Pau. Leaders in the Republic's Air Ministry had decided against including any foreigners precisely because Jover's flight expected to refuel in France. Government propagandists had for long denounced the presence of Germans and Italians on the Nationalist side; they did not want the world to see that they had Russians and Americans. Tinker thought it was all just as well.

On 16 May Jover and his Spanish pilots took off for Lérida in Aragón, where he took command of other I-15s that had been readied for the flight, plus a squadron of Rasantes led by Robert Alonso Vega. Accompanied by another Douglas DC-2 that carried their logistics, they got away for Pau on 17 May. While climbing over the ten-thousand-foot ranges of the Pyrenees, they ran into a blinding snowstorm, and it became every man for himself. The slow and clumsy Rasantes turned back for the Republic, escorted by a patrol of I-15s commanded by Manuel Zarauza, who had briefly served as one of Tinker's wingmen. Jover, the DC-2, and the rest of the I-15s groped their separate ways through the storm to clear weather in the valley of the d'Aspe, where they reformed and sped on to Pau.

After Jiménez's attempt to fly to Bilbao and the sequestering of his squadron at Toulouse, all of Europe knew that the Republic desperately wanted to fly new fighters into Bilbao and Santander. The Non-Intervention Committee's watch on southern French airfields had intensified, and their inspectors were waiting for Jover when his flight touched down at Pau. On the committee's command, the French impounded the airplanes and interned the pilots; there followed a great international tempest in a teapot. After a week of haggling, the DC-2 and the Republic's fighter planes were allowed to return to Spain, but only after the fighters had their guns removed for "humanitarian reasons"; however, just in case they were intercepted by Nationalist fighters, three of the I-15s were allowed to remain armed. The other unarmed pilots presumably would make nasty faces at the Fiats. Such was the wisdom typically displayed by the absurd international Non-Intervention Committee. So Jover led his airplanes back over the Pyrenees escorted by French fighters as far as the frontier.[4]

Meanwhile, everything remained quiet at Campo Soto, if not in the Republic itself. On 17 May, a few days after Francisco Largo Caballero had resigned as prime minister, the president of the Republic, Manuel Azaña, with the backing of the Communists, named the finance minister, Juan Negrín the sixty-seventh prime minister of Spain. Negrín, a well-known physician and able administrator with supposedly mild Socialist views, would serve as prime minister until the collapse of the Republic in February 1939. All hoped that Negrín might consolidate power against the centripetal forces of the labor unions, Anarchists, Socialists, and Communists. In the months that followed, however, he became a captive of the Comintern, and it would be Negrín's decision to transfer what remained of Spain's gold reserves to the Soviet Union in return for its continued military assistance.[5] During Negrin's stewardship the internecine political infighting continued, while the Republic's military situation deteriorated.

The day Jover left for the Cantabrian front via France, the Russians and Baumler drove into Madrid to see the long-running Charlie Chaplin film. Tinker considered going with them, even though he had already seen it. *The Gay Divorcee*, starring Fred Astaire and Ginger Rogers, was playing at a different theater, and he could give Dolores a call, but he decided instead to loaf at the duke's estate. Tinker wished them luck: that no 75-mm shells would interrupt their matinée. He wandered through the woods west of the airfield to the banks of the upper course of the Jarama River and spent time searching its banks in hopes of finding an abandoned boat. Having no luck in his search, he went swimming, but not for long. The Jarama is fed by the runoff of melting snow from the Sierra Guadarrama, and in the spring its waters are icy cold. When the Russians and Baumler returned from the city, they brought with them a rumor that Tinker and Baumler would soon be leaving Kosenkov's I-15 squadron and transitioning into the I-16 monoplane fighters. This was exciting news indeed, because hitherto only Russians had flown these high-performance airplanes.

With no flying assigned after Jover's departure for France, on 19 May Tinker and Baumler drove down to Alcalá to see Ivan Kopéts, the Soviet commander of the Alcalá region and of the air forces in the Madrid area. They were anxious to know about the I-16 rumor. The Russian sat them down, broke out a bottle of vodka, and asserted, "*Si, como no?*" Why not? Both of the American pilots had good records; Tinker had three victories and Baumler had three and one-half. In any case, he observed, in a few months more than one hundred Spanish pilots under Commandante Manuel Cascón Briega would be returning to Spain from their flight training in the Soviet Union, and there would be plenty of pilots to fly the I-15s.

On leaving the meeting, Baumler spotted a Fiat CR.32 parked on the field. The machine had been flown in by a Spanish pilot who had deserted the Nationalists. Baumler got permission to check it out and climbed into its cockpit for forty-five minutes of aerobatics, in which he did his best to wring it out. After landing, he walked away from the Fiat with the conviction that he had flown a mighty fine airplane, but when it came to climb and turn, his own I-15 was more than a trifle better.

From Alcalá the two sped up the highway to Campo X, expecting to break the big news to some of their old friends. But all of the Spaniards were gone, and a squadron of Russian I-15s occupied the field. A few old-timers with whom they were acquainted remained, however. These few were not surprised to learn that the Americans would be assigned to fly I-16s, because most of the Russian pilots were due for rotation back to the Soviet Union in the near future. There had to be a few experienced pilots to break in the new ones. At Campo X Tinker looked up Maria and learned that her sister Christina had been sent to the new airfield at Manzanares el Real. He asked if Chang had ever turned up, but Maria said she had neither seen nor heard from him after he left in March.

Disappointed at not finding any members of the old Esquadrilla de Lacalle at Campo X, Tinker and Baumler drove into Madrid, where they ran into a bunch of the Lincolns. After scrounging around until they had four bottles of Johnny Walker, they set up camp in the Hotel Florida, where everyone celebrated with a blast that went on long into the night. It was with some difficulty that they navigated their way over the secondary roads back to Campo Soto.

On the twenty-first, much to their surprise, Kosenkov gave Tinker and Baumler three days' leave and permission to go to Valencia. They hastily loaded up their car, a new Ford V-8, and hurried to Alcalá to get the necessary *salvo conductos* from the *jefe de campo* before anyone could change their minds. It was a beautiful all-day drive across New Castile to Valencia, the seat of the Republic's government on the coast of the Mediterranean Sea. When they checked into the Hotel Inglés, they were surprised to meet their former commander, Lacalle, and Barca, who had been Jim Allison's mechanic. For a moment it was like old home week.

That evening the two had supper with Lacalle, who told them that he was en route to the Soviet Union in charge of a large group of new pilot candidates who would receive their flight training there.[6] The Spaniards would receive their primary training near Kirovabad, Azerbaijan, Soviet Socialist Republic (SSR), in the southern Caucasus not far from the Turkish border. Advanced training, they learned, took place at Tbilisi and Rostov. This would be the second draft of Spaniards to go to the USSR for flight training; the first had gone earlier in the year under Commandante Cascón. It was this group that Kopéts had told them he expected to return later in the summer. In the course of their conversation, Tinker asked Lacalle about their squadronmate Chang. Lacalle shrugged and said he knew nothing but suggested that they ask at the Air Ministry downtown; surely someone there would know something.

The food and liquor in Valencia proved far superior to anything available in Madrid, and although there were shortages of luxury goods, Valencia's shop windows did not display the desperate emptiness of Madrid's. The next morning Tinker and Baumler went on a shopping spree, with soap, cigarettes, and American whiskey at the top of their lists. They also bought a Victrola, a phonograph that had to be wound by hand, and a selection of four dozen records. When they finally got to the Air Ministry to check on mail, the officials who greeted them took strong exception to their casual attire. All pilots on leave, they learned, were expected to have dress uniforms. Afterward, the two men broke down to the extent of purchasing pilots' wings for their shirt pockets. While at the ministry they asked about Chang, but no one knew anything; it was as if Chang did not exist.

In the course of the day they chanced to meet James Hawthorne, an American journalist who wrote outrageously vapid nonsense, heavily larded with heroics and tear-jerking sentimentalism, for the American Communist magazine *New Masses*.[7] He was accompanied by Robert Minor, the aging and cynical political commissar of the Abraham Lincoln Battalion, perhaps best known for his care never to get within the sound of gunfire.[8] Because of their consistent tub-thumping about "The Cause," Tinker found Minor and Hawthorne, and others like them, to be awful bores. Airplanes, their engines, the proper balance of a propeller, and the importance of bore-sighting guns Tinker appreciated, and he liked all those who understood them; but as far as he was concerned, people who talked politics all the time were the ones responsible for keeping the world in turmoil.

That afternoon Tinker and Baumler visited the U.S. Consulate to see if they might have any mail there, and to say hello to Mahlon F. Perkins, the stuffy American consul in residence. Perkins personified Cordell Hull's "moral aloofness"; he took an extremely dim view of Frank Tinker, Albert Baumler, and all the other Americans who harbored personal reasons for fighting in Spain.[9] Ever since the autumn of 1936, these disorderly Yankees had completely upset his carefully structured routine. Leaving Mr. Perkins wringing his hands, Tinker and Baumler hopped in their car and drove out to El Cabañal for some swimming and relaxation in the sun.

On their return to Valencia that evening, the two dined with Captain Townsend Griffiss, the American assistant military attaché for air in France and Spain. Only thirty-seven years old in 1937, Griffiss already was one of the Army Air Corps "old-timers." In 1924–25 he had served as an instructor of pursuit aviation for cadets at Brooks Field, Texas, when Charles Lindbergh, already an aviator, was there earning his wings as a military cadet. Ordinarily attached to the embassy in Paris, after the outbreak of the civil war Griffiss spent most of his time in Spain. This was not the first time that the American aviators in Spain met with Griffiss, and many of the experiences of Tinker, Baumler, and Dahl appeared in Griffiss' reports to the U.S. War Department—but without attribution to the pilots by name.[10]

Early in the morning of 23 May, Italian bombers based on the island of Majorca paid one of their intermittent visits to Valencia to drop a few tons of bombs. The hotel management felt obliged to awaken them for the raid, and the two were surprised by the amount of confusion. Although the city had been bombed frequently since the beginning of the war, Tinker judged its citizens to be not nearly as accustomed to the experience as the hardened Madrileños; the night attacks seemed to hold special terrors for the Valencianos.

Having slept through more than a few bomber raids, Tinker and Baumler resented being awakened. The pair advised hotel management that they were accustomed to these raids and in the future should not be awakened when they occurred. The next night, however, the Americans were almost bounced out of their beds by nearby concussions. In the morning they discovered that some heavy bombs had practically demolished a large apartment building a few doors away from the hotel. Rescue crews were digging through the ruins, and Tinker saw the shattered remains of a small child brought out. He noticed that the spectators showed no emotions whatever, which led him to remark to Baumler that human beings can become accustomed to anything.

When Tinker and Baumler returned to the Madrid area on 26 May they learned that the Republic's forces in the mountains west of Navacerrada were preparing for an offensive against Segovia, but activity at Campo Soto remained quiet. The following evening, while engaged in conversation with Kosenkov, the subject of spies came up. Tinker asked Kosenkov if he thought there might be spies in the Republican air force. No Russian of Stalin's Soviet Union could imagine an organization without spies, and he replied: "*Ciertamente!*" Only a few weeks earlier, he said, a spy had been uncovered in Lacalle's squadron.

Now Tinker and Baumler were all ears, and showed it. The Russian realized that he had said too much and attempted to change the subject, but the Americans would not let him. Kosenkov finally explained that the spy he mentioned was a pilot, a short fellow who spoke Spanish, Russian, English, and Japanese. The two realized what had happened to Chang and identified him by name.

Kosenkov replied that Chang had not spied for the Nationalists; rather, he was a Japanese agent who had gathered information for them on Soviet aircraft and tactics. Tinker asked what had been done with Chang. The Russian snapped his forefinger and thumb into the form of an imaginary pistol, pointed it at his temple, and declared, "*Fusilado!*" This aspect of the civil war was wholly unfamiliar to Tinker, and in some bewilderment he exclaimed: "You mean he's dead?" Kosenkov shrugged and replied laconically, "*Chang no hay mas.*" (Chang is no more.)[11]

It was two surprised American aviators who went up to their bedroom on the veranda that evening. Sorting it out with Baumler over a couple of whiskey and sodas, Tinker recalled that Chang was forever writing letters to a sister in Japan. Then there was the peculiar series of accidents that kept Chang out of action for extended periods. Could all of these have been bad luck? Moreover, one of

Lacalle's noteworthy characteristics was his inability to say anything without the excited use of his hands. But whenever they caught Lacalle in a lie his hands remained still. And, as he thought back upon it, Lacalle had always become very calm when anyone raised a question about Chang. Tinker and Baumler agreed that Lacalle must have known the truth all along, but kept it to himself for fear of shaking the squadron's morale.

They were still mulling over Chang's fate at breakfast when Kosenkov announced that they should prepare to pack their bags. Their squadron would be moving to Tembleque on the Toledo front shortly. Meanwhile, it would not engage in further flying operations. The Russian added that some of the old pilots of Lacalle's squadron were stationed at nearby Algete, which was just down the road and around a corner—a few miles away. Tinker immediately wanted to leave and visit them, but Kosenkov said it was too late to go; the squadron was already taking off for Santander in the Cantabrian Pocket.

On this morning of 27 May at Algete, José Riverola, who had been one of Lacalle's wingmen, led a dozen I-15s off the field and headed north for the air base of La Albericia at Santander. But over the Cordillera, the squadron became separated in the clouds. Only Francisco Alarcón's patrol of three airplanes made it directly to La Albericia. The other nine wandered off on a 26-degree course that brought them into sight of the Bay of Biscay at San Sebastian, fifty miles east of Bilbao and ninety miles east of Santander. Worse, San Sebastian had been in Nationalist hands since mid-September 1936; they were greeted by heavy antiaircraft fire and one of the I-15s took a direct hit and went down. Riverola led the rest westward down the coast to Bilbao, where they encountered a swarm of Nationalist fighters, and another I-15 went spinning to earth. Tinker's friends Justo García, José Bastida, Ramón Castañeda, and Rafael Magriña numbered among the Spanish pilots who made this flight.[12]

When word of these events reached them a few days later, Frank Tinker and Albert Baumler felt well out of it. Indeed, Bilbao would soon fall to Nationalist forces while Santander would be captured a few weeks later. Those few Republican fighters not destroyed on the ground or in aerial combat would be flown across the Bay of Biscay to France and internment. The war in the Cantabrian Pocket had become a dead end for the Republic's air force.

12

I-16s AND THE BATTLE
OF LA GRANJA

When Tinker and Baumler hauled their suitcases into the foyer of the Duke of Albuquerque's *residencia* on the morning of 28 May 1937, they discovered that it was not their squadron going to Tembleque, only themselves. But first they had to report to Ivan Kopéts in Alcalá, who would arrange air transportation for them. When they appeared before Kopéts, the Russian told them no, they were not going to Tembleque; instead, they would transition to I-16 monoplane fighters as soon as possible—in Alcalá. The Russians always did their best to package everything in a conundrum, wrap it in riddles, and tie it up with mysterious ribbons.

The Americans carried their gear to one of Alcalá's Casas de Pilotos and made themselves at home. Alcalá de Henares is a community that dates back to the Roman Empire, and its current name is derived from the Moorish al Kala, which means fortress. In the sixteenth century, Alcalá had developed into a community of monasteries devoted to scholarship and became a seat of learning that rivaled Salamanca. But by the dawn of the twentieth century it had long since slipped into decline, becoming a backwater of Spanish life and culture. In 1937 it had a population of about ten thousand persons; the anticlerical Republicans found its thirty-eight churches, twenty-one monasteries, and the buildings of its twenty-seven religious colleges to serve most usefully as barracks, hospitals, and prisons. The Casa de Pilotos that billeted Tinker and Baumler was located on the Calle de Cervantes, and in the next block Tinker found a building with a plaque on the front wall that marked it as the birthplace of Miguel de Cervantes Saavedra, the author of *Don Quixote*.

At the airfield, except for a few Spanish mechanics, they found their new I-16 squadron to be manned wholly by Russians. Its young commanding officer, a small, dark-complexioned major named Valentin Ukhov, known to be a bulldog of a fighter pilot, wasted no time with formalities; he immediately introduced them to the squadron's pilots, all of whom had been in Spain for at least six months.

Next, the Americans met their instructors. Tinker's was a small man named Ivan Lakeev[1] who had a receding hairline and mournful face. The two Americans nicknamed him "Goofy" for his physical resemblance to the character in Walt Disney's animated cartoons of the 1930s that usually appeared in the role of Mickey Mouse's straight man. Baumler's instructor was a tall, lean fellow named Lichnikov; when he smiled, which was rarely, he displayed a mouthful of gold teeth. Because he always appeared to be disgruntled, they nicknamed him "Sourpuss." Both of these men had been in Spain since October 1936 and had more than a hundred hours of combat flights in their logbooks. The frivolous nicknames had no other meaning; Tinker and Baumler respected these Russians as professionals and soon counted them among their best comrades in arms.

The Russians walked them around to a hangar and introduced them to the I-16.[2] The novelty of Nikolai Polikarpov's little monoplane fighter resided in its form, not its substance. When the prototype first flew on 31 December 1933, its airframe substance epitomized materials and engineering techniques already well into their eve of obsolescence. The fuselage was a plywood semi-monocoque of pine and birch fabricated in two vertical halves. The internally braced cantilever wing had spars of chrome-molybdenum steel alloy and ribs of duralumin; the leading edge of duralumin and the inboard sections were covered by sheet dural, but fabric covered the outboard sections and the tailgroup.

What made the I-16 truly extraordinary was its form: in a world full of biplane fighters held together by struts and wires, it was a well-streamlined cantilever-wing monoplane with retractable landing gear, flaps, a two-position controllable pitch propeller, and wing-sited guns. And its pilot sat in an enclosed cockpit. As late as 1936 the I-16 had no peers anywhere in the world. Russian ingenuity produced the world's first modern fighter airplane.[3]

For Tinker and Baumler the I-16 was a wholly new aeronautical experience. Whereas the I-15 biplane had a maximum wing loading of fourteen pounds per square foot and could be floated down to a nice three-point landing at 70 mph, the I-16 had 14 percent less wing area and a maximum wing loading of twenty pounds per square foot. By 1937, when the I-16 was five years old from the time it took shape on a drawing board, the wing loadings of new monoplane fighters had moved toward thirty pounds, but twenty was still considered high. And whereas the I-15 biplanes to which Tinker had become accustomed possessed some forgiveness, the I-16 was an unforgiving machine that demanded a pilot's every attention.

Before Tinker and Baumler were permitted to fly one of them, the Russians took them to an I-16 blocked up on wooden horses for a drill in handling the airplane's *tren escamoteable*—retractable landing gear. The Americans took turns sitting in its cockpit, practicing the raising and lowering of the landing gear. This simple but arduous procedure required some forty turns on a hand crank and about twenty-five seconds of a pilot's attention. After they had done it once, the Russians made them do it again, and again, and yet again—the repetition intended to preclude the manifold repairs made necessary by a wheels-up landing.

Although long since taken for granted, retractable landing gear in a fighter plane remained a novelty in 1937. The U.S. Navy's Grumman FF-1 biplane fighter of 1933 had a retractable undercarriage, to be sure, but the U.S. Army Air Corps had no extensive experience with this innovation until the Seversky P-35 of 1936. Meanwhile, the Russians had been flying their I-16s in squadron strength for more than a year and had had the machine blooded in Spain. Regardless of nationality, pilots with years of experience flying fixed landing gears had a tendency to forget to let the gear down in their approach to landing, and embarrassment is the least consequence of a wheels-up landing.

After Lakeev and Lichnikov were satisfied that the Americans had cranked the gear up and down enough times not to forget the existence of that small but important rotary instrument, they took them to the flight line. Baumler went up for the first flight while Tinker watched enviously from the ground. He had been aching to fly one of these rotund little machines ever since he first laid eyes on them in February, and the thirty minutes that Baumler spent orbiting the air between Alcalá and Guadalajara seemed awfully long.

When Tinker finally settled into the cramped cockpit and adjusted its seat to his height, Lakeev gave him a final check on the controls and the airplane's austere instrument panel. There were no gyroscopic instruments, not even an artificial horizon, and like the I-15 it had no fuel gauge; a pilot had to measure his fuel by wristwatch. An I-16's fuel capacity was 59.4 gallons, (356.6 pounds and 13 percent less than an I-15's tankage), which provided a trifle more than two hours in the air. Then the Russian showed Tinker a real novelty: an electric self-starter. However, sometimes it worked and sometimes it didn't, and just in case, the I-16 had a "dog" in its nose spinner to receive a Hucks starter. The plane was equipped with a two-position controllable pitch propeller, and Lakeev reminded Tinker to change pitch after his climb-out and, once again, to lower the undercarriage before landing.

Compared with the I-15, it seemed to Tinker that the monoplane took forever to get off the ground; one of the biplanes would lift off after a run of less than two hundred yards; on this first flight he used more than three hundred yards to get the I-16 into the air. Once airborne he cranked up his landing gear, and as he cranked the hurried motions of his left arm were transmitted through his body to his right hand on the control stick, and the airplane rolled, pitched, and yawed. Now he understood why the I-16s always appeared to fly such strange, undulating paths across the sky shortly after takeoff. With the airplane finally "cleaned

I-16s preparing for takeoff (*R. K. Smith Collection*)

up," Tinker pushed the throttle almost to the firewall, pulled into a climb, and found himself delighted with the I-16's ability to climb like a rocket.

Leveling out at ten thousand feet he felt out his controls in some slow turns and lazy *8*s, gradually making them faster and tighter. Most control was by elevators and ailerons only; the rudder served as hardly more than a stabilizing element, little being required even in sharp turns. Indeed, the I-16 practically refused to make sharp turns. When Tinker attempted the tight, corkscrew-like maneuvers to which he was accustomed in the I-15 biplanes, the monoplane balked, skidded across the sky, and sometimes fell off into a spin. More than ever, he now appreciated why the Russians tended to use the I-16 for slashing attacks against enemy formations and tried to avoid tangling with the nimble Fiat biplanes at close quarters.

On his approach to Alcalá, Tinker cranked down his landing gear and once again the airplane tended to bob around. Then he let down his flaps—something else he never had to do before. This early model, the I-16/5, did not have true flaps; instead, the pilot lowered its wide-span ailerons to achieve the same effect, but that resulted in a severe pitch-up. This introduced perturbation required a few landings before a pilot became accustomed to it. He came over the fence nose high and at what seemed to him an incredibly high speed, but nevertheless he touched down to a neat three-point landing. That evening he scribbled in his diary: "Flew Russian monoplane for first time today—wonderful plane—560 km/hr [347.9 mph] on straightaway at 3,000 meters [9,843 feet]—dives at 800 km/hr [497.1 mph]." For Frank Tinker, *this was flying!*

One other thing soon fascinated Tinker. Although the I-15 biplane had four guns, the I-16 had only two, but they were even more deadly. Because the I-15's had to be synchronized to fire through the propeller, their rate of fire was necessarily slower than an I-16's guns, which were mounted in the wings and sited outside the inhibiting propeller arc. He was truly amazed to discover that just one of the I-16's ShKAS machine guns had a rate of fire of 1,800 rounds per minute. When he told this to knowledgeable Americans after his return to the United States, they dismissed it as nonsense; no one, least of all the primitive Russians, possessed a machine gun that could fire that fast! Nevertheless, for its caliber, the ShKAS was one of the best airplane machine guns in the world during the 1930s, and for some years thereafter.

After speed and maneuverability, what counts in a fighter is firepower; and whereas an I-15's four guns poured 260 bullets into a target with a five-second burst, an I-16's two guns fired 300 rounds in the same five seconds. Only 900 rounds served each gun, however, and thirty seconds of continuous firing emptied its magazines. It also ruined gun barrels, and I-16 pilots were cautioned to fire in very short bursts. This was almost an unnecessary caution because at the high speeds of an I-16's attack, the best of pilots did well to hold a target in his gunsight for five seconds. Both Tinker and Baumler initially had difficulties in adjusting to this change.

The next morning the Russians gave the Americans fully armed airplanes suitable for combat and in which they were to check themselves out in aerobatics and gunnery. Before Tinker took off Lakeev climbed up on a wing, leaned into the cockpit, and reminded Tinker to lower the undercarriage before landing. Then Tinker shot off the field for thirty minutes of aerobatics and testing his guns. In these maneuvers he discovered that because of the I-16's shape and small wing area, it could not snap out of a dive like one of the biplanes; instead, it tended to squash out during a pullout, and he could feel the airplane mushing almost straight down for too many seconds before its wings and propeller got a sufficient grip on the air to end the descent and start it climbing.

In all its maneuvers along a horizontal axis the airplane responded beautifully, and its rate of roll seemed fantastic. This proved especially true of a roll to the left, which was accelerated by the gyroscopic effect of the propeller's rotation; and this was why the airplane's vertical stabilizer was offset three degrees to the right, to compensate for the engine's gyroscopic effect in normal flight. But when Tinker worked the machine through more complex maneuvers, he became increasingly aware that the I-16 was an airplane that could not be crowded; it demanded a lot of airspace, and in this experience his own flight envelope had expanded considerably.

Landing at Alcalá he found the squadron being rolled out for action. The day was 31 May; the Segovia offensive had been under way since dawn, and Ukhov's airplanes were to escort a squadron of Rasantes for a strike against the trenches around La Granja eight miles east of Segovia. The Segovia offensive, usually called the Battle of La Granja, was the abortive operation around which

Hemingway spun the story of *For Whom the Bell Tolls*. Like the other offensives against Huesca and Teruel, essentially this would be a diversionary effort. If the Republican forces managed to break through and seize Segovia, fine; but its primary object was to divert Nationalist strength in the north from the squeeze on Bilbao on the Bay of Biscay.

Tinker was told that he had just finished his "training," and his I-16 was rearmed to take part in the attack. Lakeev assigned Tinker the No. 4 slot in his patrol, and before takeoff he *again* cautioned Tinker against a wheels-up landing. Fifteen Rasantes droned out of the south, and Ukhov led his fighters to the downwind end of the field for takeoff. Because Baumler had not yet checked out in aerobatics and gunnery, the Russians kept

Ivan Lakeev (*Courtesy of Andrey Simonov*)

him grounded this day, and Tinker flew off to La Granja confident that he was the first *extranjero* to fly an I-16 with Russians on a combat mission—and most probably he was.

Segovia is about fifty miles from Alcalá, and La Granja is less than that, but the Sierra Guadarrama stands between with its formidable peaks reaching up almost eight thousand feet. Heavily laden with bombs, the slow Rasantes skirted the mountainsides while the much faster I-16s flew lazy S-turns in the cold air at 12,000 feet, weaving back and forth across the bombers' track.

It turned out to be a routine mission. No fighters appeared to challenge them. The Rasantes met some flak at La Granja but took no losses. And after the Rasantes stuttered back into their staggered formations, everyone turned for the Henares Valley. Tinker was the last to land at Alcalá and as he touched down he noticed an I-16 sitting flat on its belly near the middle of the field. Taxiing to his plane's dispersal point, he was met by his new mechanic, Pedro. Tinker jerked a thumb at the I-16 on its belly and asked, "*Que paso?*" Pedro shrugged and replied that it was one of the Russians.

Curious, Tinker started off to the operations office, but Baumler intercepted him and pulled him aside. He told Tinker that the I-16 squatting in the middle of the field had come in for its landing as nice as could be, but with its wheels up. The Russians around the operations building with him had been watching, and they all had exclaimed in unison: "*El Americano!*" But after the dust settled, who should climb out of the plane but patrol leader Lakeev.

Tinker laughed uproariously. Baumler cautioned him against attempting to rub it in, because he had already generated resentment by gloating over the mistake of the Russian calamity-howlers. But Frank Tinker never had a clear idea of discretion. Meeting a very subdued Lakeev in the operations room later, he remarked on the wheels-up landing and asked the Russian if he had gone to all that trouble simply to show him how *not* to do it. That afternoon Baumler flew his aerobatics and gunnery check, and then both Americans became bona fide members of the Soviet I-16 squadron.

In spite of the new offensive raging only forty miles away, it was a slow day at Alcalá. In part this was owed to the lack of serious Nationalist air opposition at this stage of the battle. I-16s were seldom called in for what I-15s could do, and there were at least three I-15 squadrons in the Madrid area.

The next day, on 1 June, the squadron flew three missions to the front as topmost cover for Rasantes with a squadron of I-15s sandwiched between. The Rasantes struck at targets in the vicinity of the bitterly contested heights of Cabeza Grande that overlooked the Nationalist-held village of Revenga and commanded a road to Segovia. Although Nationalist aircraft had become very active, occasionally swarming into the area on ground support missions, no Fiats rose to meet these Rasante attacks. After the Rasantes and I-15s had finished their work and headed for home, the I-16s dived down to empty their magazines into targets of opportunity.

Between sorties, while their airplanes were being refueled and rearmed, Tinker made it a custom to bring his Victrola to the field house for everyone's entertainment. Tinker and Baumler soon developed a fondness for a twelve-inch record of arias from the opera *Rigoletto*; they came to regard it as especially soothing after a hard-flown sortie, and it became their favorite *après combat* music. All dogfights ended with *Rigoletto* on the turntable. In his evocative verse "The Barrel Organ," British poet Alfred Noyes asked rhetorically if Giuseppe Verdi had ever imagined his *Il Trovatore* becoming a marching tune for the foot soldiers of London's office workers returning home at the end of a day; Verdi could not have imagined his *Rigoletto* providing the finale for battles in the skies.

Late in the afternoon of 1 June, a lone I-15 landed at Alcalá and General Jacob Smushkevich climbed out of its cockpit. After speaking with Ukhov, the Russian general sought out Tinker and Baumler and congratulated them on becoming part of Ukhov's squadron. Whatever his failings may have been, Smushkevich possessed a great sense of public relations. He called a muster of the Soviet pilots and gave them a long speech in Russian. Tinker understood none of it, but because of the happy expressions on the pilots' faces and their occasional cheering, he assumed that it was good news.

The chances are that the general's news had something to do with the imminent rotation of the Russian pilots back to the Soviet Union. Most of them had been in Spain for seven to eight months; what is more, they had every reason to believe that they would be returning to a homeland in which their hard won experience would be held in great esteem. They had the January example of seventeen returning Soviet aviators being hailed as "Heroes of the Soviet Union" for performing "difficult government tasks," which everyone knew was combat flying in Spain.

Little could these patriotic and hardworking Russian aviators have imagined the turmoil and torment that actually awaited them in their Motherland. Ten days later on 11 June, the Kremlin announced to the surprise of the world the "treason" of the Red Army's high command and that Marshal Tukachevsky had already been "tried," found guilty, and shot. This marked the beginning of Joseph Stalin's insane purge of the Red Army that decimated the ranks of its officer corps and devastated its morale; that corps would not be rejuvenated until after the German onslaught of 1941. Stalin's paranoia would judge Russians who had experienced "the world outside the USSR" as likely spies; they received especially harsh treatment on their return, and that treatment awaited many, if not most, of the veteran pilots then in Spain.

Some word of Stalin's purge of the army must have trickled into Alcalá, Albacete, and Los Alcazares before Frank Tinker left Spain two months later. Certainly before 11 June the Russians in Spain believed that they were performing an important service for the Motherland, and it never crossed their minds that their Iberian service could become a terrifying liability.

Meanwhile, the offensive on the western slopes of the Guadarrama roared on. The artillery from both sides slammed away at each other while thousands of men huddled in their trenches, and then climbed out when the barrages ceased and charged across rocky and forested terrain against a hail of fire from small arms and well-emplaced machine guns, reminiscent of the Great War. During the next few days, Italian Romeo Ro 37bis attack planes of 4-G-12 came screaming down from under caps of protective Fiat fighters to bomb and strafe the Republican trenches;[4] a few hours later the Fiats would be back, this time protecting a squadron of Czech-built Aero A-101s, big, underpowered, single-engine biplane attack bombers similar to the Rasantes, to strike again at the Republican lines.

There was bitter irony in the Nationalists' use of these Aero A-101s, which they called "Pragas," against the Republic at La Granja and Cabeza Grande, because these airplanes had been purchased with the Republic's money. A Nationalist cruiser intercepted the freighter carrying them to the Republic in

April 1937 and seized the ship with its cargo of military prizes, all of which were made useful to the Nationalist cause.

The Nationalists bombed the Republic's positions, intermixed with the Republic's air attacks on the Nationalists' earth works. Often one was scarcely finished when the other would begin; by coincidence the attacks tended to be reciprocal and seldom collided. At this time the Nationalists began to rotate a standing patrol of at least two Fiats over the front; they could harass and perhaps even break up an attack by Rasantes while Nationalist headquarters on the ground telephoned the fighter bases at Olmedo or Avila for reinforcements. After the event, the Nationalist high command regarded this as an effective technique. The Republic's field commanders depended on telephoning Alcalá for air cover only after a Nationalist air attack began. Whereas this worked well at the Jarama, it proved to be wholly unsatisfactory at La Granja, the fighters arriving too late when they arrived at all.

On 2 June, the Rasantes flew to La Granja again, and again Ukhov's squadron flew three escorts for them. The first was routine, but while refueling at Alcalá and waiting for the Rasantes to return for their second strike, two red rockets burst over the field, and Ukhov sent everyone off in a scramble to the front. It is thirty-five air miles from Alcalá to La Granja, a fourteen-minute flight at 250 mph, but when the squadron arrived, the Nationalist air forces had already finished their work and they found the sky empty.

Then they returned to the escort of Rasantes. These flights were made in the late afternoon, flying directly into the sun. While the Rasantes were at work below, dozens of Fiats popped out of the sun and swarmed among the I-16s before anyone was aware of them. Tinker thought that there were at least fifty; in fact they numbered about twenty-five—the two squadrons of the Italian group known as the As de Bastos (Ace of Clubs), led by the combat veterans Nobili and Larsimont.

In the next instant airplanes were milling all over the sky. Tinker got off several deflection shots at the Nationalists' mottled green and brown biplanes emblazoned with black discs, but he was unable to hold any in his gunsight. Unaccustomed to his guns' extraordinarily high rate of fire, he suffered from a "heavy thumb" and quickly exhausted his ammunition. When the squadron returned to Alcalá everyone was accounted for, and while the airplanes were being refueled and rearmed for their next service to the Rasantes, a phone call came in from the front that credited them with three Fiats. The Nationalists, however, recorded no losses. Then another squadron of Rasantes lumbered over the horizon from Barajas and they took off for the front again.

As they approached La Granja, the sun was low in the west, and its exaggerated light intensified the haze around the horizons. Overhead, the sunlight reflecting off a great frothy layer of cumulus clouds created a glare that rippled across the eyes. Before anyone could begin to estimate how many enemy fighters might be hiding in the midst of this dazzle, Fiats swarmed around them. Again, Tinker estimated fifty and there may have been three dozen: the two squadrons with which they had tangled earlier had since been refueled and serviced at Olmedo, and their ranks supplemented by the squadron of Degli Incerti.

Tinker got off several bursts at passing targets, this time taking care to husband his ammunition. Airplanes whirled everywhere he looked, but it seemed impossible to secure a fix on any one of them. As is so frequently the case in dogfights, it is not pilot skill that scores the kill but the other fellow's mistake sets up the victory. Tinker was beginning to miss the responsiveness of the I-15 biplane when he spotted a Fiat off his right wing whose pilot was absorbed in closing in on the tail of an I-15. Instinctively throwing over his controls, he half-rolled to the right and came down on the Fiat's rear quarter with the biplane fat in his gunsight. His first burst chopped into the Fiat's engine, setting it afire; his second burst killed the pilot as he stood up to bail out.

Rolling out of his attack, Tinker saw a formation of Rasantes below him doing their clumsy best to jink around in efforts to avoid the attacks of a half-dozen Fiats. Two I-16s were diving to the rescue and Tinker joined them, but they were already too late for one of the Rasantes, which went up in flames, rolled over on a wing, and fell toward the earth. Its gunner and pilot jumped. Tinker saw their chutes open, but because they were directly over ground forces that swept no-man's-land with crossfire between the two armies, he wondered how that pair would survive the thicket of bullets.

Meanwhile, the air had cleared of Fiats; it seemed as if they had all dived away into the setting sun. Ukhov re-formed the squadron and they climbed back to altitude and circled the area while the Rasantes and I-15s re-formed and started for their home bases. Then they dived down and buzzed the Republican trenches. This was pro forma, done in hopes of boosting morale among the Republic's ground forces. Ground troops everywhere and at all times have the psychological problem of always seeing the enemy's attacking aircraft eyeball to eyeball. These troops seldom see their own airplanes because they are usually at high altitudes or on a distant perimeter tangling with the enemy.

The Republic's army facing La Granja needed a morale booster on this day. Its offensive had already bogged down. Indeed, for the next twenty-two months these troops would sit in their wretched trenches and dugouts studying the rooftops of Segovia, its cathedral spire, and the arches of its Roman aqueduct without any hope of marching through the city's Plaza de Azoquejo as victors.

Landing at Alcalá, Tinker found himself caught in a sudden change of the wind but managed to keep everything under control until a gust slammed into the airplane during its high-speed rollout. The plane whipped around in a tight groundloop, the forces collapsed its left landing gear, and when the wing started to plow the earth, it crumpled. This was an undignified way to return from a fourth victory, but at least the Russians could not razz him for having landed with his wheels up.

When Baumler landed, he did not taxi off to his usual dispersal points but steered directly to the operations office, which told Tinker that something was seriously wrong. Baumler climbed out of his cockpit stiffly and eased himself to the ground where he gingerly worked his way out of his parachute harness. The tail of his airplane was almost chopped to pieces; fragments had ripped through the after-fuselage structure and two bullets had penetrated the nine millimeters of armor behind Baumler's seat, cutting through the heavy webbing of his parachute straps before reaching his flesh. He peeled off a bloody shirt to reveal a pair of badly lacerated shoulders. Without the protection of his seat armor he would have been gravely, if not fatally, wounded. While medics examined Baumler's bloody back, a Russian pilot named Iliev limped in with a blood-soaked leg. His trousers were cut away to reveal a limb badly slashed by dozens of fragments from explosive bullets. Ukhov packed him and Baumler off to a nearby hospital.

That evening reports from the front said that one Rasante had been lost, evidently the one Tinker saw torched, and one I-15. The I-15's pilot turned out to be a Captain Zorki. Fresh from the Soviet Union, he had been leading a squadron that was equally new to Spain. An inexperienced leader with inexperienced pilots is a poor combination; in a first combat, it was that squadron's first combat loss, and all of them had been badly mauled.

The hospital patched Baumler up quickly, and as they sat around that evening sipping cognac to the strident rhythms of *Rigoletto*, Ukhov surprised them with word that the Rasante shot down that day had been flown by an American. By this date, most American aviators had left Spain and the two had been certain that they must be the only ones left. They were even more surprised when told that the Rasante pilot was Eugene Finick; he had survived his parachute jump, came down on the Republic's side of the lines, was badly wounded, but was in a hospital and doing well. It seemed as if years had passed since Tinker had last seen Finick at Manises, yet it had been only four months.

With both of their airplanes under extensive repair, Tinker and Baumler could not fly with the squadron on 3 June, so they dashed into Madrid. The Americans' social life in Madrid had become diffused since Hemingway no longer provided a locus. The slogan *"No Pasaran!"* plastered by the thousands on the walls of the city's buildings now found itself accompanied by scrawls, daubs, and posters that exclaimed *"Pasaremos!"* (We shall pass!); but it did not look that way at La Granja.

After tracking down two prized bottles of Johnny Walker, they retired to the Hotel Florida for a testing of its water heater. Meeting some acquaintances from the Abraham Lincoln Battalion, Tinker and Baumler invited them to get in line for the bathtub; since the room was rented for all night it was a shame to let tub and water go to waste, especially when the Lincolns needed it more than the aviators.

The Lincolns were still sitting in their trenches on the lower Jarama where they had been since February. The slushy snow and icy rains of February had become the warmer rains and mud of April, and by mid-May everything had dried out and their little world had become a dust bowl. Except for occasional sniping and grenade throwing, the Jarama front had long since stagnated. They had come to Spain to fight Fascism but had been doing nothing for too long; now they wondered what it was all about: why had they been permitted to vegetate for all these months? One of their members had written a verse sung to the tune of "Red River Valley":

There's a valley in Spain called Jarama;
It's a place that we all know too well;
For 'tis there that we wasted our manhood,
And most of our old age as well.

And it went on for several more stanzas.

A new George Washington Battalion was being organized near Albacete. When it was activated, the Lincolns looked forward to being pulled out of the line for a few weeks. In fact, there were now enough Americans in Spain to create a third battalion that did not yet have a name. Some wanted to name it after Thomas Paine, others preferred Patrick Henry. Tinker suggested to them slyly that they name it after Jefferson Davis; after all, they had a Lincoln Battalion, why not name one after Jeff Davis?

That shocked the Communists among the Lincolns. They took him seriously and went to pains to explain that whereas Lincoln fought to free the slaves, Davis had been a slave owner and fought to defend that terrible institution. The International Brigades had come to Spain to free the country from Fascist slavery and would never agree to name one of its battalions after a slave-owning reactionary like Jefferson Davis. Ho hum. A serious problem with Communists everywhere, then as now, is their absent sense of humor. Tinker never understood his fellow Americans of the Lincoln Battalion. Coming to Spain to soldier in the trenches for a lousy ten pesetas a day? That was only 12 cents, $3.60 a month; no money at all and no sense to it so far as he could tell.

While Tinker, Baumler, and their Lincoln companions rolled dice, savored the Scotch, and took turns at the bathtub on this evening of 3 June, beyond the

Sierra and 125 miles to the northwest a brief but desperate drama sped toward its end. The Nationalist general Emilio Mola, the mastermind of the July insurrection, had been absorbed in directing the campaign against Bilbao when the Republic's offensive jumped off against Segovia. On this evening, he was flying to Nationalist headquarters at Burgos to consult with General Franciso Franco. His pilot, Ángel Chamorro García, flew along the Vitoria-Burgos highway, but the weather was thick, the visibility bad. Their airplane was the Airspeed Envoy that Nevil Shute had parted with so reluctantly for six £1,000 notes. Chamorro, a veteran pilot, had flown this route many times, but the worst of weather can undo the best of airmen, and he had only a split second to see the dark mountainside come rushing out of the murk and into his cockpit. The Envoy's wreckage was found near the village of Castil de Peones; there were no survivors.

In 1937 the airplane was not yet commonplace; it still possessed great novelty, and it played a unique role in shaping the Spanish conflict. It had been Luis Bolín's flight to the Canaries that provided General Franco with clandestine transportation to Morocco; an air crash at Lisbon killed General Sanjujro, who otherwise would have led the Nationalist insurrection; twenty German airplanes provided a timely airlift from Morocco that secured the Nationalists' precarious position in Andalusia; Russian fighters over Madrid in November 1936 played a vital role in rallying the Madrileños to their own defense; and now an airplane accident wiped out Emilio Mola, the only general with whom Franco had to share a measure of power. As a shaper of fate, the airplane functioned as the *deus ex machina* of the Spanish Civil War.

By the next day, on 4 June, the Segovia offensive had run out of momentum, and when Ukhov took the squadron on a patrol of the front, everything on the ground was quiet and the sky seemed empty. But as they circled a tower of cumulus a lone Fiat was spotted flying among broken clouds about 1,500 feet below them. Ukhov signaled everyone to hold formation, and then he half-rolled out into a dive after the Fiat. Tinker saw three short bursts of tracers spurt from Ukhov's wings to converge on the hapless biplane; the Fiat pulled up its nose, skidded to a stall, and fell away to spin into the dark mountainside. Meanwhile, Ukhov had zoomed back to altitude and slipped back into his place at the head of the squadron that he led back to Alcalá.

The Segovia offensive had shot its bolt and with no successes. A few square miles of useless, mountainous terrain had been taken, but Segovia remained an eternity away, and the Nationalists had not been diverted from tightening their noose around the Cantabrian Pocket. Indeed, the game was practically finished at Bilbao, with the Republic losing. A noteworthy aspect of the Segovia operations at La Granja is that the Nationalist field commanders had nothing but praise for the performance of their air force, whereas the Republic's generals complained that their air support was wholly inadequate, that bombing had been conducted from altitudes that were too high, that aircraft did not stay over the battlefield long enough, and when they called for fighter cover it usually came too late.

Like the animated mechanics back at Campo X, the Republic's high command was riven by politics. In fact, after all was said, the Soviets had the last word because they controlled the air force. Indeed, the Soviets may not have wanted this offensive to succeed because if the Republic's forces had broken through to Segovia, there was the practical problem of where they might go from there. Pushing northwest to Valladolid or southwest to Avila was in the realm of fantasies; in both cases the Republic's flanks would have been exposed and its armies had never performed well in a war of maneuver. It is likely that a breakthrough beyond Segovia would have resulted in disaster, and one way to prevent this from happening was to ration its air support and hold the operation on the short leash of the diversion it was supposed to be.

For the next five days Ukhov's squadron lounged around the field house in Alcalá on standby for alerts that never came. Divided into two sections, one stood alert by their airplanes from 4:30 a.m. until 1 p.m.; the other from 1 p.m. to 8 p.m. While on alert, they gathered under the shade of their airplanes and played cards, chess, or dominos, and Tinker introduced the Russians to Arkansas coin-pitching. Meals were brought to them in the form of bread, sausage, wine, hard-boiled eggs, and olives; they made sandwiches; and the Americans provided music on their Victrola. Once again, it did not seem like such a bad war after all.

On 10 June, a double-rocket alarm sent the squadron scrambling to its sector of the Guadalajara front. There may have been enemy aircraft in someone else's sector, but as far as Ukhov's squadron was concerned it turned out to be a false alarm. They flew back to Alcalá, cranked up the Victrola for a few spins of *Rigoletto*, and resumed their games.

Baumler learned that Finick was hospitalized in Navacerrada, a small village in the mountain pass that leads through the Sierras from Madrid to Segovia, and he and Tinker got permission for a visit. They brought along all the groceries they could find, some cognac, what English books and magazines they had, and even their Victrola. They found Finick with a swollen face, one leg up in a plaster cast, and the rest of him swathed in bandages that covered terrible burns. Finick himself, surprised to find *two* other American aviators in Spain, was delighted to see them if only to speak English for a few hours.

On his part, Tinker was surprised to learn that Finick had flown in every big fight since the Jarama and that Lacalle's squadron had been escorting Finick's Rasantes at Guadalajara. During the Segovia offensive, Finick had been flying five sorties a day, and when he was shot down he was on his fifth. His squadron had been ordered to attack targets near Revenga but had the bad luck to accidentally interrupt a half-dozen Fiats strafing the Republic's positions. Their escort of I-15s comprised a squadron of Russians new to Spain with instructions to defend the Rasantes and themselves, but not to seek combat. They took these instructions too literally, blundered into the rest of the Fiats, lost the initiative, and had to fight their way out like the Rasantes. Tinker told Finick that the Russian squadron leader had paid with his life for his want of imagination.

While the Fiats and I-15s were mixing it up, Finick and the other Rasantes plodded on to their targets, dumped their bombs, and hurried for home. But as Finick explained, when he rolled away from his target, antiaircraft fire chopped through his wings and severed his aileron controls. An airplane is extremely difficult to fly without ailerons, and thereafter he was a cripple, staggering around the sky and stuttering through turns with only his rudder. Then the Fiats closed for the kill. He did well for a few minutes, zigzagging with his rudder alone and pumping his throttle for an irregular flying speed, while his gunner in the rear cockpit discouraged the fighters from approaching too closely. Meanwhile, it seemed like Fiats were flashing past him on all sides, the yellow fingers of tracer bullets everywhere, but there were no hits. In the next instant his instrument panel exploded into junk, a fuel tank directly in front of the instrument panel erupted, and the cockpit suddenly filled with fire.

The next thing he knew, Finick said, he was falling one way, and the flaming airplane was falling in another. He pulled his ripcord, but the parachute wouldn't open. Reaching behind himself instinctively, with both hands he clawed at the canvas flap coverings of the seat pack, tearing them open. It seemed an eternity, but eventually he was seized by a back-wrenching jerk and he knew the chute had opened. But now he realized that he was afire; his leather flying suit and its fleece lining were burning, the fire fanned by his rapid descent.

While he was beating at the fires in his clothing, a Fiat dove toward him and tracers whizzed by. He had to stop beating the fires and manipulate the risers of his shroud lines left and right so he would swing back and forth, thereby becoming a more difficult target. The Fiat climbed away but rolled into a turn and came back for a second try. Then an I-16 swept in upon the scene, and the Fiat disappeared. A few seconds later, Finick came to a bouncing stop with his parachute canopy hung up in a tree, his feet dangling some twenty feet above the ground.

Before he had time to think how he was going to get out of the tree, its branches broke, and he plunged to the ground. On impact he felt no pain but heard, or felt, a *snap* from somewhere. Looking around at the crazy angle of his leg, he knew it was broken. He had begun to feel pain from his injuries when a Republican infantry patrol came tramping toward him through the forest. At first Finick was elated at not having come down in Nationalist territory, but when the soldiers heard his strangely accented Spanish they believed him to be a German and started beating him savagely. One of them leveled his rifle and was about to shoot him when an English-speaking officer appeared. Crazily enough, on this western slope of the Sierra Guadarrama, the Republican officer was an American Indian by the name of Morrison.

After Finick's identity was made clear the soldiers became terribly ashamed—almost childlike with apologies—and could not do enough for him. Morrison and his men took a long and painful time in getting Finick to a road, rough going over broken ground. There followed a long wait for an ambulance and a wild ride in the ancient vehicle over rutted roads to a mountain clubhouse that had been converted to a field hospital. When Finick reached the field hospital, the pain in his leg was fierce and burns seemed to be devouring his body; a nurse gave him a shot of morphine, and everything became warm, dark, and good.

Later, the doctors at Navacerrada told him that his leg had been set improperly at the field hospital; it would have to be rebroken and set again, which would render it about one centimeter shorter than the other. That was only three-eighths of an inch and would not prevent him from flying. Finick thought the medics had done a good job. He found the books and magazines that Tinker and Baumler had brought with them marvelous. It was good to speak English again and listen to the Victrola, if only for a few hours. It was, to be sure, great to be alive.

Tinker and Baumler said little to one another during the drive back to Alcalá. In spite of the good face everyone puts on it, visiting the wounded is always awkward and seldom pleasant. Looking at Finick, both pilots knew but for a few freak seconds of luck they could be lying in a similar bed, weighted down by plaster, smothered in bandages, and offended by the smell of their own burned flesh.

On arriving at the Casa de Pilotos the two learned that there would be no lounging around the *campo* tomorrow; the squadron was leaving for Aragon and action against Huesca.

13

FIVE DOWN, NO GLORY

While Ukhov's pilots ate a hurried breakfast on 11 June 1937, the sun remained hidden behind the distant Sierra de Altomira, but the eastern sky had begun to pale. They stepped into the Calle de Cervantes, boarded a bus, and drove through empty streets to the airfield where mechanics were readying their airplanes. The cool of the morning felt good; the stillness at the airfield seemed unreal. Then the whine of an engine being started shattered the air, the hard coughs of its ignition followed by the throaty roar of nine exhausts pulsing with the labors of hardworking pistons and valves. Another engine started, and another, and within a few minutes the air was filled with the angry sounds of a dozen engines being run up for magneto checks.

As if the engines orchestrated the day, the sun appeared out of the low eastern haze, and as dawn became daylight, Valentin Ukhov led his flock of fighters bumping through the grass to the downwind end of the field where each in its turn roared off into the rising sun. Ukhov circled Alcalá until he had gathered a half-dozen of his airplanes around him and then turned his formation east for Liria, a small town about twelve miles northwest of Valencia on the Mediterranean. Liria, 165 miles away, was a fuel stop where they would rendezvous with another Russian fighter squadron before flying to the front in Aragon.

For the next hour and twenty minutes, Tinker watched the rolling plains of La Mancha speed by the leading edges of his wings; then the terrain fell away into deep valleys and gorges bounded by arid mountains. Finally the dark Mediterranean plain appeared ahead, green with the tops of orange, olive, and almond trees, and Ukhov waggled his wings and signaled his planes into a landing circuit (see map 8.1).

At Liria airfield they found the other squadron of I-16s already there, led by a Russian major senior to Ukhov who would command the whole group. The major asked Ukhov where the rest of his airplanes were; Ukhov couldn't be sure. Lakeev led the second section, and Ukhov began stalking in and out of the operations office, glaring at the sky. Still no Lakeev. Ukhov was becoming furious.

The telephone rang. It was Lakeev. Old Goofy had missed Liria and landed at nearby Manises by mistake. He would be at Liria shortly. After Lakeev and his section of airplanes arrived, Tinker and Baumler were treated to a dramatic exhibition of Russian military discipline. Baumler had been flying with the Russians since he first arrived in Spain, and Tinker had a long relationship with them even before he had joined Kosenkov's squadron. The Americans had been favorably impressed by the pleasant informality with which the Russians operated and nevertheless managed to get things done. Now they saw something different. It was perhaps one aspect of the sinister differences then beginning to overwhelm the Soviet Union's armed forces.

When Lakeev walked casually into the operations building, the Russian major immediately got to his feet. He asked Lakeev a question, and Lakeev made the mistake of trying to laugh it off. After all, only a ten-mile difference separated Manises and Liria. But the group commander wasn't having any of it. The major snapped out a command that jerked Lakeev to attention. The pilot walked smartly to the major's desk, clicked his heels, and rattled off something in Russian that to Tinker sounded like a plebe at Annapolis answering a first classman.

Whatever Lakeev said proved unacceptable to the major, who merely answered with a "*da*," and his scowl became darker. The major's "*da*" did not mean "Yes, I understand," but rather "Yes, continue." Lakeev's next words sounded less certain, and each time he paused the major injected another "*da*." The hapless Russian pilot was obviously foundering.

Tinker and Baumler couldn't take the dismemberment any longer; they got up and left. The Russian pilots stayed for the rest of the show. Unlike the Americans, they were not foreign mercenaries and could not simply walk out from under the nose of a group commander intent on making an example of a subordinate. Perhaps some of them had personal reasons for enjoying Lakeev's humiliation; others may have been mesmerized by the new order just beginning to penetrate their careers and that soon would have a terrifying effect upon many of their lives.[1]

Lakeev somehow managed to square himself with the major and Ukhov, because when the squadrons took off for Aragon he was still leading his section of two patrols. Most likely this was owed to his being an excellent fighter pilot. Although the rules were changing in their homeland, professional ability still counted heavily with the Red Army Air Force in Spain.

From Liria, the two squadrons of I-16s followed the Mediterranean shore northward. As they overflew the village of Vinaroz the conspicuous delta of the Ebro River came into view, and they swung inland to intercept and follow its meandering track. Rising out of the high Basque country far away in the northwest, the Ebro flows between Navarre and Old Castille, and across Aragon where it begins to snake its way among the mountains and awesome gorges as it rushes to the sea. From the air, the sight is no less than breathtaking.

Near the village of Mequinenza, the airplanes' stubby shadows left the Ebro and sped up the valley of the Rio Cinca to their new base at the village of Caste-jón del Puentes, situated a few miles south of Barbastro and thirty-two miles southeast of Huesca. After the squadrons had broken up into their landing pattern and Tinker was circling for his turn to land, he was surprised and intrigued by the sight of the snow-capped Pyrenees glistening against the northern sky.

The airfield at Castejón was one of four bases the Republic had created for its offensive against the Nationalist-held salient around the city of Huesca. Although new to Tinker, this part of Spain was a familiar scene to Baumler. In April he had spent a week operating out of Balaguer, Lérida, and Castejón with Kosenkov's squadron, escorting old Fokker F.VIIb3m bombers[2] in fruitless attacks on the city of Huesca. Baumler recalled the field at Castejón being primitive but good; it was flat, hard, and had plenty of space. Its only shortcoming was its tall, tough weeds that wrapped themselves around the axles of the airplanes' landing gear, binding their accumulated girth between the wheels and the oleo legs. This undergrowth distressed the ground crews who had to cut the stuff away. In June the weeds were worse and more of a nuisance because of the I-16's retractable landing gear.

In addition to the I-16s at Castejón, there were squadrons of I-15 biplanes based at the nearby village of Selgua and at the local population center of Barbastro. And yet another I-15 base could be found at the village of Grañén off to the west. For this campaign some Rasante attack bombers would be based at Barbastro, but most of them were stationed to the south at Sariñena while the SB-2 twin-engine bombers usually operated from Sariñena and the more distant base of Lérida. As a rule, the basing of bombers depended upon the proximity of a railroad by which their heavy ordnance could be supplied easily.

The city of Huesca, some forty miles northeast of Zaragoza, is the former seat of Moorish kings and the ancient capital of Aragon. Those men of yesteryear put their seat of government at Huesca because it stands at the head of an amphitheater-like stretch of terrain that dominates the west bank of the Isuela River and a broad valley that runs off into the province of Catalonia to the east. Admirably sited for medieval warfare, Huesca's natural defenses served it equally well during the civil war of the 1930s. The Nationalists had held the city since the beginning of the war and, like Teruel, it formed a salient that jutted into Republican territory. No political leader or amateur strategist of the Republic could look at a map without raging at the sight of the brazen salient of Teruel and Huesca and dreaming of how easily they might be pinched.

The tactical situation at Huesca was the same as that at Teruel in April: the Republic thought that if it mustered enough power it could pinch off the salient. The strategic situation, on the other hand, was the same as Teruel and Segovia. The Republic would attempt yet another diversionary offensive in the naive hope that the Nationalists would divert forces from their terrible squeeze on the Cantabrian Pocket. And in this June of 1937, the squeeze on Bilbao and Santander had become desperate.

Baumler advised Tinker that when he was based at Castejón in April, the hotel facilities left much to be desired. Not much had changed. Ukhov's squadron found itself billeted on the top floor of a three-story building that held a stable of horses and mules on the ground floor. The aroma appealed to no one and loud protests were made to the squadron's commissar. This commissar was evidently a big shot in the Russian political organization in Spain, because whatever he set out to do he got done, but quickly. Tinker and Baumler nicknamed him "The Powerhouse." He had a young assistant, evidently an apprentice to the commissar trade, and Tinker named him "The Powerhouse (jg)."

The Powerhouse attacked the housing problem with full voltage, and the squadron soon found itself housed in some very pleasant quarters in Barbastro, about four miles from the field at Castejón. Barbastro possessed a population of some four thousand souls, and compared with Castejón it was a bustling metropolis. Tinker noticed that most of the houses in Barbastro appeared to have stables on their ground floors, and he assumed this to be a peculiarity of the architecture in this part of Aragon. In any case, The Powerhouses had run the animals out of the ground floor of the Casa de Pilotos, had the stable cleaned, and created a dining room on the second floor and bunk rooms on the top floor. Tinker and Baumler had a room with a balcony from which they had a stunning view of the Pyrenees.

On 12 June Tinker had his first look at Nationalist-held Huesca, escorting two dozen Rasantes to their targets around the city's dense network of ground defenses. Most of these Rasantes were the usual Russian R-5s and R-Zs, but some of them were Czech-built Aero A-101s. Although Tinker met no opposition during his three flights against Huesca, Baumler had a much more hectic day. While escorting one squadron of Rasantes, Baumler's patrol ran head-on into a flight of five Ju 52s escorted by a mixed squadron of Fiats and Heinkels. While the I-16s dove to attack the fighters, the slow and terribly vulnerable Ju 52s dumped their bombs, turned away, and their pilots put on full throttle to return to their base at Zaragoza. Meanwhile, the Nationalist fighters had swung around to meet Baumler's patrol, and for a few minutes the sky went wild with airplanes. Having successfully diverted the I-16s and given the Ju 52s time to get away, the Nationalist fighters broke off contact and turned for home.

The Nationalist fighter pilots disengaged with good reason. Unlike the Republic's air forces that had a half-dozen bases close to Huesca, the Nationalist airfields were sited along the Ebro between Zaragoza and Tudela, the closest being forty miles from Huesca, and they had only one primitive emergency field at Erla in between. After flying from Zaragoza, the Fiats did not have much fuel to expend in combat over Huesca if they hoped to return safely to base.[3]

Baumler's section had alert duty that same afternoon when the alarm sounded, and he found himself scrambling off the ground and clawing for altitude over Huesca. Another five Ju 52s (probably the same five of the morning) were finishing their work bombing Republican strong points around the city and beginning to turn for home. Their escort of Fiats and Heinkels climbed to meet the diving I-16s; a dogfight of a few minutes ensued that gave the bombers time to get away. Then the Nationalist pilots again broke it off and sped away to the southwest.

The Russian aviators had instructions not to carry a fight deeply into enemy airspace because the inevitable loss of Soviet pilots over Nationalist territory promised to embarrass the Soviet Union's loudly trumpeted policy of "nonintervention" in Spanish affairs. The Germans and Italians also claimed "nonintervention," but Joseph Stalin did not have the imagination to invent "volunteer organizations" as had Hitler with Germany's Legion Condor and Mussolini with Italy's Legionaria Aviazione. Nevertheless, more than a few Russians were shot down over Nationalist territory to become prisoners. They would be quietly exchanged for German and Italian airmen downed in Republican territory. The Russians, like Captain Zorki to his peril at La Granja, tended to take their instructions too literally. On this day, Baumler's Russian patrol leader did not attempt a pursuit of the Nationalist fighters, although the enemy must have been low on fuel and anxious to get back to Zaragoza and environs. The Russians read their orders in terms of providing fighter protection for the Republic's positions around Huesca; they had done so, and that was that.[4]

In both these combats, Baumler's section, and whatever other sections were scrambled by other Russian squadrons in the area, claimed no victories and admitted no losses. But theirs were hot fights, and they had been up against the Nationalist squadron 2-G-3, led by Joaquin Garcia Morato. With at least forty kills, he is considered by some of his contemporaries to rank among the most formidable fighter pilots of all time.[5] Although Morato made no aerial claims for himself, four of his pilots each claimed an I-16. But Morato scored another kind of victory on this first day of the Huesca offensive. Among the Republic's casualties was General Matazalka Lucasz (real name Mata Zalka), the Hungarian Communist commander of the 12th International Brigade. His brigade had been moved from the Madrid front for this campaign not only for its numbers, but also to help stiffen the resolve of the new Eastern Army made up of Catalans and Aragonians, soldiers not noted for their zeal on the battlefield. Failing to take the precaution of camouflaging his automobile, Lucasz's shiny black limousine moving swiftly at the head of a cloud of dust caught Morato's eye. He dived on it and gave the car a strafing that ran it off the road. Lucasz was killed and his chief of staff, Gustav Regler, seriously wounded.[6]

The next day was a Sunday and no bombing was done. Tinker attributed this to consideration of the religious ways of the Aragonians. More likely it was owed to a foul-up among the bomber squadrons at Sariñena and Lérida. The Nationalists showed no similar sensitivity about the Sabbath; a rocket alarm sent one of the other Russian squadrons hurrying up to the front, where they interrupted a half-dozen Ju 52s leisurely bombing Republican positions, and a squadron of Heinkel He 46s dive-bombing and strafing Republican trenches. The He 46, a single-engine, two-place, high-wing monoplane, was slow and simple "meat" for *any* fighter plane. However, attacking from high altitudes, the Russian I-16s first had to come to grips with the Fiats of Morato's 2-G-3. Neither side claimed any victories, but in the few minutes of vigorous combat Morato succeeded in covering the escape of the vulnerable Nationalist attack bombers.

On Monday the fourteenth, the Republic's attacks livened, fighters cooperating with a squadron of SB-2s. While a couple of squadrons of I-15 biplanes created a diversion by dive-bombing and strafing the trenches south and east of Huesca, the SB-2s sped in from Lérida, capped by several patrols of I-16s, to dump their one-ton loads on the rail point and highway junction at Ayerbe, a small town eight miles northwest of Huesca. Tinker guessed that the SB-2s must have hit an ammunition train. Whatever it was, it was big. A huge cloud of black smoke that could be seen for thirty miles or more came boiling up out of Ayerbe; the next day a column of smoke still marked the site of that unhappy little town.

After "Operation Ayerbe," Ukhov led his squadron back to Castejón to refuel and rearm. While ground crews crawled over the airplanes, two red rockets popped over the field. As quickly as possible, the squadron rushed back for the air over Huesca, now swarming with airplanes. Tinker guessed sixty Fiats and Heinkels. In fact, there were only about eight Fiats and six Heinkel He 51s providing cover for a half-dozen He 46s and four of the lumbering Ju 52s. But the Nationalist attack "collided" with two squadrons of I-15s that were already dive-bombing and strafing nationalist trenchworks. At a distance, there was no differentiating one from another—they were all biplanes—so Tinker assumed them all to be Heinkels and Fiats.

Caught in the midst of refueling and rearming, Ukhov's I-16s got off the ground only in spurts of one or two airplanes at a time. And by the time they all stuttered into the air above Huesca, airplanes were everywhere. Tinker found all kinds of targets; he rattled off some good bursts, at least eight of them. But in diving at high speed through and zooming out of the melee for altitude from which to begin another attack, he never had time to see if an enemy even shuddered under his hits, much less began oozing smoke, or rolled out to hit the ground.

Baumler had better luck. He spotted a Fiat whose pilot was totally absorbed in closing on an I-15. Diving in steeply from six thousand feet, Baumler had a straight run in which to frame the hapless Fiat neatly in the center of the 360-degree world of his gunsight. He squeezed off a couple of three-second bursts, sending 360 7.62-mm missiles smashing into his target. The Fiat faltered and rolled away from its attack on the I-15. Baumler followed, and a few more bursts sent the Fiat hurtling toward the valley of the Isuela four thousand feet below. After twenty minutes the Nationalist fighters, doubtless short on fuel and outnumbered in any case, worked their way out of the melee and made their escape toward Zaragoza.

That night at supper the results of the day came in. Three I-15s from other squadrons had been lost, but Loyalist front-line observers counted fourteen enemy fighters shot down. The Nationalists did not have fourteen fighters operating on the front that day, so this claim was ridiculous. Undoubtedly, two or three observers who saw the same airplane fall claimed it as "their own," which is aside from claims made by pilots. In a melee such as had occurred, two or three pilots may have fired at the same enemy at different times, in different sectors of the sky, and each would be confident that it was *he* who shot it down. On this same day over Huesca, however, the Nationalists claimed six victories and conceded the loss of four fighters, a claim more realistic than that of the Republic's.

Not until after World War II, when independent evaluators carefully dissected the Battle of Britain, did historians *begin* to realize how distorted the claims for aircraft destroyed can be. Sometimes this distortion is the deliberate result of propaganda; more often it is owed to the weaknesses of human nature. But the fact remains that concurrent to the actual event, distortion as regards aircraft shot down is inherent to the unique character of aerial combat.[7]

In the Casa de Pilotos in Barbastro, however, no pilot would ask that the day's scores be submitted to some abstruse scientific analysis. To the exhausted aviators who had bounced around in cramped cockpits all day, rushing off the ground to answer other alarms besides the one that resulted in the day's big fight, the ratio of 3:14 sounded just right. At dinner they called for a case of champagne, which was duly broken out to celebrate the day's victories. "The Powerhouse" became so carried away by the day's reported operations and the pilot's celebrations that he produced an extra case of champagne. And the celebration bubbled on well after dinner and into the wee hours.

On the morning of the sixteenth, Ukhov's squadron climbed back into the air over Huesca and provided cover for two dozen Rasantes attacking trench works northwest of the city. Orbiting the target area at ten thousand feet, Tinker was entranced by the Rasantes' tactics. The big biplane bombers plodded on well past their target, where they made a 180-degree turn and broke up their vee formations to form up in single file. Then they dove to five hundred feet and flew the length of the enemy's trenches. White puffs began filling the air around them, the first sign of antiaircraft fire Tinker had seen around Huesca, and even from ten thousand feet the stuff appeared to be thick. But the Rasantes flew on, following the axis of the trench works in single file, firing away with their batteries of 7.62-mm guns. Instead of releasing their twenty-four 25-pound bombs all at once, they loosed them in batches of six, and Tinker estimated that each Rasante wiped out about two hundred yards of trench works.

After the Rasantes had been escorted clear of Huesca and with no Nationalist fighters in evidence, Ukhov took the squadron back to empty its magazines into the trenches around the city. Then they returned to Castejón to refuel and rearm, a typical cycle in close-air support as executed in the Spanish Civil War.

A second escort flight that morning would be a similar milk run. But in the afternoon, the squadron encountered what seemed to be a "horde" of Heinkels and Fiats that came diving out of the sun. It was the same old story of previous days; the Nationalist fighters had been providing cover for a similar attack by a handful of He 46s, which had been bombing and strafing Republican trenches. Tinker estimated fifty enemy fighters, but this scene, too, was confused by a squadron of I-15s that swarmed into the combat. In his I-16 monoplane, Tinker, at a distance, was inclined to count all biplanes as Nationalist fighters until he recognized red striping on the I-15s.

The air filled with airplanes wheeling and turning in every direction. Tinker got in a few passing shots at the sharp-nosed biplanes with the white tails, their wings and fuselages marked with black discs. But he was never able to hold one in his sights for long. In a close-in dogfight the I-16 was at a distinct disadvantage with the highly maneuverable Fiat, and to some extent even with the far less-nimble Heinkel He 51. Indeed, an I-16 pilot who let himself be sucked into a turning fight with a Fiat might believe himself *muy hombre* (very much a man); but unless the Fiat pilot made a dumb mistake, sooner or later he would turn inside, and the I-16 pilot would not return to his *campo de vuelo* (airfield), but rather to the *campo santo* (cemetery).

Tinker fully appreciated this, which is why he never stayed to dogfight but kept diving through the confusion in search of targets of opportunity, then trading off the speed generated in his dive to zoom back to a high altitude, where he

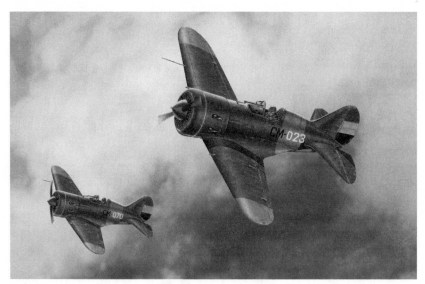

Tinker aloft in his I-16, No. 23. *(Illustration by Richard Groh)*

would flip over and begin a new attack. This was Russian fighter doctrine for the I-16 as it developed in Spain.

While Tinker swung across the sky in a steep bank, he spotted a Fiat boring in on one of the vulnerable Rasantes. He whipped around to intercept him. The Fiat's pilot saw Tinker in the same instant and rolled to meet him in an almost head-on attack. But Tinker was rolling on the inside of their turn. In a few seconds the Fiat would have its guns zeroed on his plane, but Tinker fired first and watched his two bright streams of tracers tear into the Fiat's engine, little black pieces of it flaking away in all directions. One three-second burst had reduced its engine to junk.

The two airplanes flashed past each other, Tinker climbing for altitude, the Fiat rolling around through a faltering 180-degree turn in an attempt to follow Tinker's track. The Fiat might have got off a deflection shot against him as he went through a tight, climbing turn to come back and finish it. But Tinker saw no tracers. Aside from its engine being shot to pieces, he assumed that the Fiat's pilot was either badly wounded or had died. The Fiat fell off on one wing and started spiraling toward the earth, obviously out of control, with a trail of grey-black smoke marking its descent. The fires licking out from under its engine cowling reached the fuel tank and the whole airplane disappeared in a sheet of flames and disintegrated in a ball of orange and black smoke.

The air remained alive with airplanes, and Tinker climbed back into the fight to get off shots at random targets. Then, as quickly as it started, the sky cleared except for the stubby silhouettes of I-16s and a squadron of I-15s scattered over lower altitudes.

On the earth below, Tinker saw the wreckage of a Rasante burning—one of the Czech Aero A-101s. As far as he knew, it was the only loss of the day; but the Nationalists claimed two Rasantes and one I-16.

In this afternoon air battle over Huesca Frank Tinker had scored his fifth victory, which made him an "ace." He expected no congratulations when he landed at Castejón. And indeed there were none. All he wanted was his aircraft promptly refueled and rearmed and a cup of coffee; if one of his ground crew was thoughtful enough to lace the coffee with a bit of cognac, so much the better, because it was awfully cold 12,000 feet above Huesca. In any case, there was yet another squadron of Rasantes flying in from Sariñena and another fighter cover to be flown that afternoon.

In another time in another place in a different war, public information officers would have sent their typewriters and mimeograph machines into action, and paper pushers in some headquarters would have drawn up a citation for numerous Big Brass to sign and countersign. A decoration would be authorized: "Frank G. Tinker Jr. (alias Francisco Gomez Trejo) is hereby declared an Ace!" After World War II the expression "Five Down and Glory" would be invented by the U.S. Air Force's public relations corps to celebrate these occasions. Such stuff had no place in the Spanish Civil War in the 1930s.[8]

No unusual celebrations took place in the Casa de Pilotos in Barbastro that evening. If Tinker had been naive enough to boast about his fifth victory, doubtless one of the Russians would have asked quietly, "Only five?" More important, the whole squadron had scored only five. And even this claim was optimistic. A long war still lay ahead with many more airplanes to be shot up and shot down, men to die, and victories to be claimed—and discounted. And in the bitter long run, the Spanish Civil War would not be won in the air, but on the ground, as all other wars have been won before and since. Wars may begin in the air, but they end in the mud.

In any case, Frank Tinker had not come to Spain for glory but for the money and to prove to himself that he was every bit as good a fighter pilot as he thought he was. Take the cash and let the credit go. And his fifth victory meant an extra thousand smackaroos in the bank. That's what Americans understand best. Everything else is a delusion.

Next morning on 17 June, two red rockets burst over the field at Castejón, sending Ukhov's squadron scrambling off for Huesca. They expected to find another group of Ju 52s and He 46s bombing under an umbrella of Fiats, but the sky was empty. The pilots spent the rest of the day lounging in the shade of their airplanes playing cards, swatting at flies, and cursing the heat and the insect life that infested the weeds. It was a relief to return to the Casa de Pilotos that evening, where comely Aragonian señoritas served supper. When they chose to, the girls could understand the pilots' Castillian Spanish, however butchered by primitive grammar and Russian and American accents; but the pilots were at a total loss to understand these girls who spoke Catalan, and a dialect at that, an ancient Latin amalgam of French and Spanish.

The eighteenth was the squadron's big day. It started off early with an escort of three dozen Rasantes and two dozen SB-2 light bombers for a strike against the city of Huesca itself. Heretofore, they had been attacking only the outer defenses of the city in hopes of opening a passage for the Republic's ground forces, but to little effect. After the bombers dropped their loads in the midst of the city, the fighters strafed the trenches close in around it on the way out. In one of his passes a burst of flak rocked Tinker's airplane so badly that it almost hurtled out of control, and he struggled to be certain that he was still flying the machine.[9] Others spotted this particular flak gun in a church belfry, and Ukhov re-formed the squadron for an attack. They all came screaming down, pouring tracers into the bell tower from which some of the gunners fell out and tumbled to the ground. After their pass on the church belfry, the fighters clung to the ground and sped through a hail of small arms fire before crossing the lines where they could began to climb for altitude.

When Tinker last saw Huesca, it was a "shattered and burning city," almost completely hidden by a pall of brownish-black smoke. In this battle for Huesca, Republican forces consisted mostly of Catalans whose politics embraced Anarchism. Like Italian ground forces, the Catalans and Anarchists talked a good fight, but when up against it they tended toward confusion and recrimination, and they proved no match for the Nationalist defenders of Huesca. The Loyalists had taken a few hundred yards of worthless earth here and there, but after a week and ten thousand Republican casualties on the ground, the Huesca offensive had to be written off as a failure. Huesca and its salient held fast. Indeed, the city would take its revenge some months later in March 1938, when it became one of the key jumping-off points for the great Nationalist offensive that would drive down the Ebro Valley to Vinaroz on the Mediterranean coast, cut the Republic in halves, and ultimately determine the end of the war.

Tinker did not know that the attack against Huesca would prove not only a tactical disappointment but also a strategic failure. Nationalist troops had long since broken through the so-called Ring of Steel around Bilbao, and on 19 June they had occupied the city. The battle for the Cantabrian Pocket was now half won for the Nationalists, and in the same instant the battle for Spain was half lost for the Republic. The savage attacks directed against the city of Huesca itself had nothing to do with tactics or strategy; they were simply a frustrated expression of *venganza con furia* on the part of the Republic, but it was no compensation whatever for the loss of Bilbao.[10]

Immediately after landing, Ukhov's squadron received word that operations at Castejón del Puente were finished. They would fly to Los Alcazares the next day. That afternoon and evening Tinker and Baumler spent sitting on their balcony in Barbastro breaking bread, which they ate with sardines, sipping wine poured for them by their Catalan señoritas, and looking off toward the snow-capped Pyrenees to the north. In the foreground Spanish farmers cut wheat, moving up and down the fields in their donkey carts with incredible slowness compared with American tractors and combines. Beyond the Pyrenees was France and peace, or at least no war. Less than twenty-five miles to the northeast lay Huesca, a city nearly destroyed, filled with smoke and fire, the wounded, the dead, and the dying. Looking off to the cool, pristine Pyrenees, Tinker took another sip of wine and thought once again that it wasn't such a bad war after all.

When everyone mustered at Castejón's airfield the next morning, they found Lichnikov—Baumler's Sourpuss—already in the air. The Russians' section leader had been having a lot of minor difficulties with his airplane; the mechanics had been working on it, and before flying to Los Alcazares he wanted to wring it out. Lichnikov began with easy maneuvers and then worked into some tight aerobatics: loops, snap rolls, hammerhead stalls, and spins. Then he climbed to about 15,000 feet, swung down in a screaming dive, and by this time everyone on the field was watching him. At the bottom of his pullout, the outer three feet of his left wing failed; it folded back and finally carried away. The stubby little I-16, which was not overendowed with lateral stability in any case, promptly spun into a tight left spiral.

There was still plenty of altitude for Lichnikov to bail out, but the centrifugal forces of the tight spiral apparently had him pinned in his seat. Everyone on the ground stood transfixed as the airplane came corkscrewing down through the air, crashed in the center of the field with a terrific impact, and disappeared in a great cloud of dust. An awesome silence ensued, in which no one moved; the sound of the wind whipping through the tall weeds on the field beat on everyone's ears. Then in the next instant, everyone was running toward the wreckage.

Everyone, including Tinker, ran out to the wreck. Looking back on it, he wondered why they ran. It was not burning. There was no fire to be extinguished. Nor was there any possibility that Lichnikov might be alive. Tinker arrived on the scene just as a pair of litter bearers lifted the Russian's corpse onto a stretcher. He never had imagined that a human body could be so badly mangled.

Lichnikov had served in Spain for more than eight months, longer than any other Russian in the squadron, and had fought on all of the fronts. After the squadron arrived in Los Alcazares, he was supposed to have rotated home to the

Soviet Union. By this time, Tinker had absorbed the *fatalismo Español*, and his reaction to Lichnikov's death was the same as Lacalle's toward his friend Jose Calderon's: *"Esta la guerra!"* Who knows—by dying in Spain Lichnikov may have been spared a firing squad in the USSR, or a slow death in some brutal gulag on the frozen shores of the Lena River.

While the ground crew scavenged around the crumpled airplane, the pilots went back to theirs to await Ukhov's order for takeoff. Instead, two red rockets shot into the air, which sent everyone scrambling into their cockpits and rushing for takeoff. The alarm came from the bomber base at Sariñena where there was an air raid scare. After the fighters had circled Sariñena for twenty minutes with their eyes peeled for enemy aircraft, Ukhov signaled a false alarm.[11]

When the squadron settled down among the weeds back in Castejón, Ukhov cancelled their flight to Los Alcazares. They would fly tomorrow. Tinker and Baumler spent another pleasant evening sitting on their balcony, contemplating the snow on the Pyrenees, drinking wine, and trying to penetrate the dialect of the dark-haired señoritas of Aragon.

The flight to Los Alcazares on 20 June was only a trifle more than three hundred miles, not even the distance from Randolph Field in San Antonio to San Angelo, Texas; but it was more than three-quarters of the distance from Spain's Pyrenean frontier to a point on its southernmost Mediterranean shore. The ceiling was low, and Ukhov's squadron had to fly at less than one thousand feet, which gave Tinker a marvelous view of Aragon and the provinces of Valencia and Murcia from a vantage that few ever experience. They refueled once more at Liria, and although the ceiling lifted here, the flight continued south at pleasantly low altitudes.

As the squadron pilots broke up into their landing circle and began spiraling down to landings at Carmoli airfield, a few miles south of Los Alcazares, they were suddenly introduced to the differences between Aragon and Murcia in June. Even in the short time between letdown and touchdown, their fleece-lined flying suits became terribly gooey inside; and while taxiing around the dust-filled field to their dispersal points, their sweat-covered faces became caked with dust that turned into mud. After a bath, however, Carmoli, Los Alcazares, and Murcia seemed pleasant again.

At Carmoli, Tinker and Baumler found the Soviet squadrons in the midst of a turnover. New Russian pilots fresh from the USSR had arrived by ship at nearby Cartagena a few days before, and they were busy making cross-country flights and checking out flying conditions in Spain. The old Russians with whom Tinker and Baumler were acquainted had finished their six-month tours and were being processed for their return to the Motherland. Among those relieved was Ukhov; Lakeev succeeded him as their new squadron leader.

Tinker wandered into Los Alcazares, only a village in the 1930s, and on his return to Carmoli was delighted to find Baumler in the officers' club drinking rum with Kosenkov and some of the other Russians from their Guadalajara and Campo Soto days. They, too, were on their way back to the Soviet Union, and that evening the Americans got together with them for a rousing farewell dinner.

The next morning, Tinker discovered that everyone had been granted a few days' leave. Baumler had already left for Valencia. Tinker joined Lakeev, his wingman Beyliekov, and a couple of other Russians for a stay at a special "rest house" for pilots in the village of San Juan de Alicante, not far from the Mediterranean port of Alicante. The rest house, formerly the county estate of a wealthy Alicante businessman, was lovely. Its owner, said to be a Nationalist sympathizer, had been summarily dispossessed. The usual satellite buildings attended a large, three-story manor house, all surrounded by a high stone wall that enclosed well-kept grounds and beautifully manicured gardens. The locals called it "The Villa Russia."

A doctor named Diego, assisted by his wife Carmen, operated the villa, along with a gardener and his wife who was the cook, two chauffeurs, and six señoritas—Pilar, Inez, Maria, Antonia, Juanita, and Margarita—their names carefully noted by Tinker. These girls were not necessarily at the "disposal" of the pilots but assisted with the operations of the villa, which was a hotel unto itself. It required many hands in a land in which washing machines were rare, when drip-dry fabrics did not exist, and other aspects of housekeeping had not yet become "mechanized."

The day's schedule consisted of getting up around 8:30, which was late sleeping for a group of pilots accustomed to turning out at 4:00 a.m. After breakfast they often drove to the nearby Playa de San Juan for a swim. Having sampled the beaches of California and Hawaii, Tinker was not much impressed by the Mediterranean's pebbled shore, but the water was great. Then they loafed around, talking, playing games, writing letters, or reading the villa's supply of Russian and English books and magazines until lunch, which was usually at 2:00 p.m. The rest of the afternoon was similarly theirs, to go back to the beach, use the tennis courts, perhaps play croquet on the lawn, or simply wander around the village. In the evening there were parlor games and cocktails before supper, which, in accord with Spanish custom, was not served until 8:00 p.m., and it was always a sumptuous affair. Afterward there would be music in one of the sitting rooms, the radio in another, and for those who had the enterprise to catch the eye of one of the household's señoritas, there were comfortable settees secluded among the hedgerows of the spacious garden.

This was how the Republic played host to the good and welfare of its expensive skilled labor from foreign lands: *el Norteamericanos* on contract for $1,500 per month and *los Rusos* on lease from their government in return for 315 million dollars in gold bullion, to be shipped out of Cartagena to the Soviet Union in October.

By way of contrast, at this same time members of the Abraham Lincoln Battalion—those poor suckers who "had politics" and who naively believed that they would "smash Fascism" in Spain—also enjoyed a Republican rest camp. After 116 days in the trenches, they found themselves taken for a "rest" to the wretched village of Albares, forty miles east of Madrid. There was no beach, only a creek in which to splash around. Neither radios nor English reading material were to be found, much less all the other comforts of the villa at San Juan de Alicante. There was one *bodega* in Albares, but it had no whiskey, no gin, and no cognac, much less any fancy liqueurs. It did, however, have one large vat of freshly distilled anis with which the Lincolns revived their childhood taste for licorice. Within an hour, they were so drunk that they nearly demolished the village. After they made their peace with the villagers at the direction of Steve Nelson (aka Mesarosh), the detachment's Communist leader, their entertainment would not consist of tennis or croquet but of helping the villagers harvest the local barley crop.[12] So much for the American cannon fodder inspired by self-styled "intellectuals," those who always managed to stay at home to think "great thoughts," and who explained away the Republic's military disasters in terms of a "lack of proletarian spirit."

However isolated they might be in Albares, with their miserable pay of ten pesetas a day, the Lincolns were spared the possibility of buying a bicycle. The Wright brothers had built bicycles before they built airplanes, and in San Juan de Alicante Frank Tinker was about to regress from the Wrights' invention, which he handled so well, to try his hand with their earlier product, about which he had forgotten so much. As was the case with many of Tinker's adventures on the ground, this one ended in near disaster.

14

A BICYCLE, BRUNETE, AND Bf 109s

One day everyone decided to drive into Alicante to see a movie; Tinker chose to stay at the villa and write letters, an endeavor that he lubricated with a few drinks and took no more than an hour. Eventually he wandered into the village, had more than a few additional drinks at the local *bodega,* and then discovered a bicycle shop. Deciding that the one thing he needed to make life complete on this twenty-fifth day of June 1937 was a bicycle, he purchased one and pedaled away toward a close brush with destiny.

The only feature that bothered him about his new mount was its European brakes that had their controls on the handle grips, whereas he was accustomed to the American coaster brake that engaged by backpedaling. He had mastered this problem as a midshipman while on his summer cruise to France in 1929, but now he found it harder to remember than the necessity of cranking down his landing gear.

After wheeling around the village, Tinker decided to strike out for Valencia. Baumler was in Valencia, and wouldn't *he* be surprised when Tinker wheeled in on a bike! He thought Valencia was only some thirty miles away; in fact it was about seventy-five air miles and almost twice as far by the coastal road he took. About six hours later and almost midnight, while walking the bike to the top of a steep hill, he had long since realized that he had badly underestimated the distance. At the top of the hill, he found himself looking down on the Mediterranean village of Villajoyosa, barely fifteen miles from his starting point. Swinging back into the saddle, he pedaled furiously downhill.

During the civil war, every village, however small, had local guards that checked on traffic through the town, and the traveler had to produce his *salvo conducto.* As Tinker whizzed into the village two guards stepped out of the night shouting, "*Alto!*" Tinker instinctively hit what he thought were his brakes, but backpedaling produced no results. By the time he remembered to squeeze the handle grip brakes, he had run down one of the guards and the other had whipped out a small automatic pistol and fired. In the next instant,

Tinker was on the ground, the bicycle on top of him, and he had a pain in his right side.

Investigating the pain, his fingers came away bloodied. He thought it was a hell of a thing to survive six months of combat flying only to get shot off a bicycle by some local sheriff. Fortunately, the warden's aim was not all that good, and the bullet was small and of high velocity, passing through the right side of his abdomen just below the rib cage without hitting any vital organs.

When the guards discovered that Tinker was a pilot of the Fuerzas Aereas of the Ejército Popular, and a member of one of the Russian squadrons at that, they were horrified by what had happened. They probably had fears of being stood up against a wall and shot for their blunder; their apologies were so effusive that Tinker felt sorry for them. The *alcalde,* who had the only car in town, hastened to the scene and drove Tinker to the military hospital in Alicante.

The next day, on the twenty-sixth, Baumler returned from Valencia and was astonished to find his friend in a hospital; he was even more astonished at how Tinker got there. Whitey Dahl, who had accompanied Baumler, offered some witty questions about how a fighter pilot went about getting shot off a bicycle. He sagely remarked that bicycles were very dangerous because at the low altitude in which they had to operate a parachute was useless. Whitey's appearance proved a surprise; Tinker had not seen him since March, which now seemed more like three years than three months. Whitey told of how his stomach problems took him from Madrid to Valencia, where he got permission to visit the American hospital in Paris. The American medics told him he had appendicitis and wheeled him off to surgery, after which he recuperated at Cannes with Edith. He was gone so long that the Air Ministry thought he had quit. When he finally returned, Lacalle was still in Valencia and of the conviction that Dahl had abused his trust. Whitey had to do some fast talking to obtain reassignment, but he was finally ordered to an I-15 squadron based at Guadalajara.

In Alicante, Tinker was bedded down in a ward with two dozen other patients, all recovering from combat wounds. In the bed next to him was the American Indian named Joe Morrison who had been wounded at La Granja. Morrison, ordinarily a merchant seaman, found his ship docked in Valencia when the war started, and its nervous captain sailed in great haste, leaving him stranded on the beach. For want of anything better to do, he joined the war. Wounded twice in Valencia's street fighting before Republicans secured the city, Morrison was seriously wounded during the November 1936 battles of Madrid. He had been back in the lines for only a few days of the Segovia offensive when he was shot again at La Granja. Morrison had jumped into a shallow depression that did not provide complete cover, and a Nationalist machine gun raked the right flank of his body. Peeling off his hospital shirt, he showed Tinker the scars of nine bullet wounds that started at his shoulder and stitched their way to his right foot.

One of the stories Morrison related was of his rescue of an American aviator at La Granja. The fellow was badly burned; his men took him for a German, beat him, and were about to shoot him when Morrison arrived on the scene. The story sounded familiar to Tinker, and after comparing notes it turned out that the pilot was Gene Finick. It could be a small world.

After four days in the hospital and two more recuperating at the Villa Russia, Tinker received a phone call on 2 July from Lakeev, who told him to report to Los Alcázares, north of Cartagena on the Mar Menor. After a long day's drive in a hospital car, he found Baumler and Whitey Dahl in the officers' club at the base, and Whitey was upset. He had expected a transfer to the same squadron as Tinker and Baumler, but the Russians were not agreeable. They evidently felt that Dahl's experience would be best used in one of the new squadrons recently arrived from the Soviet Union.

Orders to redeploy had not arrived by the Fourth of July, and on this day Tinker, Baumler, and Whitey refused to report to the airfield. It was not a significant breach of discipline; nothing was happening, and everyone knew it. The Americans had decided on their national holiday that a celebration was in order. The hotel in which they were billeted overlooked the Mar Menor, a vast and lovely shallow bay that is sheltered from the Mediterranean by a ten-mile hook of land. They appeared on the hotel's terrace with three Very pistols, three boxes of flares of assorted colors, and three bottles of rum; combined altogether the ensemble made an interesting threesome. They spent the afternoon lounging there, drinking rum to frequent chants of, "Yo-ho-ho and a bottle of rum, fifteen men on a dead man's chest," occasionally singing the "Star-Spangled Banner," and shooting flares. The words "the rockets' red glare" were sung especially loudly, accompanied by the popping of Very pistols and arcs of pyrotechnics across the Mediterranean blue, exploding into colors over the Mar Menor. The Americans had a good time; the hotel staff felt well entertained.

When orders arrived on the fifth, the Republic's offensive near Madrid was already some eight hours old, having begun with an artillery barrage at 3:30 a.m. Tinker and Baumler had been assigned to a Russian squadron of I-16s in which they previously served. Ivan Lakeev had succeeded Ukhov as its leader. The squadron would be one of two ordered that day to the Madrid area as reinforcements. Tinker's old wingman Beliekov appeared on the roster, but everyone else was new. The strange Russian faces struck Tinker as being substantially younger than the veterans he had known, and after flying with them he judged the newcomers to be less capable pilots than *los Rusos de antiguo*, as the expression went among the ground personnel. But in Spain they would learn—or die in the attempt.

It is 250 miles from Los Alcázares to the Madrid area, well beyond the non-stop range of an I-16, and the squadrons had to refuel en route. While landing at an airfield near the village of Sisante, the shortcomings of the new Russian pilots became manifest. One of them wiped out his landing gear in a hard landing; given the robust design of an I-16's undercarriage, this was no small achievement. Another overshot the field completely and crashed into a road embankment. The latter airplane was reduced to salvage; its pilot lay dying when the squadrons took off for Madrid.

Arriving over the valley of the Henares, Lakeev rolled his squadron out to the south, landing at Barajas, Madrid's commercial airport; the other squadron went north to Alcalá. After dispersing their airplanes, the pilots were driven up to Manzanares el Real to inspect the airfield they were to use during the days ahead. This was the same airfield that Tinker had inspected in May when the Republic anticipated using it to ferry I-15s to Santander. Then it looked small to him for biplanes; it looked smaller still for I-16 monoplanes. The site had military advantages, however; it was within thirty miles and almost due north of the battlefield, and its existence was as yet unknown to the Nationalists.

When Tinker got up on the morning of the sixth, his bullet wound gave him trouble. He attributed the discomfort to straining torn muscles climbing in and out of the cockpit with the weight of a parachute; the squadron's medic determined that although the entry wound in his back had healed, the exit hole in his abdomen had become infected. He packed Tinker off to a clinic at Barajas. The physicians grounded Tinker for a few days to spare the wound further exertion and to give it more time to heal.

When his squadron took off for Manzanares el Real on 6 July, he remained at Barajas to be driven up to the new base later. It was just as well. The landings at the small mountain airfield approximated disaster. One of the new Russians lost control of his airplane on landing, nosed over, and flipped it on its back, and all of the others had serious difficulties. Upon returning to Manzanares the next day, another new Russian dropped his I-16 through the last twenty feet of his let-down at the field; he not only wiped out its landing gear but also reduced the airplane to salvage, and in the process hospitalized himself with serious injuries.

The new Russians handled their airplanes as if they were still operating at sea level, failing to consider that they needed more speed, runway, and total control in the thinner air at higher elevations. Madrid's Barajas is about 2,500 feet above sea level, while Manzanares el Real is at some 4,000 feet; combined with the warm temperatures of a Castillian summer and pilots ignorant of the difference, this amalgam of invisible circumstances could be deadly.

While the medics examined Tinker's wound in Barajas, the Republic's offensive was more than twenty-four-hours old; within a few days it would degenerate into what has come to be called the battle of Brunete (pronounced Broo-net-tay). The Republic's plan for the offensive was practically the reverse of the one employed by the Nationalists back in December when they tried to encircle Madrid from the northwest and were stopped at the Coruña Road. The Republic's high command expected to break out in the northwest, sweep around west of Madrid to the important road junctions at Navalcarnero and Alarcón, swing south through the Nationalist forces that besieged Madrid, and cut them off from their hinterland. Success depended upon surprise and speed. Remarkably enough, surprise was complete, but speed proved sadly wanting, and the offensive exhausted itself at the village of Brunete, which is located in an arid scrubland some fifteen miles west of Madrid (see map 8.1).

On 7 July, while the offensive rumbled into its second day, Tinker rejoined the squadron, now based at Manzanares el Real; however, he would not be restored to the flight roster until the next day. The Casa de Pilotos, though hardly the former home of a *marqués*, much less a ducal estate, was comfortable enough. Christina, one of the sisters of Campo X days, had been managing the Casa de Pilotos at Manzanares since May and had now been joined by her older sister Maria. Tinker was pleasantly surprised to find them together. While Lakeev's fighters came and went from the airfield, escorting bombers to and from the front, Tinker spent the day recuperating on the front porch with the two sisters, drinking wine and talking over old times of Campo X and Azuqueca.

Lakeev's squadron had a busy time of it, and the new Russian pilots continued to have difficulties. Hard landings and groundloops proved all too common, creating hours of work for the airframe artificers who already had enough to do repairing flak damage. One Russian had an antiaircraft shell burst directly beneath his airplane; fragments shredded the underside of his fuselage, chopped through the folds of his seat-pack parachute reducing them to ribbons, and left him with bloodied buttocks. His wounds, though embarrassing and painful, were far from fatal; sent to a hospital for treatment, he was flying again within a few days.

Baumler, meanwhile, escorted Rasantes and Natacha ground-attack airplanes against traffic in the road junctions at Quijorna and Valdemorillo, and Nationalist troop concentrations near Peralles de Milla. The Natacha was an improved variant of the R-5 Rasante, recently arrived; at least three squadrons of them participated in the Battle of Brunete. Baumler numbered among those who answered a series of double-rocket alarms that called for air defense over Brunete, but all proved to be false alarms.

On the morning of the 8th, Beliekov returned with his patrol, having made a low altitude reconnaissance of Carabanchel and the Casa de Campo. The flak and small arms fire had been heavy, and their planes were riddled. Beliekov painfully struggled out of his flight jacket to reveal a blood-soaked shirt, and after the shirt was cut away an ugly piece of flak fragment could be seen imbedded in his right shoulder. A medical corpsman failed to dislodge it with surgical tweezers, so Lakeev brought a pair of mechanic's pliers to bear on the problem. With a mighty heave by Lakeev and a short cry from Beliekov, the offensive piece of steel came free; then Beliekov was sent on to a hospital in Madrid.

While Lakeev conducted surgery on site, Baumler took off leading two patrols to escort ten Rasantes in an attack against Quijorna, a small village northwest of Brunete. Halfway to the target Baumler spotted five Ju 52s off to south. They were plodding along under the escort of what appeared to be three formations of Fiats, the topmost of seven airplanes covering one of five and another of three at lower altitudes.

Baumler signaled his other patrol to continue its escort to Quijorna and turned away with his wingmen, climbing for attack altitude. He had a small advantage in having the midmorning sun behind him, but when the Nationalist formation turned north in the direction of Boadilla del Monte, they spotted him and promptly turned again, retreating toward the southeast. The two lower formations of fighters that probably consisted of He 51s carrying bombs for a ground attack, dove for the deck. The uppermost seven Fiats did not even have time to break up before the tracers of Baumler's patrol tore through their formation. Baumler saw his tracers chop into the rearmost Fiat, which fell away, stalled, and spiraled off toward the ground. The I-16s climbed right through the Nationalist formation, Baumler still seeking altitude for a diving attack, and he did not have time to see if his target hit the ground. When the I-16s rolled out at the top of their climb to dive on the enemy, the Fiats had scattered and were diving away following the bombers.

While Baumler was sweeping through the Fiats over the town of Villaviciosa de Odón, Tinker, now restored to flying status, joined Lakeev. Each of them led a patrol in the escort of fifteen Rasantes to strike at the Nationalist defenses south of Villanueva de Cañada. It was a routine operation, and after they saw the Rasantes safely back across the lines, Lakeev led the I-16s in strafing attacks against targets of opportunity in the Casa de Campo.

When Tinker climbed out of his airplane at Manzanares el Real, he was greeted by a dispirited Whitey Dahl. Dahl was flying with a squadron composed of new Russian pilots based at Alcalá; none could speak Spanish, much less English, and he was feeling very much alone. His squadron had stood down for the day, so he drove up the hill to visit Tinker and Baumler just to make sure that he could still speak English. Tinker took Whitey to the Casa de Pilotos and, when Baumler returned from yet another escort of Rasantes, the three Americans toasted Baumler's Fiat. It was his seventh victory and would be his last in

Spain. Whitey was even more cheered by an invitation to dinner, especially when told that wild duck was on the menu.[1]

After dinner, everyone retired to a veranda from which they had a marvelous view of the valley of Madrid spread out 1,500 feet below their perch on the mountainside. While they sipped cognac and coffee, Nationalist bombers, prowling invisibly through the darkness to attack Alcalá, Barajas, and other airfields in the Madrid area, provided entertainment. Scores of milky-white fingers of light swept the inky sky in search of the raiders; hundreds of orange flak bursts punctuated the night while thousands of tracer bullets laced random patterns across the sky. It was like having a box seat in the first balcony of a theatrical production, and the show went on intermittently for three hours. Only the citizens of Alcalá, Barajas, and environs, huddled in their *refugios*, could take exception to the dramatic display.

Also prowling the night air, and unknown to everyone at Manzanares, were a half-dozen I-15s under the command of a Russian named Eremenko. These pilots were especially trained for night fighting. Aside from special flame dampers on their engine exhausts and flash-guards on their gun muzzles to prevent the pilot from being temporarily afflicted by night blindness after he fired, the airplanes were no different from an ordinary I-15. They operated outside of the zone of antiaircraft fire, each fighter at a different specified altitude. Their technique was to spot a bomber as it passed through the searchlight beams, then attempt to work out an interception using the flames from its engines' exhausts for identification. The Russians' efforts proved fruitless until the night of 25 July when a Captain Yakushkin shot down a Ju 52 that fell in Nationalist territory. The next night "Captain Serov" (aka Carlos Castejón) bagged another one, its crew parachuting into Republican territory to become prisoners. Without any form of electronic guidance it was a hit-or-miss operation, but its occasional successes served to inject an element of uncertainty into the Nationalists' night bombing.

Lakeev's I-16 squadron spent the next two days shuttling back and forth across the lines, providing top cover for squadrons of Rasantes and Natachas. Sometimes a squadron of I-15s was sandwiched between, striking at Nationalist traffic on the roads between Navalcanero and Sevilla la Nueva, and at the road between Fresnedillas and Quirona, and bombing trench works around Brunete. The Republic's ground forces succeeded in taking Brunete, but the Nationalist lines hardened southeast of the town on a height called Mosquito Ridge. Republican infantry supported by artillery, tanks, and armored cars, and with complete air superiority, assaulted the ridge but the attacks were poorly coordinated, casualties were heavy, and results minimal. By its fifth day, the Republic's offensive had run out of momentum and the initiative passed to the Nationalists.

On 10 July a double-rocket alarm sent Lakeev's squadron scrambling to the front. They expected to find Nationalist bombers operating against Brunete, but the sky was empty. After cruising the area for fifteen minutes, they dived for the deck and emptied their magazines into targets of opportunity, but the flak and small arms fire was intense. One burst almost rocked Tinker's plane out of control, and in the next instant he realized that the left half of his windshield was blown away. After landing at Manzanares, he discovered that the whole left side of his airplane was practically shredded. Feeling lucky that no fragments had struck his engine, fuel tank, or himself, he remained contemptuous of antiaircraft fire. In his estimation, flak gunners never had accuracy, only luck, and their good luck was a pilot's misfortune. It was all chance, the stuff of *está la guerra*, and, for him, not worth fretting about.

All of the next day both his and Baumler's airplanes remained in the hands of the squadron's airframe artificers repairing the flak damage. So he and Baumler borrowed one of the squadron's automobiles and ran down the mountain to see Whitey Dahl at Alcalá. But Whitey's squadron had been moved from the hazardous environment of Alcalá to the seclusion of Campo Soto, and by the time they wheeled into the duke's estate, they were told that Dahl had left to see them at Manzanares. Giving up what was becoming a hunt, they went into Madrid.

When they walked into the lobby of the Hotel Florida, who should be lounging in one of its chairs but Whitey Dahl, talking with a couple of officers of the Lincoln Battalion. The Hotel Florida was no longer what it had been. During the first week of June the Nationalists lashed the city with an unusually severe bombardment. Several shells struck the Florida and one scored a direct hit on its fabulous water heater. It was an awful moment; when the pressure vessel burst, its scalding water flashed into steam vapor that filled the corridors, and many panic-stricken residents mistook it for poison gas. The long-term consequences proved worse. In wartime Madrid the water heater could not be replaced, and without hot water there was no reason to endure the Floridian "death trap"; the colony of foreign newsmen dispersed among the city's less hazardous hostelries, and the Hotel Florida as a social focus in the Spanish Civil War passed into history.

The Lincoln officers were Rollin Dart and Sandy Land; both had some experience as private pilots in the United States but found no market for their limited talents in Spain, not even flying *avionetas* in communications services, so they joined the Spanish army. The Americans decided to make a night of it, and after finding a source who produced five bottles of Piper-Heidsick Champagne for a stiff price, they walked up the hill to the Hotel Gran Vía for dinner.

There was plenty of wine with dinner, and although the food was mediocre, they had their champagne cooling in a bucket beside the table. Only fifteen miles away to the west, the men of the Lincoln and Washington Battalions were struggling through the day's suffocating heat, dragging equipment up barrancas and across arroyos while trying to regroup their forces for a predawn attack on deadly Mosquito Ridge. They had no champagne and little water—the only water was found by digging into the dry bed of the Guadarrama River. Within the next week the ranks of the Lincolns and Washingtons would be so decimated that their numbers were barely enough to make one under-strength battalion. That summer night was also hot in Madrid, but the electric fans in the Hotel Gran Vía's dining room made it tolerable. Dart and Land enjoyed it while they could.

The evening remained a pleasant one until the Americans began speculating about five attractive señoritas at a nearby table and finally managed to convince the ladies to join them. But the ladies had come in with five militia officers who resented their desertion. Some strong words were exchanged between the Americans and the *milicianos*; then fists started to fly and tables overturned to sounds of shattered crockery and glass. One of the militia officers reached for his gun, but while struggling with the flap on his holster, the Americans unholstered theirs and fired a half-dozen shots into the ceiling. The *milicianos* fled in one direction, the girls disappeared in another, and the Americans found themselves alone with some angry members of Gran Via's management. And that proved to be an expensive end of their party.

Dart and Land went back to their room in the Florida, Tinker and Baumler drove Whitey back to Campo Soto and his Russians. Although they left exchanging *hasta luegos* on the evening of 11 July, it was in fact an *adios!*; neither Tinker nor Baumler would ever see Whitey again.

When Tinker and Baumler showed up for breakfast the next day with cut lips and black eyes, Lakeev scolded them for setting bad examples for the younger pilots. Baumler was in especially bad shape. For some weeks he had been afflicted by a glandular infection around his throat; its swelling was becoming ominous. It pained him to button the collar of his flight jacket, and the fistfight had done nothing to help it.

Their airplanes were still under repair so they could only sit around the Casa de Pilotos drinking black coffee and listening to the engines of their comrades flying to and from the front. This may have been just as well. Two Russian I-16 squadrons from Alcalá flew Rasante escorts in the morning and instead of experiencing the usual milk run, it seemed to them that the whole Nationalist air force appeared. The Rasantes had to run for it and were badly mauled before they could escape, leaving the I-16 pilots to a bitter fight for survival, losing at least three of their number in the process. There seemed to be Fiats everywhere; in addition to these nimble biplanes, they encountered a swarm of the new German monoplane fighters that hitherto had been seen in force only on the Cantabrian front. The Spaniards called the new fighter a "Mayser-Schmidt"; indeed, it was the Messerschmitt Bf 109B.

This piece of bad news was barely digested at lunchtime when a double-rocket alarm rushed two patrols into the air to put a fighter cap over Madrid. Baumler's airplane was now repaired, and he led the interceptors; it was the first of five alarms he answered this day, mostly to no effect. Meanwhile, the squadron's two other patrols scrambled in reply to similar alarms over Madrid, the front, or elsewhere. Nationalist bombers now seemed to be everywhere.

In Baumler's first three scrambles, he led his wingmen to six thousand feet and scouted the triangle of Barajas-Escorial-Navalcanero, finding nothing. But on his fourth he tangled with Fiats and the new Messerschmitts over Madrid, which were flying top cover for Heinkel He 111 bombers that raced on to their targets at Barajas and Alcalá. Having done their job, the Nationalists fighters withdrew, and Baumler's interception reached no conclusions. On his fifth scramble his patrol chased after nine Italian SM.79 trimotor bombers and two He 111s, but they had too much altitude and speed to be overtaken. Meanwhile, the repairs to Tinker's airplane had been rushed to completion, and he was able to answer one alarm before sundown, a bomber threat against Alcalá; when he flew into the air above that ancient town only eighteen miles from Manzanares el Real, the sky was empty.

On this twelfth of July, the Republican offensive had shot its bolt. Its armies were only about five miles from the village of Alarcón, the primary objective, and about the same distance from the town of Navalcanero, both on the important Talavera-Madrid road, but as far as the Republic's forces were concerned, that distance may as well have been five thousand miles. In spite of having air superiority—indeed, what was tantamount to air supremacy—for all of one week, its ground forces had not attained in seven days what was supposed to have been rolled up in three. The Republic had driven a salient of about seventy square miles into Nationalist territory, and that included the hapless village of Brunete. But its reserves had long since been committed, its whole force teetered on the edge of exhaustion, and now the initiative belonged to the Nationalists. If during the first week of the offensive the Republic enjoyed what amounted to air supremacy, hereafter it had to fight hard for whatever hours of air superiority could be managed.

The Republic's offensive of 5 July 1937 had achieved complete surprise, and the Nationalists immediately became alarmed by its initial successes and obvious consequences. What the Republic's diversions against Huesca, Teruel, Segovia, and Huesca again had failed to attain, Brunete's achievements succeeded too well. The Nationalists suspended operations on the Cantabrian front, and Santander received a brief respite; men and equipment were stripped from the north and hurried south to reinforce the Madrid front. Among these reinforcements were the aviation units of the Legion Condor and the Italian Legionaria. The Legion Condor's equipment included new Dornier Do 17 twin-engine bombers and the Italians' new Savoia-Marchetti SM.79s, both types having but recently arrived in Spain. The German fighters included two squadrons of He 51s and one of the new Messerschmitts, while the Italians threw in their veteran *grupo* of three squadrons of Fiat CR.32s, whose pilots called themselves the Cucarachas, plus the equally experienced As de Basto. These elements were in addition to Morato's 2-G-3, Spanish-manned squadrons of Junkers Ju 52 bombers, He 51s modified for ground attack, miscellaneous squadrons of clumsy Heinkel He 45s and He 46s, and the somewhat more versatile Romeo Ro 37bis ground-attack planes.

Tinker's morning of 13 July started with an escort of a squadron of SB-2s to a target near Navalcarnero. The bombers had just finished dropping their half-ton loads when Lakeev spotted five Nationalist bombers overhead, cruising above ten thousand feet. Liberated from their bomb loads, the SB-2s were capable of dashing for home by themselves, and Lakeev signaled his squadron into a climb to intercept the bombers. They were new bombers never before seen on the Madrid front, evidently Dornier Do 17s that could run away from a pursuit at 220 mph. Because of their advantage in altitude and speed, Lakeev's squadron could not close to an effective gun range within any reasonable time and distance; he abandoned pursuit, and the pilots returned to their base on the slopes of the Sierras.

After refueling, Lakeev led his squadron back into the air to rendezvous with a squadron of SB-2s and two squadrons of Natachas en route to the front. The SB-2s dumped their loads on the Nationalists in Boadilla del Monte while the Natachas bombed and strafed troops on the road between Boadilla and Mosquito Ridge. Far from being a replay of Guadalajara, the well-disciplined Spanish regulars promptly took cover alongside the roads, from where they turned their rifles on the low-flying attack planes. Flak and small-arms fire was thick.

The air war heated up in the afternoon when the day's sun gauge shifted to the advantage of the Nationalists, and then it became hotter still. It was another case of attacks meeting head-on. Lakeev's squadron was flying top cover for two squadrons of I-15s loaded for dive-bombing, and a squadron of SB–2s, when the sky in the southwest suddenly became filled with specks glinting in the afternoon's sun. There were formations of Junkers Ju 52s and Heinkel He 111s en route to bomb Brunete and escorted by a swarm of Fiats, He 51s, and what Tinker called the new "Mayser-Schmidts."

The appearance of the Bf 109B in substantial numbers in Spain during the spring of 1937, first in the north and now on the Madrid front, suggested to the rest of the world that Hitler's Reich had this high-performance fighter well

Messerschmitt Bf 109B, No. 6-15, Legion Condor (*Courtesy of Sergei Abrosov*)

along in series production and available in such large numbers that it was no inconvenience to the Luftwaffe to dispatch Bf 109s to Spain in squadron strength. In truth, the Bf 109's presence in Spain was a hurry-up job dictated by the He 51's miserable performance against the Russian fighter planes.

As early as December 1936, three preproduction prototypes of the Bf 109 were rushed to Spain for combat trials, joined by three more in January 1937. After a seven-week combat evaluation, which all survived, they were shipped back to Germany. When production models of the Bf 109B-2 became available, two squadrons were shipped to Seville and Cadiz in April 1937, the airplanes being assembled at Jerez de la Frontera and Tablada, and then rushed into service on the Cantabrian front to assist with the push on Bilbao. Their presence in Spain would prove a significant factor in changing the character of the air war, and not just in Spain, but throughout Europe for the next fourteen years. But this impending alteration in aerial combat was impossible to imagine in the summer of 1937.[2]

At 15,000 feet above the parched plain of the Guadarrama, Tinker was about to acquire insights to this change as Lakeev's squadron and the Nationalist fighters sped toward each other at a combined speed of five hundred miles per hour. In an instant the sky was awhirl with airplanes. Diving and climbing through the fracas, Tinker found himself unable to hold a target. His Russian wingmen were new pilots; he did not know how much he could expect from them, and he was trying to be careful this day—to the extent that carefulness in these circumstances can mean anything. What is more, he was flying with essentially one eye because his other eye was puffed up with various hues of purple from the exertions of the night before.

Then he saw a lone I-15 being chased by a vee of three Messerschmitts;[3] signaling his wingmen into a right echelon, he half-rolled into a dive to the rescue. But before he could bring one of the attackers into his gunsight, smoke started to pour from the I-15; it staggered across the sky and started for the ground, apparently out of control. No parachute appeared.

By this time, Tinker had the leading Messerschmitt square in his gunsight and sent two bright streams of tracers into the target, sparkling as they chopped their way through the duralumin skin of the enemy's fuselage; then the whole airplane erupted in flames. Meanwhile, his wingmen had caught the leader's right wingman between them; they failed to set it afire, but it went down out of control. When Tinker turned his attention to the remaining Bf 109, it had already rolled away and was diving to escape.

After landing at Manzanares, Tinker reported seeing the loss of one I-15 and then stood his wingmen to a round of drinks; he was pleased by their teamwork, which turned out to be unusually good. Until this mission he and the wingmen had been relative strangers, but the patrol's neat dispatch of the two Bf 109s created a bond that transcended language barriers; it was a good beginning. Eventually word came in from the front that ground observers had seen a dozen assorted Fiats, Heinkels, and Messerschmitts hitting the ground; two Fiats were lost in a midair collision. The score sounded good until Tinker was called to the telephone and was told that the one I-15 lost this day was Whitey Dahl's.

In fact, as Dahl later related to a newspaper reporter while in captivity, he had been flying in a patrol of four airplanes when they were jumped by Messerschmitts. Two of the other I-15s promptly went up in flames. The third Russian pilot evidently died in his cockpit, because without any sign of smoke, his airplane went out of control and dived into the ground. Whitey said he had attempted to jink his way out of the Messerschmitts' coordinated attacks and reach Republican territory when they got him; his engine began smoking and finally caught fire. He bailed out and landed in an orchard, amidst a band of Moorish troops who beat him with rifle butts and were about to shoot him when three Spanish officers came on the run. They knocked the guns away, took command, and brought him to a nearby airfield. Ever since his rescue by the Spanish officers, Dahl said, he had been treated with courtesy. He was one of twenty Republican aviators confined in the prison at Salamanca; most were Spaniards, but among them were three Frenchmen and eight Russians.

Believing that Whitey was flying alone when the three Messerschmitts attacked, Tinker suspected that his Russian wingmen had either been incapable of staying with him or had wandered off to do their own hunting. He and Baumler blamed the high command for Whitey's loss, for putting him in a squadron that was new to Spain and one in which he had no common language. Once airborne, however, all communications among squadron members took place with hand signals, and the assumption was erroneous. Lacalle had judged Dahl a superior pilot, better than Tinker, but he had to discount his cockpit skills in terms of irresponsibility. Aside from an overwhelming personal charm that inspired confidence among his peers, he wanted for the tougher qualities of leadership. After all, during his three months in France, Dahl had run up more than a few bills that were overdue for remittances; his American friends could also suppose that he left the squadron with the intent to ring the cash register again by himself.

Much of the discussion that evening turned on the new German fighter. No one had been much impressed by its maneuverability, but it was too early to form hard judgments about this. What most impressed them was its tracer pattern—three streams of shells. Its two wing guns suggested a rate of fire as heavy as the I-16's, but the center gun that fired through the propeller hub seemed ominous: it suggested a 20- or 37-mm canon. In fact, it was only another 7.9-mm machine gun, but this was one more gun than the I-16 carried. The consensus held that the Messerschmitt was an airplane best kept at one's twelve o'clock position.

Shortly after dawn on the fourteenth, Lakeev had the squadron in the air escorting Rasantes to Brunete. The flak was thick, but no enemy fighters appeared in the air to complicate matters, nor was there any fighter opposition during a second mission before noon. In the morning, the Republic's air forces had the advantage of the sun behind them, and Nationalist air opposition rarely developed until afternoon when the sun gauge had shifted to the latter's advantage.

Returning to Manzanares el Real after the day's second mission, the pilots encountered a stiff crosswind on the field. One of the new Russian aviators touched down to a wing-smashing groundloop that brought the *jefe del campo* running out with a flag with which he waved off the rest of the squadron. When this occurred, they were supposed to divert to Alcalá. Tinker knew the mountainside winds of Manzanares to be fickle, but he had no desire to spend the night in the valley's heat, so he circled a few more times. The crosswind not only refused to go away, it built up in intensity so he had to give it up. When Tinker landed at Alcalá, however, there was no sign of the squadron. While his I-16 was being refueled a Russian armorer told him that his squadron had mistakenly put down at Barajas six miles away to the west. As Tinker climbed into his cockpit, he thought that this activity was a poor way for anyone to observe a twenty-eighth birthday—chasing around Spain after a bunch of pilots who could not tell the difference between Alcalá and Madrid's Barajas.

While Tinker taxied to the downwind end of the field, two red Very flares burst overhead. Enemy bombers had been observed in the vicinity. The Russian fighters based at Alcalá already were moving, the airplanes of the alert patrol rolling into their takeoff runs, so Tinker fell in behind them. But the alarm had come too late. While in their climb-outs that took them over Barajas, Tinker looked down to see a chain of black geysers of earth exploding across a corner of the city's commercial airport; almost directly overhead at 12,000 feet or higher, he could see a half-dozen Do 17s. There was no point in chasing these twin-engine bombers; by the time the fighters reached an attack altitude, the sleek, swift Dorniers would be over the Sierras and almost halfway to their base at Avila.

After the interception broke off, Tinker landed at Barajas expecting his squadron mates to be flocking in, but he learned that they had been sent on to a new airfield near the village of Campo Real ten miles away to the east. Tinker was unfamiliar with it, and being an auxiliary dispersal field, it would be camouflaged and hard to identify. The hour was late, he was tired of chasing around, so he parked his airplane and went into Madrid.

The Hotel Florida without its water heater no longer appealed to Tinker, and this evening he spent the night in the government's special quarters for pilots among the cellars of the Prado Museum. At the beginning of the siege of Madrid, most of the Prado's priceless paintings and sculptures had been removed from the city; the less portable artifacts were stored among the heavy vaulting of the museum's cellars. The Republic was confident that not even "Fascist criminals" would risk destroying Spain's art treasures, and there was no safer place in Madrid to billet valuable aviators than in the Prado Museum.

At the foot of his bed, Tinker found facing him a life-size statue of the Venus del Delfin in the company of an equally large figure of Hermes. A pity, perhaps, that he could not have had Goya's painting of *Saturno devorando a su hijo* hanging in his room; although done in the 1700s, no other item of the graphic arts provides as much terrifying insight into the essence of Spain's civil war of the 1930s. As the Nationalists moved into their counteroffensive and the night bombings of the airfields in Madrid's vicinity increased in tempo, Tinker used this room frequently, but he never became entirely accustomed to waking up under the stares of the Grecian deities.

After Tinker flew from Barajas to Campo Real the next morning, on the fifteenth, Lakeev greeted him with a bawling out for not getting to the new field the night before. The Russian had snarled off only a few declarative sentences when the airfield filled with shouts and running figures. Five enemy bombers had appeared almost directly overhead. Campo Real proved not to be the secluded spot that many persons had thought. All of the squadron's planes were moving before the bombs began falling, and all were off the ground when they started their ugly, earth-shaking march across the terrain beyond the field's perimeters. The bombardiers' aim was poor; they failed to put one crater in the landing ground. Although Lakeev's squadron chased after the raiders, an interception was hopeless; once again the bombers were too high and too fast to be overtaken.

Shortly after the squadron returned to Campo Real, the bark of antiaircraft guns sounded from Alcalá, Torrejon de Ardoz, and Barajas across the valley. Another five Nationalist bombers were cruising across the blue in shallow dives, their target apparently Barajas. Tinker and everyone else scrambled back into the air and clawed for altitude. The squadron was able to head off the bombers before

Savoia-Marchetti S.79 bombers (*National Air and Space Museum, Smithsonian Institution*)

they reached Barajas, and when the bomber pilots recognized the imminence of a successful interception, they jettisoned their bombs and turned away for the Sierras at full throttle.

The new Nationalist bombers that appeared in force on the Madrid front during the Battle of Brunete were little different from the Heinkel He 111s that had been operating in Spain since February; because they operated in what seemed to be large numbers and with greater frequency, everything about them seemed new to Madrid's defenders. Relative to bomber operations conducted only three years later during the opening phase of World War II, however, these air raids seem quaint. An attack force ordinarily consisted of a half-dozen bombers; twelve made for a big raid; a force of two dozen or more constituted a massive assault.

The twin-engine Dornier 17s and trimotor Savoia-Marchetti 79s had been added to the He 111s. While the Ju 52s and SM.81s no longer could be operated in daylight without fighter escorts, the performance of these new bombers, suddenly operating intensively and in what seemed to be large numbers, was disturbing in the extreme. Except as it might occur by accident, their high speeds made them invulnerable to interception; there seemed to be no effective defense against them.

The bombers penetrated the Republic's airspace from high altitudes that in 1937 was about 15,000 feet, and they passed unseen and oftentimes unheard by ground observers. Nearing the target, they throttled back their engines and made their final approach in a practically silent power glide. Within a mile of the target they put on power, leveled into their bombing runs, dropped their loads, and then sped away at minimum weight and maximum power combined with a shallow dive that yielded 250 mph.

This technique had been used in World War I to squeeze maximum speed out of underpowered biplane bombers; but when employed with superior horsepower and the fine, streamlined form of the modern airplane, it produced dramatic results. The net product was a "Baldwin bomber," a self-defending bomber that "will always get through."[4] Before electronic means of detection and tracking became practicable, its "silent approach" was terrifying to civilian populations and demoralizing to defending forces. This was especially true in the Madrid area with Nationalist bomber bases located within fifty miles of the salient. They could speed across the Sierras with a ton of bombs, hit any target within a twenty-mile radius of Alcalá, and be parked back on their airfields within fifty minutes of takeoff, no more than fifteen minutes of their flight being over enemy territory.

If the bombers achieved surprise, and they invariably did, the Republic's fighters only began to get off the ground when the attackers entered their bomb runs. The fighters might reach an attack altitude by the time the bombers had finished their work, and the fighters were in a position to attack only after the bombers were exploiting full power to run for home. A stern chase is a long chase, and even with an advantage of 50 mph the I-16s were hard put to overtake the bombers before they had slipped into Nationalist airspace. Without radar to provide early warning and direction of flight, a fighter pilot's life under a sustained bombing offensive, even with the relatively small forces deployed in Spain, slowly degenerated into an exhausting series of exercises in futility. This was especially so in the Madrid salient, where the enemy's attacks could come in from Torrijos, Avila, and Soria, some 270 points of the compass.[5]

After two fruitless efforts to intercept the new bombers, Lakeev's squadron was waiting for the arrival of Rasantes to be escorted to the front, and Lakeev was talking with Baumler about the latter's throat infection. It had become worse, and Lakeev decided to send Baumler to a clinic in Alcalá. All of the fighters had been warmed up except Lakeev's; its engine was still ticking over and he could hear little beyond immediate earshot. Everyone else heard the thrum of aero engines and saw two SB-2s overflying the field; Baumler also saw them but said nothing. Then the Rasantes appeared on the horizon, and the *jefe del campo* fired off a Very flare, the squadron's signal to start engines for takeoff.

Because of the frequent no-warning bomber attacks, everyone was on edge, and when Lakeev heard the flare pop he asked, "*Que pasa?*" Baumler replied, "*Apparatos de bombaderos,*" nodding in the direction of the SB-2s. When the

Russian looked up and saw sleek twin-engine bombers where he expected to see single-engine biplanes, he automatically sprinted for a nearby slit trench and literally dove into it. After Baumler explained what had happened, Lakeev felt foolish, but the "silent approach" raids had become real enough that no one was inclined to tease the Russian about his quick reflexes.

Shortly after Baumler's Ford disappeared down the road to the east, the anti-aircraft guns at Barajas and Alcalá started putting up a barrage. There was no time for brooding over his departure; it was time to go back to work.

15

ENOUGH IS ENOUGH!

Cameo Real is on a plateau between the Henares and Tajuna River valleys, and although ten miles away from Alcalá and Barajas, in a day when there were only open fields between, its elevation provided a good general view of the two main airfields and their satellites near Torrejon de Ardoz. Squinting at the northern sky, Tinker saw a half-dozen specks speeding among thin, broken clouds. Then he saw geysers of earth erupting from the airfields followed by the sounds of bomb detonations. A few hours later he witnessed another attack on Alcalá by Nationalist bombers sneaking in via the "silent approach."

Because the squadron was in stand-down for maintenance and repairs on 16 July, Tinker and some of the other pilots drove over to Alcalá for lunch, where they found the damage from the two air raids to be nil. To achieve surprise, the bombers flew too high to achieve accuracy; the silent attacks often proved more demoralizing than dangerous to an airfield's equipment or personnel. But several attacks a day usually achieved a corrosive effect on those in the target area, and there was always a chance that the bombers might hit something. Tinker learned that Ivan Kopéts had carried his contempt for the high-flying bombers too far. While standing outside a shelter to observe one of the attacks, some promiscuous bomb splinters nicked him badly enough to send him to the hospital.

While at Alcalá Tinker's commander, Ivan Lakeev, and two other Russian "old-timer" pilots were called to headquarters, detached from the squadron, and given orders to Carmoli airfield near Cartagena on the Mediterranean. All had served more than eight months in Spain; this was the first step in their return to the Soviet Union.

That evening the air raid alarms sounded again and again in Madrid and throughout the Henares Valley. From Campo Real's heights, everyone sat around drinking wine, talking, and watching the searchlights probe the sky for enemy bombers. The flak bursts and tracer bullets slashed at the darkness, and the occasional flashes of bombs detonated on the terrain in the vicinity of Barajas, Alcalá, and their satellite airfields. While watching the deadly display, Tinker thought of

Baumler's departure, of Lakeev and the veteran Russians being detached, and he felt more alone than ever. What he did not realize was that these night raids and the increasing tempo of the enemy's attacks by day and night was the overture to a Nationalist counteroffensive at Brunete.[1]

The morning of 17 July started with a double-rocket alarm that sent the squadron chasing off to the front, where they intercepted a half-dozen He 111s flying under a cloud of Fiats and Messerschmitts. For the next thirty minutes, the sky was a mad tangle of airplanes. In this fight, Tinker discovered that although the new Bf 109s could run away from him and his I-16 in a dive, he could overtake the German fighter in level flight, outclimb it, and roll inside of its turns. Tinker spotted one of the Bf 109s diving on a patrol of I-15 biplanes and rolled in behind him, followed by his Russian wingmen. The German pilot must have recognized his peril in his rearview mirror, because he broke off his attack and tried to escape in a climbing turn. That proved a fatal mistake.

Tinker threw over his controls, neatly turned inside the track of the angular German fighter, and with a squeeze of his thumb he squirted a few hundred rounds into the Messerschmitt's Jumo engine. Small, dark bits and pieces of the engine cowling flew away under the hail of bullets; Tinker fired again, and the engine exploded into flames. The Messerschmitt rolled over on its back, its cockpit canopy opened, and the pilot dropped out to take to his parachute.[2]

Jinking for altitude, Tinker searched the sky for passing targets but found none. What seemed to be a bunch of Fiats appeared, loitering around at a higher altitude some distance away, but they refused to come down and join the fracas. It is likely, however, that these "Fiats" were in fact Romeo Ro 37bis ground-attack planes that had no place in a dogfight at any time, and their pilots were smart enough to know it.

The Messerschmitts and I-16s were still mixing it up, but they were spread out all over the sky. This was something new. With the maneuverable, tight-turning biplanes such as the Fiat CR.32 and the I-15, dogfights were cozy affairs conducted in a relatively confined airspace. Indeed, they much resembled real dogfights, in which two canines are placed in a small pit and they circle one another at close quarters until one makes a mistake, giving the other an opening. The I-16 monoplanes were at a disadvantage in these close-in fights and were restricted to flying top cover, from which they might choose a target, dive through the melee to pick it off, and then zoom back to altitude to scan the fight for another target.

But with the I-16s fighting Messerschmitts and both airplanes being less maneuverable than the biplanes, their greater speeds and wider turning radii served to spread the fight all over wide areas. Thus, in Spain, over the battered and burning village of Brunete, the dogfight envelope established in World War I was torn asunder. A new dogfight envelope emerged with dimensions that became commonplace in World War II. No similarly historic expansion would occur again until November 1950, when swept-wing jet fighters—with much higher speeds, greater radii of turn, and substantially less maneuverability—tangled with one another in the sky over North Korea.

At dinner that evening in Campo Real, the day's returns came in. The Republic claimed one bomber, two He 51s, and two Bf 109s, while admitting the loss of one I-15. Tinker thought it a disappointing score for a half-hour's fight; what it suggests is that the monoplane fighters had a difficult time coming to grips with one another.

That night held another series of air raid alarms while Nationalist bombers prowled the darkness trying to drop their loads on Republican airfields, but again without much success. On the other side of the lines west of Madrid, the roads were packed with Nationalist troops on the move, and hundreds of trucks and horse-drawn vehicles advanced toward the front. When the sun finally rose to throw an angry light on the morning of 18 July, it brought with it another day of suffocating heat, and at 7:00 a.m. the Nationalist artillery opened up with a forty-five-minute bombardment. The Nationalist counteroffensive at Brunete had begun.

At Campo Real the day started with an escort mission taking Rasantes up to the front. Tinker later recalled 18 July as his "hardest day's work in Spain." Although he flew only three sorties, they totaled four hours and ten minutes of flying time, and each sortie met stiff opposition.

When they arrived over Brunete, a swarm of Fiats and Heinkel He 51s met their attack. The Rasantes were left to their own devices, and the I-16s turned to meet the Fiats slashing through their formation and breaking it up. This initial fight did not last long; after five minutes, the Fiats broke off contact and sped away toward Torrijos. The He 51s stayed for another twenty minutes to lose at least one of their number. Diving in and out of the melee, Tinker got off only passing shots at the more nimble biplanes. Although the He 51 was at a disadvantage against the I-15 and totally outclassed by the I-16, in the hands of a halfway decent pilot it could nevertheless be jinked around to escape the attacks of the less maneuverable monoplanes. In the midst of this confused fight, Tinker saw a parachute floating down with airplanes whirling all around it. He wondered what was going on in that pilot's mind—assuming the man was still alive.

After refueling and rearming at Campo Real, the familiar Very flares burst over the field. The squadron dashed up to its sector of the Brunete salient, where it found two dozen Messerschmitts strafing Republican ground forces. The Germans, absorbed in their labors, were all milling around at low altitudes without a top cover—easy targets for the I-16s that came screaming down from 12,000 feet, cutting through them like a scythe and zooming back for altitude from which to repeat the attack. But within a few minutes the fight had dispersed across miles of sky, and the scattered Messerschmitts started working their way south toward Navalcanero from where they scurried off to their base at Escalona.

The I-16s hurried back to Campo Real to refuel and rearm for an escort of Rasantes. Everyone was enthusiastic about the fight with the Messerschmitts, a total of five victories being claimed. The Nationalists admitted the loss of only one, however, and its German pilot was taken prisoner.

Tinker reported that he had fired on a strange monoplane fighter unlike a Messerschmitt. It was bulkier in its fuselage, had short, rounded wings, and its wings had a peculiar downward slant from the fuselage before they turned up normally. This "mystery plane" turned out to be a Heinkel He 112, the fifth and only prototype sent to Spain for combat evaluation. And when the He 112 pilot, Max Schulz, returned to his base near Escalona after operating over Brunete on this day, his engine seized, and he wiped it out in a crash landing. How much Frank Tinker's short burst of fire may have contributed to that engine failure is something that can never be known with certainty, but Salas says the airplane was badly shot up.[3]

A few minutes later nineteen Rasantes roared over the field, and the squadron swarmed into the air to escort them to the front. The city of Madrid passed below, then the Casa de Campo, and the awful smudge of Brunete came in sight. The ground battle was marked by great clouds of dust hanging lazily in the summer air and pillars of smoke leaning against an almost windless day. The Rasantes cruised at 5,000 feet; the I-16s capped them at 12,000 feet, snaking back and forth in leisurely S-turns above the attack planes' slow passage. As they lazily rolled out of one turn and into another, an I-16 started waggling its wings furiously, a signal that rippled through the formation. Dead ahead, the sky was dark with airplanes all diving toward them, and in the next instant, the air was filled with Fiats and Messerschmitts. It seemed to Tinker that they had been "attacked by everything the enemy had in the air."

The Rasantes rumbled on to their target, where they were badly mauled by flak and Fiats. Overhead, the outnumbered I-16s twisted and turned through an hour's fight that gradually spread itself out over fifteen miles of the front between Brunete and El Escorial. A lone Dornier Do 17 bomber returning from a reconnaissance mission over Republican territory suddenly appeared in the mad whirl of fighters and bored on through. Tinker managed to fire one good burst into the Dornier as it crossed his sights, and almost everyone else in the squadron who had an opportunity shot at it. The bomber flew on out of the fight but certainly not unscathed.

As the fight thinned out, Tinker looked down across one of his wingtips and spotted a Fiat skirting the base of a large cumulus cloud, and he promptly rolled into a dive after it. The Fiat's pilot saw him, and he half-rolled into a dive for escape. This was a mistake. If the Fiat pilot had exploited the greater maneuverability that he possessed he probably would have gotten away, but there was no escape from an I-16 in any form of straight-line flight. Tinker almost had too much speed, because as he rolled into his dive he built enough g-forces that he almost blacked out.

In their long dive toward the earth, Tinker worked the Fiat into the center of his gunsight and fired. He could see his tracers chopping the biplane to pieces, but there was no smoke, no trail of vaporizing fuel or radiator water. He fired again with no visible results. The hard, parched foothills of the Sierras were rushing up at him at more than 300 mph, and Tinker knew that the pullout characteristics of an I-16 were miserable compared with the Fiat's. He gave up the chase and pulled out of his dive, feeling the stubby fighter wallow through a few seconds of sickening squash-out before its wings and propeller got a fresh grip on the air.

Pulling out into a climbing turn, Tinker swung around to make sure that he had no unwelcome company on his tail and then started spiraling down after the Fiat. The Fiat was still going down, straight down, and apparently under full throttle. It hit the earth with awful force and disappeared in a ball of fire, leaving a great cloud of dust and a column of smoke to mark its point of impact.

That evening, Tinker was only too glad to flop into his bed at the feet of Venus and Hermes in the Prado. The Fiat, his eighth victory, did not find a commissar to produce a case of champagne for a celebration this evening. When he reported his claim for the Fiat, it was greeted with a nod and a tired smile and that was it. Everyone in the squadron, including Tinker, was wrung out and dead tired. The past few days had been long ones. Up at 4 a.m., three or four escort missions every day, otherwise standing by in flight suits in the dust and insufferable heat in various stages of alert until sundown. And there were the Nationalists' relentless "silent approach" raids and their own futile efforts at interception; initially a nuisance, the raids eventually became unnerving. Everyone looked forward to sundown, a bath in Madrid, a supper—now eaten in unusual silence—and then at an early hour rolling into the sack.

The next morning, on 19 July—the fifteenth day of the battle and the second day of the Nationalist counteroffensive—Tinker turned out at 4 a.m. for the trip to Campo Real. As usual, there was no enemy air opposition in the morning when the Republic had the sun gauge, but, as usual, there was plenty of flak. While the Rasantes skimmed the trenches, strafing their hapless occupants and loosing scores of fragmentation bombs, the I-16s orbited the target area at 13,000 feet, jinking around among the flak bursts. Then one I-16 took a direct hit, an unusual occurrence. The hit flamed its fuel tank, and the airplane burst into a ball of fire that went rocketing across the sky for a hundred yards, where it dissolved into a long cloud of oily black smoke that spat out bits and pieces of the aircraft. It was all over in two or three seconds. The pilot never had a chance and was probably incinerated in his cockpit. A flak gunner's luck, thought Tinker, holding fast to his contempt for the ugly black puffs filled with deadly steel splinters.

After refueling at Campo Real, a double-rocket alarm sent the squadron scurrying back into the air to intercept bombers over Barajas. Again, as usual, the alarm had arrived too late, and the high-flying bombers were already well on their way back to Avila. A column of black smoke hung over Barajas and it appeared as if the bombers had finally scored some serious hits, but it was only the burning carcass of a battle-damaged Rasante being used for salvage.

A few hours later, the squadron again rushed into the air, this time to intercept five Italian bombers approaching Alcalá. They were still clawing for altitude when the bombers—new Savoia-Marchetti S.79s—loosed their loads,[4] and Tinker watched with interest as the line of bombs churned up a half-mile of sod. He was climbing through 12,000 feet when he spotted the bombers. They were about 3,000 feet directly above him and speeding away toward the north. He had no chance of gaining an attack position, so in sheer frustration he stood his I-16 almost on its tail and squeezed off a long-range deflection shot. This proved too much for his war-weary engine; hanging by its propeller as it was, it stalled and quit.

Tinker pushed over into a dive for flying speed and to keep his propeller windmilling, and he labored over his wobble pump, ramming fuel into the silent engine. His steep glide kept the propeller turning at 1,000 rpm; he had compression, but the engine simply refused to fire. Losing altitude fast, he gave up on the engine and cranked down his landing gear for a dead-stick landing at Alcalá, whose field was off his right wingtip. Then he saw another line of bombs suddenly start churning up ugly geysers of dirt, dust, and debris across Alcalá's landing ground, and he looked up to see a pair of twin-engine bombers cruising at 15,000 feet, the sun glinting off their propeller arcs. It promised to be a very messy landing, but he was now down to 1,500 feet and turning into the final leg of his approach to the cratered airfield; he had long since run out of options.

Suddenly the powerplant coughed and sputtered, and the whole airplane gave a terrible shudder when the engine, its cylinders flooded with fuel, practically exploded back to life. Tinker was certain that only six or seven of its nine cylinders were operating, but these were enough. He eased his controls into a shallow bank and nursed the balky machine through a gentle turn away from Alcalá. The ten miles to Campo Real were long ones, but not as long as that one mile of approach to the happily aborted landing at Alcalá.

After taxiing up to the maintenance trucks and cutting his switch, Tinker climbed out of his cockpit and rounded up Gregoric and Pedro to put them to work on the engine. The mechanics had it in good enough shape within an hour so that Tinker was able to join the squadron in its last flight of the day—a chase after five bombers over Alcalá. Once again, the alarm was too late; the bombers too high and too fast; and the fighters were only climbing through 12,000 feet when the raiders faded into the gloom of the Sierras.

The Nationalist raids seemed to come in spurts, so the squadron climbed to 15,000 feet and orbited the Madrid area for forty minutes in anticipation of an encore, but the Nationalist air force had called it quits for the daylight hours. After sundown they returned for an evening performance, striking again at the Barajas-Alcalá area, but at Campo Real everyone was too tired to sit up and watch the show.

At sunrise on 20 July a pair of Italian S.79s buzzed across Campo Real, followed by a second and third pair. They had apparently done their bombing elsewhere and were now hurrying back to Soria. Tinker had the alert duty, and he hurried off the ground to chase after the first pair with two new Russia wingmen. While overflying Guadalajara, they finally closed to gun range but started firing too soon and exhausted their ammunition. Hits were scored on one bomber, and its right engine started trailing thick black smoke. The bomber's rear ventral gunner, a nervous fellow, assumed that smoke meant fire, and he was not interested to see when or if it would reach the fuel tanks. Disclaiming the rest of the crew, he clambered out of his gun pit and took to his parachute. But when he jumped he pulled his rip cord too soon, and the parachute canopy fouled on the plane's tail assembly. The pilot nevertheless managed to retain control, putting the SM.79 into a shallow dive and holding to his speed for Soria—with the unfortunate gunner spinning along behind in his parachute harness.

En route back to Campo Real, Tinker saw another pair of S.79s loosing their bombs on Alcalá, the bomb line cutting across a corner of the field, but with empty guns he and his wingmen could only fly on by. Another pair of S.79s had struck at Barajas, but the airfield was empty of planes The only damage done at Alcala was to the Fiat CR.32 that a Nationalist defector had supplied. Other fighters based on other airfields managed to intercept and shoot down one of the bombers, so except for holding reveille on the Henares Valley, the S.79s' sorties were relatively fruitless.

West of Madrid, the Nationalist counteroffensive pushed on, taking a few hundred yards here, another hundred yards somewhere else. The fighting was bitter, but on this day Tinker's squadron made no flights to the front; it was held on alert at Campo Real for the air defense of the Madrid area. In the afternoon a bomber scare rushed the squadron into the air, and the fighters orbited Madrid for forty minutes waiting for attackers who failed to appear. Suspecting that the enemy would strike at Campo Real that night, all pilots were ordered off the field at sundown to sleep in the Prado Museum. This, too, proved a false alarm, but everyone's nerves had become a bit ragged.

As evidence of how jumpy Tinker had become, early the next morning he spotted two twin-engine bombers approaching the field. There was no alarm, but he was not inclined to wait for it and immediately scrambled into the air with his two wingmen. While they climbed to an interception, the bombers made no effort to run away, and as Tinker closed to gun range the bombers made no attempt at evasive action; their rear gunners were passive. Tinker brought one bomber into his gunsight when he suddenly recognized it as an SB-2. In this instant he felt every bit as foolish as Lakeev must have felt in his SB-2 scare of a few days earlier. With all of the hit-and-run Nationalist air attacks of the past four days, however, it was even more foolish to take chances when in doubt.

While Tinker and his wingmen were refueling, two red Very flares popped over the field. The squadron rushed into the air, but the alarm was caused by a pair of Heinkel He 70F photo-reconnaissance planes, and they were flying too high and too fast for interception. After landing and being serviced, the squadron resumed its escort of Rasantes to the front, flying two missions in the afternoon without a sign of the Nationalist air forces. This was unusual because the enemy usually was most active in the afternoon, a time of day when he had the sun over his tailplanes. The first phase of the Nationalist counteroffensive had spent itself, and without retaking the village of Brunete—then hardly more than a heap of rubble. However, a second phase was being prepared and would not be long in coming.

By this time, the last of *los Rusos antiguos* had rotated out of the squadron, on their way to a warm—or cold—welcome in the USSR. The new squadron leader who relieved Lakeev did not lead the squadron in the air but flew as an ordinary pilot under the command of one of the old Russian veterans. But the new squadron leader did command the squadron's personnel on the ground. Among its pilots, Frank Tinker remained the only veteran left, and now he was told that he would lead the squadron in the air. This came as a staggering surprise, but Tinker had no doubts about his combat abilities. His assumption of aerial command duties is probably the only occasion in the history of the Red Army Air Force when an American—and a graduate of the U.S. Naval Academy, at that—led one of its squadrons into combat. But his tenure as a Soviet squadron leader would not be for long. Ever since the departure of Baumler and Lakeev, he had been trying to make up his mind about his future, and with the last of the old Russians gone, he came to a decision: It was time to leave Spain. At least for a while.

When Baumler left for the hospital, Tinker really missed someone—anyone—with whom he could speak English. Although his Spanish had become fairly good, he was by no means fluent, and the Spanish that he and the Russians

used among themselves is best described as "Espanglaisruso." Even the Spaniards were hard put to understand this Russo-American mangling of their
mother tongue. In any case, the newly arrived Russians had not yet learned even
a primitive Spanish, and the only persons Tinker had to talk with were Gregoric,
the Russian chief mechanic, another Russian nicknamed "Smoothie," who was
the chief airframe artificer, and his own personal mechanic, Pedro. And Tinker
knew that Gregoric and "Smoothie" would rotate back to the USSR shortly.

Few things can be more corrosive to the spirit than a sudden loneliness in
the midst of a crowd, especially if one has obvious common interest with that
crowd. In his new loneliness, Tinker realized that he was tired, and he was wise
enough to admit it to himself. Most of the Russians rotated after six months
and, unknown to him, the Germans of the Legion Condor rotated on a similar
schedule. He had been in Spain for almost seven months. He had experienced
more than enough combat flying, and enough is enough. That evening he wrote a
letter to the Air Ministry, giving them the required ten days' notice to terminate
his contract.

Shortly after Tinker finished his letter, the chief Russian language interpreter in the Madrid area visited him. The Russian had good news and bad news.
Whitey Dahl was alive; he had managed to parachute to safety and had landed
unhurt—but he came down in Nationalist territory and was now a prisoner in
Salamanca. The Russian nevertheless expressed confidence that Whitey would
eventually be exchanged for a Nationalist aviator held by the Republic. Taken in
sum, this was good news, and it permitted Tinker to tear up the several unfinished draft letters of condolence to Edith Dahl. He did not, however, tear up his
letter to the Air Ministry; he became more determined than ever to leave Spain.

The next morning, 22 July, the squadron stood down while its airplanes were
overhauled. Aerial squadron leader Tinker requisitioned a car and driver from
the motor pool and drove over to Alcalá to see if he had any mail. The car, an
ancient Graham-Paige, found its driver doing well just to nurse it along the
primitive back roads to the town. While he was at the field house, the phone
rang with a warning of two enemy bombers approaching. Without an airplane at
Alcalá, Tinker joined the groundlings in the *refugio*.

After sitting in the stuffy air raid shelter for almost an hour without hearing
any bomb detonations or an all clear, Tinker became impatient with the enemy.
Collecting his driver, they got back in the car and headed off toward Madrid.
About two minutes later, the antiaircraft guns began barking at the sky, and
through their noise came the scream of falling bombs. The driver hit his brakes,
and he and Tinker jumped out of the car in search of the usual ditches alongside
the road. Both were dismayed to find only shallow gutters, but they flopped into
them and made every effort to make themselves as small as possible.

As bad luck would have it, they were caught between the bomb lines of two airplanes; only being caught on one of the bomb lines could have been worse. The bombs shrieked down and burst with dizzying detonations that smashed at their eardrums and showered them with dirt and debris. Then the world became incredibly quiet. Tinker dazedly got to his feet with a terrible ringing in his head. An I-16 and a fuel truck could be seen burning on the airfield. His driver was shouting at him with great excitement, but Tinker could barely hear the man; for the moment his eardrums were almost nonfunctional. Their car's roof and sides were shredded by bomb fragments. They got in; its engine still worked, and they hurried on to Madrid.

Tinker paid a visit to the Hotel Florida, where he failed to muster any familiar faces. Everyone he knew, the journalists, the Lincolns, had left. Then he looked up Dolores for an evening on the town, making the rounds of sundry bars and nightclubs. He needed it. But tomorrow was a flying day, and by midnight he had returned to the company of his marble Venus in the cellars of the Prado. He subsequently would recall this bombing at Alcalá as his most terrible experience in Spain, even worse than being caught in the bombardment of the Grand Vía. And that evening he made an unusual entry in his diary: "very nerve wracking."[5]

The next morning, on the twenty-third, the pilots drove out to Campo Real before daylight. Tinker was trudging across the field with his parachute when he heard a great commotion and saw men running for the bomb shelters. Looking up, he saw a sky paling with the dawn and two S.79 bombers almost directly overhead. Buckling on his parachute, he jumped into the cockpit and buttoned up its sides. When he hit his electric starter and it cranked the engine with unusual vigor, he muttered, "Good boy, Pedro!"; when the engine immediately fired, he thanked the deity Himself.

Roaring down the field, Tinker reached flying speed when two red rockets popped over the *caseta de mando*. He felt his wheels leave the ground, reached down to crank up the landing gear, and looked around to see who else was getting away. It was then that he saw three bombs box in the place where his airplane had been parked.

Only three other planes got rolling in response to this surprise attack. Two made it into the air. The third was in its takeoff run when a bomb exploded directly in its path. The blast flipped the plane over, and it went skidding across the field on its back, its engine wrenched off in the mad passage. By some miracle, its Russian pilot crawled out of the wreck and managed to limp back to the field house. His only physical injuries were a few cuts and bruises and a bomb splinter in one shoulder, but he was in such a state of psychological shock that he remained out of action for more than a week.

The other two fighters formed up on Tinker, and they chased after the S.79s. But the trio of 750-horsepower Alfa Romeo engines in each of the Italian bombers sped them homeward for Soria at 270 mph and at an altitude of 15,000 feet. Tinker and his wingmen only began to overhaul them north of Guadalajara and had no chance of closing to accurate gun range before they could be well into Nationalist airspace. Carefully sighting on one bomber, Tinker again pulled up the nose of his I-16 in an attempt at a long-range shot that might drop his fire into the enemy, but after firing only a few bursts, his guns jammed.

With the field at Campo Real freshly cratered, Tinker led his wingmen to Alcalá where they put themselves at the service of the squadrons based there. Here they were told that Campo Real's only casualties, other than the badly rattled pilot, were two Spanish mechanics who got peppered with bomb splinters, and Gregoric who was dead. A bomb exploded only fifteen feet away from the Russian mechanic, ripping away his whole left side. While waiting for medical attention, he reached around with his right hand and fumbled through the gore that had been his rib cage. Concluding that he was a dead man, Gregoric unholstered his pistol and shot himself.

At Alcalá, Tinker's day would be a slow one, but one punctuated by a Russian visitor. There were no operations to the front. This downtime occurred in spite of a renewed Nationalist offensive against the Brunete salient, one that succeeded in overrunning the ruined village by late afternoon. Tinker, meanwhile, sat in the shade of his airplane's wing, his back supported by the landing gear's tire; he was playing his accordion for the other pilots and ground crew on alert when the Russians' chief inspector of aircraft came along. After examining Tinker's airplane, he condemned it as a fighting machine. Its engine was in sore need of a major overhaul, and its airframe was so full of flak and bullet holes and temporary patchwork that he thought its structure at risk to fail. The Russian pointed at the I-16's fuselage and then at Tinker's accordion, and with appropriate gestures he made it clear that he thought both had about the same structural integrity.

Tinker knew that his airplane was not in the best shape, but the details elaborated by the Russian visitor came as sobering news: three base bolts in the engine mounts were cracked, the landing gear's retraction mechanism was practically finished, his machine gun barrels were worn smooth and the guns' firing mechanisms were all but gone.

Next, the Russian wanted to know why the airplane's dangerous condition had not been reported. There would be no real answer. Tinker squeezed off a refrain from *Rigoletto* on his accordion, smiled, and said he liked his airplanes this way. As the disgruntled inspector stomped off, Tinker accompanied his footsteps with some of the opera's martial music. The local commander directed that the airplane should be flown to Los Alcázares immediately and traded in for a new one. Tinker got away the next morning, on the twenty-fourth, and after a two-and-one-half-hour flight, with a stop for refueling at Albacete, he touched down at Los Alcázares. Given what the inspector had told him, he half expected the plane to fall apart at any time during the 250-mile flight and was delighted to arrive safely. At the airfield's maintenance depot, he turned over his old No. 23, the instrument of his last four victories, to the chief of aircraft maintenance for a complete rebuilding. Then he headed off to the pilots' hotel.

At the hotel he was amazed to encounter Justo García, his wingman from Guadalajara days. He was even more surprised after Justo excused himself with an *una momento* and returned with Riverola, Gil, and Alarcón. The last Tinker had heard of them was when they had flown to the Cantabrian front in May. He assumed that they had either been taken prisoner when Bilbao collapsed in June or had been trapped in the pocket around Santander (which, indeed, would fall to the Nationalists before end of August). Riverola explained that they had simply turned over their airplanes to other pilots on the northern front, and then were flown back to the Levante. Not all made it back, however; Rafael Magriñá had been killed during the ferrying operation.[6]

The alumni of the Esquadrilla de Lacalle had come a long way since February, just six months past. Both Gil and Riverola were now captains and stationed at Carmoli airfield for transitioning to I-16s, after which they would be working up their own squadrons. This was the first Tinker heard of all-Spanish I-16 squadrons being created. He learned that Lacalle had indeed gone to the Soviet Union, taking with him almost two hundred young Spaniards for training as pilots, aircrews, and ground crews. Gil had been a close friend of Whitey Dahl, had heard that he had been shot down, and was pleased to know that Whitey had survived. He assured Tinker that in spite of what he might hear, no aviators were executed, especially foreigners. The Republic had too many German, Italian, and Spanish Nationalist pilots in its own prisons. The foreign aviators were always exchanged—sometimes even the Spaniards. Lacalle's veterans had a pleasant dinner together with many toasts drunk to Whitey Dahl's escape from an unpleasant death, to Lacalle's work in Russia, to Whitey's eventual exchange, to their own *buena suerte*. And so it went into the evening.

The next day, 26 July, Tinker went out to Los Alcázares, where the Russian engineers advised him that others were picking up airplanes and he would have to return on the morrow. That day they had a new I-16 ready. It was No. 239. The three-digit number suggested that it was "right off the boat" from Odessa—as compared with old No. 23, which had probably arrived in Spain in November 1936. No. 239 certainly looked to be new; but when Tinker ran up its engine, the sounds issuing from beneath the cowling gave him a strong suspicion that the new airframe had a secondhand power plant, and one not properly tuned at that. More work for Pedro when he got back to Madrid, and he took off within the hour.

It was two hours and twenty minutes' flying time from Los Alcázares to Alcalá, plus a fuel stop at Albacete. The war on the Madrid front had quieted down considerably. The Nationalist counteroffensive had finally rolled up the Republic's salient, and the front had stabilized at approximately the same place from where the Republic began its offensive in June. The Republic's net gain was about three square miles, for which it paid the fearsome price of 20,000 casualties. The Nationalists lost 13,000 men during the three-week slaughter. On this twenty-seventh of July, both sides were digging elaborate trench works from which they would face one another in static warfare until what was left of the Republic finally collapsed in the spring of 1939.

On the afternoon of 28 July, the alarm sounded when four S.79s were spotted at a very high altitude almost over the airfield. The squadron was off before the bombs started falling, but otherwise it made no difference; it was the old story of the bombers being too high and too fast. With Alcalá cratered, Tinker's squadron landed at Barajas. By this time, Tinker had come to the conclusion that the principal purpose of these raids was psychological, to wear down the fighter pilots, and anything else achieved was secondary. On this point he thought they were relatively successful; the most recent draft of Russian replacements appeared obviously jittery.

After a night in the Prado's cellar with Venus and Hermes, the squadron drove out to Barajas in the dark of the morning to be ready for flying by sunrise. It was a quiet morning. There were no Rasantes to be escorted on 29 July. Groups of pilots and mechanics sat around under the shade of the airplanes playing cards, chess, or dominos, happy to sniff at the slightest breeze that stirred the day's hot, dusty air. Then two red Very rockets burst in the blue, sending each one scrambling for his airplane.

Tinker was fed up with the bombers always getting away, and he led the squadron in a hard climb to 20,000 feet from where he was certain they could see and dive upon any attackers. The I-16s had oxygen equipment in their cockpits, and the squadrons had oxygen masks, but some Soviet functionary in Odessa had forgotten to include the oxygen systems' regulators when everything was shipped to Spain, and without regulators the available equipment was useless. With the deadly threat of anoxia imminent among his pilots, Tinker could stay at this altitude for only a moment—just long enough to scan the horizons and the scene below to see that there were no bombers. It was another false alarm.

Rolling into a steep dive, Tinker took the squadron screaming down to oxygen aplenty at 4,000 feet where he signaled them into their landing pattern. That

16,000-foot dive practically tore the heart out of Tinker's uncertain engine, and for the rest of the day Pedro and his assistants swarmed over its problems. There were no more alarms. The sun went down behind the Sierras, and after dinner at Barajas everyone climbed on board a bus for their bunks in the Prado. Tinker wondered about that wretched engine in No. 239. But unknown to him this evening, it was going to be another pilot's problem. He had made his last flight in Spain.

The next morning Tinker and his patrol had the predawn alert duty. At 7 a.m. they were relieved and went to breakfast. While at breakfast Tinker was called to the telephone. Ivan Kopéts told him that a new Russian pilot was on his way to Barajas. Tinker should check him out on his airplane and then consider himself relieved.

After checking out the new pilot, Tinker celebrated by going into Madrid for a bath. Arriving back at Barajas in the afternoon, he was just in time to see two red Very flares go sailing up from the *caseta de mando*. But they were no longer his red rockets. He watched the squadron scramble to life and rush off the field; he felt his role as spectator to be a strange one.

Overhead he saw five bombers cruising across the blue—Heinkel He 111s. He went to the *refugio* with the rest of the ground crews. The bombs did a great job of churning up the sod at a distant end of the airfield but scored no material damage. After the "all clear," he collected his baggage and hurried up to Azuqueca and Campo X, where a Ford Tri-Motor was parked on the field, its engines ticking over. It was the plane to Valencia. But the air raid's delay made him too late, passengers had taken all of the Ford's seats, so he hauled his gear back to the Casa de Pilotos in Alcalá. This was just as well. He was in no great hurry to reach Valencia, and there were people he wanted to see before he finally left Madrid.

Tinker spent a week at Alcalá, and it proved to be anything but dull. The Russians had begun withdrawing their squadrons from the well-known bases at Barajas and Alcalá and dispersing them among less-conspicuous satellite fields, while other squadrons transferred to the Levante. In a few days, Tinker had the Casa de Pilotos almost to himself. Before the Russians left, however, they placed dozens of dummy airplanes around Barajas and Alcalá, and a couple of times every day soldiers moved the dummies to new positions around the fields. At least once a day, high-flying Nationalist reconnaissance airplanes overflew the area to take photographs, followed by high-flying bombers that tried to bomb the dummy airplanes. The hazards to ground personnel were no less than if the planes were real, and Tinker paid many visits to the *refugios*.

There were good-byes to be made to old friends and acquaintances at the Hotel Florida, Chicote's, the Hotel Gran Vía, Molinaro's, and the Miami Bar. And there was Dolores. One day he drove up to Campo X where the sisters Maria and Christina had but recently been reassigned to the management of the *finca.* Tinker wanted to give them his prized Victrola and records, but the girls could not understand it in terms of his need to reduce his baggage, and to them the gift seemed so extravagant that they felt obliged to refuse it. This was too bad. He finally gave it to a Spanish interpreter who had been of great assistance to the American aviators.

Early on the morning of 5 August, Tinker finally got away from Alcalá on board a truck en route to Albacete, where he arrived in time for a late breakfast. Here he chanced to meet "General Douglas" again. Smushkevich was shocked to learn that Tinker had to ride as a passenger in a truck and gave him the loan of a new Ford V-8 sedan for the rest of his trip to Valencia.

Tinker had a week in Valencia while the Air Ministry shuffled the papers that concluded his contract. There was no quibbling about money; the Republic paid him every peseta and centime called for under its terms. While in the city, Tinker looked up Derek Dickinson, who had been with him at Los Alcazares in January. Dickinson had failed to qualify as a fighter pilot but was accepted for reconnaissance airplanes, and he later became a flight instructor at Manisas. Meanwhile, he had taken a Spanish wife whose wit and charm held Tinker in thrall. It was against the law to take firearms out of Spain, so Tinker gave Dickinson his 9-mm automatic pistol and left his bulky leather flying clothes and a few other personal effects with him. After a few months in the States, Frank Tinker fully expected to return to Spain and retrieve them.

En route back to the Hotel Regina, Tinker stopped at the Vodka Cafe, an establishment for which Americans and air force people had an affinity. Inside, he found little Barbeitos, whom he had not seen since Jiménez tried to take the old squadron to the Cantabrian front and met with the fiasco in France. But when Tinker saw the man seated next to Barbeitos, he thought he was seeing a ghost. It was Manuel García Gómez, the Guatemalan shot down near Cifuentes and supposedly dead for four months. He was no longer the same Gómez, however; he looked like a victim of the wrath of God.

Gómez told Tinker that the five Fiats had indeed made short work of him. They shot up his engine, which started smoking badly and then caught fire, but he managed to lose the Fiats among the clouds; then he dove for the ground. Everything went well until he touched down, and then the whole airplane burst into flames. The ground was rough and in his rollout the wheels hit something that flipped the plane over on its back, and he was thrown out of the cockpit. But for this he thought it likely that he would have burned with the wreck. As it was, among other tissue damage, his left hand was badly burned while getting the plane down, but he felt lucky that no bullet had even grazed him.

Within the hour, Gómez continued, strange-speaking soldiers challenged him, and he realized that he was in enemy territory. They were Italians and determined to shoot him, when an officer intervened. Then he was shipped off to prison in Salamanca where he was formally tried, found guilty of "crimes against Spain," sentenced to death, given a reprieve, and then marched back to his cell. His time in prison had been terrible. He got just enough to eat to stay alive, and the burns on his hand did not receive proper treatment. Now his left hand was almost useless. After four months he, Bastida, who had been captured in the north near San Sabastian, and a Yugoslav pilot named Ferác were traded for three Italian aviators held by the Republic. Gómez did not believe that he would be flying again for a long time. Maybe never. All he wanted now was to get back to Guatemala or maybe to Mexico.[7] Gómez's experiences made Tinker wonder how Whitey Dahl was getting along in the prison at Salamanca.

Before leaving Valencia, Tinker dropped in to see Mahlon F. Perkins, the U.S. consul, in case he had any mail at the consulate. After exchanging pleasantries, Perkins was pleased to remind Tinker that back in the States he might be prosecuted for violating all kinds of laws as a result of his prolonged military labors in Spain. The consul recited a litany of legalistic "thou shalt nots" for American citizens abroad, and for a moment it seemed to Tinker that the "Land of the Free" had a law against everything. Perkins said the penalties could be as much as a $1,000 fine and three years in jail. That last prospect was something to think about.

On the August morning of Friday the Thirteenth, Tinker hauled his luggage off the crowded train from Barcelona and carried it into customs at Port Bou on the French border. He had no difficulties getting out of Spain; the Italians on Majorca did not even bother to see him off with a small air raid, but when he hopped the shuttle train to Cerbere, he knew that he was in France because there was nothing but difficulties. His phony Spanish passport was good enough for anyone disembarking from the marvelous *Normandie*, but it excited nothing but suspicions when used to enter France from turbulent Spain. It took twenty-four hours to straighten out matters with the authorities in Perpignan, and then he was on his way to Paris.

Tinker had taken his first step toward home on the road back from Port Bou. Fighting an enemy with real bullets that he understood so well was finished; fighting State Department functionaries with paper bullets, for which he had no talent at all, was about to begin. He would lose this battle and temporarily end up a "prisoner of peace."

16

LOOKING FOR A WAY HOME

On the morning of the frantic French vacation-time Sunday of 16 August 1937, Frank Tinker carried his suitcase off the train from Perpignan and into the noisy confusion of the Gare d'Orsay. It was the height of the tourist season and the middle of a three-day weekend; the Paris International Exposition was running at full tilt, and most of Europe seemed to be in motion on the station's Rue de Anatole France. Tinker found a free taxi with difficulty; he went to the Hotel St. Anne where Albert Baumler was staying.

On arriving, Tinker learned that Baumler was out, so he checked in and bought a copy of the Paris edition of the *Herald-Tribune* to find out what was going on in the world. The famous Russian arctic aviator, Sigismund Lavenevsky, and his crew of five had disappeared while attempting a transpolar nonstop flight from Moscow to New York; Cyril McNeile, creator of the Bulldog Drummond detective stories had died in London at age forty-nine; Japanese cruisers in the Whangpoo River had shelled the Chinese sections of Shanghai. When Chinese aircraft attempted to bomb the Japanese ships, the bombs fell in the international settlement and killed hundreds of civilians. By comparison, the day's news from Spain seemed dull stuff.

Tinker's immediate interest was the newspaper's shipping news. The French Line's *Lafayette* was sailing from LeHavre for New York on the twentieth, the *DeGrasse* on the twenty-fourth, and the *Normandie* on the twenty-fifth. He thought he should be able to make the *DeGrasse*.

When Baumler returned at 1:00 p.m., he was sporting a thick swatch of bandages around his neck and had visibly lost weight. He had undergone surgery and still remained an outpatient at the American hospital in nearby Neuilly; the medics had found an infected salivary gland that had become gangrenous. Baumler had gotten out of Spain none too soon; another thirty days and the condition might have slipped beyond control.

They spent the long weekend sightseeing, including the International Exposition, ending their tours each day at that popular Parisian hangout for Americans of the interwar years, Harry's New York Bar at 5 Rue Daunou. Harry's advertisements made it easy for newcomers to find the place: "Just tell your cab driver 'Sank Roo Doe-Noo!'" It was in Harry's that bartender Fernand Petiot combined a 50/50 mixture of vodka and tomato juice and invented the "Bloody Mary" in 1924.[1] Harry's had an ongoing beer-drinking contest. Anyone could participate, and the bartender was always ready to produce a stopwatch and whistle for the clientele's attention. In the summer of 1937, the record was slightly more than one-half gallon in eleven seconds, a record that neither Tinker nor Baumler felt up to challenging.

While skimming the theater pages of his *Herald-Tribune* in search of an evening movie, an announcement that *Rigoletto* was being performed at the Academie Nationale de Musique et de Danse caught Tinker's eye. Selections from *Rigoletto* had provided their favorite *après combat* relaxation. Neither had experienced the complete opera, and now they determined to "have it all." Hurrying to the opera house, they found the performance sold out but managed to buy two tickets from a scalper. Tinker later remarked that "the opera fulfilled all of our expectations." They were only slightly disappointed to find it sung in French instead of the Italian lyrics that they had taken pains to memorize.

With the long holiday finished, Tinker concluded the business he had at the Spanish Embassy and then accompanied Baumler to the Gare St. Lazare and the boat train for LeHavre. Unlike Tinker with his phony Spanish passport, Baumler had a genuine American document, but it was stamped NOT VALID FOR TRAVEL IN SPAIN. Of course his passport now displayed vivid stamps showing that he had entered Spain in December 1936 and exited in July 1937. Secretary of State Cordell Hull's minions might take exception to this. To avoid any possible difficulties with U.S. authorities, Baumler had purchased a ticket to sail on the Canadian Pacific liner *Duchess of Richmond* for Montreal. The Canadians wouldn't care if he had been to Spain or Ulan Bator, and from Canada he could easily fly to Newark, New Jersey, and no one at Newark's airport cared about Spain either.

With Baumler gone, Tinker found himself alone again. He booked passage on the *DeGrasse* and then went to the U. S. Embassy. Using his Spanish passport he expected to pass himself off as Francisco Gomez Trejo and obtain a tourist visa for the United States. But once at the embassy he had the bad luck to encounter a naval attaché who recognized him from his Navy days on board the USS *San Francisco*. Once seen in action, no one forgot "Salty" Tinker; formally identified as Frank Tinker, he could no longer play the role of Gomez Trejo. Now he found himself in a foreign land without an effective passport. Somehow it seemed as if his luck always began to run out as soon as he climbed out of an airplane's cockpit, and the further he moved away from airplanes and into the world of well-ordered affairs, the worse his luck became.

At this point, had he thought about it, Tinker should have emulated Baumler and immediately sought a tourist visa from the Canadian Embassy—or from the Mexican Embassy, since the Mexicans were inclined to be flexible with anything relating to the Spanish Republic. But among Frank Tinker's shortcomings was his lack of guile.

At the Naval Academy, Tinker had been exposed to a course in international law, and he knew that any American citizen who can identify himself as such is entitled to a passport if caught abroad without one. But only the embassy's counselor, Tinker learned, had authority to confirm such an identification, and he wouldn't be available until he returned from vacation the following Monday.

On leaving the embassy Tinker wandered back to Harry's New York Bar, where he chanced to meet Lieutenant Lindell H. Hewett of the U.S. Navy on leave in Paris. Hewett had graduated from the Academy a year before Tinker entered as a plebe. They were enjoying a conversation when they were interrupted by the appearance of Vincent Schmidt. He approached Tinker with overwhelming camaraderie, but Tinker coldly refused to accept any of it. Indeed, Schmidt was broke. Certain that Tinker had just come from Spain presumably loaded with back pay, Schmidt sought a loan. Tinker told Schmidt to go to hell; Hewett was surprised by his acquaintance's fierce anger. Tinker then explained how Schmidt tended to develop "engine trouble" whenever enemy fighters appeared, and he had run off at Teruel, leaving the vulnerable attack bombers to fend for themselves. The Spaniards subsequently paid Schmidt for his "service" and told him to leave the country.

When Tinker finally met the embassy's forty-two-year-old counselor on the morning of 24 August, the encounter proved most unpleasant. Robert Murphy, a Roman Catholic who had worked his way up in the WASPish gentleman's club that was the U.S. Foreign Service between the world wars, proved entirely unsympathetic. Years later Murphy wrote a book in which he styled himself as a "diplomat among warriors."[2] On this day he had a warrior standing in front of him in the person of Frank Tinker.

But Murphy's principal problem in 1937 was keeping track of the clandestine traffic in U.S. passports that had grown out of the Spanish Civil War. Recovering the passports of American volunteers killed in Spain especially concerned him. Communists dominated the hierarchy of the International Brigades, and the State Department knew that the passports of their dead members were turned over to the Comintern for its use in Soviet espionage and infiltrating agents back into the United States.[3] Frank Tinker's attempt to enter the States on a fraudulent Spanish passport unquestionably angered Murphy, even though by using it and not getting killed in Spain Tinker had actually done him a twofold favor—but the embassy counselor failed to appreciate this.

Tinker produced documents from the Naval Academy, the Army Air Corps, Pensacola, and the Fleet; all of which Murphy judged to be inadequate proof of citizenship. Tinker next tried to explain that to hold a commission in the U.S. Navy a person had to be citizen, and on this point one of the naval attachés upstairs might be consulted. "I don't need outsiders telling me how to run my office," Murphy snapped. What Tinker had to do, Murphy continued, was find some American citizen who would take an oath to the effect that he knew Frank Tinker in fact to be an American citizen; the naval attachés that might know him, being part of the embassy, were disqualified from performing this service.

A baffled and angry Frank Tinker stalked out of the U.S. Embassy and into the Place de la Concorde. He was reminded of a piece of wisdom he heard while he was sailing merchant ships: "When in serious trouble in a foreign port go to the British consul who will treat you as a person with a problem, whereas the U.S. consul will treat you as the problem."

With Baumler gone, Tinker knew no one in Paris who could identify him. Meanwhile, the *DeGrasse* had sailed, and there was no hope of catching the *Normandie* the next day. But once again Arkansas luck stood with him. When he walked into Harry's that evening, who should be holding forth from one of the barstools but Tinker's Madrid acquaintance, Ernest Hemingway. Told of his passport dilemma, Hemingway volunteered to make the identification.

Even with a well-known figure like Ernest Hemingway vouching for his identity the next day, Murphy remained vindictive to the last. Although he paid a passport preparation fee of ten dollars, Tinker was not given the document. Instead, Murphy had it delivered to the U.S. consul in LeHavre, who would give it to the purser of whatever ship on which Tinker sailed, and the passport would be collected from the purser by a State Department agent on Tinker's arrival in New York. This initiated the first move in the mechanics that would make Frank Tinker Cordell Hull's temporary prisoner.

That evening Tinker again joined Hemingway, who took him to a special showing of the documentary film *The Spanish Earth*. Archibald Macleish and Lillian Hellman wrote the film's storyline, but Hemingway wrote its narration and delivered it on the film's soundtrack. Supported by the Comintern and directed by the Dutch Communist Joris Ivens, it is essentially a heavy-handed propaganda film aimed at generating sympathy for the Spanish Republic. Painfully "arty" and overloaded with lugubrious sentimentalizing of "The People," much of its presentation breaks readily into the realm of dullness—although Hollywood's contemporary notables expressed their admiration of it.[4] The film uses some excellent combat footage, most of it from the battle of Guadalajara. Tinker, who had rejected "The Cause" and its vociferous adherents who "had politics," appeared to buy the message: "Just to see the picture is to get a better idea of what is going on in Spain than could be gotten by reading reams of literature."

Concurrently, on 24 August, the Republic launched a massive offensive against Belchite in Aragon, and for a few days the Spanish Civil War was again front page news. Belchite, sited between Teruel and Huesca, is similarly a mountain stronghold, and the Republic's offensive ultimately degenerated into another costly stalemate.

On 26 August Tinker finally caught the boat train out of the Gare St. Lazare, sailing for New York on the French Line's *Champlain*, the same ship on which Hemingway had arrived in France. Having made her maiden voyage in 1932, the *Champlain* was still a new ship. She was 28,000 tons and had accommodations for 623 passengers in cabin class and 334 in tourist. A comfortable enough ship, but without first-class cabins and having a speed of only nineteen knots, the *Champlain* was not in a class with the well-remembered speed queens of the North Atlantic seaway. Tinker's crossing took eight days.

It was on board the *Champlain* that Tinker started writing what he called his "memoirs," a chronicle of his experiences in Spain later published as the book *Some Still Live*. Besides having the record of his flight log, he had kept a diary of sorts on a 6x8-inch page-a-day calendar on which he made short, telegraphic notes. In writing his book he followed his calendar-diary closely; when the two are placed side by side it is manifest that he wrote directly from it, expanding on its short entries with memories only a few months old. It may seem odd that a man of only twenty-eight years should be writing a "memoir," but Frank Tinker did not command a profound vocabulary, and he was probably hard put for a better word.

On 5 September 1937, when the *Champlain* steamed through the Narrows of New York Harbor and moored at the French Line pier at the foot of West Forty-Eighth Street, a State Department agent came on board, collected Tinker's passport from the purser, and attempted to interrogate him about Spain. Tinker first demanded his passport. The bureaucrat was not about to give it up, so Tinker refused him any information. This would be the last he saw of his passport, and for the next ten months in the "land of the free and the home of the brave" he would remain without one.

From Manhattan, he crossed the Hudson to Jersey City, checking into Journal Square's Plaza Hotel, familiar from his coastwise tanker days. A telegram from his father awaited him, saying that the newspapers had reported that the Nationalists had tried Whitey Dahl and condemned him to death. Disturbing news indeed, but Tinker knew well that this account represented only one-half of how "the system" worked in Spain.

Tinker bought a 1936 Studebaker coupe and left Jersey City for Arkansas. In those years nothing in the United States approximated a four-lane interstate highway. All long-distance driving took place over what would be considered in the 1960s "secondary roads"; they meandered all over the countryside and through every small town along the way. His trip to DeWitt took four days.

In DeWitt before mid-month, he remained a celebrity of sorts, but as more than a few million American veterans have discovered, there are few smaller coins in American life than that of a war hero. The parades barely disperse before everyone wants to know when he is going to do something "useful." If his experience occurred in someone else's war, so much the worse for him. Nevertheless, in the months that followed, Tinker's various activities kept him in the public eye in his hometown and the state capital of Little Rock, as well.

DeWitt had changed but little since Tinker departed for the U.S. Navy eleven years before. This tiny rural town near the border with Mississippi still numbered fewer than 1,500 souls, and its occupants all engaged themselves in farming (primarily soybeans and rice), in rice milling, and in the services related thereto. They also still maintained the starched Protestant façade that prompted Frank Tinker's sisters to vacate the place as soon as they were able. But Tinker found the small town well suited to the hunting, fishing, and practical jokes that he enjoyed. Moreover, compared with Spain, its pace of life proved much to his liking. He moved in, temporarily, with his parents, and thereafter stayed at the Cooper Hotel on DeWitt's central square and in several rented homes, all with a return address of 214 Shotgun Terrace. There is no such street in DeWitt, but the town's postmaster obviously entertained Tinker's sense of humor and saw that he received his mail.

Tinker's seven months in Spain had yielded $11,250 in wages and $8,000 in bonuses, a total of $19,250 in 1937 dollars. Considered in 2010-dollar equivalents, it is $291,435—quite a tidy sum! It might be thought that Tinker would look around for something in aviation. In nearby Stuttgart, Arkansas, two brothers had a large crop-dusting operation.[5] Given Tinker's flying skills and the money he had to invest, it could be assumed the brothers might have been interested in taking him into the business. Tinker never went near the place. He did purchase a "filling station" on the road to Stuttgart, but because he operated it as an absentee owner, the business soon failed. Meanwhile, new and old friends eagerly embraced him, all anxious to assist in the labor of spending his money; to be sure, within two years, most of it was gone.

Concurrently, Whitey Dahl's plight continued to stutter through the pages of the daily press. The outside world was unfamiliar with the quiet processes for exchanging aviation prisoners, and this ignorance permitted the American news media to whip up a glitzy melodrama about the fate of Harold Dahl. From her suite in the Riviera's Hotel Miramar, Edith Dahl rushed on stage to sing an impassioned plea for Whitey's life. The American form of this drama demands a "mother" as a vital constituent, and from Champaign, Illinois, Ida Dahl appealed to the moral sensibilities of Cordell Hull to save her son. Edith, in turn, wrote a carefully publicized personal appeal to General Francisco Franco: "Please don't destroy my happiness," she begged. And for a moment the U.S. State Department ran in circles to preserve Whitey's torso from a fusillade of 7.7-mm rifle bullets. This wretched drama enjoyed a four-month run in the pages of the *New York Times* and other newspapers that kept it on the national scene throughout the autumn of 1937.

There was never a chance of Dahl being shot. But from his prison cell in Salamanca, Whitey did nothing to help his case. Shortly after his capture the Nationalists took him to General José Varela, who was curious to learn about the American mercenary aviator. Dahl told Varela that he didn't give a damn about the politics of either side; he was flying for the money, and if the Nationalists would meet the Republic's pay scale he would be pleased to fly for them.

Although probably true, it was the wrong thing to say. Both sides of the Spanish Civil War took their politics with deadly seriousness and put great store by honor, a quaint notion that in America was fast becoming passé. Dahl's indiscretions shocked his interrogators. He further reduced their estimates of him by telling them anything they wanted to know about the Republic's air operations. However useful this information may have been, his behavior disgusted them. Nor was this enough; relative to the American air attaché's periodic liaisons with American aviators in Spain, Dahl also "confessed" that Captain Townsend Griffiss had intervened with the Republic's Air Ministry in Valencia on behalf of U.S. pilots in Spain, a charge that embarrassed the captain, his offices in Paris and Valencia, and the U.S. War and State Departments.[6]

William P. Carney, who covered the Nationalist side of the war for the *New York Times*, finally obtained an interview with Dahl. Although charitable to Whitey in what he wrote for public consumption, he told Claude Bowers, the U.S. ambassador to the Republic, that "the fellow is utterly shameless." This led Bowers to conclude that "the man is a thoroughly bad sort," but "worthless as Dahl is himself, his execution might cause unfortunate controversy at home in the press."[7] In fretting over this, the State Department showed itself woefully ignorant of the process by which captured aviators were subjected to public "show" trials and then quietly exchanged. Although determined to save Dahl's life, State Department officials would not have objected if the Nationalists kept him imprisoned forever—as they almost did.

On 7 October 1937, along with three Russian aviators, the Nationalists formally tried Dahl for "rebellion against Spain," found him guilty, sentenced him to death, granted him a reprieve, and held him for exchange. As a result of the hoopla surrounding his case, however, and the Nationalist propaganda exploiting

Tinker and a friend in DeWitt, 1938
(*Family photograph*)

his indiscretions, the Republic's air force had no further use for Harold Dahl. Its officials saw no logic in exchanging a perfectly good enemy aviator for this unseemly American who had not only dishonored the Republic, but who probably would not return to combat. Whitey Dahl thus remained an unwilling prisoner of Nationalist Spain for more than a year after the civil war ended.

For Tinker, life in Arkansas hardly quieted down. Shortly after his return he joined DeWitt Lodge 157 of the Masons, and subsequently participated in its activities. He spoke to the DeWitt Study Club, a woman's organization, and entertained them with his accordion. Tinker also addressed the DeWitt Rotary Club on his adventures in Spain and played his accordion for them, as well. Like the Masons, the Rotary Club contained a number of his high school classmates, with whom he reestablished friendships. But for the most part he worked on his memoir throughout the late fall of 1937 until the end of the year. Although its form left something to be desired, its substance was a model of informative writing. Hard put for a title, one day he remarked of his fellow aviators: "Most of them are dead but some still live." To which his sister Lucille replied, "There's your title: 'Some Still Live.'"

With his memoir finished, Tinker inquired about a return to Spain, but the Republic's Ministry of Defense replied that the government now had adequate numbers of Spanish pilots, and his assistance was no longer needed. Ironically, this surfeit of aviators was owed to Lacalle, who had returned to Spain from the Soviet Union in late February 1938 with a couple of hundred freshly trained pilots and aircrews. In any case, there was the problem of how Tinker expected to get to Spain without a U.S. passport. Nevertheless, he still possessed the documentation of Francisco Gomez Trejo. It had worked once. U.S. authorities were not fussy about people *leaving* the United States; Gomez Trejo might do it again.

Meanwhile, Derek Dickinson returned from Spain, spinning a story about how he had a one-on-one aerial "duel" with Bruno Mussolini, the aviator son of the Italian dictator. It was all hogwash. Never mind that Bruno Mussolini had built his career around multi-engine airplanes and was not a fighter pilot; never mind that at the time of the alleged "duel" Bruno was engaged in preparations for a well-publicized transoceanic flight from Italy to Brazil; the mainstream news media lapped up Dickinson's fantasy.[8] Concurrently, Orrin Dwight Bell, the drunk who failed to shape up in Spain, burst into print among the pages of *Liberty* magazine with wild tales of deeds he never performed for the Republic's air force.[9] With his own memoir moving toward print, Tinker found these accounts amusing.

Rejected by two publishers, in early 1938 Funk & Wagnall's accepted *Some Still Live*, the book coming on the market in the spring of the year together with a four-part serialization in the *Saturday Evening Post*.[10] Until television siphoned off advertising revenues in the 1960s and destroyed the *Post's* economic foundation, forcing an end to its publication, this magazine was practically a fixture in every middle-class American home. In England, Lovat Dickinson purchased the book's British Empire rights and produced a British edition, and in Sweden *Some Still Live* was published in translation as *Några Leva Än*. Altogether, Tinker's book was well received. Immediately after its appearance 20th Century Fox offered to buy the movie rights, but Tinker failed to seize this singular opportunity. Six months later a general European war appeared imminent, and the Spanish Civil War suddenly became as old as last week's meat loaf.

Nevertheless, that war temporarily came alive again in American newspapers when in March 1938 the Italians treated Barcelona to three days of around-the-clock terror bombing that shocked the world. In April the Nationalists burst out of the Teruel salient, punching through the Republic's defenses in Aragon to reach the Mediterranean shore at Vinaroz. This not only separated the Levante from Catalonia, it also cut off Valencia, the Levante, and Madrid from direct overland communications with France. Cut in two, the Republic's defeat now appeared inevitable.

With interest in Spain revived for a moment, in May the Columbia Broadcasting System (CBS) invited Tinker to New York to appear on *We The People*, a weekly thirty-minute radio program that focused on current events.[11] His sister, Toodles, wanted to see the big city so he took her along. Driving to Memphis, they boarded a Douglas DC-3 of American Airlines for Newark. (Until LaGuardia Airport opened in December 1939, Newark, New Jersey, served as New York City's commercial air terminal.) Their 960-mile flight took almost seven hours.

At CBS, newscaster Floyd Gibbons[12] took them in tow and introduced them to Gabriel Heater, the program's master of ceremonies.[13] The program had to be rehearsed, but its maudlin "horrors of war" script irritated Tinker; he thought it reeked of mindless pacifism. Had he felt that way about the war, he never would have gone to Spain, *Some Still Live* could not have been written, and CBS would have had no interest in him.

He wanted to tell the world what an incredible experience it had been. What it was like to go corkscrewing across the sky at 280 mph behind four PV-1 guns to kill the other guy before he killed you, to watch the groundlings scurry around in panic at a squeeze of his thumb, and then to exchange the deafening 2,000 rpm of an R-1750 engine for a Victrola's 78 rpm and the emphatic sounds of *Rigoletto*. Yes sir, *that's* what it was all about. He asked for numerous changes in the script but was granted only a few.[14]

After rehearsal they had lunch at the Glass Hat, a fashionable eatery in Belmont Plaza that was a favorite with radio people in the late 1930s, and here aviation writer, artist, and illustrator Clayton Knight, who had flown as a fighter pilot in World War I, joined them. Knight did the illustrations for the serialization of Tinker's story in the *Saturday Evening Post* and the dust jacket for *Some Still Live*; now he planned to feature Tinker in his weekly "Hall of Fame of the Air" that he drew for the King Features Syndicate in collaboration with Eddie Rickenbacker. (The feature appeared in the newspapers a few weeks later.)

That evening Tinker and Toodles met Albert Baumler for dinner. Baumler had just finished a training course with United Air Lines that promised a copilot's job, but he was still trying to get back into the Army Air Corps. While engaged in the course, he had been contacted about a scheme for clandestinely flying airplanes to Spain. Pilots were needed. He wanted to know if Tinker might be interested, and of course he was.[15]

The radio broadcast took place on 5 May 1938, and it went well. Later, at the Stork Club, a night spot on the eve of a glittering heyday enjoyed in the 1940s, Walter Winchell, the influential gossip columnist, interviewed Tinker.[16] With the radio production finished, Tinker put Toodles on a plane for Memphis and joined Baumler for a drive to Newcastle, Delaware, and a visit to the Bellanca Aircraft factory.

In 1934 Giuseppe Bellanca designed a long-distance racing plane for the MacRobertson Race from England to Australia, but it failed to fly in that contest. He subsequently developed it into his Model 28-90 as a ground-attack plane. In 1936 agents of the Spanish Republic ordered two dozen of them. To evade U.S. neutrality laws they were described as "mail planes," Air France being the ostensible customer.[17] The U.S. State Department unraveled this subterfuge, and the airplanes were subsequently sold to China. Undeterred, in 1938 the Republic's agents tried again, ordering twenty-two, and this time the export licenses were taken out in the name of an organization in Greece as the ostensible customer; but this approach, too, was thwarted.[18] Next, the firm studied the possibility of clandestine transatlantic delivery flights from some point in the United States directly to Republican Spain. Tinker and Baumler represented prospective pilots.

The transatlantic flight had to be nonstop. As of 1938, aside from inevitable political complications, no facilities to serve landplanes existed in Newfoundland or the Azores. From Newcastle, Delaware, to Madrid is about 3,800 miles, and with an average speed of 160 mph, it would take 23.7 hours. Bellanca airplanes were noted for their efficiency in long-range cruising, however, and the 2890 could accommodate 610 gallons of internal fuel, giving it a still-air range of 4,000 miles to dry tanks. And a beneficial tailwind could be expected flying west to east. After discussions with Bellanca engineers and studying the 2890's performance data, they decided that the number of airplanes to be moved and the chance of bad weather militated against the plan unless numerous qualified pilots could be obtained.[19]

Tinker and Baumler left Newcastle and drove to Annapolis in mid-May. Here they met with Lieutenant Commander Edwin F. "Bunny" Cochrane, editor of the Naval Academy Alumni Association's new magazine, *Shipmate*. Cochrane was a naval aviator, an airship pilot, had been on board the airplane-carrying airship *Macon* when it went down in the Pacific in 1935, and had recently retired from active duty. He was fascinated by Tinker's stories of Spain and urged him to write them up for *Shipmate*. From Annapolis Tinker continued to Washington, where he and Baumler had an appointment with Fernando de los Rios, the Republic's ambassador to the United States, a meeting that discussed the prospects of ferrying airplanes to Spain.

In Washington he also sought to resolve the passport situation that held him captive within the United States. Since his return, he had been conducting a guerilla war of sorts via the mails with one R. B. Shipley in the State Department about gaining possession of the passport that he had paid for in Paris. Visiting the State Department he was surprised to discover that "R. B." was a woman. Unbeknownst to Tinker, fifty-three-year-old Ruth B. Shipley already was notorious for inflicting her personal judgments on passport applications. She played a devious game of delay or denial toward any persons she had heard about and whose reputations she disliked.[20] Regrettably, she had heard of Tinker's military activities in Spain and, not surprisingly, they met with her firm disapproval.

Tinker did not regain his Paris passport. Instead, Shipley made him pay again for a new one, and although its ten-dollar fee may not sound like much, in 1938 it represented a week's pay for thousands of Americans.[21] Shipley also made him sign an affidavit that, under pain of prosecution, he would not attempt to use the passport for travel to Spain. Finally, the passport was stamped NOT VALID FOR TRAVEL IN SPAIN OR CHINA.[22] But as Albert Baumler had demonstrated by traveling via Canada, caveats such as this meant nothing in the real traveler's world.

Returning to Arkansas near month's end, in possession at last of his restricted passport, Tinker was shown a copy of the *American Magazine* that contained another bloated account of Orrin Dwight Bell's fictitious exploits in Spain.[23] Tinker had had little to say about Bell in *Some Still Live* beyond, "He had not been able to pass the flight tests and had been sent back to the United States," which seemed innocent enough. These few words, however, reduced Bell's twice-told adventures to a pack of lies; in fact, Tinker recalled, Bell "stayed so tanked up on anis and cognac while he was still in primary, when the others were breaking into fighters," but he had omitted this "out of consideration for the old boy." Bell felt otherwise and initiated a libel suit against Tinker and his publishers.

Tinker suspected Bell was aiming at an out-of-court settlement, "because if he went to court, his reputation won't be damaged, it will be ruined." By way of a defense, Tinker obtained affidavits from Allison and Baumler; from his prison cell in Spain even Whitey Dahl wrote letters denouncing Bell. In the face of all this, the "Bell Suit" faded away.

As regards the Bellanca transatlantic ferrying operation, Tinker and Baumler were also expected to recruit other pilots. Tinker tracked down Jim Allison in Texas, where he was flying for an oil company. Allison had recently returned from China, operating Vultee V-11 attack planes out of Hankow with a squadron of mercenaries flying for the Chinese air force, such as it was. Allison was game for the Bellanca scheme, and Tinker was curious about China. Allison gave him some American contacts but said that the man to get in touch with was a Major Claire Chennault. By midsummer, however, plans for the ambitious Bellanca transatlantic ferrying operation had faded away.

All the while during late 1937 and 1938, when he was not traveling, Frank Tinker engaged himself in and around DeWitt, Arkansas. He resumed hunting and fishing in the fields, forests, and waterways of the White River at nearby St. Charles. In early 1938 Tinker met and became a friend of Lemuel C. ("L. C.") Brown Sr., who had a farm seventeen miles east of DeWitt, near St. Charles. The two frequently hunted and fished together, accompanied by Brown's twelve-year-old son, L. C. Brown Jr. In the spring of 1938 Tinker purchased the remnants of a Curtiss JN-4 "Jenny" two-place biplane and, with parts fashioned at the Johnson mechanic shop, cobbled it together in a field provided by another cooperative farmer just outside DeWitt. Nearly every Saturday, L. C. Jr. recalled, the family would pack a picnic lunch and drive in their Dort automobile over to the field where Tinker kept the Jenny. Tinker would "borrow" the Dort's magneto, install it on the engine of the Jenny and, assisted by L. C. Sr. who cranked the propeller, take to the air. The only admonition was that the aviator return before dusk so that the Browns could retrieve the magneto and get back to the livestock before dark. These weekend Jenny flights over DeWitt and the surrounding area, where

Tinker's Jenny (*Courtesy of L. C. Brown Jr.*)

no man had an airplane, much less could fly one, brought other families with picnic baskets to the field, and the event soon became a major local attraction. Tinker eventually purchased a magneto, but try as he might, he never could convince the elder Brown to fly with him in the Jenny.[24]

On 1 June 1938, sponsored by John Smith, Tinker was elected a member of the Delta Nu Chapter, Local No. 48, of the Kappa Alpha Phi International Young Men's Fraternity in Hot Springs, Arkansas.[25] Smith, the son of one of the Smith brothers, now owned the rice mill in DeWitt in which Frank Tinker Sr. served as the chief engineer and manager. About ten years older than Frank Jr., he had spent a good deal of time with the Tinker family over the years and numbered among Frank Jr.'s "hunting buddies." Later that month, Tinker joined his Rotarian companions in a practical joke that caught the attention of the *Arkansas Gazette* in Little Rock. W. L. ("Pink") Kennedy, editor of the *Grand Prairie Leader*, the newspaper of record in Stuttgart, frequently panned the people of DeWitt as country bumpkins in his column. Despite this record, he accepted an invitation to speak at a DeWitt Rotary Club banquet on 20 June. While addressing those assembled, "two rough-looking individuals, one armed with a shotgun and the other with a pistol, appeared at the door and demanded to see him." Kennedy dashed from the lectern toward the back door, where he was met by a third man armed with a revolver. He was escorted back "to the dining room and sat down among fellow Rotarians, who soon broke into laughter."[26] Whether Stuttgart's "Pink" Kennedy continued to take jabs at DeWitt in later columns is not recorded.

During the 1930s, along the banks of the White, Arkansas, and Mississippi Rivers, there remained hundreds of small houseboat communities, floating villages in which children were born and could spend a lifetime without experiencing a home with fixed foundations, much less a cellar. They were the shantyboat folks of a distinctly lower class, possessed of a culture all their own. Without

Setting out on the White River with Susie Q (*Family photograph*)

electricity or any other modern convenience, they ordered their own communities, carried their own firearms, and dispensed their own "river justice"; no lawman ventured into their communities alone. All of them made their living from fish and mussels (the shells used for buttons) brought in from the river and sold in nearby towns. Not until the 1930s did these novel people begin to send their children to public schools. Townsfolk referred to them as "the river rats," but no "outsider" dared call them that to their face.

In July 1938 Tinker bought a canoe, named it *Arkansas Traveler*, and accompanied by a pet terrier, "Susie Q," shoved off from Whitemore's Dock at St. Charles, Arkansas, on the thirty-first. From St. Charles he paddled down the White River to its junction with the Arkansas River, then on to the Mississippi and down to New Orleans. He had wanted to make this trip, he said, "ever since my first reading of *Huckleberry Finn*," and his river foray was prominently reported in Little Rock's *Arkansas Gazette*. The Mississippi still remained a colorful stretch of water in 1938, having more in common with the world of the 1890s than it would have with the mid-twentieth century. Besides the communities of houseboat people, there were still steamboats and lots of them, each with its own distinctive whistle, a crew with its own special *esprit*, and each a family unto itself. And among these steamboats were scores of sternwheelers, including the mighty *Sprague*, the largest sternwheeler the world has ever known. Built in 1901, the 1,480-ton *Sprague* with only 1,600 steam horsepower set an all-time record, successfully pushing a string of 61 barges of some 67,000 tons, their mass being 485 by 1,160 feet long, almost four times the length of a football field. South of Vicksburg, Tinker met the *Sprague* pushing upriver with a typically awesome tow.

Mark Twain could have made himself at home on the Mississippi River of 1938. The same could not be said of 1948, just a decade later, by which time the lure of the automobile and slump in demand for mussels and fish took houseboat folks away from their less mobile dwellings, and the river echoed to the anonymous bleats of diesel boat horns. The *Sprague* would be retired in 1948, and within a few years all but a few sternwheelers had slipped into American history.

All of the houseboat people were hospitable toward the strange young man in the canoe from "upriver," who could speak in their idiom. But often as not, Tinker camped on islands and sandbars, catching fish or shooting ducks and turtles for dinner. It took almost four weeks for Tinker to reach New Orleans, and then things started to go awry. The evening before he arrived, Susie Q went missing. Although he appealed for her return in an interview published in the *New Orleans Picayune*, it was not to be. He bought a small outboard motor for his return upriver, but it never worked well, and by the time he reached Baton Rouge it had reduced itself to junk. He finally packed up the canoe and had it shipped to DeWitt while he boarded a passenger train. His bucolic adventure was subsequently written up for the *Arkansas Gazette*, which serialized it in six of its Sunday feature sections, and that inspired him to start another book about the Mississippi's riverine dwellers.

While Tinker cruised down the Mississippi in July–August 1938, the earthly remains of Ben Leider also made their last cruise. Officials of the Communist Party of America decided that Leider must have been the first American aviator killed in the Spanish Civil War, and that this event had not been adequately exploited. They had Leider's corpse exhumed from its resting place on the east bank of the Jarama and trucked to Valencia, where it was loaded on board the British freighter *Fredavore*. Transhipped at Lisbon on board the American Export Lines freighter *Excambion*, it was offloaded in Boston and turned over to the care of the New York, New Haven & Hartford Railroad.

Leider's coffin arrived in New York City's Grand Central Terminal on the evening of 18 August 1938, where it was greeted by some two thousand persons. These included an honor guard of 125 veterans of the Abraham Lincoln Battalion. Leider the individualist had never belonged to the Lincolns, but in the station's grand concourse any recollection of this might have spoiled the moment. To the beat of muffled drums they marched his coffin to Times Square, and

Tinker on arrival in New Orleans, late August 1938 (*Family photograph*)

then up Broadway to a memorial service in Carnegie Hall. Some three thousand persons jammed the auditorium, and another two thousand stood in the street outside listening to the proceedings over loudspeakers.

Rabbi Benjamin Plotkin read a dignified eulogy, and then some half-dozen others felt the need of adding to it. These included the artist Rockwell Kent, the war correspondent Jay Allen, and the dreadful opportunist Frederic Lord, who was lucky enough to be possessed of sobriety on this evening; finally, a number of Party members became aware that what should have been a solemn moment had been transformed into a noisome circus of political declamation that had dragged on for hours, and they ended it. On Sunday, 21 August, Ben Leider's remains were finally laid to rest in Mount Hebron Cemetery in Flushing, Queens.[27]

On returning to DeWitt from New Orleans in early September, Tinker must have realized that his life had significantly slowed down. His *Some Still Live* was past tense; his moment as a "celebrity" had unquestionably diminished, although his doings still commanded press attention. An article in the *Arkansas Democrat* described him as unassuming, well liked by his fellow townsmen, "just another of the home town boys."[28] At that time he began writing a weekly column on foreign affairs for the *DeWitt Record* newspaper, called "Tinkering Around," which he continued producing until the end of February 1939.[29] And, responding to Ed Cochrane's request, Tinker contributed an article to *Shipmate* on the effectiveness of antiaircraft fire that appeared in the following year. Alluding to his exploration of opportunities in China, he concluded: "Well Maties—this will probably be my last article for a while. I would like to continue the series but urgent business is at hand. However, if it turns out well there may be more of them in the Future."[30]

But there was no going back to Spain. Even if he could, there was no point to it. In early September a frightfully expensive Republican offensive of six weeks, which attempted to break through Nationalist forces holding the right bank of the Ebro River and reunite Catalonia with the Levante, had exhausted itself. Now the initiative belonged to the Nationalists. To the extent that the Republic had any future, it was grim.

By that time the fate of the Republic's disastrous Ebro offensive was no longer news; the world's attention riveted on German threats against Czechoslovakia. A general European war seemed imminent. The crisis dragged through the month of September, with the prime minister of Great Britain flitting between England and Germany in a Lockheed airliner while attempting to "appease" Adolf Hitler. The notorious Munich Agreement, in which the Anglo-French leaders gave Nazi Germany the keys to Czechoslovakia and all of southeastern Europe, finally resolved the "Czech Crisis." In Britain, the news media hailed this success as "peace for our time"; that unhappy "peace" would last not quite eleven months.

Back in Dewitt, Tinker got the harebrained idea of exchanging himself to the Nationalists for Whitey Dahl so that Whitey could be reunited with Edith and be home by Christmas. He actually made this proposal in a letter addressed to General Francisco Franco, with a copy sent to Secretary of State Cordell Hull. The Nationalist seat of government in Burgos made no reply; Cordell Hull dismissed Tinker as a "misguided young man," and, because it concerned Whitey Dahl, he was probably right.[31]

There is no question about the offer of an exchange being a serious proposition, and it bespoke a measure of desperation. Although he had begun to receive small sums in royalties from the sale of his book, Tinker's life in rural Arkansas seemed to have reached a standstill; jail in Nationalist Spain might be more interesting than feeling confined within the United States. In response to remarks by people around him, he was inclined with increasing frequency to answer them with a shrug and the Spanish idioms *Sin novedad!* (Nothing's new!) or *Quién sabe?* (Who knows?).

If he needed a reminder of the extent to which his life now flew in slow circles, he got it in a telegram from Albert Baumler asking Tinker to meet him at the Memphis airport on 8 November. It was 2nd Lieutenant Albert Baumler, U.S. Army Air Corps, who landed at Memphis, seated at the controls of a Douglas

0-43 observation airplane on a flight from Mitchel Field in New York. After spending two days with Tinker in DeWitt, Baumler flew back to New York.[32] Baumler certainly seemed to have his career boresighted, whereas Tinker stared at life through a cracked prism. Although Frank Tinker was too much of a loner to measure his life by the achievements of others, by the end of 1938 he doubtless felt that he was slipping off the ragged edge of infinity on a tangent to nowhere.

But he was not without viable options. E. Burke Wilford, president of the Pennsylvania Aircraft Syndicate, read Tinker's story in the *Saturday Evening Post* and was favorably impressed. Involved in early rotary wing developments, his syndicate focused on the autogiro and was part of a well-financed group that had many channels into Pennsylvania's aviation industrial complex.[33] He invited Tinker to drop by for a visit. Later yet, Wilford offered Tinker a letter of introduction to the commanding officer of Wright Field, the Army Air Corps' test and development center. And if Tinker would meet him in Washington, it would be his pleasure to introduce Tinker to General Henry H. Arnold, the new chief of the Army Air Corps.

Wilford clearly thought Tinker had something to offer aviation, and he in turn offered what others would recognize as a key to many opportunities. In spite of his Navy fiasco, this might have led to a commission in the Army Air Corps, which, after 1934, Tinker had claimed as his new heart's desire. But in his heart of hearts he may have had a glimmering that he could no more adapt to the Air Corps' peacetime discipline than he had to the Navy's. Frank Tinker functioned best under the pressures of life-or-death chaos, from which he established his own order. This was predicated expressly on the violent work at hand and the survival of himself and his immediate associates—his wingmen and the squadron. Peacetime military establishments do not operate on this basis. Whatever his own reasons may have been, Tinker, always erratic in peacetime, failed entirely to follow up on Wilford's generous invitations.

Meanwhile, on the Iberian Peninsula, the Spain that Tinker knew ceased to exist. In late December 1938, the Nationalists started rolling up the Mediterranean shore for Barcelona and the French frontier. In this dark hour, Tinker's old squadron leader Lacalle was named chief of the Republic's fighter aviation—as if Lacalle could bring off a miracle. By that time the Soviet aerial contingents had left for the Soviet Union, and Lacalle had only eighty-four fighters remaining and not all of them serviceable, whereas the Nationalists had more than two hundred. It was a one-sided struggle destined to fail.

On 16 January 1939, the Nationalists occupied Barcelona, and the telephone system, the heart of Lacalle's early-warning network, was lost. Now reduced to a mixed bag of forty-three airplanes, Lacalle retreated to an airfield at Viljuiga near the French frontier for the sole reason of organizing a withdrawal into

France. On 6 February the airplanes took off, Lacalle in an I-15 with Jose Bastida as his wingman. Intercepted by Messerschmitts of the Legion Condor, they had to fight their way across the Pyrenees. North of this mountain barrier they were intercepted by French fighter planes. There would be no shooting, but the French pilots tried to direct them to the airport at Perpignan.

Lacalle knew that hundreds of thousands of refugees from the Republic had overwhelmed Perpignan and its hinterland, and that the local French had long since become jaded to their desperate condition and inclined to treat these Spaniards as they would diseased cattle. Certain that his pilots would get better treatment at more-distant Toulouse, he pressed on, and within the hour they landed their riddled I-15s at the military airfield at Toulouse-Francanzal, where their war ended. The French Armée de l'Air treated them as brothers, but political considerations determined their ultimate fate, which dictated confinement in an internment camp.[34]

Although the newspapers were full of Catalonia's disaster and the Republic's imminent collapse, Tinker never learned of Lacalle's plight. A few weeks later, on 27 March 1939, the Spanish Republic formally surrendered, and on the twenty-eighth, Nationalist troops swarmed across the Casa de Campo, through the ruins of University City, and into the Plaza de España to march up the Gran Vía without a shot being fired.

During this time someone brought Tinker a copy of the current *Reader's Digest* that carried an article by Derek Dickinson. It contained more lurid details of his alleged "duel" with Bruno Mussolini.[35] Its narrative read like a hodgepodge plagiarized from the romantic stuff of *Flying Aces* or *Air Stories*, popular pulp magazines of the 1930s. In fact, the article was such a ridiculous pack of lies that on this occasion it offended him. He wrote a sharp letter to the magazine, detailing the article's many impossibilities; the editor's reply made it clear that the *Digest* was not inclined to let anything like facts stand in the way of a "good yarn." In all, between September 1938 and April 1939, Tinker spent some seven months in DeWitt, dividing his time among acquaintances and hunting and fishing.

With the spring of the year came Derby Day in Lexington, Kentucky, and Tinker left DeWitt for the bluegrass country for two weeks in mid-April to watch the horses run in circles. If he thought he was a "gambler" he should have learned he was in fact a "loser"; this experience, which concluded with the Kentucky Derby on 2 May, cost him some five hundred dollars.

From Kentucky he retired to the spa of Hot Springs, Arkansas, to visit with members of Kappa Alpha Phi and another Hot Springs acquaintance, Sue Owens. Here someone apparently taunted him about his ability to actually fly an airplane, so he went to the Hot Springs airport on 15 May and rented one. Tinker had never obtained a civil pilot's license, but he could be very charming with his "soft soap" approach, and he had his identification cards from Randolph Field and Pensacola. After airport manager John Stover had Tinker checked out by a flight instructor, he approved the rental.

The airplane was a Piper J-3 Cub, an extremely docile machine. With a gross weight of 990 pounds and a wing loading of only 5.6 pounds per square foot, compared with what Tinker was accustomed, he found it more like controlling a leaf in the wind than flying an airplane. Its 40-horsepower Continental engine had only one-half the power produced by one cylinder of the Wright Cyclones that had rushed him across the skies of Spain. But pound for pound the J-3 was probably the most versatile flying machine of its modest class. In those years Piper Cubs came only in one color, yellow.

After takeoff Tinker flew over downtown Hot Springs, treating its citizens to a ten-minute aerobatic display of loops, snap rolls, barrel rolls, chandelles, a few brief spins, and even some inverted flight.[36] Aerobatics over a populated area violated everything the Civil Aeronautics Authority's regulations had to say on the subject, but the nearest CAA inspectors were far away in Dallas and St. Louis. In 1939 long-distance telephone calls cost dearly, and no one in Hot Springs became sufficiently upset to file a complaint. An airplane was still enough of a novelty in 1939 that everyone enjoyed the show.

The next day, anyone who knew Frank Tinker would have been puzzled by his behavior on Hot Springs' Central Avenue, the city's main drag. He walked its length from the old Como Hotel to the Whitington Avenue junction, almost two miles. Walking slowly, he appeared to be making a surveillance, stopping frequently, always looking up as if there was something of extraordinary interest among the rooftops and telephone wires. Those on Central Avenue paid scant attention to him on this day, but there was no missing his passage on the next.

On Wednesday, 17 May 1939, he returned to the airport and again hired the Piper Cub. Flying to the downtown area, he circled his target a few times and then dove on the Como Hotel, pulling up over the Arkansas Bank, which he orbited in tight circles while assessing the street traffic. To spectators it appeared as if his inside wingtip must be scribing circles on the bank's roof. Then he dove into Central Avenue, under the telephone wires, and, nearly at street level, roared up the boulevard beyond Whitington Avenue, where he climbed back into the blue. Stover, the airport manager, happened to be in a shop on Central Avenue. He heard the airplane coming but refused to believe his ears; when he saw a yellow streak flash past the store's front windows, he thought surely he was out the price of a Piper Cub.[37]

After Tinker landed the Piper Cub, he turned it in without a word, got into his car, and drove away. Confident that it was expedient to leave Arkansas, he kept on going all the way to Cameron, Texas, for a brief visit with his sister

Toodles. He continued to San Antonio and Randolph Field, where Baumler now served as a flight instructor. After a few days he pushed on toward California. Meanwhile, Baumler determined through his Air Corps sources that Tinker's flat-hatting of Hot Springs' Central Avenue had not created the great uproar that he feared. He telegraphed this information to Tinker in El Paso where Tinker, unfortunately, received it and decided to return to Arkansas.

This would prove a final turning point in Frank Tinker's life. The best thing that had happened to him in a year was the sudden conviction that he had to get out of Arkansas. Since December 1938 he had written a couple of times to Major Claire Chennault in China in quest of work similar to his employment in Spain. Since the summer of 1937 Chennault and a small group of Americans had been operating a flight school for the Chinese government in an effort to build up a Chinese air force, an effort complicated by the snake pit of China's internal politics and the Japanese invasion of that country. By early 1939 the Japanese had seized all of China's seaports and the Chinese government was isolated in Chungking. Its only overland communications with the outside world turned on the railroad to Hanoi in French Indo-China, the treacherous Burma Road to Lashio, Mandalay and the port of Rangoon, or over the desperate truck route north across Mongolia to the Soviet Union. Irregular air communications were flown by night across Japanese occupied territory to British Hong Kong.[38] At this date, Chennault was hurting for airplanes but also would have welcomed a flight instructor with combat experience.

As yet, Tinker had no reply, though he had made plans for a move to the West Coast in pursuit of a course to China and a return to aerial combat. Indeed, he had begun to act on it after leaving Hot Springs for points west. He knew that letters were problematic at best. In those days, it took a letter three weeks to cross the Pacific by steamship. An exchange of correspondence could run to two months. Pan American Airways' air-mail service from San Francisco to Hong Kong operated only once a week and took nine days. Between Hong Kong and Chennault's address in Chungking anything could happen to a letter, assuming Tinker sent it air mail. Surface mail would be routed through Hanoi—or via Rangoon and over the Burma Road, which was almost as bad as putting a letter in a bottle and tossing it off the Golden Gate Bridge.

Since his return from New Orleans in late August of 1938 he had been vegetating in a benign hometown environment, where he was the big frog in a very small pond, and one in which he was not only tolerated but indulged by the townsfolk. However, instead of pressing on to Los Angeles from El Paso, where he could make "China connections," in late May 1939 he returned to Arkansas and the swamp of illusions. For reasons of his own, on his return from Texas he did not go directly to DeWitt; on 2 June he checked into Little Rock's McGehee Hotel.

From Room 1013 in the McGehee, he wrote to Louis Sullenberger of the Western Air College in Alhambra, California (part of the Los Angeles metropolitan area), telling of his difficulties in trying to reach Chennault; he hoped Sullenberger would provide a better "Chennault connection." He wrote to the Chinese consul in San Francisco. He wrote to friends in the east saying he expected to be in Washington, D.C., by the end of the month. And he continued to work on his new book about the Mississippi River shantyboat people. For this project, Ed Cochrane of *Shipmate* had offered to put him in touch with a friend at McGraw-Hill; Tinker thanked him and wrote in reply that he would see him in Annapolis in a few weeks.

But in this first week of June 1939, Frank Tinker's calendar and clock were running out fast. Within a few days, they would stop among the fouled-up circuitry of the McGehee Hotel's telephone switchboard.

17

QUIÉN SABE?

Tuesday, 13 June 1939, was a slow day at one of the city's best hostelries, Little Rock's eight-year-old McGehee Hotel. An early summer had long since become a scorcher, and on this day the red stuff in shaded thermometers stood at ninety-two degrees; it was a hundred in the sun. When the stillness of the lobby wasn't being interrupted by the muffled *whop-whup-whup* from the swinging screen doors that opened to Markham and Main Streets—whose intersection locals styled "the Broadway of Mid-America"—there was only the faint whir of a dozen electric fans and the occasional ring of a cash register to be heard. The day's nuisance occurred just before noon, when the hotel's telephone switchboard broke down.

The switchboard's repairs were finished by two o'clock, after which one of its lights came on, and refused to go out. It was Room 1013. The telephone operator recognized the room as Mr. Tinker's. Everyone knew about him. He was the aviator who flew in the Spanish war and wrote a book. Some of his stories even appeared in the *Saturday Evening Post*. And anyone in Little Rock who read the *Arkansas Gazette* knew all about his canoe trip down the Mississippi. He was a nice young man, albeit a bit of a strange one. Some people called him "eccentric." Others said he was daft in the head, rattled by his war experiences. After all, normal people don't fight in other people's wars. Normal people don't fly airplanes down the main street of Hot Springs scaring everyone half to death.

But however erratic his behavior could be, those who knew him would concede Tinker to be a most colorful and uncommon young man. Through sheer perseverance, he had risen from a teenage enlisted seaman, through the U.S. Naval Academy, to the officers' wardroom—then pressed on to claim the wings of a naval aviator and become a superlative fighter pilot and a published author. More unusual still, he possessed extraordinary people skills—skills that allowed him to deal and move with relative ease among Navy compatriots, foreign combat pilots, left-wing literati in Madrid and Paris, and the rural folk of Arkansas, Mississippi, and Louisiana, who embraced him as "one of their own."

Tinker had already made two phone calls that morning. Now his light was on again. His phone was off its hook, but he wasn't answering. Maybe his circuit still remained out of order. Or maybe he'd tried to call out while the board was out of order, got tired of waiting, and went off, leaving the receiver out of its cradle. His room key wasn't in his mailbox, so it seemed likely that he was in the tenth-floor room; but then, he might have gone out, taking the key with him.

The hotel operator called a bellhop and told him to get a passkey and to check the telephone in 1013. When the bellhop entered Room 1013, he found Mr. Tinker clad only in his undershorts and sprawled on the unmade bed, its sheets streaked with fresh blood. A long-barreled revolver was on the seat of an armchair a few feet away from the bed. The telephone receiver was out of its cradle. Mr. Tinker hadn't stirred. "Mr. Tinker?" the bellhop called. He did not really expect a reply, and he got none. The bellhop fled and called the manager.

Frank Glasgow Tinker Jr., age twenty-nine years, ten months, and twenty-nine days, was dead of a gunshot wound. One shot had been fired from a .22-caliber target pistol that Tinker had bought only a few months earlier. In addition to the .22, the police found a fully loaded .45 Colt automatic in his luggage.

The medical examiner found an entry wound below the heart, from where the bullet ranged downward into the lower abdomen without an exit. It hit no vital organs. Frank Tinker had slowly bled to death.

Speaking with police at the scene, the occupant of an adjoining room reported hearing "a sharp report" shortly after 1 p.m., but assumed that the noise occurred because someone had "dropped a light bulb." After discussing the matter with detectives, Dr. John N. Roberts, deputy coroner for Pulaski County, judged Tinker's death a suicide.[1]

Tinker's body was returned to DeWitt into the custody of the Essex Brothers Funeral Home the next day—Wednesday afternoon, 14 June.[2] Dealing with their own particular grief, Tinker's parents would be consoled by his sisters from Louisiana and Texas, and by Albert Baumler, who flew in from San Antonio in a Douglas O-25C, an obsolete biplane that Randolph Field retained as a "squadron hack." The town's leading citizens, including members of the Masons and the Eastern Star, joined the Tinker family at the funeral and burial the next morning in the DeWitt Cemetery.[3] Tinker's brothers at Kappa Alpha Phi served as pallbearers. A newspaper clipping held by Tinker's family reported, "Wilford Harper of Stuttgart sang 'Anchors Away,' a favorite song of Mr. Tinker." The funeral book lists among his friends that telephoned condolences a Miss Sue Owens of Hot Springs and Miss Gladys Henry of San Antonio.

Frank Tinker Sr. retired from the Smith Brothers Rice Mill a few months later, and he and Effie moved to Hot Springs in December. The Tinker family never accepted the verdict of suicide, nor did anyone else who knew Tinker well.[4] There is much to be said for their exceptions. However capricious and erratic his behavior could be, and however "eccentric" he may have become after Spain, Frank Tinker did not have a suicidal personality. Moreover, while at the hotel, he had been working on his new book about the boat people that inhabited the White, Arkansas, and Mississippi Rivers, and had scheduled a trip to the East Coast. Finally, as Tinker himself had demonstrated throughout a fractious life, he was by all instincts a survivor.

Familiar with firearms, if Tinker had decided to commit suicide, it is unlikely that he would have used a .22 when he had a .45 available—a handgun that he was seldom without. Nor would he have attempted it by shooting himself in the abdomen. In Spain he had been shot by a small-caliber bullet and was flying again within a few days. Moreover, he was always something of an exhibitionist. Once determined to kill himself he doubtless would have tucked the muzzle of his .45 under his chin and blown his brains all over the ceiling, his last thought being, "This'll give 'em all a 'Wow!'"

Consider this: while in Little Rock and Hot Springs, Tinker ran with a fast, hard-drinking, hard-partying crowd, many of them gamblers. However illegal it might be, gambling was big stuff in these cities. Doubtless one or more of their number inspired him to flat-hat Hot Springs Central Avenue. Maybe Tinker did it to win a wager—maybe to wipe out a gambling debt. After a hard Monday night or maybe the whole weekend, it is not difficult to imagine Tinker waking up to a terrible hangover on Tuesday and phoning a friend or two in Little Rock to drop in around noontime and share a bit of the "hair of the dog." He did make two phone calls before noon.

To be sure, the day was stinking hot and the hotel had no air-conditioning. On this point the upscale McGehee Hotel was not unusual; in 1939 mechanical air-conditioning existed only in new movie theaters, a few big department stores, and hotels built within very recent years. The room's windows were open; circulation created by one of the three-hundred-some ceiling fans, of which the hotel boasted on its letterheads, provided relative coolness. Given the day's heat and familiar male visitors, skivvies served as an adequate uniform of the day.

It is not hard to imagine Tinker and his friend, or friends, sitting around sipping whiskey and swapping stories around noon, with Tinker telling about getting shot off his bicycle in Villajoyosa, Spain. He had the scars to prove it and did not have to peel off a shirt to make his point. Meanwhile, a friend has picked up the .22 target pistol and is playing with it. From a standing position he aims it at Tinker seated in the armchair and says, "You mean like this?" Before Tinker can shout, "Hey! That thing's loaded!" the trigger is pulled through its double action, and Tinker has a bullet in his gut.

The McGehee Hotel *(Courtesy of the Arkansas History Commission®)*

At this point Tinker would examine his new wound. It is similar to the one received in Spain, but this bullet failed to exit. And Little Rock is not Villajoyosa. In the United States, gunshot wounds require an explanation to officialdom, and there will be questions, or maybe even forms to be filled out. Many bureaucrats of this world like to wax their egos over the subject of passports; others do it with respect to minor errors on income tax forms; still others in small towns take a special interest in shuffling papers over gunshot wounds.

Instinctively sensing complications, Tinker tells his friends to clear out. It will be simplest if he handles it by himself. He will wait a few minutes and then call for help.

They leave. He waits. When he picks up the telephone the switchboard doesn't answer. He clatters the phone's cradle. Still no answer. Maybe the operator had to leave the switchboard to handle a problem at the front desk. He tries again. No answer. He leaves the receiver out of its cradle so the operator will see his room illuminated on her switchboard as soon as she returns.

Meanwhile, he is losing blood. The wound begins to ache. He shudders with a sudden chill that signals the onset of shock. A terrible cold grows from deep within him; an icy sweat breaks out on his face. It is no longer the same as Spain. Everything's terribly wrong.

The phone is still dead. He stands up, which is the wrong thing to do. The sudden motion and fractional g-forces drain the reduced blood supply away from his brain; once standing, his heart must work harder, accelerating blood loss. His vision is blurred, and he is dizzy. But if he can get to the door, to the hall, to the elevators, he will have help. But he has lost too much blood. Staggering toward the door, he collapses on the bed and slips into unconsciousness.

When the operator's voice finally came scratching in the telephone receiver's earpiece asking for Mr. Tinker, Mr. Tinker was no longer there.

In all the years after 1939, no one ever came forward to admit that he accidentally shot Frank Tinker. But why should he? Such an admission would only have provided a few weeks' grist for the functionaries of Little Rock's law enforcement agencies. It would not restore Frank Tinker's life.

Eighty days after Tinker died, Hitler's Germany invaded Poland, triggering a European war that eventually expanded into World War II. Between the events on the Polish frontier and the Japanese attack on Pearl Harbor, there were twenty-seven months filled with opportunities for ostensibly "neutral" American aviators who possessed expertise in hunting other men across the skies from behind a battery of machine guns.

Frank G. Tinker Jr., graduate of the Naval Academy, missed the ample aeronautical employment opportunities of World War II. How he would have performed in the chaos of 1939–45, how long he would have survived, and what he

Headstone in the DeWitt Cemetery (*Courtesy of Cargill Hall*)

might have become had he lived to 1945 and beyond will always remain useless speculation. His small measure of immortality is owed to his book *Some Still Live*, which provides posterity with a rare, firsthand account of cockpit aviation and military aerial tactics in the Spanish Civil War.

The sum of what he might have become in a future he never had, and the actual circumstances of his death, is had in two cryptic words carved into the granite of his DeWitt tombstone: *Quién Sabe?*

EPILOGUE

The calendar and clock stopped for Frank G. Tinker Jr. on 13 June 1939, but I think it abrupt, if not rude, to leave the reader stranded at the cemetery in DeWitt, Arkansas. Tinker's world marched on toward World War II, and its performers and institutional constituents moved along their respective timelines toward their own unique destinies. The reader may find it interesting to know what happened to the principals who left Tinker behind in 1939; perhaps not surprisingly, many of them endured disappointments, hard times, and early deaths. A brief summary of their lives, to the extent known, appears below in alphabetical order.

Acosta, Bertrand Blanchard (1 January 1895–1 September 1954), a record-setting aviator in the 1920s, had his last fling on the world's stage in Spain. After returning to the United States in the late 1930s, during World War II he sailed away on a stormy sea of alcoholism that compounded his marital problems, provoked revocation of his pilot's license, got him a series of short jail sentences, and finally put him on skid row. During 1946–50 he dried out in California at a Catholic monastery dedicated to the restoration of broken men, but on returning to New York he relapsed to embrace his path of self-destruction. Learning of his friend's situation, Admiral Richard Byrd raised money to send Acosta to a Colorado sanatorium in 1952. On 1 September 1954 Acosta died of tuberculosis in the hospital of the Jewish Consumptive Relief Society in Denver, Colorado. He was fifty-nine years old.

Allison, James William Marion "Tex" (1 October 1905–27 March 1946), returned to the United States after Spain, made contact with the Wallingford Corporation of Hong Kong that recruited mercenary aviators for service in China, and traveled to China in mid-1937. There he flew Northrop 2E attack airplanes and Martin 166 twin-engine bombers with the so-called International Squadron made up of mercenaries that operated in the vicinity of Hankow. In

China he flew with Vincent Schmidt, who apparently put on a slightly better show there than he had in Spain. Allison left China and went to Colombia, where he found aviation dominated by German interests associated with the Sociedad Colombo Alemana de Transporte Aéreo (SCDTA) that Peter Paul von Bauer, an Austrian industrialist, had established in 1919. When it was discovered that Allison had flown for the Spanish "Reds," he was asked to leave the country. Returning to the United States, by September 1938 he was back in Texas working for Booth-Henning Aircraft Distributers based at Love Field in Dallas, and he was flying for the Texas Pipeline Company in Houston, a subsidiary of Texaco. In late 1940 Allison turned up in Canada, where he signed on with the Atlantic Ferry Organization created to fly Lockheed Hudson bombers from Canada to Great Britain. In February 1941 he made his first transatlantic flight, ferrying Hudson bomber T9441 from Gander, Newfoundland, to Prestwick, Scotland; this was the first of many such transoceanic deliveries he made during the war. After the war Allison again sought his fortune in South America. On 27 March 1946 he died a suicide in Lima, Peru. He was forty-one years old.

Baumler, Albert John "Ajax" (17 April 1914–2 August 1973), perhaps Frank Tinker's best friend, briefly attended New York University on his return from Spain before joining the Army Air Corps, which on 20 June 1941 was subsumed in a reorganized U.S. Army Air Forces (USAAF).[1] On 20 February 1941 the service promoted him to first lieutenant. At that time the U.S. government quietly permitted agents of the Chinese government to recruit among American military aviators on active duty in an effort to create a special fighter group for service in China. This unit became the American Volunteer Group (AVG), best remembered as the Flying Tigers. The first contingent arrived in Rangoon, Burma, in the late summer of 1941, where it was organized under the command of Major Claire Chenault. Its pilots received $600 a month (with a $500 bonus for every Japanese airplane destroyed). Although this was a hundred dollars more than the base pay of a brigadier general in the U.S. Army, it by no means measured up to the pay of the Spanish Republic. Baumler was recruited for the AVG in October when he was flying A-17s, P-36As, and P-39Ds from the Army airfield at Myrtle Beach, South Carolina. In the event, however, he would become the only AVG volunteer who failed to reach China in 1941.[2]

On 25 November 1941 Baumler was released from active duty and within a week arrived in San Francisco where, at Pan American Airways' Treasure Island seaplane base, he boarded the *Philippine Clipper* for Singapore. This flight at best involved eight days with overnight stops at Honolulu, Midway, Wake, Guam, and Manila. On this flight he also would serve as custodian of a special cargo of spare parts consigned to the AVG.

On the morning of 8 December (the seventh in Hawaii, east of the International Date Line), the *Philippine Clipper* took off from Wake Island for Guam, but when word came over the radio of the Japanese air attack on Pearl Harbor, the *Clipper* was recalled to Wake. A few hours later, thirty-six Japanese twin-engine bombers hit Wake Island, inflicting heavy casualties and extensive damage. Remarkably the big *Clipper*, moored conspicuously at the end of a pier jutting into the island's lagoon, survived the attack with only a few bullet holes. Baumler volunteered his services to Commander W. Scott Cunningham, USN, the island's commanding officer, but the air raid had destroyed seven of the twelve Grumman F3F fighter planes based on Wake, and Cunningham now had a surplus of pilots.

Navy personnel unloaded the AVG spare parts, loaded the PanAm ground staff on Wake along with its passengers on board the *Clipper*, and it flew back to Midway and eventually to Hawaii, where Baumler reported for active duty with the Army Air Forces. He was assigned to the 45th Pursuit Squadron (15th Pursuit Group), which was operating P-36As from Wheeler Field. A short time later, on 27 December, the service ordered Baumler back to the United States to assist in ferrying fighter planes to China. A transpacific movement was now out of the question, so the airplanes, fifty P-40Es and their crews, were moved by freighter to Takoradi in what was then the British colony of the Gold Coast (now the Republic of Ghana), where they arrived in mid-March 1942.

On 26 March Baumler made his first test flight at Takoradi in one of the newly-assembled P-40Es, and on the twenty-seventh he took off from Accra leading a flight of nine airplanes. They flew to Kunming, China, via Khartoum, Cairo, Karachi, and Calcutta, a track of 8,210 miles; it took twenty-five days, which included sixteen days of flying with twenty-nine landings. Baumler's cockpit time was exactly fifty hours.

On 12 April 1942 Baumler began flying with the AVG as an attached USAAF officer. He scored his first victory in China, shooting down an Ki-27 fighter, on 22 June.[3] After the AVG disbanded on 14 July, he flew pursuit airplanes for the USAAF China Air Task Force, which would become General Claire Chennault's Fourteenth Air Force (5 March 1943). In a daylight action on 30 July, he destroyed another Ki-27. That same night, in the vicinity of Hengyang, he crept into a Japanese bomber formation and, guided by their exhaust flames, shot down two twin-engine Ki-48 Lily bombers in rapid succession. On 3 September he scored his fifth victory by downing a Ki-43 fighter. In January 1943 the service promoted him to major and on 5 March ordered the ace transferred from combat duty to the United States, reporting to the director of intelligence at USAAF headquarters at Bolling Field in Washington, D.C. Shortly thereafter the USAAF posted Baumler on a three-month tour of the country to promote the sale of war bonds.

In the summer of 1943 the USAAF assigned Albert Baumler to Wright Field in Dayton, Ohio, where he flew and evaluated captured enemy warplanes. Among his decorations by this time were the Silver Star, Distinguished Flying Cross with an Oak Leaf Cluster, the Bronze Star, and the Air Medal. At Wright Field, however, he found himself a raggedy-edged square peg in a world of sleek, round holes, and he soon blundered into a series of scrapes well known to Frank Tinker. In the wee hours of 21 July he became involved in a minor fracas in the Lord Lansdowne Night Club in Dayton, Ohio. Unfortunately this was not an isolated incident, and it resulted in a September court-martial. Instead of sending him back overseas as a fighter pilot, the local commanders confined him stateside. Unable to secure orders to return to combat, Baumler found rebellion in distilled spirits. A major at the time, he was still a major confined to CONUS commands when the war ended in 1945. He had served in the USAAF on a temporary commission granted in 1938, and on 6 November 1945 he was unceremoniously discharged without an invitation to become a member of the regular postwar Army Air Forces. But military airplanes and military action were all he knew. On 5 February 1946 he enlisted in the U.S. Army as a private. Meanwhile, in 1947 the separate U.S. Air Force was established, and when he re-enlisted in 1950 it was with the Air Force. He subsequently rose to the rank of master sergeant and served pilots during the Korean War as a ground controlled approach (GCA) operator. He retired from the Air Force on 30 September 1965. A few years later he had the misfortune to interrupt a robbery of his rural home near Denison, Texas, and the burglars beat him nearly to death. Baumler was never the same man afterward, and he died alone on 2 August 1973. He was fifty-nine years old. (Baumler's papers are held in the archives of the National Museum of the United States Air Force and in the National Air and Space Museum.)

Bell, Orrin Dwight "O. D." (5 September 1899–5 August 1943), on receiving word of Frank Tinker's death, renewed his lawsuit against the Curtiss Publishing Company and managed to win a small out-of-court settlement. After the attack on Pearl Harbor brought the United States directly into World War II, Bell flew as a civilian contract pilot for the Army Air Forces' Ferry Command. If his performance in Spain can be taken as a guide, it may be assumed that his conduct as a contract pilot was hardly exemplary. On 5 August 1943 he died of a heart attack at his home in Annadale, Staten Island, New York. Exaggerating his place in life to the last, his obituary claimed that he had shot down a German zeppelin while flying for the Royal Flying Corps as a teenager in World War I. He was forty-six years old.

Carnahan, Lucille Tinker (1907–2004), Frank Tinker's older sister, never returned to Arkansas. She married Leo Carnahan of Cloutierville, Louisiana, in 1934. At her home in Cloutierville, Lucille permitted Richard Smith to examine Tinker's papers and answered many of his inquiries over the years about her brother's activities in Spain. She taught library science and children's literature at nearby Northwestern State Teachers College (now Northwestern State University) in Natchitoches for more than twenty years, and she received the National Clio Award for History for a biography of Alexis Cloutier. She died in 2004 at ninety-seven years of age.

Class of '33, for all its early trials, proved to be the Naval Academy class that the "stars fell on"; eighty-five of its members retired as admirals, three as Marine Corps generals, and one (Thomas L. Moorer) became chief of naval operations and later chairman of the Joint Chiefs of Staff. In June 1983 some 200 of its members (of the original 432) mustered on the Naval Academy's grounds to observe their fiftieth anniversary. Also present were about one hundred widows and two dozen non-graduates (those who resigned or were dismissed before graduation), and a good time was had by all. For a few hours "Salty" Tinker "The Mohammedan" was well remembered.[4]

Dahl, Harold E. "Whitey" (29 June 1909–13 February 1956), was released from Salamanca prison on 22 February 1940, almost a year after the Nationalist victory in Spain. He arrived in New York City on 18 March on board the American Export Lines freighter *Exiria*. There he was met by the press and his "wife" Edith, then appearing in nightclubs as "the woman who melted Franco's heart," who was anxious to squeeze the moment for the last drop of publicity. She gave him a cool reception and immediately left the scene, later confiding to reporters that they had never been married. The next day, New York City police greeted Whitey at his hotel with papers for his extradition to Los Angeles, where he was still wanted for his rubber checks. After New York City officials determined that the bad checks related to gambling debts and that the cost of transporting him to the West Coast under guard exceeded the amounts he owed, they dropped the California charges.

A few weeks later on 26 May, Dahl arrived in Ottawa, Canada, where he enlisted in the Royal Canadian Air Force (RCAF) and became a flight instructor. On 26 July 1941 he married Eleanor Robbins Bone of Belleville, Ontario; they subsequently had three children. Meanwhile, he rose to the rank of squadron leader (equivalent to a U.S. major) and was assigned command of the Ferry Command's station at Para, Brazil, an important servicing stop for airplanes being ferried from North America to Africa and points north and east via the bulge of Brazil. Once again, as a result of "irregularities" in the selling of RCAF property at the station, Dahl found himself crosswise with authorities. Brought to court-martial in early 1945, he was found guilty and dismissed from the service.

Between 1945 and 1952 Dahl flew for the Venezuelan airline Avianca, an employment that terminated under another shadow when he suddenly had to "leave" Venezuela. He subsequently flew in Europe for Swissair, but in 1955 a bar of gold bullion worth $54,385 disappeared from a flight between Geneva and Rome on which he was captain. Picked up later in the Hotel Ritz in Paris with a comely stewardess and a considerable sum of cash, he was charged with theft, tried in Switzerland, found guilty, and sentenced to two years in prison. Given his freedom pending an appeal and urged to leave, he returned to Canada where he found employment with Dorval Air Transport, a Canadian bush airline that had a contract for the aerial resupply of the DEW Line, a chain of distant early warning radar stations spread across the Canadian Arctic intended as a trip wire in the event of a Soviet bomber surprise attack over the North Pole. On 13 February 1956 he was flying from Baffin Island to Fort Chino, Quebec, in a Douglas DC-3 CF-BZH when he faced an in-flight engine emergency and had to make a forced landing in the wilderness, twenty-five miles short of his destination. It was a bad landing among trees, and the wreckage was not found until the eighteenth. One of the two passengers on board perished and so did Whitey Dahl. He was forty-six years old.[5]

Dickinson, Derek D. "Dick" (17 February 1897–November 1966), left Spain on 15 February 1938 and returned to New York City, where he told reporters that he had fought to a draw in an aerial duel with Mussolini's son Bruno, a claim dutifully reported in *Time* magazine (28 March 1938). After Tinker's death, the forty-two-year-old Dickinson contacted his sisters and offered to *sell* them (ostensibly for "storage costs") certain personal effects that Frank had left with him in Valencia in anticipation of his return to combat. Baumler advised the sisters against having anything to do with him.

Before long his letterhead bore the caption "Captain Derek Dick Dickinson, Free Lance, Military Master Pilot, Adventurer, Writer, and Lecturer," but he apparently failed to find any application for these talents in World War II. He would have been forty-three years old at the time of the Japanese attack on Pearl Harbor, which was a bit long in the tooth for the military services. Dickinson disappeared entirely from the historical record at this time, and his activities before he died in Binghamton, New York, in November 1966 are currently unknown. He was sixty-nine years of age.

The U.S. Army's intelligence service had a dossier on Dickinson that established him as a spinner of self-serving fairy tales. His immortality is owed solely to the article he wrote about his fanciful aerial duel with Mussolini published in the magazine *For Men* (February 1939) and reprinted in *Reader's Digest* (March 1939). Every now and then a writer who does traffic in aviation subjects will trot out this rotten chestnut and pass it off as "history," and a new generation is gulled into believing it actually happened.

Finick, Eugene R. (22 April 1912–30 June 1991), returned to the United States in late 1937 with a Spanish wife, the nurse who looked after him during his long hospitalization. His only public gesture was an article he wrote for *True* magazine in 1940, a sober and credible narrative corroborated by information that came to light only years later. Thereafter, he fades from ordinary sources of information. Finick died in New Milford, Connecticut, on 30 June 1991 at seventy-nine years of age. His wife, Sagrario Crespo Guerrero Finick (1914–2007), is interred next to him in a Sherman, Connecticut, cemetery.

The **Florida Hotel** at No. 4 Plaza de Callao fell on even harder times after 1937, as did all of Madrid until well after the civil war ended in March 1939. It gradually revived as a first-class hostelry, but it was undone by Spain's prosperity of the 1960s when it was adjudged too small relative to the strategic ground it occupied in downtown Madrid. The Florida was demolished, and today the Galerías Preciados, a department store, stands on its site.

Franco, Francisco (4 December 1892–19 November 1975), led Nationalist forces to victory in 1939 and ruled Spain for the next thirty-six years, guiding it through a precarious neutrality during World War II and an almost equally uncomfortable decade thereafter, when "Fascist" Spain was treated as a pariah by the victorious Allies and their UN associates. The Fascist label was applied mostly by foreigners, usually those of a Leftist political persuasion, but it had little or no reality in Falangist Spain. Critics missed the point: Franco was first and last a Spaniard, and his only concern was for Spain. He may not have managed all that he might have for his country, but he knew that only time could heal the awful wounds of 1936–39; he not only gave Spain that time, he enforced it.

The young man of forty-four years in 1936 was eighty-three years old in 1975. And by the 1970s most Spaniards had begun treating their civil war as most Americans started treating theirs by 1901: the subject and its excesses were being examined clinically and with the universal conviction that it must never happen again. Indeed, by the 1970s, Spaniards were producing the best historiography of the Spanish Civil War; unfortunately, little of it has been translated into English.

The inflammatory stuff of Communism versus Fascism and their manifold nuances remain mostly the plaything of foreigners who claim for themselves the mantle of disinterested intellectuals, and this is unlikely to change any time soon.

On 19 November 1975 Francisco Franco died in Madrid. He was two weeks shy of eighty-four years of age.

Gaylord's Hotel at No. 3 Alfonso XI, the Madrid palace of the Kremlin's mightiest, was demolished in the late 1960s; today an office building stands on its former site.

Gran Vía, Madrid's main east–west artery, was renamed Avenida Jose Antonio shortly after the Nationalist victory. Jose Antonio Primo de Rivera y Saenz de Heredia (b. 1903) was the eldest son of the dictator Primo de Rivera who served as the de facto ruler of Spain during the twilight of the monarchy. After 1933 Jose Antonio founded and became the heart and soul of the Falange Española, Spain's uniquely Spanish Fascist party.[6] Madrileños responded to the name change in the same way that New Yorkers did when Sixth Avenue was renamed Avenue of the Americas in 1941; Avenida Jose Antonio constitutes a legal postal address, but by word of mouth it is still universally known as the Gran Vía.

The Hotel **Gran Vía** at No. 25 Avenida Jose Antonio (postal address), long since cleared of its Anarchist staff, is still functioning as a hostelry on the corner of the Gran Vía and the Calle de la Montera; now known as the Senator Gran Vía Hotel, its rathskellar is gone, the dining room is now on the second floor, and its cuisine is much improved over that of 1937.

Griffiss, Townsend (4 April 1900–15 February 1942), assistant military attaché for air to France and Spain, was not seriously embarrassed by Whitey Dahl's mindlessness. In September 1938 he returned to the United States where he attended the Air Corps Tactical School at Maxwell Field. On graduating in June 1939 he was assigned to the Office of the Chief of the Air Corps and directly attached to the Office of the Assistant Secretary of War. In 1940 Lieutenant Colonel Griffiss was posted to the Office of the Army Chief of Staff and ordered to London, England, in May 1941 as a member of a special Army observers group that evaluated foreign airplanes. After Germany declared war on the United States on 11 December 1941, he worked with Army Air Forces representatives who laid the groundwork for the arrival of the Eighth Air Force in Britain.

In November 1941 Colonel Griffiss led a confidential mission to the Soviet Union, flying via the Mediterranean, Cairo, and Teheran to Kubyshev, just east of Moscow. At that moment the German Army was nearing the gates of

Moscow, and most of the Soviet government's functions had evacuated to Kuby-shev. Colonel Griffiss, representing the U.S. government, sought to arrange ferry routes for Lend-Lease American aircraft requested by the USSR. But even with the Soviet Union in near extremis and wanting desperately for war matériel, he found the Russian negotiators unreasonably difficult and unable to agree on any aerial routes that might avoid "sensitive areas" of the USSR, which seemed to be most of the country. In the absence of any progress, Colonel Griffiss was recalled to Britain in late December.

On 15 February 1942 Colonel Griffiss was on board a Consolidated LB.30A Liberator bomber converted to transport use. The plane was operated by British Overseas Airways Corporation, flown by Captain Humphrey Page with a crew of five, and there were three other passengers in addition to the colonel. En route from Cairo to Whitchurch (near Bournemouth), England, nonstop, they flew closely around German-occupied France over the Atlantic. Approaching the British coast near Eddystone Light in the vicinity of Plymouth, British radar picked up the Liberator, and a flight of fighters scrambled to identify the contact. Two Spitfires from a Polish squadron made the interception.

At this date barely a hundred B-24 Liberator bombers operated anywhere in the world, and since the summer of 1941 only a half-dozen operated in Britain; it remained a very rare bird. The Polish aviators mistook the Liberator for a long-range German intruder and shot it down off Eddystone Light. There were no survivors; no bodies ever were recovered. Colonel Griffiss, a promising Army Air Forces "fast burner," was forty-two years of age.

On 29 January 1948 the Air Force base at Rome, New York, coincidentally established in February 1942, was named Griffiss Air Force Base in the colonel's honor. It is another coincidence, but appropriate, that a primary mission of Griffiss AFB is the refinement of electronic warfare techniques.

Hemingway, Ernest (21 July 1899–2 July 1961), is well enough known that little need be said about his career after Spain in 1937. Hemingway learned of Tinker's apparent suicide in July 1939 and lamented it. Mentioning Tinker's death in a letter to a friend, he said that "he had often enough argued himself out of sui-cidal impulses. . . . [T]he important thing was not to let discouragement tempt you into taking the easy way out."[7] Nevertheless, as had his father before him in 1928, at the age of sixty-one he died of suicide on 2 July 1961.

At about 7:30 a.m. on that date, at his home in Ketchum, Idaho, near the resort of Sun Valley, Hemingway blew his head away with both barrels of a twelve-gauge shotgun. The reader should note that this is how a person familiar with firearms does the job, not by shooting himself in the abdomen with a .22 target pistol. Hemingway was nineteen days short of sixty-two years of age.

Hull, Cordell (2 October 1871–23 July 1955), continued to serve President Roosevelt as secretary of state. His finest hour probably occurred during those moments that straddled high noon on Sunday, 7 December 1941, when he received the Japanese emissaries who had come to deliver a message that U.S. Navy code breakers had already given him. At 12:50 p.m. East Coast time, (7:50 a.m. in Hawaii—the attack occurred at 7:48 a.m.), Washington, D.C., had received word of the Japanese surprise attack on Pearl Harbor. The Japanese emissaries knew nothing of the attack; they had orders to deliver their message at 1:00 p.m. East Coast time, which was 8:00 a.m. in Hawaii, but they were delayed because their own code clerks were late in deciphering the whole message, especially its last, crucial section. Hull received the two emissaries with a straight face, as if nothing had happened, and only after they had delivered their message did he tell them, with anger appropriate to the occasion, of the attack on Pearl Harbor. This unexpected news was a bona fide surprise to the Japanese emissaries; unknown to Hull, the two men had been betrayed by their own countrymen.

In poor health for some years, Hull retired on the seventy-third anniversary of his birth, 2 October 1944, living afterward in Washington, D.C.'s Wardman Park Hotel (now the Sheraton Four Points), where he wrote his two-volume memoirs. In 1951 he suffered a severe stroke. His wife preceded him in death in 1954, by which time he was a semi-invalid. On 23 July 1955 he died in the Bethesda Naval Hospital; he was eighty-three years of age.

Ingersoll, Royal Eason (20 June 1883–22 May 1976), the commanding officer of the *San Francisco* when Frank Tinker was ship's officer, subsequently served with the Navy's War Plans Division, 1935–38, returning to sea as commander of Cruiser Division Six, 1938–40, when he became assistant to the chief of naval operations. During World War II he served as commander in chief Atlantic, creating the U.S. Navy's antisubmarine warfare organization that helped win the Battle of the Atlantic. He retired with the rank of admiral in April 1946 and died in Bethesda, Maryland, on 22 May 1976; he was ninety-two years of age.

Knight, Clayton (1891–17 July 1969), the aviation illustrator who created the artwork for the dust jacket of Frank Tinker's book, in 1940 organized the Clayton Knight Committee that successfully recruited Americans for the Royal Canadian Air Force and contract pilots for the Atlantic Ferry Organization. He later served as a war correspondent in Great Britain and witnessed the D-day invasion of Hitler's Europe. On 17 July 1969 he died in Danbury, Connecticut; he was seventy-eight years old.

Koch, Charles August (28 November 1894–5 September 1983), made his last flight for Republican Spain on 19 March 1937 while based at Tembleque; his stomach again rebelled against its long exposure to Iberian cuisine, and he was hospitalized. His contract was formally terminated on 8 April 1937, after which he returned to the United States and resumed his career as a "gypsy engineer." Finding nothing with his former employer, Seversky, he went to nearby Grumman, whose people steered him to the Canadian Car & Foundry (CCF) at Fort William, Ontario. CCF had created an aircraft subsidiary and was building FF-1 fighter-bombers under license; the customer for the FF-1s was supposedly Turkey, but their destination in fact was Republican Spain.

In 1938 Koch went back to Seversky on Long Island and then signed on with Barkley-Grow Aircraft in Detroit; in 1941 he became a technical adviser to the Automotive Committee for Air Defense, an organization that guided automobile makers in the manufacture of airplanes and airplane parts. He subsequently worked at Ford's Willow Run factory building B-24s. At war's end he was back in the New York City area, where he found employment in diverse fields of engineering, including railway equipment. He died in Long Island City, New York, on 5 September 1983, three months short of eighty-nine years of age.

Kopéts, Ivan Ivanovich (aka "José") (19 September 1908–22 June 1941), one of the first four Soviet pilots to arrive in Spain (September 1936), served ten months and returned to the USSR on 17 June 1937. According to unofficial sources, Kopéts flew some two hundred sorties and was credited with two personal aerial victories and four shared victories. He was awarded the Order of the Red Banner on 2 January 1937. Only one year older than Frank Tinker, this devout Communist senior lieutenant returned wearing military issued clothing identical to that in which he had arrived. According to Lacalle, "All the Russian pilots, without exception, had an exorbitant enthusiasm for watches, clothes, shoes, and other clothing articles, and they took great amounts of everything when they were ordered to return to their country. Kopéts was the only exception." His subsequent rapid rise through the military hierarchy proved to be spectacular: on 20 June 1937 the Red Army Air Force promoted him to colonel (skipping the ranks of captain and major). On 21 June he was accorded the title Hero of the Soviet Union and received the Order of Lenin. That same day he was named a deputy commander of Air Forces in the Leningrad Military District, and in December 1937 he became a deputy of the Supreme Soviet. Lacalle, while returning to Spain with the second group of Spanish pilot-trainees via Murmansk in late January–early February 1938, arranged to pay a courtesy call on Kopéts in Leningrad. "Our visit was very brief and cold. José was seated behind an extremely luxurious desk while I stood in front of him. Despite our [former] great intimacy and the confidence that had existed between us, we were like two dummies without anything to say. Smiling, we said hello and good-bye. That was all." Kopéts subsequently was promoted to kombrig (equivalent to a brigadier general) and served as commanding officer, Air Forces Eighth Army, during the Soviet-Finnish War of 1939–40; on 10 April 1940 he was named commander, Air Forces of the Belorussian Military District, received a second Order of Lenin on 19 May, and on 4 June was promoted to komdiv, a major general.[8]

On 23 November 1940 Kopéts received orders to attend courses for the advancement of command personnel at the General Staff Academy in Moscow. In March 1941, however, he requested release from these courses and a return to command the air forces of the Belorussian Military District. His request was granted, and it made him the unfortunate general in charge of Soviet aviation in northwestern Russia at the time of the German surprise attack. On 22 June 1941 the Luftwaffe destroyed most of his air force, some six hundred airplanes on the ground, and the survivors gave an almost equally dismal performance in the air. In Stalin's Russia the punishment for presiding over a military disaster of this magnitude was invariably a bullet in the back of the head, delivered in a cellar of an NKVD prison. Well aware of this denouement, late in the evening of 22 June (some accounts say early on 23 June) Kopéts chose suicide. He was thirty-two years old.

Kosenkov, Ivan Ivanovich (1911–3 September 1938), returned to the Soviet Union in late August 1937, having served some ten months in Spain. He flew 150 sorties (180 hours) and is credited with one aerial victory and one shared victory while there. Kosenkov was awarded the Order of the Red Banner on 28 October 1937 and received an accelerated promotion to captain in February 1938. On 2 March he was awarded a second Order of the Red Banner and subsequently served as commander of the 45th Fighter Air Regiment (IAP) stationed in Azerbaijan on the Caspian Sea. He perished on duty on 3 September 1938, presumably in an airplane accident. He was twenty-seven years of age.

Lacalle, Andrés García (4 February 1909–7 May 1980), remained for months in a French internment camp and refused to consider the Soviet's offer of sanctuary in the USSR. Many other interned Spanish pilots, the younger ones in particular, whose experience in Russia, if any, had been limited to training camps, elected to emigrate and later fought for the Soviet Union in World War II. But Lacalle, who had spent time there and moved among the upper echelons of the Soviet military apparatus, judged that country to be "the largest jail in the world," and he preferred internment to it.

The French released Lacalle in December 1939. He left Toulouse and, traveling via Bordeaux and Casablanca, made his way to Santo Domingo, Dominican Republic, where he spent the next fourteen years. Meanwhile, he married and fathered three children, two boys and a girl. In 1954 he and his family moved to Chile and in 1958 to Mexico City, where he established Sederias Europa, a successful business that specialized in fine fabrics and draperies. Lacalle died in Mexico City on 7 May 1980; he was seventy-two years of age.

Lakeev, Ivan Alexeevich (10 February 1908–15 August 1990), after serving ten months in Spain, returned to the Soviet Union on 13 August 1937. He had flown 312 combat sorties, could claim twelve aerial victories, and had been twice awarded the Order of the Red Banner (2 January and 4 July 1937). After the military purges that began in June of that year, Lakeev numbered among the fortunate returnees in November to receive the title Hero of the Soviet Union, accompanied by the Order of Lenin. Promoted to major he was placed in command of the 68th Fighter Squadron, then the 16th Fighter Air Regiment (IAP) in the Moscow Military District. In March 1939 Lakeev was named acting head of the Department of Fighter Aviation, Chief Directorate of the Red Army Air Force, and in April he was sent to attend courses for advancement of command personnel at the General Staff Academy. He next served as deputy commander of fighter aviation, 1st Army Group, once again under Jacob Smushkevich, during the Khalkin Gol River operations against the Japanese in Mongolia, where, flying I-16s, he gained two more aerial victories. He was awarded a third Order of the Red Banner and the Order of the Red Banner of the Mongolian Republic. On his return from Mongolia in October 1939, he was promoted to colonel and appointed deputy chief of Flight-Technical Inspection, Directorate of Combat Readiness, Red Army Air Force, and subsequently took part in the aerial operations against Finland in the Soviet-Finnish War 1939–40.

Promoted to major general on 4 June 1940, Lakeev was named inspector general of the Red Army Air Force and in August led the "Red Five" formation at the air parade in Tushino. Dismissed from this position in April 1941, he was reassigned in demotion as deputy commander of the 14th Mixed Aviation Division (SAD) stationed in Lutsk, Ukraine. During the German surprise attack on 22 June 1941, the 14th SAD suffered heavy losses and once again Lakeev was dismissed as commander, but he was not arrested. In September he was reassigned as deputy commander of Fighter Aviation, Air Defense (PVO) of the South-Western Front, and he participated in aerial battles in southern Ukraine and Donbas. Named commander of the 524th Fighter Air Regiment (IAP) in October, he participated in combat on the Carelian Front and in the defense of Leningrad. After March 1943 he commanded the 235th Fighter Air Division of the 2nd Air Army and participated in the battles for Kursk, Dnieper, and the liberation of Western Ukraine, Southern Poland, and Czechoslovakia. He remained in command of the 235th, redesignated in 1944 as the 15th Guards Fighter Air Division (GIAD), until September 1947. He served in command positions thereafter, last as assistant to the commander of the 22nd Air Army, Northern Military District (in Petrozavodsk). He retired from the Soviet Army Air Force in 1955 with the rank of major general[9] and lived in Moscow after his retirement; Lakeev died on 15 August 1990 at eighty-two years of age.

Marquésa Del Valle (dates unknown) and her infant son spent the war as members of Madrid's thousands of "invisible refugees," clandestinely supported and hidden by friends who could not be identified with them or any prewar upper classes of the Nationalist cause. Theirs was a dark and precarious existence, lived out in cellars, attics, and secret rooms. Only after the Nationalist occupation of Madrid in March 1939 did these persons dare to emerge from the hiding places in which they had survived for almost three years. The family's *finca*—Campo X—near Azuqueca was returned to her, much the worse for wear. When Smith interviewed her in 1972, she was living in Madrid; her son, the new *marqués*, occupied the *finca*, its modest buildings still identifiable as the Campo X described by Frank Tinker almost a half-century earlier.

The Hotel **McGehee** in Little Rock in which Frank Tinker died, and known to locals as the Ben McGehee, passed out of existence as such on 1 June 1947 when its name was changed to the Hotel Grady Manning, memorializing the man who founded Southwest Hotels, Inc., the chain that erected the building in 1931. In the 1960s the economic decay of downtown Little Rock overtook the aging hotel, and by the end of the 1970s urban renewal overwhelmed it. In 1980 the hotel was demolished, thus joining the Florida and Gaylord's in the rubble of history. The city's new convention center and the Excelsior Hotel now stand on its former site.

Morrison, Mary Elizabeth "Toodles" Tinker (8 December 1915–5 October 1975), Frank's younger sister, married William A. "Bill" Morrison on Thanksgiving Day in 1938 and eventually moved from Cameron to Austin, Texas, where her husband served as a justice on the state court of criminal appeals for many years. They had a daughter, Marcia Tinker Morrison (10 December 1947–), and separated in 1968, after which she returned to Louisiana. She died in New Orleans on 5 October 1975. "Toodles" was fifty-nine years of age.

Morrow, Guy Marion (11 June 1909–9 December 1962), Frank Tinker's roommate at the U.S. Naval Academy, completed flight training at Pensacola, Florida, was designated a naval aviator on 10 June 1936, and joined the First Marine Brigade at Quantico, Virginia. He subsequently flew in combat in the Pacific during World War II and later in Korea. Morrow was awarded the Bronze Star for his service in World War II and the Legion of Merit and the Distinguished Flying Cross during the Korean War. He married and had three daughters and retired from the Marine Corps as a colonel in February 1959. Morrow died on 9 December 1962 at Bethesda Naval Hospital in Maryland. He was fifty-three years old.

Pumpur, Petr Ivanovich (aka "Colonel Julio") (25 April 1900–23 March 1942), having arrived in Spain on 13 October 1936, rotated home to the Soviet Union on 11 May 1937. Credited with two personal aerial victories and three shared victories, he was awarded Hero of the Soviet Union on 4 July 1937. About that time he was promoted and appointed a commander in the Air Forces, Moscow Military District, and in November 1937 Commander of Air Forces, Special Red Banner Far Eastern Army. Pumpur next served as the chief test pilot of Aircraft Factory No. 1 between December 1938 and late 1939, when he was named chief of the Directorate for Combat Readiness of the Red Army Air Force. On 4 June 1940 Pumpur was promoted to lieutenant general and placed in command of Air Forces, Moscow Military District. After General Rychagove was relieved of command, in mid-April 1941 the government accused Pumpur of "incompetence" in organizing and training pilots, and dismissed him from his command. Shortly before the German surprise attack, on 31 May 1941, General Pumpur was arrested and charged with participating in an "anti-Soviet conspiracy." Confined to Saratov Prison, the NKVD executed him on 23 March 1942. At the time of his death he was nearly forty-two years of age.

Rosmarin, Joseph (7 February 1900–7 December 1972), continued flying transports for the Spanish Republic until November 1937, when he and his wife returned to the United States, after which he became a fixed-base operator with a flying service at New York City's Floyd Bennett Field. He made headlines on 14 March 1940 when a passenger on board his airplane ran forward, seized the controls, and started screaming that he wanted to die. Unable to subdue the man during the struggle that ensued, Rosmarin managed to fly the airplane to a safe ditching in Jamaica Bay. The distraught passenger got his wish in the water; Rosmarin survived but lost his airplane.

In 1942 Rosmarin joined the Army Air Forces and flew with the Air Transport Command, operating cargo airplanes on transatlantic flights to Africa and Europe. He was discharged with a physical disability in 1947, but a few years later he was made to carry an undeserved political scar in the "Red Scare" of the early 1950s as a result of his flying for Republican Spain. Thereafter, he found no openings in aviation and had to make a living as an upholsterer. He died on 7 December 1972 in the veterans' hospital at West Point, New York, at the age of seventy-two.

Rychagov, Pavel Vasilevich (aka "Palancar,") (15 January 1911–28 October 1941), one of the first pilots to arrive in Spain, returned to the USSR in February 1937. While in Spain he served as a pilot and squadron commander and accumulated 105 hours of combat sorties in I-15 fighters. He is credited with eight personal aerial victories and fourteen shared victories. Awarded Hero of the Soviet Union on 31 December 1936, on his return he was appointed commander of the 109th Fighter Squadron in the Kiev Military District. In November 1937 Rychagov was sent to China to command Soviet fighter pilots in air combat against Japanese aerial forces. There, he served as an adviser on fighter aviation while participating in combat operations. The next month, in December, he was elected to the Supreme Soviet. On 8 March 1938 Rychagov was awarded the Order of the Red Banner, and, during the same month, appointed commanding officer, Air Forces Moscow Military District. In April, however, he was reassigned as commanding officer, Air Forces Primorsk Group of Forces, Far Eastern Front, where his air forces engaged in the "incident" with the Japanese at Lake Khasan in August. He next served as commanding officer, Air Forces of the 9th Army during the Soviet-Finnish War (November 1939–March 1940). He was awarded a third Order of the Red Banner on 21 May 1940, promoted to lieutenant general on 4 June, and appointed deputy head, later head (in August) of the Main Directorate of the Air Force, People's Commissariat of Defense.

In February 1941 Rychagov was named deputy people's commissar of defense for aviation; on 12 April, however, owing to the high accident rate in the Red Army Air Force, he was demoted and posted to the General Staff Academy. Immediately after the Luftwaffe destroyed almost all of the Red Army Air Force on the western frontier, on 24 June Stalin had Rychagov arrested and the secret police executed him along with his wife, major Maria Nesterenko, and other air force officers on 28 October 1941. Sixteen months after Stalin's death, in late July 1954, Rychagov's name was "rehabilitated." At the time of his death he was thirty years old.

Shipley, Ruth Bielski (1885–3 November 1966), continued to rule her office in the State Department, which grew in size, importance, and power as a consequence of the wartime development of global air transportation and the postwar air travel boom. In 1951, the heyday of the McCarthy Red Scare, the slim, bespectacled Shipley had her knuckles rapped by Senator Pat McCarran (D-Nevada) and members of his Internal Security Subcommittee of the Senate's Committee on the Judiciary when they accused her and the State Department of being "soft on Communism," specifically, of having been lax by permitting known American Communists, Communist sympathizers, and left-wingers to travel from the United States to the Soviet Union through third countries.

The foreign travel procedures and restrictions that she formulated and over which she presided are considered precursors of the contemporary State Department's terrorist "No-Fly" List," although in her day she could and did deny passports outright. Among those denied was the American artist and illustrator Rockwell Kent, a man much enamored of the feeble-minded politics of the far left and who, in 1938, spoke in Carnegie Hall at the gala memorial service for Ben Leider. After a court battle stretching over seven years, the U.S. Supreme Court in 1958 held that, yes, indeed, as a U.S. citizen Rockwell Kent was entitled to a passport.

On 30 April 1955, after forty-seven years in civil service, twenty-seven of those years in command of the Passport Section, Shipley retired at the mandatory age of seventy. The *New York Times* termed it an "abdication." President Franklin Roosevelt had called her a "wonderful ogre"; Senator Wayne Morse (D-Oregon) more pointedly described her as "tyrannical and capricious"; and after her retirement a State Department employee remarked, "We reached a point where an American citizen could try unsuccessfully for two-and-a-half years to obtain a passport without ever being able to find out why he could not get one." On 3 November 1966 Shipley died in a Washington, D.C., nursing home; she was eighty-one years of age.

Smushkevich, Jacob Vladimirovich (aka "General Douglas") (14 April 1902– 28 October 1941), arrived in Spain in October 1936 and served as the "senior adviser" to the commander of the Republican Air Force. While in Spain, according to unofficial data, he personally flew 115 combat sorties in I-15 fighters. Awarded the Order of Lenin on 3 January 1937 and named a Hero of the Soviet Union on 21 June, he returned to the USSR in September of that year. In early 1938 he completed courses for the advancement of command personnel at the Frunze Military Academy. Badly injured in a flight training accident on 30 April, Smushkevich, after his recovery in June, was named deputy commander of the Chief Directorate, Red Army Air Force. Subsequently, between June 1938 and August 1939, he served as commander of aviation, 1st Army Group, during the conflict with the Japanese at the Kolkhin-Gol River, in which the Soviets won two vital air battles and air supremacy over the Kolkhin Gol steppes. For this achievement he was awarded Hero of the Soviet Union for the second time. On

11 September 1939 Smushkevich was appointed commanding officer Air Forces, Kiev Special Military District, and, on 19 November, chief of the Red Army Air Force. During the Soviet-Finnish War he coordinated actions of Soviet aviation at the front lines.

In August 1940 Lieutenant General Smushkevich was demoted and "reassigned" as inspector general of the Red Army Air Force and, from December 1940, assistant chief of the general staff for aviation. On 8 June 1941, while in hospital for treatment of recurrent problems with injuries suffered in his 1938 airplane accident, the NKVD arrested Smushkevich. He was subsequently "eliminated," shot on 28 October of that year along with Rychagov and other high ranking aviation officers, although the Soviets later "rehabilitated" his name in 1954—small comfort to the deceased recipient. He died at forty years of age.

SS *Champlain*, the ship that returned Frank Tinker to the United States in August 1937, continued in transatlantic service into World War II. On 17 June 1940, the last day of the Battle of France and on the eve of the French surrender, the *Champlain* took part in a frantic evacuation that occurred from French ports in the Bay of Biscay. That day the *Champlain* ran upon a German air-dropped magnetic mine and sank near La Pallice in the Gironde Estuary, just below the city of Bordeaux.

The **Telefónica Building** at the beginning of the twenty-first century continues to command the heights of the Gran Vía. Although other tall buildings erected since the 1960s interrupt its azimuth, nevertheless, its rooftop parapets continue to provide a breathtaking view of Madrid and the Casa de Campo. Even though its masonry has been painstakingly patched, the visitor who examines it with a careful eye has no difficulty in finding scores of pockmarks from the shrapnel of 1936–39.

Tinker, Frank Glasgow, Sr. (14 November 1871–19 August 1957), never accepted the verdict of suicide in the death of his only son, nor did his wife Effie, and neither of them ever got over the loss. He and Effie moved from Little Rock, Arkansas, to San Antonio, Texas, after World War II, and in 1951 to Austin, Texas, where Frank Senior died on 19 August 1957. He was eighty-five years of age. Effie Henry Tinker (b. 13 July 1884) survived him by seven years; she died in Natchitoches, Louisiana, on 7 March 1964, three months shy of her eightieth birthday. Both are interred at Memorial Park Cemetery in Austin, Texas.

Ukhov, Valentin Petrovich (16 January 1908–9 June 1957), returned to the Soviet Union in July 1937. While leading his I-16 squadron in Spain, Ukhov was credited with two aerial victories and two shared victories. He was awarded the Order of the Red Banner that July and the Order of Lenin in March 1938. Promoted to the rank of colonel, he was given command of the Borisoglebsk Flight School, where he remained until late 1940. From March 1941 until January 1942 he commanded the 61st Mixed Air Division (SAD), and from January to June 1942 he commanded the air forces of the 61st Army. In June Ukhov assumed command of the 210th Guards Fighter Air Division (GIAD—later redesignated the 3rd Guards Fighter Air Division). On 4 February 1944 he was promoted to major general, and from June until the end of World War II he commanded the 10th Guards Fighter Air Division; he remained in command positions after the war.

In 1950, however, the NKVD arrested Ukhov on "political grounds" and, after "interrogation," sent him to a prison camp. Released from prison after Joseph Stalin's death in March 1953, Ukhov's name was "rehabilitated" in July of that year. He subsequently served as an instructor of military education at the Moscow Energy Institute from September 1953 until he retired in September 1955. In poor health after his release from prison, Ukhov died on 9 June 1957 at forty-nine years of age.

USS *Lexington*, on which Tinker traveled from the East Coast to the West Coast in 1928, along with her sister ship *Saratoga*, became the backbone of the Navy's carrier forces during the 1930s. When Japan attacked Pearl Harbor on 7 December 1941, the *Lexington* was 420 miles southeast of Midway and en route to that island to fly off a Marine Corps bombing squadron. On 8 May 1942, in the Battle of the Coral Sea, the *Lexington* was hit by torpedo planes and dive-bombers; within seven hours the fires were out of control, and the carrier had to be abandoned. The fires and the *Lexington* burned into the night, and she finally had to be sunk by torpedoes from the destroyer *Phelps*.

USS *New York*, the battleship that Tinker joined on the West Coast and on board which he made fireman 2nd class, was twenty-five years old when World War II started in 1939; between 1939 and 1941 she participated in the undeclared U.S. efforts against German submarines in the North Atlantic. In 1942 her guns supported the invasion of North Africa. Already obsolescent by 1920 and regarded obsolete by 1940, the *New York* was thirty-two years of age in 1946 when she served as a target ship in Operation Crossroads, the Able (air burst) and Baker (underwater detonation) atomic tests conducted at Bikini Lagoon on 1 and 25 July, respectively. The old girl survived both explosions but eventually sank as a result of unchecked progressive flooding.

USS *San Francisco*, the only ship on which Tinker served as a commissioned officer, was moored to a pier in Pearl Harbor's East Loch when the Japanese attacked on 7 December 1941 but escaped serious damage. Afterward, however, in a night action on 13 November 1942, during the long and bloody battle for Guadalcanal and when the *San Francisco* was the flagship of Admiral Daniel Callahan, she came to grief under the guns of the Japanese battleship *Kirishima* and was practically shot to pieces, suffered unusually heavy casualties, and was lucky to escape. The ship was rebuilt at the Mare Island shipyard and returned to service before the end of the Pacific War. When decommissioned into the Reserve Fleet on 10 February 1946, the *San Francisco* sported seventeen battle stars. In March 1959 the ship was stricken from the Navy List and sold for scrap. During her rebuilding in 1943, however, the steel dodger around her bridge, riddled with shrapnel holes, was carefully removed and later installed on a memorial at Point Lobos, known locally as "Lands End," just below Fort Miley at the south side of the entrance to San Francisco Bay. It is a certainty that during his officer-of-the-deck watches in 1935, Frank Tinker logged more than a few hours leaning on that steel dodger.

USS *Texas*, the first ship of Tinker's Navy career, was twenty-five years old when World War II started in 1939, and, like the *New York*, during 1940–41 she participated in the undeclared U.S. efforts against German submarines in the North Atlantic. The *Texas* also participated in the invasion of North Africa in November 1942, and on 6 June 1944, D-day of the Allied invasion of Hitler's Fortress Europe, she served as flagship of the bombardment forces, and her guns helped clear Omaha Beach at Normandy for the amphibious assault forces. In 1946 the Navy decommissioned the ship, moved it to Houston, and transferred temporary custody to the State of Texas. In early 1948 the *Texas* was maneuvered into a loch, excavated, and dredged into San Jacinto State Park adjacent to the Houston Ship Canal, and on 21 April the thirty-four-year-old battleship was formally decommissioned as a ship of the U.S. Navy and turned over to the State of Texas, which continues to maintain her as a memorial.

Zakharov, Georgiy Nefedovich (aka "Rodriges Kromberg") (24 April 1908–6 January 1996), another one of the first pilots to arrive in Spain, served as a flight commander of I-15 fighters; he rotated back to the Soviet Union on 7 April 1937, where he became a close friend of Pavel Rychagov. While in Spain he was credited with five aerial victories (two personal and three shared) and was awarded two Orders of the Red Banner (2 January and 17 July 1937). A senior lieutenant, he was appointed commander of a detachment of the 109th Fighter Squadron in the Kiev Military District. During the fall of 1937 he was recalled to Moscow to conduct combat tests of the I-15bis. From the end of November until April 1938 Zakharov commanded a Soviet fighter group in China. Promoted to captain on 20 January 1938, and flying an I-15bis and an I-16 in combat, he achieved two more shared aerial victories in twenty sorties against the Japanese at Lake Khasan. Zakharov received an accelerated promotion to colonel on 16 July 1938, was appointed commander of air forces, Siberian Military District, in September, and on 14 November was awarded yet another Order of the Red Banner. Between May and November 1940 he completed courses for the advancement of command personnel at the General Staff Academy.

On 4 June 1940 Zakharov was promoted to major general, and from November he commanded the 43rd Fighter Air Division (IAD) of the Western Special Military District based in Minsk. In October 1941 he was dismissed from his combat command and sent to Ulan Ude to command a flight school. In April 1942 he was reassigned as commander of the Tashkent School of Gunners and Bombardiers. Recalled to combat in March 1943, he returned to the front as commander of the 303rd Fighter Air Division (IAD), which later hosted the Free French Squadron "Normandie." By war's end he had completed 153 sorties in 48 separate engagements and received credit for two aerial victories and three shared victories; on 19 April 1945 he was awarded Hero of the Soviet Union. Zakharov continued to serve in the Soviet Army Air Force after the war, graduated from the General Staff Academy in 1950, and thereafter held a number of important command positions. He retired as a major general in 1960 and lived in Moscow until his death on 6 January 1996. He was eighty-seven years of age.

Appendix 1

CHRONOLOGICAL HIGHLIGHTS
OF THE SPANISH CIVIL WAR

1936

17 July	The Spanish army in Morocco rose against the Spanish Republic, which provided a signal for similar uprisings in metropolitan Spain.
19 July	Francisco Franco, who had been flown to Africa from the Canary Islands, arrived in Spanish Morocco.
26 July	At Bayreuth, Germany, Adolf Hitler agreed to assist Franco and the insurgents, and the next day twenty Junkers Ju 52 transport-bombers were flown to Morocco.
27 July	Benito Mussolini, dictator of Italy, also agreed to assist the insurgents and on 30 July twelve S.81 bombers flew to Morocco, three being lost en route.
5 August	The first German military contingent consisting of eight men and six Heinkel He 51 fighter planes arrived in Cadiz.
8 August	France closed its frontier to munitions destined for Spain.
14 August	Nationalist insurgents took the frontier city of Badajoz, cutting the Republic's communications with Portugal.
5 September	Nationalists captured the Spanish frontier town of Irún, cutting off the Republic's northern provinces of Guipuzcoa, Alava Vizcaya, and Asturias from France and isolating them in what became known as the Cantabrian Pocket.
Early September	After weeks of assisting the Spanish Republic through Communist-front organizations in Europe, Stalin decided that the Soviet Union would provide direct but covert military assistance.
15 September	The freighter *Neva* arrived in Alicante with the first load of Soviet weapons and airplanes.
22 October	Soviet airplanes flew their first combat missions in Spain.

24 October	German and Italian bombers executed their first attacks against Madrid.
2 November	Soviet fighter planes made their first appearance in the air defense of Madrid.
6 November	The Republic's government fled to Valencia from Madrid.
7 November	The Nationalist siege of Madrid began.
15 November	Nationalist forces crossed the Manzanares River and gained a lodgment in Madrid's suburb of University City; the battle for University City ended in a stalemate this day.

1937

3–9 January	A Nationalist attempt to encircle Madrid from the west ended in the Battle of Coruña Road.
6 January	The U.S. Congress acted to forbid the export of munitions to Spain.
6–28 February	A Nationalist attempt to encircle Madrid from the south ended in the Battle of the Jarama and a stalemate.
8 February	Nationalist forces captured the city of Málaga on the Mediterranean.
8–18 March	A Nationalist attempt to overrun Madrid from the north ended in the Republic defeating an Italian army at the Battle of Guadalajara.
15–23 April	A Republican offensive against Teruel failed to take the city or to divert Nationalist forces from a successful offensive in the Basque country.
26 April	Bombers of the Legion Condor struck the Basque town of Guernica, coincidentally creating a formidable legend for the folklore of aerial bombardment.
30 May–3 June	An abortive Republican offensive in the Sierra Guadarrama aimed at Segovia became bogged down at La Granja.
11–19 June	A Republican offensive against Huesca failed to take the city or to divert Nationalist forces from their successful drive on the seaport and industrial center of Bilbao in the Basque country. On 19 June Nationalist forces occupied Bilbao.
6–26 July	A Republican offensive northwest of Madrid degenerated into the Battle of Brunete.
18–26 July	The Nationalists mounted a counteroffensive at Brunete, after which the military situation stalemated.

24 August– 6 September	A Republican offensive in Aragon managed to take Belchite but failed to reach its goal of Zaragoza.
26 August	Nationalist forces seized the coastal resort of Santander on the Bay of Biscay and Basque resistance began to crumble.
21 October	Nationalist forces occupied the ports of Gijón and Avilés and established control over the province of Asturias; the Cantabrian Pocket ceased to exist.
15 December– 8 January	A Republican winter offensive in Aragon succeeded in taking the fortress city of Teruel.

1938

17 January– 20 February	A Nationalist counteroffensive in Aragon retook the city of Teruel.
9 March	A Nationalist offensive in Aragon broke through Republican defenses and drove down the Ebro Valley for the Mediterranean Sea.
17 March	France opened its frontier to munitions for the Spanish Republic.
16–18 March	During a period of fifty-three hours, Italian bombers based on the Island of Majorca launched thirteen air raids against the city of Barcelona. Although no single attack included as many as a dozen bombers, the repeated waves of attacks demoralized the citizens and shocked the world.
15 April	Nationalist forces captured the town of Vinaroz on the Mediterranean, cutting the Republic in two and isolating Catalonia from the Levante.
25 July–2 August	A Republican offensive across the Ebro River ended in a stalemate; Nationalist counteroffensives of 7 August–4 September, and 30 October–18 November, drove the Republican army back across the river.
30 September	In Munich, Germany, representatives of France and Great Britain gave Adolf Hitler the keys to Czechoslovakia, thereby delaying a general European war for eleven months.
29 December	The Nationalists launched an offensive north of the Ebro River aimed at rolling up Catalonia.

1939

26 January	Nationalist forces captured Barcelona.

10 February	Nationalist forces occupied all of Catalonia and took control of the major border crossing points to France.
27 February	France and Great Britain recognized the Nationalist government.
5 March	The Republic's political leaders, now based at the village of Elda in the province of Alicante, boarded airplanes and fled to France.
28 March	The Nationalist army marched into Madrid and took possession of the city without a shot being fired within a hundred miles of the Gran Vía.
29 March	The city of Valencia surrendered to Nationalist forces.
1 April	On "All Fools Day" the Nationalist government formally declared the civil war to be over.

Appendix 2

MILITARY AIRPLANE MARKINGS IN THE SPANISH CIVIL WAR[1]

Republic (Loyalist) Air Force

The Republican tricolor of red, yellow, and purple bands appeared on the rudder. A broad red band circled the fuselage aft of the cockpit, and the wingtips were painted red.

Nationalist Air Force

A black Saint Andrew's cross painted over a white background appeared on the rudder. A white Saint Andrew's cross appeared on each wing, often inside a black roundel, with the wingtips often painted white. A black roundel appeared on the fuselage behind the cockpit, sometimes with a unit emblem or Nationalist Yoke and Arrows device within it.

Appendix 3

TINKER PUBLICATIONS

Frank G. Tinker Jr. *Some Still Live* (New York: Funk & Wagnalls Company, 1938).

———. *Some Still Live, Experiences of a Fighting-Plane Pilot in the Spanish War* (London: Lovat Dickson, Ltd., 1938)

———. "Some Still Live," *Saturday Evening Post,* Vol. 210

No. 41 (9 April, 1938): 5–7, 74–76, 78–80, 82.

No. 42 (16 April, 1938): 10–11, 86, 88, 93–94.

No. 43 (23 April, 1938): 16–17, 55, 58, 61–62.

No. 44 (30 April, 1938): 18–19, 31, 33–34, 36.

———. "I Fought in Spain," *Popular Aviation,* Vol. 23, No. 3 (September 1938): 10–12, 82.

———. "Tinkering Around," a weekly column on "foreign affairs" that appeared in *The DeWitt Record* newspaper between September 1938 and February 1939.

———. "Planes in Spain," *Model Airplane News,* Vol. 20, No. 1 (January 1939): 6–7, 47–48.

———. "I Was Bombed!" *Popular Aviation,* Vol. 24, No. 2 (February 1939): 13–15.

———. "The Case for the Dive Bomber," *Popular Aviation,* Vol. 24, No. 3 (March 1939): 28–30, 79-81.

———. "Anti-Aircraft in Spain," *Shipmate* (March 1939): 7, 21.

———. "Monoplanes vs. Biplanes—Again," *Popular Aviation,* Vol. 26, No. 2 (February 1940): 50–51, 70, 73.

Appendix 4

TINKER AERIAL VICTORIES

Date	Tinker A/C	Enemy A/C	Vicinity
3/14/37	I-15	Fiat	Guadalajara
3/20/37	I-15	Fiat	Guadalajara
4/17/37	I-15	Heinkel	Teruel
6/2/37	I-16	Fiat	Segovia
6/16/37	I-16	Fiat	Huesca
7/13/37	I-16	Me 109	Madrid
7/17/37	I-16	Me 109	Madrid
7/18/37	I-16	Fiat	Madrid

5 Fiat CR.32
2 Me 109B
1 Heinkel 51

Total: 8 (in addition, there is 1 He 112 probable on 18 July)

NOTES

Preface

1. An accounting of Smith's life, publications, and contributions to the historiography of aeronautics can be found in R. Cargill Hall with David Alan Rosenberg, "Richard K. Smith: An Appreciation," *Air Power History* (Summer 2004): 30–37.—RCH

Introduction

1. In Spain, however, civil war memories grow fainter thanks to an Orwellian-titled "Law of Historical Memory" *(Ley de Memoria Histórica)* passed in 2007 by Spain's Chamber of Deputies that directed the removal of all symbols of the Franco era.

2. Hugh Thomas, *The Spanish Civil War* (New York: Harper & Row, Publishers, 1961), 165–70, details Nationalist atrocities. As regards the Left's implacable war against the clergy, more than 6,800 religious were killed, half in the first six weeks of the war. See Julio de la Cueva, "Religious Persecution, Anticlerical Tradition and Revolution: On Atrocities against the Clergy during the Spanish Civil War," *Journal of Contemporary History*, Vol. 33, No. 3 (July 1998): 355–69. The French aviator Antoine de Saint-Exupéry witnessed cleric cleansing while accompanying a former radical anticleric in Spain, which caused him to become an enthusiastic priest rescuer. See Antoine de Saint-Exupéry, *Airman's Odyssey* (New York: Reynal & Hitchcock, 1942), 164–74.

3. A case in point is the careless-to-the-point-of-irresponsible use of the words "Fascism" and "Fascists" to describe the Nationalist cause and any who supported it. In retrospect, only the Falange—which opposed Franco as often as it supported him—was truly Fascistic, and it was but one constituent element of a much broader coalition of nationalists, monarchists, religious, free-market democrats, and land owners (small, medium, and large) who opposed the Madrid government. For a careful explication of the word and its applicability to Spain, see Stanley G. Payne, *Fascism: Comparison and Definition* (Madison: University of Wisconsin Press, 1980).

4. See, for example, Thomas, *The Spanish Civil War*; and Stanley G. Payne's *Falange: A History of Spanish Fascism* (Stanford: Stanford University Press, 1961); *The Spanish Revolution: A Study of the Social and Political Tensions That Culminated in the Civil War in*

Spain (New York: W. W. Norton & Co., 1970); *Fascism in Spain, 1923–1977* (Madison: University of Wisconsin Press, 2000); especially *The Spanish Civil War, The Soviet Union, and Communism* (New Haven: Yale University Press, 2004); and *The Collapse of the Spanish Republic, 1933–1936: Origins of the Civil War* (New Haven: Yale University Press, 2006).

5. Though it must be said that the Nationalist air chief, Teniente General del Ejército Alfredo Kindelán, had an exceptional grasp of air power and air doctrine, as evidenced in his *Mis Cuadernos de Guerra* (Madrid: Editorial Plus Ultra, 1945), 139–70, and he wrote widely after the war on air power and air doctrine topics.

6. Ted Morgan, *Reds: McCarthyism in Twentieth Century America* (New York: Random House, 2003), 176. Morgan was the Comte St. Charles Armand Gabriel de Gramont in 1932; his diplomat father, a hero of the French resistance, perished in an aircraft accident in 1943. Morgan himself served in the French Army, coming to the United States, taking American citizenship in 1977, and changing his name as well.

7. Maochun Yu, *The Dragon's War: Allied Operations and the Fate of China, 1937–1947* (Annapolis: Naval Institute Press, 2006), 13.

8. Morgan, *Reds,* 177.

9. Alan Bullock, *Hitler and Stalin: Parallel Lives* (New York: Vintage Books, 1993), 733. For Stalin and Soviet involvement, exploitation, and withdrawal from Spain, see Ronald Radosh, Mary R. Habeck, and Grigory Sevostianov, eds., *Spain Betrayed: The Soviet Union and the Spanish Civil War,* a volume in the Yale University Annals of Communism series (New Haven: Yale University Press, 2001); and Payne, *The Spanish Civil War, The Soviet Union, and Communism.*

10. For Soviet military operations in the Far East, see the previously cited Yu, *The Dragon's War,* 10–23; Marshal Georgi Zhukov, *Marshal Zhukov's Greatest Battles* (New York: Harper & Row, 1969), 147–89; A. Y. Kalyagin, "Along Unfamiliar Roads," and S. V. Slyusarev, "Protecting China's Airspace," in Y. V. Chudodeyev, ed., *Soviet Volunteers in China, 1925–1945* (Moscow: Progress Publishers, 1980), 194–284; Alvin D. Coox, *The Anatomy of a Small War: The Soviet-Japanese Struggle for Changkufeng/Khasan, 1938,* No. 13 in the Contributions to Military History series (Westport, Conn.: Greenwood Press, 1977), 177–96, 205–9, 361–74; also Alvin D. Coox, *Nomonhan: Japan Against Russia, 1939,* 2 vols. (Stanford: Stanford University Press, 1985), 397, 683–89, 779–841, 881–83, 1069–70; and Edward J. Drea, *Nomonhan: Japanese-Soviet Tactical Combat, 1939,* No. 2 of the Leavenworth Papers series (Ft. Leavenworth, Kans.: Combat Studies Institute, U.S. Army Command and General Staff College, 1981), 69–99.

11. See, for example, Colonel I. T. Starinov, "Homecoming," in Seweryn Bialer, ed., *Stalin and His Generals: Soviet Military Memoirs of World War II* (New York: Pegasus, 1969), 65–79. This unhappy episode underscores the wisdom of Andres Garcia Lacalle, who declined an invitation to resettle in the Soviet Union, as recounted in chapter 16 of this biography. For an account of what happened to Soviet aviators mentioned in this biography who returned from Spain to the USSR, see the epilogue.

12. Thomas, *The Spanish Civil War,* details their sorry fates; see 621–22.

13. For Mussolini, see John Gooch's magisterial *Mussolini and His Generals: The Armed Forces and Fascist Foreign Policy, 1922–1940* (Cambridge: Cambridge University Press, 2007), 318, 322–24; R. J. B. Bosworth, *Mussolini* (New York: Oxford University Press, 2002), 315–17; and F. W. Deakin, *The Brutal Friendship: Mussolini, Hitler, and the Fall of Italian Fascism* (Garden City, N.Y.: Anchor Books, 1966), 5, 8.

14. See H. R. Trevor-Roper, ed., *Hitler's Secret Conversations, 1941–1944* (New York: Farrar, Straus and Young, 1955), 422–23, 492–93.

15. Stanley G. Payne, *Franco and Hitler: Spain, Germany, and World War II* (New Haven: Yale University Press, 2008), 91.

16. For Franco and Canaris, see John H. Waller, *The Unseen War in Europe: Espionage and Conspiracy in the Second World War* (New York: Random House, 1996), 14, 169, 258, 264–65.

17. Regarding German-Soviet negotiations leading to the Non-Aggression Pact, see Raymond James Sontag and James Stuart Beddie, eds., *Nazi-Soviet Relations, 1939–1941: Documents from the Archives of the German Foreign Office* (Washington, D.C.: Department of State, 1948), 1–78; for the shattering of Leftist unity at this time, see Harvey Klehr, John Earl Haynes, and Fridrikh Igorevich Firsov, eds., *The Secret World of American Communism*, a volume in the Yale University Annals of Communism series (New Haven: Yale University Press, 1995), 267–69.

18. Thomas, *The Spanish Civil War*, 206

19. Trevor-Roper, *Hitler's Secret Conversations*, 493; see also Paul Preston, "General Franco as Military Leader," in *Transactions of the Royal Historical Society*, 6th Series, Vol. 4 (London: Royal Historical Society, 1994), 21, 26–28, 32–35.

20. Jesus Salas Larrazabal, *Air War Over Spain* (Shepperton, UK: Ian Allan, Ltd., 1974 ed.), 30–37.

21. See Gerald Howson, *Arms for Spain: The Untold Story of the Spanish Civil War* (New York: St. Martin's Press, 1998), and his earlier *Aircraft of the Spanish Civil War, 1936–1939* (Washington, D.C.: Smithsonian Institution Press, 1990), 292–300.

22. Pierre Cot, *Triumph of Treason* (New York: Ziff-Davis Publishing Co., 1944), 351–56. Decoded intercepts of Soviet message traffic reveal that in the fall of 1940 Cot approached American Communist Party chief Earl Browder about working for the Soviets; see Document 63 in Klehr, Haynes, and Firsov, eds., *Secret World of American Communism*, 233–37. Afterward he was reputedly recruited into the NKVD with the code name Daedalus; see Herbert Romerstein and Eric Breindel, *The Venona Secrets: Exposing Soviet Espionage and America's Traitors* (Washington, D.C.: Regnery Publishing, Inc., 2000), 303–4; and Peter Jackson, *France and the Nazi Menace: Intelligence and Policy Making 1933–1939* (Oxford: Oxford University Press, 2000), 192–94, and notes 48–51.

23. For Malraux's role in Spain, see Curtis Cate's sympathetic *André Malraux: A Biography* (New York: Fromm International Publishing Co., 1995), 234–52.

24. Cipher message, Stalin to Kaganovich, 6 September 1936, Document 159 in R. W. Davies, Oleg V. Khlevniuk, E. A. Rees, Liudmila P. Kosheleva, Larisa A. Rogovaya, and

Steven Shabad, eds., *The Stalin-Kaganovich Correspondence, 1931–36,* a volume in the Yale University Annals of Communism series (New Haven: Yale University Press, 2003), 351.

25. See "Joint Resolution to Prohibit the Exportation of Arms, Ammunition, and Implements of War from the United States to Spain," in S. Shepard Jones and Denys P. Myers, *Documents on American Foreign Relations, January 1938–June 1939* (Boston: World Peace Foundation, 1939), 547–48.

26. For Soviet-German relations, see G. W. F. Hallgarten, "General Hans von Seeckt and Russia, 1920–1922," *Journal of Modern History,* Vol. 21, No. 1 (March 1949): 28–30; H. W. Gatzke, "Russo-German Military Collaboration During the Weimar Republic," *American Historical Review,* Vol. 63, No. 3 (April 1958): 566–67; Generalleutnant Friedrich von Rabenau, *Seeckt: Aus seinem Leben, 1918–1936* (Leipzig: Hase & Koehler, 1940), 15–52, 97, 306; James S. Corum, *The Roots of Blitzkrieg: Hans von Seeckt and German Military Reform* (Lawrence: University Press of Kansas, 1992); Manfred Zeidler, *Reichswehr und Rote Armee, 1920–1933: Wege und Stationen einer ungewöhnlichen Zusammenarbeit* (Munich: R. Oldenbourg Verlag, 1993); and Aleksandr M. Nekrich, *Pariahs, Partners, Predators: German-Soviet Relations, 1922–1941* (New York: Columbia University Press, 1997).

27. For a case study, Squadron Leader Brian Armstrong, "Through a Glass Darkly: The Royal Air Force and the Lessons of the Spanish Civil War, 1936–1939," *Royal Air Force Air Power Review,* Vol. 12, No. 1 (Spring 2009): 32–55.

28. A. S. Yakovlev, *Fifty Years of Soviet Aircraft Construction,* NASA Technical Translation TT F-627 (Jerusalem: Israel Program for Scientific Translations in Association with the National Aeronautics and Space Administration, 1970), 19.

29. Captain Didier Poulain, "Aircraft and Mechanized Land Warfare: The Battle of Guadalajara, 1937," *Journal of the Royal United Services Institute,* Vol. 83 (May 1938): 362–68; Maurice Duval, *Les Leçons de la Guerre d'Espagne* (Paris: Librairie Plon, 1938); and F. O. Miksche, *Attack: A Study of Blitzkrieg Tactics* (New York: Random House, 1942). The Miriam Sigel Friedlander Papers, Marjorie Polon Papers, and the James Lardner Papers, all of the Abraham Lincoln Brigade Archives (ALBA) at the Tamiment Library, New York University, contain correspondence from various veterans graphically relating the physical and psychological effects of air attack. These (and other Lincoln documents) can be accessed online at http://www.alba-valb.org/resources/digital-library.

30. Tom Wintringham and J. N. Blashford-Snell, *Weapons and Tactics* (Baltimore: Penguin Books, 1973 ed.), 165.

31. Miksche, *Attack,* 73.

32. For example, in Robert A. Rosenstone's *Crusade of the Left: The Lincoln Battalion in the Spanish Civil War* (New York: Pegasus, 1969), and Alvah Bessie and Albert Prago, eds., *Our Fight: Writings by Veterans of the Abraham Lincoln Brigade, Spain, 1936–1939* (New York: Monthly Review Press, 1987). Rukeyser, a Leftist activist best known for her poetry (much of which was inspired by an early interest in aviation), was, by coincidence, in Spain upon the outbreak of the revolt. See Jan Heller Levi, ed., *The Muriel Rukeyser Reader* (New York: W. W. Norton and Company, 1994), 2, 52–54, 119–20. The international volunteers figure prominently in André Malraux' *Man's Hope* (New York: Random

House, 1938, reprinted by Bantam, 1968), a translation of *L'Espoir*, first published in 1937 and based on his experiences with the Escuadrilla España.

33. Ted Morgan, *Reds*, 175–82 (quote from 177).

34. For the American volunteers in Spain, see Cecil Eby, *Between the Bullet and the Lie: American Volunteers in the Spanish Civil War* (New York: Holt, Rinehart, and Winston, 1969), and his sequel, *Comrades and Commissars: The Lincoln Battalion in the Spanish Civil War* (University Park: The Pennsylvania State University Press, 2006). For a useful examination of American airmen as a group, see John Carver Edwards, *Airmen Without Portfolio: U.S. Mercenaries in Civil War Spain* (Westport, Conn.: Praeger, 1997).

35. For Hollywood in this time period, and *The Spanish Earth* episode in particular, see Ronald Radosh and Allis Radosh, *Red Star Over Hollywood: The Film Colony's Long Romance with the Left* (San Francisco: Encounter Books, 2005).

36. Emeric Pressburger, *Killing a Mouse on Sunday* (New York: Harcourt, Brace & World, 1961), reissued in paperback under the title *Behold a Pale Horse*, 1964.

37. Often to the shock of cinemagoers anticipating a more traditional retelling of the Loyalist myth, as the author personally witnessed in London shortly after the film's release.

38. The previously cited Larrazabal, *Air War Over Spain*, and José Larios [Fernandez], *Combat Over Spain* (London: Neville Spearman, 1966), both offer an informative look at the air war from a Spanish perspective.

39. Frank G. Tinker, *Some Still Live* (New York: Funk & Wagnalls, 1938); for other examples, see Eugene Finick, "I Fly for Spain," *Harpers*, Vol. 176 (January 1938): 138–48; and Frederic B. Acosta, "The Yanks in Spain," *Popular Aviation* (May 1938): 37, 92

40. One myth holds that Loyalist mercenary Derek Dickinson fought a thirty-minute duel against Bruno Mussolini, pilot-son of the Italian dictator, forcing the Italian to drop a white scarf and quit; the fight never took place. Martin Caidin, to his discredit, recycled this nonsense in *The Ragged, Rugged Warriors* (New York: Ballantine Books, 1966), 8–30. For a good overview and assessment of the Spanish volunteers, see Sterling Seagrave, *Soldiers of Fortune*, a volume in the Time-Life Epic of Flight series (Alexandria, Va.: Time-Life Books, 1981), 41–65

41. For an example, see Seagrave, *Soldiers of Fortune*, 46. One of the most accurate portrayals of the mind-set and actions of a mercenary airman in Spain is in a novel: Ernest Gann's tellingly entitled *Benjamin Lawless* (New York: William Sloane Associates, 1948).

42. As is evident by reviewing the previously cited Larrazabal, *Air War Over Spain*, 184–307; Von Hardesty, *Red Phoenix: The Rise of Soviet Air Power, 1941–1945* (Washington, D.C.: Smithsonian Institution Press, 1991 ed.), 49–50; Scott W. Palmer, *Dictatorship of the Air: Aviation Culture and the Fate of Modern Russia*, a volume in the Cambridge Centennial of Flight series (Cambridge: Cambridge University Press, 2006), 246–47; K. E. Bailes, "Technology and Legitimacy: Soviet Aviation and Stalinism in the 1930s," *Technology and Culture*, Vol. 17, No. 1 (January 1976): 68–70; Raymond L. Proctor, *Hitler's Luftwaffe in the Spanish Civil War*, No. 35 of the Contributions in Military History series (Westport, Conn.: Greenwood Press, 1983); and Angelo Emiliani, Giuseppe F. Ghergo, and Achille Vigna, *Spagna 1936–39: L'aviazione Legionaria* (Milan: Intergest, 1973).

43. R. Cargill Hall with David Alan Rosenberg, "Richard K. Smith: An Appreciation," *Air Power History* (Summer 2004): 37.

Chapter 2. The Ragged Edge of Infinity

1. Except as indicated, all information relating to Frank G. Tinker Jr., his family life, and years at the Naval Academy is taken from his collected papers and letters held by his sister, Lucille Tinker Carnahan, or drawn from the recollections of his two sisters and former classmates. [Note: after Lucille Carnahan's death in 2004, Tinker's collected papers passed to her niece, Marcia Tinker Morrison.—RCH]

2. The reader may be interested to know that the Native American name of Natchitoches is pronounced Nack-ah-tish.

3. The USS *Texas*, a veteran of Vera Cruz (1914) and both world wars, is the last dreadnought in existence; now a museum ship, it is open for public viewing at San Jacinto State Historic Site in Houston, Texas.—RCH

4. For an excellent account of this contest, see Thomas G. Foxworth, *The Speed Seekers* (London: Macdonald & Janes, 1975); more comprehensive as regards the Schneider contests is David Mondey, *The Schneider Trophy: A History of the Contests of the Coupe d'Aviation Maritime Jacques Schneider* (London: Robin Hale, 1975).

5. The Navy maintained two of these schools, one at Hampton Roads, Virginia, the other at San Diego, California. Not only did the Navy lose the services of those sailors and Marines sent to these schools, officers had to be detailed to them as teachers. It appears that slightly more than one-half of the original contingents washed out before the end of the six months; washouts immediately returned to the Fleet.

6. See Richard K. Smith, *First Across! The U.S. Navy's Transatlantic Flight of 1919* (Annapolis: Naval Institute Press, 1973). NC refers to the Navy seaplanes marshaled for this operation to fly across the Atlantic Ocean.—RCH

7. See Richard K. Smith, *The Airships* Akron & Macon: *Flying Aircraft Carriers of the United States Navy* (Annapolis: Naval Institute Press, 1965).—RCH

8. Taken from Charlton L. Murphy, ed., *Reef Points: The Annual Handbook of the Regiment of Midshipmen*, Vol. 27 (1930); a pocket-sized booklet of 160 pages and 3x5 inches, it is revised annually to include the scheduled events of the current academic year and it serves as a guidebook for the plebes. As a source of information for historians, the whole series of these little books is rich in insights to life at the Academy.

9. Guy Marion Morrow, born 11 June 1909, went on to complete flight training at Pensacola in 1936 and was designated a naval aviator; he flew with Marine Air in World War II and Korea. Morrow retired a colonel and died on 9 December 1962. He was fifty-one years old.—RCH

10. Tinker's idea of "modern dancing," where the partners hold one another in an embrace, was distinct from square dancing, about which he had no qualms and did enjoy.

11. The "commission problem" is discussed at length in U.S. Congress, House of Representatives, Committee on Naval Affairs, *Hearings on Sundry Legislation Affecting The Naval Establishment,* "Hearings on HR-8083, Providing for the Appointment as Ensigns

in the Line of the Navy and Midshipmen Who Graduate from the Naval Academy in 1932" [No. 246], 72nd Cong., 1st Sess., 1932, 745–75.

12. It is doubtful if these observations are original with Tinker; they probably echo estimates at large within the Naval Academy. As regards the poor condition of the U.S. Fleet, at this date they are essentially correct.

13. Smith's interview with Captain Elliot L. "Jesse" James, USN (Ret.), at his cattle farm near Selma, Alabama, 30 March 1971.

14. See William L. White, *They Were Expendable* (New York: Harcourt Brace, 1942). The book, made into a movie under the same title, found Robert Montgomery playing the leading role backed up by John Wayne; for a review, see the *New York Times*, 21 December 1945 (25:2).

15. The *New York Times*, 2 June 1933 (5:1).

Chapter 3. Army, Navy—And Out!

1. The dollar of 1933 had about twelve times the purchasing power of the same depreciated scrap of paper of a half-century later. A rough index is the price of gold, $35 an ounce in 1933, fluctuating around $400 an ounce in 1983. [The price of gold exceeded $1,000 an ounce in 2009.—RCH] In 1933 an apprentice seaman received $21 a month, a midshipman at the Naval Academy $75, and an ensign (without allowances, longevity, or flight pay) $125. [Using the Unskilled Wage index, the same figures for 2008 were $1008.30, $3,604.63, and $6,007.72.— RCH]. All information relating to Frank G. Tinker in this chapter is taken from his papers and his service records; the latter include four distinct items: (1) as a Navy enlisted man, (2) as a midshipman, (3) as a commissioned officer in the Navy, and (4) his Army 201 file as an air cadet, all of which are stored in the National Personnel Records Center in St. Louis. The *San Antonio Express* newspaper was useful, and the logbook of the USS *San Francisco* (CA-38) provided an elementary chronology. It, along with the logbooks of other Navy ships, is in Record Group 24, National Archives. In many instances the recollections of his classmates at Annapolis and Randolph Field proved vital.

2. The *Air Corps Newsletter*, Vol. 17 (29 August 1933): 196, describes the first contingent of ex-midshipmen; that of Vol. 17 (30 October 1933), 220, describes Tinker's class that included the ex-midshipmen Garrett S. Coleman, Charles W. Fiedler, Samuel R. Mathes, and Raymond P. Zimmerman. Thomas E. Norris is also listed, but at the last minute he took a job with the Glenn L. Martin Company installing turrets in B-10 bombers for $14 a week.

3. The contemporary term for airplanes that provided close air support of the infantry.—RCH

4. *Annual Report of the Chief of the Air Corps*, 1934. Although this item may be found shelved as an independent document, it also will be found invariably as a part of the annual *Report of the Secretary of War* to the president; the latter is submitted to Congress where it becomes part of the congressional serial set.

5. For the airmail fiasco, see Norman E. Borden Jr., *Air Mail Emergency* (Freeport, Maine: The Bond Wheelwright Co., 1968), which is a reasonably good account; a comprehensive history of this mess in all of its aspects does not yet exist.

6. "West Point of the Air," *Popular Mechanics,* Vol. 62, Part 1 (July 1934): 17–30, 116; Part 2 (August 1934): 25–30.

7. For a review of this film see the *New York Times,* 6 April 1935 (10:1).

8. The *Randolph Field Tee,* (May 1934): 2.

9. The *New York Times,* 29 March 1934 (2:2); 27 May 1934 (22:5), and 4 June 1934 (4:2).

10. It seemed hopeless but was not impossible; however, it involved a gamble. Although the number of Air Corps officers was limited, a loophole in the law permitted it to have (theoretically) an infinite number of air cadets, or at least as many as money could be obtained to support. After winning their wings, a select number of cadets stayed on in the Air Corps performing the duties of an officer at a cadet's pay until openings occurred among the ranks of 2nd lieutenants; this could go on for a year or more. Of the ex-midshipmen, Francis R. Drake declined the Navy's invitation to return and chose to go the "infinite air cadet" route. But by 1936 he despaired of obtaining an Air Corps commission and returned to the Navy; he retired as a captain in 1964 and died 12 March 1975.

11. "Black shoes" referred to U.S. Navy regular officers.—RCH

12. *Syllabus for Training Naval Aviators and Student Naval Aviation Pilots, Flight School and Ground School* (U.S. Naval Air Station, Pensacola, 1 May 1935); a copy of this thirteen-page booklet was obtained from Lee M. Pearson, former historian, Naval Air Systems Command.

13. Using the Unskilled Wage index, a total of $159.38 per month in 1934 would equate to $6,432 monthly in 2008. The 1934 sum of $1,900 per annum amounts to $76,600 in 2008 Unskilled Wage dollars.—RCH

14. Being put in "hack" is a form of non-judicial punishment for officers; he is relieved of all duties and confined to his quarters for a period of days.

15. The "Army bunch" that went to Pensacola and their subsequent duty assignments were: Richard T. Black to the cruiser *Astoria*; Jesse B. Burkes to the battleship *Mississippi*; Garrett S. Coleman to the battleship *Colorado*; Paul D. Duke to the battleship *Arizona*; Charles W. Fielder to the cruiser *Chester*; Robert C. Hird to the battleship *California*; Elliot L. James to the cruiser *Pensacola*; George P. Koch to the cruiser *Tuscaloosa*; John N. Ogle to the cruiser *New Orleans*; James R. Reedy to the cruiser *Northampton*; James A. Smith to the cruiser *Portland*; and Raymond P. Zimmerman to the battleship *Nevada.*

16. For details of this aspect of Trapnell's career, see Richard K. Smith, *The Airships Akron & Macon: Flying Aircraft Carriers of the U.S. Navy* (Annapolis: Naval Institute Press, 1965).

17. A scarf ring consisted of a half-around (180-degree) iron ring fixed to the aft side of the rear cockpit, from which rear-firing machine guns could be suspended.—RCH

18. A summary of Tinker's court-martial is published in *Martial Orders for Year Ending December 31, 1935* (Washington, D.C.: Government Printing Office, 1936), CMO5, 4. The full transcript is held by the Navy's Judge Advocate General, Washington, D.C.

19. Frank Tinker's sister, Lucille Carnahan, for reasons of her own, withheld this information from Richard Smith, and it only came to light when Marcia Tinker Morrison, who inherited the Tinker collection from Lucille, uncovered it among his papers

in 2010. (The officiant, Reverend McIntegart, later became the fourth Catholic bishop of Brooklyn.) The newspaper clipping is without an exact date or identification, other than a penciled "1936," but Martha Rothenhofer was born and grew up in DeWitt, Arkansas, wrote part-time for the *DeWitt Era-Enterprise* in the 1930s, and also taught penmanship and typing at the DeWitt high school. Moreover, had it been any other newspaper, the town of DeWitt, Arkansas, would have been mentioned. Frank Tinker had left DeWitt to join the Navy immediately after he graduated from high school, and he may not have been all that well known to most townsfolk, though his family was well recognized because of their "different ways." His mother, as have many proud mothers before and since, took this occasion to inflate her son's record at the Naval Academy, when in fact his academic record had him in the bottom quarter of the class.—RCH

20. Certificate of Discharge from the Standard Shipping Company, 21 June 1936, in New York City. Tinker left as a 3rd Mate, whose "Character" and "Ability" were judged "Very Good."—RCH

Chapter 4. Of Planes and Spain

1. Registration listed in A. J. Jackson, *De Havilland Aircraft Since 1915* (London: Putnam Books, 1962), 338. Two 200-horsepower Gipsy Six inline engines powered this airplane. Ibid., 340. The secret arrangements made for this flight during the first week in July are covered in Jose Larios, *Combat Over Spain: Memoirs of a Nationalist Fighter Pilot, 1936–1939* (New York: The MacMillan Company, 1966), 21.—RCH

2. Luis Bolin, *Spain: The Vital Years* (Philadelphia: J. B. Lippincott, 1967), 50; chapter 5 recounts this flight in detail.

3. For information on the Spanish armed forces Smith relied on Jesús Salas Larrazábal, *La Guerra de España desde el Aire*, 2nd rev. ed. (Barcelona: Ediciones Ariel, 1972), and Ramón Salas Larrazábal's four volumes of *Historia de Ejército Popular de la República* (Madrid: San Martin, 1973).

4. Another good source of information on Spain and its armed forces on the eve of the war is in the U.S. War Department, General Staff, Military Intelligence Division Files, Record Group 165, National Archives; file 2093 treats aviation in Spain. There are similar files for other nations.

5. Spain purchased one Boeing 281, the export version of the P-26A. Although its gross weight was 23 percent lighter than the Fury and its power-to-weight ratio 10 percent better, its wing loading was 20 percent higher and it was not as maneuverable as the British biplane. Also, it could not use the Hispano engine without an extensive and expensive redesign.

6. Francis K. Mason, *Hawker Aircraft Since 1920* (London: Putnam, 1961), 168–83, 196–201.

7. *Foreign Relations of the U.S., 1936* (Washington, D.C.: GPO, 1954), Vol. 2, 474–76. In mid-1936, CASA negotiated a contract for fifty M-139s, eight pattern aircraft, and the balance to be manufactured at Getafe; Pratt & Whitney engines were to be manufactured by Elizalde, S.A., in Barcelona. (Military attaché reports of 5 October 1935 and

13 February 1936, f/2257-S-35, RG-165, National Archives.) The Republic sought to avoid payment in dollars and the deal was suspended. When it tried to revive the purchase on 10 August 1936, the State Department intervened and no Martin bombers went to Spain except in the imaginations of Nationalist propagandists.

8. Nevil Shute, *Slide Rule: The Autobiography of an Engineer* (New York: Morrow, 1954), 205-10.

9. Ibid., 201, 224–25; and H. A. Taylor, *Airspeed Aircraft Since 1931* (London: Putnam, 1970), 57, 65–66, 71–72.

10. Some of these activities are described in Richard P. Traina, *American Diplomacy and the Spanish Civil War* (Bloomington: Indiana University Press, 1968), chapter 8; and Félix Gordón Ordás gives his point of view in volume 1 of his memoirs, *Mi Política en España* (Mexico City: Figaro, 1961).

11. There is a huge file on these export efforts, applications for export licenses ordered alphabetically by names of the applicants, in the U.S. State Department File 711.00111 Licenses, National Archives.

12. United States Department of State, *Foreign Relations of the U.S., 1936*, Vol. 2 Europe (Spain), 536–8.

13. Concurrently, Cuse arranged the sale of the Christy suspension system and a pattern chassis to the British War Ministry, and it was used in British tank designs. Smith's conversations with Robert Cuse in Mexico City, October 1973.

14. Contemporary newspapers carry a day-to-day account of this little drama; documents are in State Department File 711.00111 Licenses, Vimalert Corp., National Archives. When signed by the president, the statute made it unlawful to ship arms to Spain "or to any other foreign country for transshipment to Spain."

15. This episode is detailed in Richard Sanders Allen, *The Ship That Ran Against Congress*, 1978.

16. Salas, *La Guerra de España*, 83–84, and the contemporary newspaper press usually took note of these flights. In books about the Spanish Civil War, no end of attention is lavished on the $316 million in Spanish gold shipped from Cartagena to Odessa in the Soviet Union in October 1935, whereas the bullion that went to France is practically ignored.

17. Rafael A. Permuy Lopéz, *Air War Over Spain: Aviators, Aircraft and Air Units of the Nationalist and Republican Air Forces 1936–1939*. (Hersham, Surrey, UK: Allan Printing Ltd., 2009; translated from Spanish by Juan Carlos Salgado), 32.—RCH

18. Luis Bolin, *Spain: The Vital Years*, 159–76; and Jesús Salas Larrazábal, "Los Savoia-81, Primeros Aviones Extranjeros que se Incorporaron al Ejército Nacional," *Revista de Aeronáutica y Astronáutica*, No. 388 (March 1973): 186–90.

19. Hellmuth Günther Dahms, *Der Spanische Bürgerkrieg, 1936–1939* (Tübingen: Wunderlich, 1962), 101–3; and Fritz Morzik and Gerhard Hümmelchen, *Die deutschen Transportflieger im Zweiten Weltkrieg* (Tinkerfurt am Main: Bernard & Graefe, 1966), 3ff.

20. H. R. Trevor-Roper, ed., *Hitler's Secret Conversations, 1941–1944* (New York: Farrar, Straus and Young, 1955), 493.

21. Lopéz, *Air War Over Spain*, 32.—RCH

22. The term Wehrmacht is the collective name for Germany's armed forces (Heer [Army], Luftwaffe [Air Force], and Kriegsmarine [War Navy]), although many incorrectly refer to the Army as the Wehrmacht.—RCH

· 23. The Legion Condor was a combined volunteer Luftwaffe and Heer unit, with the air side directed by Hugo Sperrle and the ground forces by Oberstleutnant (Colonel Lieutenant) Wilhelm Ritter von Thoma, who reported to Sperrle.—RCH

24. Lopéz, *Air War Over Spain*, 25–26.—RCH

25. D. C. Watt, "Soviet Military Aid to the Spanish Republic in the Civil War 1936–1939," *Slavonic and East European Review*, Vol. 38 (June 1960): 536–41, is the original contribution to illuminating this subject; however, Jesús Salas Larrazábal, "Intervención Soviética en la Guerra de Liberación," *Revista de Aeronáutica y Astronáutica*, No. 379 (June 1972): 428–38, provides better developed data and a good discussion; a decent overall view is Robert H. Whealey, "Foreign Intervention in the Spanish Civil War," in Raymond Carr, ed., *The Republic and The Civil War in Spain* (London: Macmillan, 1971), 213–38.

26. As popularized by the news media in the United States, this expression became totally divorced from its Spanish origins and came to mean *German* espionage anywhere in the world.

27. In 1936 radar was under concurrent development in Britain, France, Germany, and the United States, occasionally by two agencies within one country. In Britain the Air Ministry was the prime developer, and in September 1936 a crude radar set was used in the RAF's annual air exercises. In France the developing agency was similarly the Air Ministry, but French efforts lagged far behind the British. In both Germany and the United States the navies developed radar for gun laying; the Luftwaffe's and the U.S. Army Signal Corps' developments were for aircraft detection. The word "radar" is the abbreviation for Radio Detection and Ranging and is of American origin. Because "radar" spelled backwards is "radar," it could sound meaningless and made a good code word. Without radar, air operations in Spain bear more relationship to the operations of World War I than to those of 1939–45, but in their romantic obsession with "arrow-planes" this is a "lesson" of the Spanish Civil War that historians have not yet learned.

28. The *New York Times*, 11 November 1932 (4:4).

29. Although this was their first time over Madrid, Soviet aircraft first went into action on 29 October, when SB-2 twin-engine bombers struck at Nationalist airfields and I-15 fighters were used in cooperation with Republican ground forces. At the same time Russian tanks in the vicinity of Esquivias made an abortive effort to break up the Nationalists' right flank.

30. Both men stayed in Spain but a short time. They rotated back to the USSR in the early Spring of 1937.—RCH

31. Salas, *La Guerra desde el Aire*, 130.

32. By far the best description of this is José Manuel Martínez Bande, *La lucha en torno a Madrid* (Madrid: Editorial San Martín, 1972); in English there is George Hills, *The Battle for Madrid* (New York: St. Martin's Press, 1976), which draws heavily on Martínez Bande.

33. Thomas G. Foxworth, "Bertrand B. Acosta," in Paul Matt, ed., *Historical Aviation Album* (Temple City, Calif., 1969), Vol. 6, 51–56 and Vol. 7, 108–12; Acosta's own "story" was sold to the Universal News Service and three installments appear in the *Schenectady* (N.Y.) *Gazette*, 5, 7, and 12 January 1937. Lord exaggerated his experiences in "I Faced Death in Spanish Skies," *Flying Aces*, Vol. 26 (June 1937): 8–10, 75–77; and (July 1937): 8–10, 75–76.

34. Actually, the quote is attributed to David Hannum who headed a syndicate that purchased controlling interest in the Cardiff Giant, which competed with a similar hoax perpetrated by P. T. Barnum.—RCH

35. Details of the CPUSA recruitment and training (such as it was) of this initial Lincoln Battalion cadre in New York City, and the cadre's voyage to France on the *Normandie* in late December 1936, is contained in Cecil Eby, *Between the Bullet and the Lie: American Volunteers in the Spanish Civil War* (New York: Holt, Rinehart and Winston, 1969), 5–12.

Chapter 5. La Esquadrilla de Lacalle

1. The "Communist International," or Comintern, served as the international arm of the Communist Party. Formed in Moscow in March 1919, it became deeply involved in the Spanish Civil War. For that history, see Stanley G. Payne, *The Spanish Civil War, The Soviet Union, and Communism* (New Haven: Yale University Press, 2004), chapters 1–4.—RCH

2. Except as noted, the basic information contained in this chapter through chapter 15 that relates to Frank Tinker is taken from his book *Some Still Live,* his diary and flight log, and miscellaneous writings. Similarly, the basic source for the air war is Jesús Salas Larrazábal, *La Guerra de España desde el Aire,* hereafter abbreviated as Salas, *La Guerra,* and Andrés García Lacalle, *Mitos y Verdades: La Aviación de Gaza en la Guerra Española* (Mexico City: Ediciones Oasis, 1973), hereafter abbreviated as Lacalle, *Mitos y Verdades.*

3. There are no hard and fast rules about this. Usually the patronym is used; but in the case of "Gomez," which is a rather common name like "Jones" or "Brown" (but not as common as "Smith"), a man may choose to use his more distinctive matronym or the two in combination, such as "Gomez Trejo"; Anglo-Saxons usually find this confusing.

4. The province of Catalonia is populated by Catalans, an ancient people who have their own language, history, and culture; most do not consider themselves Spaniards. The same is true of the Basques. Both historically resent the rule of Madrid, and both nourish a cultural nationalism that occasionally becomes hyper-political to the distress of Spain as a whole. Under the Republic, both Catalonia and the Basque provinces were given autonomy.

5. For some miles on both sides of the Franco-Iberian frontier at Cerbère–Port Bou and at Hendaye-Irun, there is a two-rail system that provides both gauges, permitting French equipment to operate a distance into Spain and Spanish equipment to operate a distance into France. Ordinarily Tinker's train would have gone through to Port Bou

and he would have had to change trains there; only the war and the charade of French "neutrality" dictated this change at Cerbère.

6. After its occupation of Eastern Europe in 1945, the Soviet Union built five-foot-gauge strategic railways into Poland and East Germany.

7. Norman E. Borden Jr., *Air Mail Emergency: 1934* (Freeport, Maine: The Bond Wheelwright Co., 1968), 136.

8. There is a large file on Whitey Dahl in U.S. State Department Records, File 852.2221, Dahl, Harold E., in the National Archives.

9. Salas, *La Guerra,* 43–44.

10. Both Tinker's flight log and his diary identify this man as Walter Katz, but in his book *Some Still Live* he describes him as "a Spanish pilot," probably to protect Katz's Austrian identity.

11. Tinker's diary says there were "nine charter members" of this Anglo-American squadron, but he identifies only seven and not all of them completely. The American named "Nolde" was probably Nolte Caldwell; he did not stay in Spain beyond January 1937. Because Tinker only heard these names spoken and rarely saw them on paper, his spelling is often phonetic (e.g., he recorded the Koolhoven airplane in his flight log as a "Cojo-joven," the way it might be corrupted in Spanish; and the Spanish pilot Luis Bercial has his name spelled "Berthial" the way it is pronounced in Castilian). Obviously, this can lead to some confusion.

12. Jimmy Collins, *Test Pilot* (Garden City, N.Y.: Doubleday, 1935), which is for the most part a collection of his newspaper columns. He was killed 20 March 1935 while testing the Grumman XF3F.

13. Lacalle, *Mitos y Verdades,* 154. Weeks later he discovered that among the crewmen who died in this Ju 52 was Sergeant Quintin Segovia, one of his best friends of the prewar air force, going back to their flying school days together. Also killed was Captain Ruiz de Alda, a heroic figure of Spanish aviation as a result of his being Ramón Franco's copilot during their great transatlantic flight to South America in 1926 (a year before Lindbergh's sensational flight to Paris and when Lacalle was only seventeen years old). Discovering that one has been responsible for the deaths of old friends and acquaintances injected inevitable bitterness into many a Spanish fighter pilot's "victories" and a disinclination to talk about them even decades later. Foreigners such as Tinker did not have to be bothered by this. Indeed, Tinker assumed that all German-built airplanes were flown by Germans, all Italian-built airplanes were flown by Italians, and it was as simple as that; the real pain of the civil war could not be his.

14. Aside from Tinker's brief information, Finick's experiences are taken from his "I Fly for Spain," *Harper's,* Vol. 176 (January 1938): 138–48; and "Bombers Aloft," *True Magazine,* Vol. 5 (August 1939): 73–93; both are relatively sober and check out against other sources.

15. "Polikarpov's Natasha," *R.A.F. Flying Review,* Vol. 13 (June 1958): 6–7.

16. Information on Schmidt from public sources is negligible; there is a squib in "Aviation People," *Aviation,* Vol. 7 (April 1938): 57. There is no question about his getting around and being on the scene in these various places; fragmentary data suggests that he

was one of those disreputable types that CIA officers would hire for covert projects and otherwise to pad their payrolls.

17. Although Tinker does not mention Schmidt in *Some Still Live*, in August 1937 he had an angry head-on collision with Schmidt in Paris in which there was a reference to Schmidt having run from a fight, leaving Tinker and others to fend for themselves. This is the only occasion on which such a confrontation could have occurred, and for reasons of his own, Tinker chose to cloak him in anonymity. Schmidt seems to have stayed in Aragon and Catalonia; Colonel Lacalle had never heard of him.

18. In January 1937 the peseta was worth about twelve cents U.S.

19. "Nieuport-Delage Fighters," *R.A.F. Flying Review*, Vol. 16 (November 1961): 44–47; "One-And-a-Half Nieuport-Delage," *R.A.F. Flying Review*, Vol. 18 (September 1963): 32–34; and D. Balaguer, "Spanish Fighters," *Air Pictorial*, Vol. 28 (November 1966): 408–12.

20. Lacalle, *Mitos y Verdades*, 523–24, has some bitter words about "victories."

21. Lacalle, *Mitos y Verdades*, 134–39, 174ff.

22. See John Erickson, *The Soviet High Command, 1918–1941* (London: Macmillan, 1962), and Robert Conquest, *The Great Terror: Stalin's Purges of the Thirties* (New York: Macmillan, 1968). And among the pages of Alexander I. Solzhenitsyn's novels and his trilogy of *The Gulag Archipelago*, Soviet veterans of Spain are frequently identified among the prisoners of the Soviet Union's post-1945 labor camps.

23. "Polikarpov's Chato," *R.A.F. Flying Review*, Vol. 12 (May 1957): 13, 52; and "Chato and Chaika, Polikarpov's Elegant Fighters," *Flying Review International*, Vol. 23 (January 1968): 44–48. A further difference is that the I-15 carried 68.6 gallons, or 412 pounds of internal fuel, whereas the F4B carried only 55 gallons (330 pounds) internally. Unlike bombers and transports, which often juggle their fuel loads against payloads, a fighter's fuel tanks are normally full at takeoff.

24. After almost two years of negotiations, in April 1933 Curtiss-Wright sold an open-ended (no per-unit royalties) manufacturing license for the R-1750-E Cyclone air-cooled radial, 750 horsepower, and the V-1570 Conqueror, a liquid-cooled engine of 650 horsepower. In late 1933 fourteen Russian engineers started training at C-W's Paterson, New Jersey, factory to learn American manufacturing techniques, and later two dozen C-W engineers went to the Soviet Union to assist with the establishment of a new factory near Moscow that manufactured the M-25; see the *New York Times*, 12 November 1933 (15:1). The Russians got a good engine but by no means the latest; in 1933 C-W had already up-rated the Cyclone to the R-1820 (an additional 70 cubic inches), and its "G" model produced 1,000 horsepower.

25. See Herschel Smith, *Aircraft Piston Engines* (New York: McGraw-Hill, 1981), 107–8, 137.

26. Salas, *La Guerra*, 130.

27. Obituary, *New York Post*, 1 March 1937, 1; *Ben Leider: American Hero* (New York: Ben Leider Memorial Fund, ca. 1938); and Ruth McKenney, "Ben Leider: In Memoriam," *New Masses*, Vol. 31 (21 March 1939): 8. The latter two items are Communist Party exploitations of Leider.

28. Lacalle, *Mitos y Verdades*, 206–10; and Smith's conversations with Colonel Lacalle in Mexico City, October 1973.

29. His full name is Hidalgo de Cisneros y López Montenegro, and in some Anglo-American books he is cryptically referred to as "General Montenegro," creating confusion with the Russian who succeeded Jakob Smushkevich as the commander of Soviet air force units in Spain and who used the nom de guerre of "Montenegro."

30. After the 1940s the spy stories of Eric Ambler would be used as the baseline, but in the 1930s Oppenheim (1866–1946) provided the model.

Chapter 6. First Blood over the Jarama

1. The Very pistol and its flares are owed to Lieutenant Edward Wilson Very (1847–1910), who graduated from the U.S. Naval Academy, class of 1867, resigned from the service in 1885, and invented the system of pyrotechnic signals that continues to be identified with his name.

2. The basic squadron consisted of nine airplanes, the other three being "spares" to take up the slack with respect to casualties, mechanical breakdown, and the like.

3. For comparative data see "The Luftwaffe's First Fighter," *R.A.F. Flying Review*, Vol. 17 (November 1961): 26–27, and (December 1961): 61; "Fiat of the 'Thirties," *Flying Review International*, Vol. 20 (March 1965): 49–51, 54; and "Chato and Chaika; Polikarpov's Elegant Fighters," *Flying Review International*, Vol. 23 (January 1968): 44–48.

4. The basic source for the Battle of the Jarama is José Manuel Martínez Bande, *La lucha en torno a Madrid* (Madrid: Editorial San Martin, 1970); in English there is George Hills, *The Battle for Madrid* (New York: St. Martin's Press, 1976), which draws heavily on Martínez Bande.

5. The reader may find it useful to know that Azuqueca is pronounced Ah-soo-kay-kah.

6. Jesus Salas Larrazabal, translated by Margaret A. Kelley, *Air War Over Spain* (London: Ian Allan Ltd., 1969), Appendix 39, "Summary of Recorded Executions," 357.—RCH

7. Smith's interview with the former Marquésa del Valle, in Madrid, October 1972.

8. The ratings and ranks of the Ejército Popular (People's Army) were: Cabo (corporal); Sargento (sergeant); Brigada (master sergeant); Alférez (2nd lieutenant); Teniente (1st lieutenant); Capitán (captain); Comandante (major); Teniente Coronel (lieutenant colonel); Coronel; and General.

9. "Bavarian Motor Works Gets Wasp and Hornet Manufacturing Rights," *Aviation*, Vol. 25 (20 February 1928), 162. One of the little-known and less-appreciated aspects of World War II is that, as a result of prewar licensing arrangements, practically all of the combatants' airplanes flew with the principles of the Hamilton-Standard controllable pitch or its constant-speed propeller.

10. Herbert Feis, *The Spanish Story: Franco and the Nations at War* (New York: Knopf, 1948), 269. During 1936–39 Texaco delivered 1,866,000 tons of petroleum products to Nationalist Spain; it is an old joke in the oil business that Texaco issued its first credit card

to Francisco Franco. Also illuminating is John R. Hubbard, "How Franco Financed His War," *Journal of Modern History* (December 1953): 399–408.

11. Lacalle, *Mitos y Verdades,* 206–11; and Smith's conversations with Colonel Lacalle in Mexico City, October 1973.

12. Named after its British inventor, Arthur C. W. Aldis (1878–1953), this shuttered lamp was used in aerial applications to radiate light signals in red, green, or white, and steady or flashing. Messages were limited to basic instructions: "take off," "land," "stop," and such.—RCH

13. Thirty-some years later Lacalle's recollection of his first contact with a fleet of Ju 52s was remarkably similar to Tinker's of the moment: "For the first time in my life I saw close at hand twelve huge bombers formed up in a line of patrols [i.e., vees of three] . . . it was a 'monstrous thing,' an inflexible compact mass, incomprehensible, as if suspended in the sky." *Mitos y Verdades,* 191. The occasion was 18 November 1936, when he was flying with Ivan Kopéts' squadron; the Ju 52s were striking at the north-northeast section of Madrid.

14. A brief description of this same action by a Nationalist who crewed on board one of the Ju 52s is José Larios, *Combat Over Spain* (New York: Macmillan, 1966), 100.

15. Cecil D. Eby, *Between the Bullet and the Lie: American Volunteers in the Spanish Civil War* (New York: Holt, Rinehart and Winston, 1969), 42. Here the bombers are described as Capronis. No Caproni bombers were used in Spain, but Caproni Ca.101s had been used in Italy's war with Ethiopia in 1935–36 where their operations were widely publicized, which established a stereotype, and this evidently carried over to International Brigade reportage in Spain.

16. In *Some Still Live,* Tinker says that there were eighty-five Heinkels, almost three times as many as there actually were, but he says he obtained this estimate only later. In his book he consistently overestimates the number of enemy fighters his squadrons encounter, but when it is appreciated that a fighter pilot has no time in which to "study" the subject, makes his estimates with glances of two or three seconds that are probably fifteen to thirty seconds apart, and in the meantime everything is in motion, it is likely that one formation may be counted twice. He also identifies the enemy fighters as Heinkels; in Smith's conversations with Colonel Lacalle in Mexico City, October 1973, he also insisted that they were Heinkels and does so in his *Mitos y Verdades.* However, Jesús Salas had access to Nationalist records and makes it clear that the aircraft were Fiats, two Italian squadrons and one patrol of Spaniards; *La Guerra,* 164–65. This is one of those niggling things that recur with some frequency in this subject.

17. Tinker writes in *Some Still Live* of Leider being the first to leave the circle, followed by Allison and Dahl, but this did not happen. It seems to have been his way of doing something "nice" for the memory of Ben Leider, and it is the only incident in his book that Smith found that may be taken as deliberate fabrication. The complete circumstances of Leider's demise remain something of a mystery.

18. Lacalle, *Mitos y Verdades,* 226; Larrazabal, *Air War Over Spain,* 121–22.—RCH

19. This "turning point" as sensed by the Nationalists is described in Larios, *Combat Over Spain,* 101–2, who, with some emotion, describes it as a "historic day"; it is treated more clinically by Salas in *La Guerra,* 164–65.

Chapter 7. Hot Baths, Hemingway, and He 111s

1. With a poor knowledge of Spanish, Tinker did not realize that in Spain a *hospital de sangre* is the general term for a field hospital, and in civil life it is used to describe a first aid station.

2. In his diary, Tinker remarks of Leider's death: "killed by scope," meaning, the telescopic gunsight.

3. The first six months of the war has many unpleasant stories about aviators who parachuted to what they thought was safety, only to fall into the hands of a savage mob. People on the ground who had been bombed and strafed often did not care to distinguish between friend and foe (one aviator was as bad as another!), and they quickly became frenzied crowds that exorcised their anger by beating up, mutilating, and eventually murdering any airman unlucky enough to fall into their hands. José Larios, a Nationalist pilot, tells in his *Combat Over Spain* (New York: Macmillan, 1966), 53–64, of the brutal murders of the Spanish crew of the Ju 52 that Lacalle shot down near Toledo, after they had bailed out. The *New York Times*, 3 September 1936 (2:3), tells of an Italian pilot, Ernesto Monico, shot down near Talavera de la Reina, who bailed out and came down near the village of Calero. Surrounded by peasants who sought to take him prisoner, he allegedly pulled out his pistol and shot himself. It is more likely that the peasants mobbed him, murdered him with his own pistol, and officialdom found it good public relations to call it "suicide."

That period is a catalogue of atrocity stories against aviators, many true and others duly exaggerated if not fabricated. One beloved by sensationalists and rediscovered by hack writers every ten years or so is that of a Nationalist airplane parachuting a box into Madrid that contained the bloody and mutilated remains of one José Gallarza, a Republican aviator shot down over Nationalist territory; see the *New York Herald-Tribune* (Paris edition), 17 November 1936 (1:1). It is probably no coincidence that this story appeared during the first battles for Madrid, when Republican propagandists labored mightily to heap opprobrium on the Nationalists by way of cultivating "public opinion" abroad. However, neither Lacalle (who was in Madrid at that time), nor Salas, nor any other Spanish source written during the years thereafter, makes any reference to such an incident. Anglo-American hack writers love it nevertheless, and they see to its decennial revival as part of the bloody apocrypha of the Spanish Civil War.

4. Lacalle, *Mitos y Verdades*, 187–88; and Salas, *La Guerra*, 135.

5. This "hail of bullets" may seem "quaint" relative to World War II experience, but these three bombers could bring to bear a total of six guns against a single line of fighters peeling off one at a time in a predictable "textbook" attack; the fighters may as well have been clay pigeons on a shooting range. This is why "The Book," as it was written during the interwar years, eventually was thrown away.

6. In *Some Still Live* Tinker expresses his belief that Bercial (while leading the third patrol he would have been at least one airplane behind Tinker) was shot down by the bombers; but Salas, *La Guerra*, 165, says that the Italian fighter pilot Guido Nobili claimed this victory, which suggests that at least one of the Fiat escorts moved in on the rear of Lacalle's attack. What is more, when Smith interviewed Dr. Salas in October 1972,

Salas told him that he could find no Nationalist record of a Ju 52 crash-landing on the western shore of the Jarama on this date. Perhaps Tinker got this secondhand. In any case, it is typical of many such conflicts of information.

7. Levante refers to Spain's Mediterranean Coast, at least that part still controlled by the Republic in early 1937, which, after the loss of Málaga, extended roughly from Almería north to Port Bou on the French border.

8. Hemingway's biographer, Carlos Baker, dates the author's arrival in Madrid on 20 March. Tinker's memoir *Some Still Live*, based on his diary and an annotated calendar that he kept, dates their first encounter on 25 February. Most likely the two first met on 25 March during a period of bad weather that grounded Tinker's squadron; I can find no explanation for this chronological disconnection.—RCH

9. Carlos H. Baker, *Ernest Hemingway: A Life Story* (New York: Scribner's, 1969), 343.

10. Ibid., 309.—RCH

11. Ernest Hemingway, "Night Before Battle," *Esquire* (February 1939), collected in Hemingway, *The Fifth Column and Four Unpublished Stories of the Spanish Civil War* (New York: Bantam Books, 1970), 165–200, originally published by Scribner's (1969) in a library edition.

12. Hemingway, *The Fifth Column,* Act 2, Scene 4.

13. Sefton Delmar, *Trail Sinister: An Autobiography* (London: Seeker & Warburg, 1961), Vol. 1, passim.

14. Hemingway had been indifferent to left-wing politics until he fell under the influence of Gellhorn, who would "educate" him in Popular Front propaganda. Stephen Koch, *The Breaking Point: Hemingway, Dos Passos, and the Murder of José Robles* (Berkeley, Calif.: Counterpoint Press, 2005), chapter 4.—RCH

15. For another account of the Hotel Florida during the war, see John Dos Passos, "Room and Bath at the Hotel Florida," *Esquire* (January 1938): 35, 131–32, 134.—RCH

16. Information on Baumler is taken from his biographical file that Smith assembled during 1969–71 in the library of the National Air and Space Museum, Washington, D.C.; data from his personal files, including his flight log from Spain, and Smith's conversations with Albert Baumler in Texas in March 1971.

17. Lacalle, *Mitos y Verdades*, 139.

18. A low-wing Italian monoplane with fixed landing gear, the Savoia-Marchetti S.81 bomber was powered by three radial engines of 650 horsepower to 750 horsepower, depending on the manufacturer, and was frequently confused with its more capable counterpart, the trimotor S.79, which had retractable landing gear. Its crew of five included a pilot, copilot (who doubled as bombardier), a radio operator (who also served as dorsal gunner), an armorer, and a flight engineer; the latter two manned between them the ventral and waist guns (see photo 6). The S.81 carried a maximum bomb load of 4,400 pounds internally (with 2,000 pounds as the standard bomb load) and possessed a combat radius of 465 miles, with a maximum speed of 211 mph. These machines began to be delivered to the Nationalists in quantity in the late fall of 1936. Gerald Howson, *Aircraft of the Spanish Civil War, 1936–1939* (London: Putnam Aeronautical Books, 1990), 273–76.—RCH

19. To be sure, five twin-engine, twin-tail Junkers Ju 86 bombers also were sent to Spain in early 1937 for combat evaluation. As it turned out, their Jumo 205 diesel engines proved marvelous for long-distance cruising, but they were not responsive to the power surges demanded in combat conditions, which caused the airplane subsequently to be relegated to less demanding operations; see William Green, *Bombers and Reconnaissance Aircraft of World War II* (Garden City, N.Y.: Doubleday, 1968), Vol. 10, 35–36.

20. Ibid., Vol. 9, 97–101; and Dario Vecino, "New Light on Heinkels in Spain," *R.A.F. Flying Review*, Vol. 14 (July 1959): 24–26.

21. Ernst Heinkel designed the He 70 low-wing monoplane with retractable landing gear to compete in civil service with the Lockheed 9B Orion that Swissair began using in 1932. Powered by a single BMW twelve-cylinder glycol-cooled vee engine, an He 70G Blitz Lightning at empty weight still weighed more than a fully loaded 9B Orion. Howson, *Aircraft of the Spanish Civil War*, 179–80.—RCH. See also "The Blitz: Heinkel's Elegant Trendsetter," *Air International*, Vol. 8 (February 1975): 89–92.

22. Blanch's "defection" was judged significant enough to warrant treatment by the *New York Times*, 17 December 1936 (22:2); other related information is in Lacalle, *Mitos y Verdades*, 252–53.

23. Lacalle, *Mitos y Verdades*, 199.—RCH

Chapter 8. The Debacle of Guadalajara

1. The best treatment of Guadalajara is José Miguel Martínez Bande, *La Lucha en Torno a Madrid* (Madrid: Editorial San Martin, 1969); in English the best is George Hills, *The Battle for Madrid* (New York: St. Martin's Press, 1977), which draws heavily on Martínez Bande; and John F. Coverdale, *Italian Intervention in the Spanish Civil War* (Princeton, N.J.: Princeton University Press, 1976), which shines fresh light on the Italian side.

2. Although the methods of modern weather forecasting were first used to serve military operations during World War I, the subject has no literature; to what extent meteorology was used with respect to operations in the Spanish Civil War (Guadalajara in particular) remains unknown.

3. In a day when concrete runways have long since become taken for granted, the problems of operating from grass airfields in wet weather cannot be overemphasized, especially in a time when airplanes experienced dramatic increases in operating weights. The average weight of a World War I fighter was about 2,000 pounds, a twin-engine bomber 12,000 pounds; by 1937 the same had increased to upward of 4,000 pounds and 25,000 pounds, respectively, which increased wear and tear on the sod. A first-class grass airfield designed for intensive operations had to be properly engineered with miles of drain tiles laid under the earth with runoffs, catchments, and even pumps to carry away the inevitable water, and a species of grass with a thick and deep root system had to be selected for development of a durable sod. Ordinary grass on ordinary terrain was no more than an ornamental carpet that soon shredded under heavy usage. The airfield at Campo X, sited thirty feet above and immediately adjacent to the Henares River, had excellent

drainage, but it could not hold up under intensive wet-weather operations. On the eve of World War II, concrete runways remained the exception rather than rule throughout Europe. In the spring of 1936 the new airport at Rhein-Main, Germany, opened with great fanfare as Europe's most modern, and it had a sod landing area.

4. See John Erickson, *The Soviet High Command, 1918–1941* (London: Macmillan, 1962), passim. Lacalle provides further insights in *Mitos y Verdades*, 26, 34, 50, 134–39.

5. The SB-2, a breakthrough design at the time of its introduction, possessed twin machine guns in the nose, a single-gun dorsal turret, and a ventral gun position as defensive armament. It carried a crew of three (pilot, navigator/bombardier/gunner, and radio operator/gunner). The maximum range (around 700 miles), bomb load (2,000-plus pounds), and speed (200-plus mph) varied with upgraded in-line engines. Dario Vecino, "Tupolevs in Spain," *R.A.F. Flying Review*, Vol. 19 (June 1963): 37–38.

6. Most accounts of the Spanish Civil War written in English assume a pro-Republic point of view, and in order to exaggerate the magnitude of the Italian defeat at Guadalajara they build up the CTV with equipment equivalent to a German panzer division of 1939–40, when this clearly was not the case; the first good examination of the CTV in English is Coverdale's *Italian Intervention*, and his evidence is emphatic on this point.

7. A Fiat CR.32 had tankage for 95 gallons of fuel; at a cruising speed of 180 mph its combat radius was about 230 miles with an endurance of 2.5 hours.

8. The reader will recall that on 18 February Whitey Dahl's I-15 experienced a similar structural failure; this may be coincidence or it may indicate that the I-15 wanted for redundancy in that part of the fuselage structure that carried the tailgroup.

9. Herbert Matthews, *Two Wars and More to Come* (New York: Carrick & Evans, 1938), 254. Twenty years later Matthews admitted in his *Yoke and the Arrows* (New York: George Brazillier, 1957), 36, that his enthusiasm (i.e., bad guesswork mixed with a left-wing bias), seemed a bit foolish; but in 1957 he was about to embark on his great love affair with Fidel Castro, whom he promoted as the imminent liberator of all Latin America; readers of the *New York Times* had to swallow that too. Matthews died in September 1977.

10. Ernest Hemingway, "The Spanish War," *Fact* (June 1937): 47.

11. Texas encompasses 267,338 square miles; the whole Iberian Peninsula including Spain and Portugal is 230,223 square miles, and Spain alone encompasses only 194,883 square miles.

12. See "Polikarpov's Natasha," *R.A.F. Flying Review*, Vol. 13 (June 1958): 6; and Finick's article "Bombers Aloft," which provides good descriptions of its operating techniques.

13. Herbert Matthews, *Two Wars, More to Come*, 272–73.

14. José Larios (aka Marquis of Larios and Duke of Lerma), *Combat Over Spain: Memoirs of a Nationalist Fighter Pilot, 1936–1939* (New York: The MacMillan Co., 1966), 82–83.—RCH

15. The People's Commissariat for Internal Affairs (Narodnyy Komissariat Vnutrennikh), the Soviet Union's Secret Police. For a penetrating account of Orlov's role and his operations in Spain, see Stanley G. Payne, *The Spanish Civil War, The Soviet Union, and Communism* (New Haven: Yale University Press, 2004), 205–8.—RCH

16. Larios claims that a Russian general Kleber directed Miaja. Kleber may have done so as commander of the XI International Brigade and later the 45th Division, but he reported to General Goriev. Larios, loc cit.—RCH

17. A recent, insightful account of the air war in the battle of Guadalajara appears in Richard P. Hallion, *Strike from the Sky: The History of Battlefield Air Attack, 1911–1945* (Washington, D.C.: Smithsonian Institution Press, 1990), 97–102.—RCH

18. Ibid., 101.—RCH

19. A perceptive contemporary analysis is Jack W. Rudolph, "Guadalajara: An Aerial Counterattack," *The Infantry Journal,* Vol. 45 (March–April 1938): 109–14.

20. Robert S. McNamara's concept of a "body count" was unheard of in 1937; Latin armies tended to have poor bookkeepers, and casualty figures for Guadalajara vary. Both sides appear to have lost about two thousand dead.

Chapter 9. Rail Targets and Rural Relaxation

1. Lacalle, *Mitos y Verdades,* 139, 231 note 2.

2. Ibid., 259; and Smith's interview with Colonel Lacalle in Mexico City, October 1973.

3. Salas, *La Guerra,* 471 passim; after the Republic collapsed in March 1939, Zaruaza numbered among the Republican aviators who chose to go to the Soviet Union, where he subsequently died in a flying accident.

4. *New York Herald-Tribune* (Paris edition), 7 April 1937 (5:3). (This account is also described, albeit less graphically, in Cecil D. Eby, *Comrades and Commissars: The Lincoln Battalion in the Spanish Civil War* [University Park: The Pennsylvania State University Press, 2007], 119–20.—RCH)

5. This unusual book of maps is among the Tinker papers now held by his neice.

6. See Walter Mittelhozer and Balz Zimmerman, "Six Mois de Service Aerien Rapide Zurich-Vienne," *L'Aeronautique,* Vol. 13, No. 165 (February 1933): 31–33; for an "outsider's" impression, see Ernst Heinkel, *Stormy Life: Memoirs of a Pioneer of the Air Age* (New York: E. P. Dutton Co., 1956), 120–21.

Chapter 10. Action at Teruel and on the Gran Vía

1. Lacalle, *Mitos y Verdades,* 398; Alonso Santamaría later died in an accident at Sabadell; Juan Comas survived the war but lost a leg as a result of a Nationalist air attack on the airfield at Monjos in September 1938.

2. Salas, *La Guerra,* 462–64. It deserves mention that Jesus Salas, an aeronautical engineer by profession and a historian by avocation, was the younger brother of Ángel Salas the aviator and ace. In 1936–39 Jesus was too young to participate in the war.

3. Regarding Kosenkov's "little lie," Salas in *La Guerra,* 194–95, observes that the Nationalists recorded no losses over Huesca on that day.

4. Because the Soviet I-15 fighter proved superior in speed, rate of climb, and maneuverability, in early 1937 the Legion Condor began retrofitting its He 51Bs with racks to

carry six small bombs and using the airplanes for close-air support/ground attack. The Bf 109 would succeed them as fighters.—RCH

5. The true offensive against Teruel would not take place until 15 December 1937, in the dead of winter, and would prove to be one of the bitterest battles of the war. The Republican forces numbered some 100,000 men and by January they had taken the city. By 22 February 1938, however, the Nationalists recaptured it and the Republicans withdrew. Nationalist casualties are estimated at some 57,000, while the Republican casualties approached 85,000. The ten-week battle for Teruel proved to be a picture of devastation and a major, if not the decisive, Republican defeat.

6. Salas, *La Guerra*, 195–96. Salas, who had access to official records, makes clear Tinker's confusion of the moment.

7. Ibid., 196.

8. Dos Passos and Hemingway fell out about this time, and later would have nothing to do with each other. Stephen Koch, *The Breaking Point: Hemingway, Dos Passos, and the Murder of José Robles* (Berkeley, Calif.: Counterpoint Press, 2005).—RCH

9. Cecil Eby, *Between The Bullet and The Lie: American Volunteers in the Spanish Civil War* (New York: Holt, Rinehart and Winston, 1969), 67. Hemingway so despised André Marty, the Communist commander of the International Brigades, whom he first met at Brigades headquarters in Albacete, that he was banned from the Hotel Florida. The American author described him as modeled "from the waste material you find under the claws of a very old lion." Carlos Baker, *Ernest Hemingway: A Life Story* (New York: Charles Scribner's Sons, 1969), 310.

10. *Esquire* magazine originally published Hemingway's short stories of the war in 1938–39; they were subsequently collected in Ernest Hemingway, *The Fifth Column and Four Unpublished Stories of the Spanish Civil War* (New York: Bantam Books, 1970).

11. Although essentially reportage, the only contemporary description of Gaylord's, including its atmosphere, is in Hemingway's novel *For Whom The Bell Tolls*, chapter 18.

Chapter 11. Kosenkov & Co.

1. Lacalle, *Mitos y Verdades*, 173–98; and Salas, *La Guerra*, 125–48.

2. In *Some Still Live*, Tinker spelled this Russian surname as "Kosokov."—RCH

3. Lacalle, *Mitos y Verdades*, 301–3. Unknown to the pilots, at that time the French air minister, Pierre Cot, ran a covert operation that supported Republican aviation and their internment was out of the question. Cot's front man in this secret operation, Jean Moulin, may well have made the original arrangements for the servicing and refueling of the I-15s in France. Moulin would later be executed by the Gestapo in 1943 while directing the French Resistance.—RCH

4. Stanley G. Payne, *The Spanish Civil War, the Soviet Union, and Communism* (New Haven: Yale University Press, 2004), 305; and Salas, *La Guerra*, 214–18.

5. Hugh Thomas, *The Spanish Civil War* (New York: The Modern Library, revised edition, 1999), 631–32, 645–47. More recent scholarship, based on records held in Soviet archives, finds Negrín a pro-Communist before he became prime minister, and Soviet

subversion of the government far greater than the Republic's apologists ever knew. These events are well covered in Payne, *The Spanish Civil War*, 217–20, and chapter 10.—RCH

6. Lacalle left Spain for the USSR with his Spanish aviation cadets shortly thereafter. These cadets, who trained as pilots in the Caucasus and at Kharkov in European Russia, found themselves practically prisoners on their training bases. Except for occasional, carefully controlled tours of the "Soviet paradise," they were never permitted into nearby towns. Lacalle, meanwhile, was hospitalized for heart surgery, recovered better than ever, and attended a Soviet command and staff school. He and his graduated airmen returned to Spain in February 1938, at which time the Republic found itself, owing to combat attrition, with far more pilots than it had Soviet aircraft for them to fly. After the Republic collapsed in the spring of 1939, Lacalle and many other Republican aviators ended up interned in France. The Soviets offered them refuge in the Soviet Union; quite a few accepted, and most of them subsequently flew with the Red Army Air Force during World War II. Lacalle declined the offer; instead, he chose a precarious existence as an international refugee, which took him eventually to the Dominican Republic, Chile, and finally to Mexico.

When speaking with Colonel Lacalle in October 1973, Smith asked him why he chose not to go to the USSR. He replied, "I had been there and found the Soviet Union to be the biggest jail in the world!" He added that virtually all of those Spaniards who accepted the Soviet invitation had never before been to Russia.

7. Cecil Eby, *Between the Bullet and the Lie: American Volunteers in the Spanish Civil War* (New York: Holt, Rinehart and Winston, 1969), 72–73.

8. Ibid., 105, 109–10, 169–70.

9. Ibid., 1–3, 13 (note 10), 16.

10. An exceptionally perceptive officer, Griffiss' G-2 reports are models of the genre. In a report dated 21 February 1937 he lucidly described the Russian presence in Spain, and affirmed that "the Russians *are* the [Spanish] Air Force." Moreover, he asserted, aerial combat operations in Spain clearly demonstrated that "the peace time theory of the complete invulnerability of the modern type of bombardment airplane no longer holds. The increased speeds and modern armament of both the bombardment and pursuit planes have worked in favor of the pursuit. The bombardment gunner is at a terrific disadvantage due to this same speed and to the difficulty of accurate aim. Pursuit must be employed to protect bombardment or, it is better to say, bombardment must rely upon pursuit for its protection." Coming from a fighter pilot, an Army Air Corps staff committed to a doctrine of high altitude, daylight strategic bombing would ignore this recommendation until the fall of 1943, when losses of self-defending unescorted bombers on missions deep into Germany reached 25 percent, at which time the Army air forces equipped long-range fighters with drop tanks to escort American bombers. Captain Towsend Griffiss, "Special Report on Spanish Government Air Force," 21 February 1937, 11, 21 (file 170.2278.21, U.S. Air Force Historical Research Agency). The Griffiss attaché reports and those of others as well are collected in a single reference work by Colonel Byron Q. Jones. A copy of this compendium is on file in the library holdings of the U.S. Army Military History Institute, Carlisle Barracks, Pennsylvania.—RCH

11. For whatever reason, Kosenkov was quite wrong. According to Lacalle, Chang not only survived the war but as of late 1972 was living in Barcelona "enjoying life and good health, according to Tarazona, who personally spoke with him, which caused me great satisfaction." Lacalle, *Mitos y Verdades*, 205.—RCH

12. Salas, *La Guerra*, 218; Lacalle, *Mitos y Verdades*, 263–64. In the Cantabrian Pocket there were pilots without airplanes, so after ferrying in these I-15s, Riverola and his pilots flew back to the eastern part of the Republic via Air Pyrenees, a commercial airline that was the Republic's last link with the Basque provinces. Bastida, who had been captured, was later exchanged for an Italian aviator held by the Republic. He served as Lacalle's wingman when, on their last flights in February 1939, they fought their way over the Pyrenees to internment in France.

Chapter 12. I-16s and the Battle of La Granja

1. In *Some Still Live*, Tinker spelled his name as "Lockiev."—RCH

2. Throughout the civil war, the Republicans referred to the I-16 as the *Mosca* (Fly), while the Nationalists called it the *Rata* (Rat).—RCH

3. William Green and Gordon Swanborough, "Soviet Flies in Spanish Skies," *Air Enthusiast Quarterly*, Vol. 1, No. 1 (1976): 1–16. Neither the National Air and Space Museum nor the National Museum of the USAF has an I-16, but one is on display in the Hiller Aviation Museum in San Carlos, California.—RCH

4. The Italian firm of Meridionali designed and built this two-place reconnaissance biplane with fixed landing gear in 1934. The original Ro 37 had a Fiat twelve-cylinder inline water-cooled vee engine. The improved Ro 37bis mounted a nine-cylinder radial engine and, fitted with bomb racks, was used as an attack bomber. Jonathan W. Thompson, *Italian Civil and Military Aircraft, 1930–1945* (Los Angeles: Aero Publishers, Inc., 1963), 198–201.—RCH

Chapter 13. Five Down, No Glory

1. Regrettably, during research Smith was unable to locate even a hint as to who this Russian major may have been.

2. According to Howson, the Republic converted two of these 1920 high-wing tri-motor transport relics into bombers. They were used one last time in June 1937 in daylight sorties with Rasantes against La Granja de Revenca and Hill 1220 in the Sierra de Guadarrama, before being retired. Gerald Howson, *Aircraft of the Spanish Civil War, 1936–1939* (London: Putnam Aeronautical Books, 1990), 147.—RCH

3. Salas, *La Guerra*, 226–30

4. Before the Russian "advisers" left the Soviet Union in 1936, Stalin told them to "stay out of range of artillery fire," meaning, do not create any embarrassment for the USSR. For the aviators, however, this proved absolutely impossible.

5. Jose Larios, *Combat Over Spain: Memoirs of a Nationalist Fighter Pilot, 1936–1939* (New York: The MacMillan Company, 1966), 171–80.

6. General Lucasz had been one of Ernest Hemingway's favorites in Spain, a man whose company he much enjoyed. Carlos Baker, *Ernest Hemingway: A Life Story* (New York: Charles Scribner's Sons, 1969), 310, 312.—RCH

7. In the Battle of Britain (July–October 1940) the RAF claimed 2,692 German airplanes destroyed; actual German losses were 1,733, 35 percent less than British claims.

8. The French bestowed on their pilots who had scored five or more aerial victories in World War I the title "ace." The U.S. Air Service elected not to glorify one branch of military aeronautics over another (e.g., reconnaissance or bombardment) and refused to adopt that identifier. Nevertheless, "ace" was informally applied by the U.S. Army air forces in World War II and thereafter. USAF Historical Study No. 73, *A Preliminary List of U.S. Air Force Aces, 1917–1953* (Montgomery, Ala.: USAF Historical Division, Air University, 1962), 1. A few years later, Gene Gurney wrote a book on aces that popularized the term: Gene Gurney, *Five Down and Glory* (New York: Ballantine Books, 1958).—RCH

9. The full German name for "flak," Fliegerabwehrkanone, identifies an antiaircraft gun.—RCH

10. Comparisons would be made with the Nationalist bombing of Guernica in April 1937. During the Spanish Civil War Communist and Communist-front propaganda proved incredibly effective in making most of the world believe that only the Nationalists conducted "terror bombing"; the truth is that both sides proved good at it.

11. It is likely that this "false alarm" was deliberately created to divert the attention of the pilots from Lichnikov's death and prevent them from sitting around and brooding over it.

12. Cecil Eby, *Between the Bullet and the Lie: American Volunteers in the Spanish Civil War* (New York: Holt, Rinehart and Winston, 1969), 123–27. (For a more self-serving account, see Steve Nelson, James R. Barrett, and Rob Ruck, S*teve Nelson, American Radical* [Pittsburgh, Pa.: Pittsburgh Series in Social and Labor History, 1992].—RCH)

Chapter 14. A Bicycle, Brunete, and Bf 109s

1. The airfield at Manzanares, the reader will recall, lay alongside the Embalsa de Santillana, the manmade lake of some twelve square miles that provides Madrid's water supply. It also was home to several hundred ducks similar to the American mallard. Lakeev had gone off with a shotgun and bagged a dozen of the birds before sundown; it was Maria's and Christina's pleasure to have the cooks prepare them for dinner.

2. For a recent survey of the Bf 109, its introduction in Spain, and the resultant alteration in aerial tactics, see Alfred Price, "Spanish Baptism of Fire," *Aeroplane Monthly*, Vol. 38, No. 7 (July 2010): 42–45; see also, Key Wixey, "Luftwaffe Eagle: A Production History of the Messerschmitt Bf 109," *Air Enthusiast* (July/August 2000): 24.—RCH

3. By July–August 1937, owing to a shortage of Bf 109Bs, the Luftwaffe abandoned the vee of three in favor of two pairs; the wingman flew about 130 feet apart from his lead while escorting bombers—close enough to allow him to observe his leader's hand signals (still no radio). Werner Moelders devised this basic flight element in Spain; the Germans termed the one line–abreast pair a Rotte, while two pairs formed a Schwarm. During

combat, pilots found that a two-airplane fighting unit maneuvered more easily than a vee of three aircraft. English-speaking aviators called this flexible formation "finger four," and before long most major air forces adopted it. David Baker, "A Luftwaffe Perspective: The Views of Adolf Galland," *Aeroplane* (July 2000): 49–50; see also Alfred Price, "Spanish Baptism of Fire," 43.—RCH

4. Named after the British politician Stanley Baldwin who, in a famous speech before the House of Commons on 30 July 1934, declared that defense against swift, modern bombers was impossible since "the bomber will always get through." He advised that "the only defense is offence, which means you have to kill more women and children more quickly than the enemy if you want to save yourselves." Denis Richards, *The Royal Air Force 1939–1945*, Volume 1, *The Fight at Odds* (London: HMSO, 1993), 1–2.—RCH

5. The introduction of radar early warning of aerial attacks in 1940–41 in England and Germany ended the advantage of surprise; fighters would be aloft and waiting for the bombers to arrive. Radar changed the aerial equation dramatically, and fighter cover for bombers, first introduced in Spain, soon became indispensable.—RCH

Chapter 15. Enough Is Enough!

1. Lacalle identifies June–July 1937 as the turning point in the air war in Spain, in part owed to a lag in Soviet deliveries of airplanes to the Loyalists, in part to less experienced Loyalist pilots, and in part to the increased deliveries of advanced German and Italian airplanes to the Nationalists. *Mitos y Verdades,* 51–52. Rafael A. Permuy Lopéz, however, avers that the Soviets replaced the fighters lost in the Cantabrian Pocket, and continued deliveries of I-15s and I-16s until August 1938, although all Soviet personnel were repatriated to the USSR at that time, during the battle of the Ebro. Lopéz, *Air War Over Spain: Aviators, Aircraft and Air Units of the Nationalist and Republican Air Forces 1936–1939* (Hersham, Surrey, UK: Allan Printing, Ltd., 2009; translated from Spanish by Juan Carlos Salgado), 76–77.—RCH

2. The German pilot was Uffz Guido Höhness of 2./J88 who had shot down three Republican aircraft in one day, on 12 July. He may well have become overconfident in his own prowess and supposed superior performance of the Bf 109.—RCH

3. Although he did not mention it in his book, in an article he wrote later, "Planes in Spain," *Model Airplane News,* Vol. 20 (January 1939): 6–7, 47–48, Tinker described a low-wing monoplane with wing roots about a quarter of the way up the sides of the fuselage, and the wings had an unusual gull upturn to them. However garbled, this description is enough to identify the Henkel He 112V5 that was in Spain at this date for experimental combat evaluation. According to Salas, *La Guerra,* 242, on this day of 18 July it landed back at its Escalona base so badly shot up that it crash-landed and was wrecked; the German pilot, Max Schulz, walked away from it. A year later in 1938 Germany provided the Nationalists with two squadrons of much-modified He 112Bs. See "The Mysterious Heinkel He 112," *Flying Review International,* Vol. 22 (February 1967): 387–91; and for a Spanish pilot's experiences with the squadron, J. L. Jimenez Arenas, *Cadenas del Aire,* 325ff.

4. Designed by Alessandro Marchetti in early 1934, the S.79 low-wing, trimotor mono-plane mounted Alfa Romeo 126 RC 34 radial engines *and* retractable landing gear. The bomber first entered combat in Spain in late April 1937. With a top speed of 255 mph, the S.79 could easily outrun almost all fighters of the time. Adapted as a bomber with a crew of five, it carried two dorsal 12.7-mm machine guns (forward and rear firing) in the hump over the pilot's cabin. A blister beneath the fuselage contained a rear-firing ventral machine gun of the same caliber and the bombsight. The internal bomb bay could carry two 1,100-pound or five 550-pound bombs suspended vertically. By July 1937 the S.79 was the only bomber with sufficient speed that the Nationalists could use during daylight hours. Gerald Howson, *Aircraft of the Spanish Civil War, 1936–1939* (London: Putnam, 1990): 270–72.—RCH

5. Tinker recounted this moment of terror in "I Was Bombed!" *Popular Aviation*, Vol. 24 (February 1939): 13–15.—RCH

6. According to López, with the Nationalist conquest of the Cantabrian Pocket, the Republic lost more than two hundred airplanes operating on the Biscay coast, 40 percent of the available I-15s and I-16s in the inventory. Only seven airplanes managed to escape to France: two I-15s, one I-16, and four other miscellaneous. *The Air War Over Spain*, 63.—RCH

7. Lacalle, *Mitos y Verdades*, 263–64.

Chapter 16. Looking for a Way Home

1. Fernand Petiot (1899–1975) eventually immigrated to the United States and from 1933 until his retirement in 1966 he served as the head bartender at New York City's plush St. Regis Hotel. He conceived the Bloody Mary in an effort to do *something* with vodka, the tasteless liquor that thousands of White Russian refugees introduced to Paris in the early 1920s.

2. Robert Murphy, *A Diplomat Among Warriors* (New York: Pyramid Books, 1964). Murphy's later career is described in this volume.

3. Ibid., 43–44.

4. Ronald and Allis Radosh, *Red Star Over Hollywood: The Film Colony's Long Romance with the Left* (San Francisco: Encounter Books, 2005), 56–57.—RCH; for contemporary opinion, a review of *The Spanish Earth* appears in the *New York Times*, 21 August 1937 (7:2), and it was treated as a Sunday feature, 22 August 1937, Pt. 10 (3:1). Prints of this film are held by the Library of Congress, the National Archives, and New York City's Museum of Modern Art, and they may be rented from Films, Incorporated, 440 Park Avenue South, New York, NY, 10016.

5. See Maybry I. Anderson, *Low and Slow: A History of Crop Dusting in America* (Clarksdale: Mississippi Agricultural Aviation Assn., 1986), passim.

6. Letter, Assistant Military Attaché for Air Griffiss to State Department, 2 August 1937, War Department Records No. 2093-215, National Archives, as cited in Allen Herr, "American Pilots in the Spanish Civil War," *American Aviation Historical Society Journal*, Vol. 22, No. 3 (1977): 169. Dahl later retracted his confession and, after an investigation, Griffiss was exonerated. Ibid.—RCH

7. Aside from many newspaper accounts, most of which make Dahl seem like a victim, the gritty side of the saga of Whitey Dahl is contained in State Department file 1930–39, 852.2221/Dahl, Harold; Record Group 59, National Archives.

8. "Duel," *Time*, Vol. 31 (28 March 1938): 15. Disseminated by *Time*, the Dickinson fabrication inevitably passed on to the wire services, which spread it from coast to coast and locked it into "history." For example, the popular aviation writer Martin Caidin · repeated and embellished it in his widely read book *The Ragged, Rugged Warriors* (New York: Ballantine Books, 1966), 27–30, complete with an evocative drawing of the mythical "encounter" by Fred Wolff.

9. Orrin Dwight Bell, as told to Frederick G. Painton, "I Fly in the Spanish War," *Liberty*, Vol. 14 (18 December 1937): 6–8, 10–11; (25 December 1937): 15–17; and Vol. 15 (1 January 1938): 37–39. *Liberty* at that time was a popular magazine equivalent to the tabloid newspapers sold at supermarket checkouts since the 1950s.

10. See appendix 3, Tinker Publications.—RCH

11. During the 1930s *We The People* was the radio equivalent of television's *Sixty Minutes* or *20-20*.

12. Floyd P. Gibbons (1887–1939), a newspaperman of some thirty years' experience, initially made a name for himself by providing an eyewitness account of the torpedoing of the troopship *Laconic* on 25 February 1917, and later being wounded in World War I's Battle of Belleau Wood, resulting in his loss of an eye. Thereafter he wore an eye patch that became his "trademark." Moving into broadcast radio in the 1930s, he originated and popularized the breathless, staccato form of telegraphic speech that supposedly lent "excitement" to the news and became widely imitated by other radio newscasters. He is perhaps best remembered for his biography of Manfred von Richthofen, *The Red Knight of Germany*.

13. Gabriel Heater (1890–1972) was a popular radio newscaster of the 1930s and into the 1950s, when television eclipsed radio news as a big-time evening feature. Heater achieved a conspicuous place in the social history of radio broadcasting during World War II when his sepulchral voice usually opened a newscast with the words "There's good news tonight . . . ," which became widely mimicked and for some years served as a popular conversational cliché.

14. Transcript of "We the People," Audio-Scriptions, Inc., Radio Recording Studios, 5 May 1938, in the Tinker records.—RCH

15. This proposition coincided with another plan that surfaced in May–June 1938, ostensibly supported by President Roosevelt, to fly large numbers of American airplanes via Canada to France, where they would be moved across the border to the Spanish Republic. France had made this possible by opening the frontier with Spain to military shipments on 17 March. Dominic Tierney, "Franklin D. Roosevelt and Covert Aid to the Loyalists in the Spanish Civil War, 1936–39," *Journal of Contemporary History*, Vol. 39, No. 3 (2004): 299–313.—RCH

16. Walter Winchell (1897–1974), a New York newspaperman who circa 1924 "invented the gossip column" and its elliptical form of writing, specialized in the affairs of the show business herd and what was known as "cafe society." His heyday circumscribed

1936–56, when some eight hundred newspapers carried his column, and he had a network radio news program in which he used Floyd Gibbons' rat-a-tat-tat form of speaking. A distinctly unpleasant person, Winchell was the archetype of the overweening "media man" who could "make careers" and despoil reputations with but a few words.

17. Many details of these transactions are contained in the State Department file 1930–39, 711/00011, Licenses, Bellanca Aircraft Corp., Record Group 59, National Archives. For a description of the Bellanca 28-90 and a more readily available account of the whole imbroglio, see "The Bellanca Flash," *Flying Review International,* Vol. 22 (December 1967): 1068–69.

18. After 1922 the U.S. government required licenses for the export of airplanes and any form of aircraft accessory to China and Mexico; this was to ascertain the "end-user" of the products and to prevent warlords and revolutionaries from creating their own air forces. After 1934 and the U.S. Senate's extensive investigation of the munitions industry, popularly characterized by the Democrats as the "merchants of death," licensing was expanded to cover all nations, policed by a Munitions Control Board in the State Department. See Murray Stedman, *Exporting Arms: The Federal Arms Export Administration, 1934–45* (New York: King Crown Press, 1960).

19. Bellanca officials subsequently tried exporting the airplanes to France in October, and, via Amtorg Trading Corporation, to the Soviet Union in January 1939, all to no avail. Ultimately, the airplanes were sold to Mexico in March 1939, by which time the Spanish Civil War had ended. Ibid., 101–2.—RCH

20. Ruth B. Shipley (1885–1966), who headed the State Department's Passport Division for twenty-seven years and until her retirement in 1955, was infamous for her capricious denials of passports to anyone whose behavior or beliefs she disliked. Over two decades, thousands of Americans were "tried" *in camera* within the limitations of Shipley's shriveled imagination and denied passports. Inevitably, these were public figures of some kind, such as Frank Tinker who published a book, whereas those who took care to be "anonymous" (such as the discreet Baumler) escaped her attention. In the 1950s her behavior provoked a series of significant court cases that turned on a citizen's right to a passport. For Shipley's obituary, see the *New York Times,* 5 November 1966 (31:2).

21. The Fair Labor Standards Act of 1938 established the federal minimum wage, initially twenty-five cents an hour x 8 hours = $2.00 x 5 days = $10.00 per week.

22. After July 1937 an undeclared war existed between China and Japan; it raged on until it became part of the Pacific War in December 1941. Meanwhile, the State Department discouraged American travel to China.

23. Orrin Dwight Bell, as told to George W. Campbell, "I've Stopped Killing for Money," *American Magazine,* Vol. 31 (21 March 1939): 35, 80–83. Campbell was a U.S. naval aviator, an airship pilot, who did a lot of freelance writing.

24. Interview with L. C. Brown Jr., 7 August 2010, in Hot Springs, Arkansas. L. C. recalled his father asking Tinker if he one day would fly to the moon. To which Tinker replied, "I will make that flight, L. C., when you can bring the fuel up to me!"—RCH

25. *The Kappa,* Vol. 12, No. 4 (July 1938): 13 and 28.—RCH

26. "Newspaper Columnist Butt of DeWitt Rotarians' Joke," *Arkansas Gazette*, Little Rock, 21 June 1938, no page indicated on the clipping.—RCH

27. Regarding Ben Leider, see the *New York Times,* 2 August 1938 (11:3); 14 August 1938 (23:6); 19 August 1938 (6:5); and 22 August 1938 (13:5).

28. "Run of the News," *The Arkansas Democrat*, Little Rock, 25 November 1938.

29. Many of his columns evinced a naiveté regarding events in Europe. As late as January 1939 he advised readers that France, unwilling to see a German-Italian puppet state on its border, would enter the Spanish Civil War on the side of the Republic.—RCH

30. F. G. Tinker Jr., '33, "Anti-Aircraft in Spain," *Shipmate* (March 1939): 7–21.—RCH

31. Correspondence on this subject relating to Tinker appears in State Department Records, 1930–39, file 811.79652/Tinker, Frank G.; other material is in file 852.2221/Dahl, Harold, Record Group 59, National Archives.

32. The Baumler-Tinker reunion was dutifully reported in the *Arkansas Gazette*, Little Rock, on 11 November 1938.—RCH

33. Rarely does anyone think of Pennsylvania as being a locus of aviation manufacturing, but in the 1930s it was the center of American rotary-wing development that turned on the Pitcairn and Kellett aircraft companies; it had Lycoming and Jacobs engines, Keystone Aircraft, subsequently displaced by Fleetwings, Piper Aircraft, and the U.S. Naval Aircraft Factory. It also was headquarters for Penn Central Airlines, and there was Alcoa, Gulf Oil, SKF Bearings, and the powerful banks of Pittsburgh that were movers and shakers in the world of aviation finance; see William F. Trimble, *High Frontier: A History of Aeronautics in Pennsylvania* (Pittsburgh, Pa.: University of Pittsburgh Press, 1982).

34. Lacalle, *Mitos y Verdades,* 501–10. According to a contemporary Army Air Corps intelligence report, Lacalle and his surviving pilots were "interned in the concentration camp of Argeles," where an unnamed Air Corps officer interviewed them regarding the air war. For details, see "Aviation in the Spanish Civil War," no author identified, 13 August 1940 (file number 170.2278-21, U.S. Air Force Historical Research Agency). This too is an excellent survey, one that underscores the prior recommendations of Townsend Griffiss.—RCH

35. Derek Dickinson, as told to Edwin C. Parsons, "My Air Duel with Bruno Mussolini," *Reader's Digest* (March 1939): 34–37. Parsons was a World War I fighter pilot and an ace (eight victories); he should have known better.

36. Because of the characteristics of its gas tank and filler cap, the early model Cub could not be flown inverted for very long.

37. *Arkansas Gazette*, Little Rock, 18 May 1939; and Smith's conversation with John Stover in 1973; he had vivid recollections of this event. In 1939 the factory price of a Piper Cub was $995.

38. Martha Byrd, *Chennault: Giving Wings to the Tiger* (Tuscaloosa: University of Alabama Press, 1987), 89–103. Of the half-dozen biographies of Chennault, this magnificently done 450-page book gives the best treatment of Chennault's formative pre-1941 years, which other authors skate over so they can reach as quickly as possible the treadmill of popular excitement provided by World War II.

Chapter 17. *Quién Sabe?*

1. "Frank G. Tinker, Noted Aviator, Ends Life Here," *Arkansas Gazette*, Little Rock, 14 June 1939 (1:3). All of the pre-1960 Little Rock (Pulaski County) coroner reports were destroyed in a flood in the late 1950s. We have only the contemporary *Arkansas Gazette* newspaper account to go by.—RCH

2. Tinker knew the Essex family well. In fact, he had rented a home just across the street from the funeral home for a period of time. Interview with Cooper Essex, 6 August 2010, in DeWitt, Arkansas.—RCH

3. Many years later, in October 1998, the American Fighter Aces Association would name Tinker a "credited American Ace"; in 1999 he was inducted into the Arkansas Aviation Hall of Fame.—RCH

4. Some recent works suggest that Tinker "got politics" and became an ardent Republican while in Spain, and that the Nationalist victory in early 1939 and his inability to return to "fight the Fascists" might have driven him to suicide. Nothing could be further from the truth. Unsurprisingly, no direct evidence that would undergird such a fanciful notion is ever cited. See, for example, John Carver Edwards, *Airmen Without Portfolio: U.S. Mercenaries in Civil War Spain* (North Charleston, S.C.: Global Book Publisher, second edition, 2003), passim.—RCH

Epilogue

1. Its military members, enlisted and officers, remained commissioned in the U.S. Army Air Corps.—RCH

2. During July–September 1941, three separate detachments, each totaling some sixty pilots and ground crews, sailed from San Francisco for Rangoon, Burma, a voyage of about six weeks. Japan had long since occupied China's seaports, and China's lifeline to the outside world was through the port of Rangoon, the railway to Lashio, and finally a treacherous highway—"the Burma Road"—that twisted over the mountains to Kunming, China. A primary function of the AVG was to defend the Burma Road against Japanese air attacks.

3. When Baumler left Spain he had four confirmed aerial victories. With this victory he became an ace and the first (if not the only) American to shoot down airplanes from all three of the Axis powers.—RCH

4. Smith attended this reunion in Annapolis, Maryland.—RCH

5. According to John Edwards, "Edith Rogers Dahl went to Australia in 1959 with a revue company, 'Ziegfeld Follies,' settled down in Sydney working the night club circuit and cruise ships. She died on November 17, 1985, at the age of eighty-one, always remembered as 'The Blonde Who Spiked the Guns of General Franco's Firing Squad.'" John Carver Edwards, *Airmen Without Portfolio: U.S. Mercenaries in Civil War Spain* (North Charleston, S.C.: Global Book Publisher, second edition, 2003), 114.—RCH

6. Seized and imprisoned by the Republic's Communists on the eve of the Army's uprising in March 1936, he was tried after the uprising in July and judged guilty of

conspiracy against the Republic; sentenced to death by firing squad, on 20 November in a prison in Alicante he was "eliminated." This act was considered so politically sensitive that it was kept a secret for many months. When it became public, the execution was widely publicized as an arbitrary and provocative Communist act, and it proved extremely embarrassing to the Republic's more moderate elements. Rivera's death did Franco a favor, however, for the two likely would have clashed over the leadership of Spain.—RCH

7. Carlos Baker, *Ernest Hemingway: A Life Story* (New York: Charles Scribner's Sons, 1969), under "EH's plans and departure for Wyoming," 627.—RCH

8. The Red Army Air Force abandoned the ranks of kombrig and komdiv, introduced in 1935, in favor of general officer ranks in 1941.—RCH

9. Shortly after World War II the Red Army Air Force was redesignated the Soviet Army Air Force.—RCH

Appendix 2

1. Military airplanes on both sides also sported factory numbers and squadron emblems on the fuselage or on the vertical stabilizer. The emblems could be a top hat, a pair of dice, and the like. Drawn from Larios, *Combat Over Spain*, 52; and Howson, *Aircraft of the Spanish Civil War*, 30–31.—RCH

INDEX

About the Authors

Richard K. Smith served as an engineer in the U.S. Merchant Marines before completing his academic degrees in history at the University of Illinois and University of Chicago. He subsequently served as a curator at the National Air and Space Museum, collected and organized the papers of Hugh L. Dryden for Johns Hopkins University, and taught the history of aeronautics in the engineering department at the University of Maryland before retiring to Wilmington, NC. Smith is the author of *The Airships Akron & Macon: Aircraft Carriers of the U.S. Navy* and the award-winning *First Across! The U.S. Navy's Transatlantic Flight of 1919*. He died before completing *Five Down, No Glory*.

R. Cargill Hall is Emeritus Chief Historian of the National Reconnaissance Office, an intelligence arm of the Department of Defense. Previously he served in various history positions for the Air Force History and Museums Program. Still earlier he served as historian at the Jet Propulsion Laboratory, California Institute of Technology, for NASA. He is the author of *Lunar Impact: A History of Project Ranger* and *Lightning Over Bougainville: The Yamamoto Mission Reconsidered*.

The Naval Institute Press is the book-publishing arm of the U.S. Naval Institute, a private, nonprofit, membership society for sea service professionals and others who share an interest in naval and maritime affairs. Established in 1873 at the U.S. Naval Academy in Annapolis, Maryland, where its offices remain today, the Naval Institute has members worldwide.

Members of the Naval Institute support the education programs of the society and receive the influential monthly magazine *Proceedings* or the colorful bimonthly magazine *Naval History* and discounts on fine nautical prints and on ship and aircraft photos. They also have access to the transcripts of the Institute's Oral History Program and get discounted admission to any of the Institute-sponsored seminars offered around the country.

The Naval Institute's book-publishing program, begun in 1898 with basic guides to naval practices, has broadened its scope to include books of more general interest. Now the Naval Institute Press publishes about seventy titles each year, ranging from how-to books on boating and navigation to battle histories, biographies, ship and aircraft guides, and novels. Institute members receive significant discounts on the Press's more than eight hundred books in print.

Full-time students are eligible for special half-price membership rates. Life memberships are also available.

For a free catalog describing Naval Institute Press books currently available, and for further information about joining the U.S. Naval Institute, please write to:

Member Services
U.S. Naval Institute
291 Wood Road
Annapolis, MD 21402-5034
Telephone: (800) 233-8764
Fax: (410) 571-1703
Web address: www.usni.org